FREEDOM'S BANNER

FREEDOM'S BANNER

*How peaceful demonstrations have
changed the world*

PAUL HARRIS

CRUX
PUBLISHING

Published in November 2021 by Crux Publishing Ltd.

ISBN: 978-1-913613-10-5

CONTENTS

INTRODUCTION

Demonstrations are marches or open-air meetings in support of a cause. This book is about the history of peaceful demonstrations, and how they have changed the world. It is not about riots, rebellions or revolutions, although it does deal with the connections and the boundaries between such events and demonstrations. Equally, it is not about processions or parades which have been organised by the government or the authorities. It is about demonstrations organised by people who are not part of the power structure of the state. In other words, it is about the kinds of marches or meetings which are intended to right wrongs, or to get action taken by those in power about issues of concern to those taking part in the demonstration.

This kind of demonstration is something rather new in human history. There does not seem to be any record of it in the world of ancient Greece or Rome. Nor is it recorded in medieval Europe. Street protests were always common, some more violent than others. However the peaceful political march or assembly seems not to be recorded anywhere in the Western world until almost the end of the eighteenth century. The first record in Europe of a deliberately peaceful demonstration, where people coming were told to leave all their weapons behind, so that no-one would question their peaceful intentions, was in 1795 in London. There was something similar to the modern demonstration centuries earlier, in medieval China, organised by students, as described further in Chapter 19 of this book. However that tradition died out in the sixteenth century, and was not revived in China until the 1890s, when Chinese students were already heavily influenced by exposure to ideas from Europe, including the idea of peaceful demonstrations. The demonstration as it has evolved in the modern world can therefore be traced to late eighteenth century England, roughly coinciding with the Industrial Revolution. This is not a coincidence. For reasons which I explain, the conditions which led to the world's first industrial revolution also favoured

1

the emergence of peaceful demonstrations, although there were also many other factors involved, arising from England's particular political system, and from other events at around that time.

From England, the habit of holding demonstrations to get across one's point of view spread gradually around the world, though at a rather uneven pace, with people adopting it much sooner in some countries than others. It spread because its use in England proved, by the early nineteenth century, to be startlingly successful. Without the peaceful demonstrations of the "Days of May" in 1832, England would not have become a democracy when it did. Demonstrations were not always as effective in other places. There were spectacular successes, such as Gandhi's campaigns in India. There were also catastrophic failures, such as by the Armenians in Constantinople in 1895; by the Pan African Congress at Sharpeville in South Africa in 1961; and by the Tiananmen Square students' movement in Beijing in 1989. In this book I try to assess why some demonstrations succeeded in achieving their objectives, while others failed.

I became interested in demonstrations while working as a Hong Kong barrister, in a case where I represented the Chinese Buddhist spiritual movement, Falun Gong. A group of Falun Gong supporters held a hunger strike on the pavement outside a government building in Hong Kong, to protest against the persecution of Falun Gong practitioners in Mainland China. The Falun Gong demonstrators were dragged away and arrested by the police. The police then charged them with pavement obstruction, enforcing a law usually used against owners of unlicensed street hawker stalls. I decided to defend the demonstrators by reference to the constitutional right of freedom of assembly, which in Hong Kong includes a specific "right of demonstration". I argued that this must include some limited right to obstruct a pavement for the purpose of a demonstration, so long as the obstruction was reasonable in the circumstances. I looked for a book which would explain to me what the "right of demonstration" actually was, and where the idea of such a right came from. I searched for a long time in libraries, and eventually realised that there was no such book to consult, as none had been written. When the case was over, with the demonstrators all found not guilty, I decided to write one.

Lawyers look for information about demonstrations mainly in books about criminal law, in the sections dealing with "public order" offences, such as riot, rout, affray, disorderly behaviour, criminal trespass and breaches of by-laws. There are even specialised legal works which deal with nothing else. However the emphasis in such books is, understandably, on what offences might be committed by demonstrators who break the law. They are not concerned with demonstrators who observe the law and do not commit offences.

Other information about demonstrations can be found in books by sociologists and political scientists, who sometimes write about demonstrations as part of studies of protest. Unfortunately, most of these writings ignore the important distinction between demonstrations which are deliberately trying to keep within the law, demonstrations which do not care whether or not they are legal, and demonstrations which deliberately set out to break the law. In this book I try to analyse these differences and their significance. Sociology and political science books also tend to be dull, written in a turgid academic style which saps the life out of dramatic events and situations. With laborious effort they transform the gripping into the soporific.

There are also some good practical books about how to organise your own demonstration, such as the American Civil Liberties Union Handbook "The Right to Protest".

This book is none of these things. It is a short history, intended to be readable, which tries to explain, by looking at the historical record, why we have demonstrations today, why we should continue to do so, and why we should treat the right to hold demonstrations as something of value which we need to protect.

The book tells the story of where the idea of the peaceful demonstration came from and how it spread. It charts how demonstrations rapidly became part of the culture of countries as diverse as Australia, the United States and Russia, and how this affected their history in important ways. It contrasts this with other countries, such as Germany, where the idea of demonstrations failed to catch on for a long time, with equally important historical consequences. It describes how being able to hold a peaceful demonstration gradually came to be recognized as a human right. It looks at different types of demonstrations and explores the characteristics of successful demonstrations. It also looks at the continual tension between two different approaches to demonstrations, between those which want to stay within the law, and those which deliberately set out to break laws which they believe to be unjust.

Demonstrations began to emerge in the mid-eighteenth century from the traditional London political riot. Their beginnings can be seen in the "Wilkes and Liberty" riots in support of the politician John Wilkes in the 1760s and in marches by discontented London workers, such as the Spitalfields silk weavers, in the 1770s. However the first clearly recognizable modern demonstrators were the supporters of the London Corresponding Society, at the time of the French

Revolution, who deliberately campaigned peacefully for Parliamentary Reform, believing that being seen to be peaceful would help their cause.

The huge peaceful meetings of the London Corresponding Society broke no law, but terrified the authorities so much that the Society was suppressed. After a gap of a few years during the Napoleonic wars, the Society's peaceful demonstration technique was then revived, and used to great effect, by other Parliamentary reformers in the years after the Battle of Waterloo in 1815.

Most prominent among these reformers was Henry Hunt, known as "Orator Hunt", who developed the technique of using his oratory to attract a huge crowd to a deliberately peaceful meeting, which, by its sheer size, always carried with it, the implied threat that, if the demands of the meeting were not met, something less peaceful might happen at some future date. Daniel O'Connell adopted the same technique in Ireland, with his "Monster Meetings", in support of his successful campaign for Catholic emancipation in the 1820s. The technique was again used, on an even bigger scale, in the campaigns which led to the 1832 Reform Act, and again in another big campaign in the 1860s, which led to the second Reform Act of 1867.

Marches and meetings of this kind were just called "marches" and "meetings" until the word "demonstration" first entered the English language to describe them in 1839. After that "demonstration" quickly became the normal term to use.

The concept of "freedom of assembly" developed in the United States at the time of American independence, and the "right of the people peaceably to assemble" is enshrined in the First Amendment to the United States constitution. However when the constitution was enacted, and for many years, afterwards the rights guaranteed by the First Amendment did not include the idea of a peaceful march. Demonstration type marches began in the USA in the late nineteenth century, arriving from the British Isles, perhaps surprisingly, via Australia, but it was not until the twentieth century that such marches became protected by the First Amendment.

Demonstrations on the British model only became popular in France nearly a century after they became popular in the British Isles. About the same time as they caught on in France, they were introduced to Russia, and soon became common there. In due course they were skilfully used by Lenin and the Bolsheviks to capture power, only for all protest demonstrations in Russia to be ruthlessly suppressed as soon as the Bolsheviks were in control. In Germany, in contrast to France and Russia, demonstrating was scarcely used as a technique until the twentieth century, and did not become popular until long after the Second World War. The lack of any tradition of peaceful street demonstrations helped the Nazis come to power, as it meant that respectable Germans did not go demonstrating, and politics in the street was therefore the preserve of armed gangs like the Nazi Brownshirts and their Communist opponents, the Red Flag Fighting Front.

The idea of demonstrations reached the Ottoman Empire at the end of the nineteenth century, where its novelty generated a mixed reception. It was viewed with horror by the authorities in Constantinople, and as a result played a key role in the Armenian tragedy. However it had happier consequences when it reached nominally Ottoman, but actually British-controlled, Egypt at around the same time. Peaceful demonstrations, in which Muslims and Christian Copts demonstrated together, were used effectively by the Egyptian independence movement of Dr Zaghloul Pasha, and were instrumental in obtaining partial independence from the British colonial government in 1922.

After looking at developments in these and other countries, the book returns to United Kingdom and important demonstration movements of the twentieth century, including the Women's Suffragists of the years before World War One, the hunger marchers of the 1930s, and the early environmental demonstrators who took part in the Kinder Scout Mass Trespass in 1932. It goes on to look at parallel developments in the United States, including the first ever march on Washington DC by "Coxey's Army" in 1896, the Bonus Marchers of the Great Depression in 1932, the Negro March on Washington in 1941, and then the great campaigns of the Civil Rights Movement which in turn inspired developments around the world from Northern Ireland to Thailand.

Mahatma Gandhi's unique role in the history of demonstrations deserves a chapter to itself, including an exploration of what it was that made Gandhi's approach successful, and where its limitations lay. The success or failure of later attempts to apply Gandhian methods is charted, from Sharpeville to Greenpeace, as well as the variant of Gandhian passive resistance known as "People Power", most famous from its successful use against President Ferdinand Marcos in the Philippines.

After the Philippines comes China. No history of demonstrations would be complete without a detailed look at the complexities which lay behind the Tiananmen Square Massacre in Beijing in 1989, and at demonstrations in China both before and after that date, including the extraordinary demonstrations for democracy which took place in Hong Kong in 2019.

Finally, the book reaches the present day with the emergence of demonstrations organised through social networking sites, the Arab Spring, and the continuing obstruction faced by demonstrations in most countries, including the emergence of objectionable new British police tactics against demonstrators, such as "kettling". I end with an assessment of the role of the peaceful demonstration in society and in the political process.

The law about demonstrations is an interesting subject to lawyers. I described it at length in an earlier book, "The Right to Demonstrate" (Rights Press: 2007). However as the present book is not intended for lawyers, I have only covered a few points about the law in one chapter. Traditionally, English law has not protected demonstrations, unless they happened to take the form of presentation of a petition. That changed when the European Convention on Human Rights became part of English law in 2002, but the extent to which the right to demonstrate is protected is still slowly being worked out on a case by case basis, with some disappointing results. In the United States legal protection goes back a little further, to the landmark Supreme Court case of <u>Shuttlesworth v City of Birmingham</u> (No. 6) in 1965 (a case, which like my Falun Gong case in Hong Kong, concerned the prosecution of demonstrators for pavement obstruction). Demonstrations are protected in the US, but by a cumbersome procedure whereby almost all demonstrations require a permit, but permission must not be unreasonably refused. The European Convention on Human Rights has protected the right to demonstrate across Europe, but in much of the world demonstrations remain either unprotected or outlawed. In many countries taking part in a demonstration still carries serious risk to life.

One of the unfortunate aspects of studying the history of demonstrations is that those which end in tragedy are often well-documented, the subject of investigations, research reports and much attention by historians. The large majority which pass off peacefully, in contrast, are often forgotten. The demonstrators go home, hang up or throw away their banners and placards, and move on to something else. The fact that there ever was a demonstration about a particular issue in a particular place may not have been recorded by anyone. Even if recorded, it may only have merited a short summary paragraph in an obscure local newspaper. For this reason the present history is inevitably slanted towards the more dramatic and frequently tragic demonstrations.

The historical record would be much better if there was somewhere in the world a "Museum of the Demonstration", where demonstrators could deposit information about their demonstration to form an archive. This would soon grow into something of great value to many people as a source of information. I hope that this book, and the extraordinary series of events it portrays, will encourage someone to create one.

Sadly, it is certain that around the world, as well as the demonstrations which have been forgotten because they did not end in tragedy, there have been others which did end in tragedy but have been forgotten because the authorities responsible for killing the demonstrators made sure that nothing was known about what happened. No one who has read Gabriel Garcia Marquez's great novel about Colombia, *One Hundred Years of Solitude* can forget the description of the crowd of demonstrators gunned down by troops, who take away all the bodies of the dead in the middle of the night. The military authorities then claim that they know nothing of the whereabouts of hundreds of people who have completely disappeared, and whom they have actually killed. This is something not confined to the imagination of a great novelist. From the first massacres of demonstrators, authorities involved in such practices have always tried to cover up and deny. At one of the earliest, the Peterloo Massacre of 1819, the Manchester magistrates, who had ordered the troops to charge the unarmed crowd, unsuccessfully tried to prevent news of their action and its consequences from reaching the newspapers, by arresting *The Times* reporter who was present at the scene. One hundred and forty years later, the South African police are thought to have reduced the official death toll of the Sharpeville massacre by secretly disposing of the bodies of some of the dead. There must have been times when attempts to hide all evidence of an atrocity of this kind succeeded so well that the massacre is unknown to history. Nor is this type of event confined to history. The 2013 massacres of demonstrators by the Sisi regime in Egypt were on an even bigger scale than Tiananmen Square, and have been followed by aggressive attempts by the regime to suppress the truth about them. One book can make only a tiny contribution to tackling this horrible phenomenon. I hope however that the book will alert people to its existence, as well as the existence of other techniques, such as use of government agent provocateurs to create trouble, which are widely used by governments of different political persuasions to discredit demonstrators. Just how widely these techniques are used may come as a surprise to some readers. At least, if they are known about, observers should be better equipped to draw conclusions about events.

My other hope, in writing this book, is that more people around the world will share my final conclusion, which is that the right to hold a peaceful demonstration is a good thing, and that it should be universally respected and jealously guarded. I hope that this in turn will reduce the number of occasions when peaceful demonstrators are attacked and killed or injured, simply for coming out in public to make a protest.

CHAPTER 1

THE LONDON CORRESPONDING SOCIETY

The modern idea of the peaceful demonstration, as a means of bringing about political change, was born in London in the age of the French Revolution. The chain of events leading to its birth can be traced much further back in history, to Magna Carta, to the right to petition the king to right wrongs, and to the English constitutional struggles of the seventeenth century. However, it was the drama and conflicting passions of the French revolutionary era – what Dickens called "the best of times and the worst of times" – that finally brought it to life. All the great peaceful protest movements of the last two centuries and more draw on the ideas and tactics of protesters in 1790s London. The inspiration for the "Arab spring", the Orange Revolution in Ukraine, Martin Luther King's Civil Rights Marches, Gandhi's satyagraha and his Salt March to Dandi, and the marches and campaigns of the Suffragettes, can all be traced back to a public meeting held by the London Corresponding Society, in St George's Fields, Southwark, just south of the river Thames, on the afternoon of 29 June, 1795.

St George's Fields no longer exists. Its grass is long buried beneath the nondescript streets and buildings around St George's Circus, between the Elephant and Castle and Waterloo. However, in the eighteenth century, it was London's main open-air meeting place. The Methodist preacher, George Whitfield, gave a sermon to a huge gathering there in 1759. On 10 May, 1768, a crowd gathered there in support of John "Wilkes and Liberty" Wilkes, imprisoned in the nearby King's Bench prison, before it was dispersed by soldiers with loss of life. In 1780, the members of the Protestant Association assembled there, before marching to Parliament, under the leadership of Lord George Gordon, to present their petition against Catholic emancipation, whose rejection led to London's worst riots of the century.

Unlike the meetings involving Wilkes and Gordon, the London Corresponding Society's meeting began and ended peacefully. As the *Morning Post* newspaper reported the following day:

"Yesterday about two o'clock, upwards of fifty thousand people assembled in St George's Fields, pursuant to public notice, to take into consideration the necessity there was for a Parliamentary Reform. At three o'clock Mr Jones, a medical gentleman, took the chair" (This was John Gale Jones, who styled himself "Citizen Jones" after the manner of the French Revolutionaries)…"On this occasion we claim some praise in recommending temperance and caution to the Public, which was productive of the moderation which happily distinguished one of the most numerous meetings ever assembled in the country on a political occasion."

The newspaper reported how the speakers at the meeting talked about the necessity of reform of Parliament, and how maintaining "order and decorum" was necessary to achieve this aim; how an address to the king and an address to the nation, moderate in tone, were delivered by the speakers, and how some spectators watched on horseback while others viewed the proceedings from adjacent houses. It also records that both the keepers of the King's Bench prison, and the Life Guards on Horse Guards Parade, were armed in case the crowd turned violent, while the City and Surrey Militia were also ready to intervene if required.

The *Morning Post* account captures the tension of the occasion. It hints at, but does not fully explain – because it would have been understood by all its readers that morning without explanation – the conflicting impulses of the reformers and of those afraid that reform would rapidly transform itself into riot and revolution.

Six years earlier, the French Revolution had started with the storming of the Bastille prison by the Paris mob. For everyone who dreamed of reform of England's corrupt system of government, the early stages of the French Revolution, dominated by reformers tackling every form of abuse and of aristocratic or clerical privilege, were an inspiration and a model. They were a beacon of hope that, if things could change so far in France, they might change equally fast in Britain. In Wordsworth's famous words, "Bliss was it in that dawn to be alive, but to be young was very Heaven".

England in 1795 was not a repressive autocracy like pre-Revolutionary France. Its form of government was a limited constitutional monarchy, ruled by the king in Parliament, with everyone subject to the rule of law. This system had been established since the Glorious Revolution and the Bill of Rights of 1688, just over a century earlier, which was itself the culmination of a previous century of struggle between the Stuart kings and the people. In England there were no "lettres de cachet" signed by an anonymous official, confining a person to prison without trial for years on end, as there had been in France before the fall of the Bastille. The words "continental" and "despotism" were linked in eighteenth century English conversation. Pride in England's liberties was widespread and deep rooted. However, the convulsion of the French Revolution drew attention to the many obvious abuses and defects that nevertheless existed under the English system of government.

The most glaring of these defects was the corrupt and unrepresentative eighteenth century Parliament, with its "rotten boroughs" – seats in Parliament bought and sold for cash or favours – and its landowner members voting for their own interests against the interests of the majority of the nation. High food prices, vast spending on unnecessary pensions paid to useless people to do non-existent jobs, neglect of the needs of the poor, unwillingness to support any reform that threatened a vested interest, and the small voter franchise (4% of the population) which completely excluded most people from the political process, made Parliament an obvious target for reform.

As the French Revolution developed, however, the prospects for achieving reform in England grew less. By 1791, the moderate, reforming, Girondin group in the French Assembly had lost power to the extremist Jacobins, and the Revolution had descended into the bloodbath of the Terror. All established institutions were overthrown, and cartloads of innocent victims were dragged to execution on the guillotine for no crime other than the class into which they had been born. As a result, initial widespread enthusiasm for the Revolution in England evaporated, replaced for many people by the assumption that, if a process of reform were started in England, it would follow the same horrifying course as in France. The abolition of the French monarchy and the execution of King Louis XVI in 1793 brought this revulsion to its climax.

Fear of the violence of the French Revolution was coupled with traditional English anti-French feelings when war broke out between Britain and France, a few days after the execution of Louis XVI. Suddenly, advocacy of a French-style revolution in England became a kind of double treason, not just treason against the established order, but treason in support of a foreign power in time of war.

The strongest advocates of Parliamentary Reform in England were the members of the London Corresponding Society. Its name and purpose as a "Corresponding Society" was derived not from the French Revolution, but from the American Revolution fifteen years earlier. Then, the Boston Corresponding Society had been used by politicians in Boston, who wanted independence from

Great Britain, to correspond with like-minded societies in other American cities, and build up a united independence movement. In conscious imitation of Boston, the London Corresponding Society was started in 1792 by a London-based Scottish shoemaker, Thomas Hardy. It aimed to promote Parliamentary reform by linking up with other similar societies around Britain, of which the most active outside London was in Sheffield.

From a handful of founder members, the Society grew rapidly for two years. In early 1794, it attempted to organise an English National Convention to press for reform, despite the recent prosecution for sedition of the leaders of a Scottish Convention for the same purpose. The government of Prime Minister William Pitt the Younger reacted by arresting Hardy and the leading members of the Society in February 1794, and imprisoning them in the Tower of London to await prosecution.

Hardy and his colleagues were not the first prominent supporters of the French Revolution to be prosecuted in England for their political views. Two years earlier, in 1792, the government had prosecuted Tom Paine, author of the best-selling book, *The Rights of Man*. Paine's book was a riposte to Edmund Burke's *Reflections on the French Revolution*, an influential book which had highlighted the post-French Revolution atrocities and done much to turn the English political class against the Revolution. Burke believed that any Revolution would inevitably be controlled by unscrupulous demagogues, who would lead astray the mass of the people, whom he contemptuously referred to as "the swinish multitude". Paine's best-seller was a powerful restatement of the principles of liberty, equality and fraternity which represented the ideology of the French Revolution. It created a reaction close to panic in the British Government. Within weeks of its publication, Paine was charged with sedition and subsequently convicted. He had, however, taken the wise precaution of departing for the United States of America just before his book appeared, and he remained there in safety for many years.

Paine was an unqualified Republican. From his perspective, the immediate removal of King George III was heartily to be desired. The London Corresponding Society, however, appealed to a wider range of opinion. There were no opinion polls in the 1790s, but certainly many, and possibly most, of its members and supporters simply wanted to reform Parliament, to make it more representative and more effective. This was also the position taken by many of its speakers. As the unpopularity of the French Revolution and of France grew, the Society was increasingly careful to dissociate itself from ideas of violent revolution or of a complete overthrow of the existing order. However, this did little to help it in the eyes of Pitt the Younger and his government.

Pitt saw the Society as an instrument of subversion which would do Revolutionary France's war work for it, weakening and demoralising the British war effort. On the Continent, the French Revolutionary armies were strong, motivated and achieving victories. The risk of invasion of England was real. So was the risk that France would foment a revolution in England, by exploiting domestic English political discontent. Pitt planned to reduce this risk by breaking the Society and its influence. His chosen method was to have its leaders prosecuted for treason, and, he hoped, found guilty and executed.

Arrested along with Hardy were the Reverend John Horne Tooke, who had helped him found the Society, the novelist and dramatist Thomas Holcroft, the Unitarian Minister Jeremiah Joyce, the bookseller and pamphleteer Thomas Spence, the lecturer and poet John Thelwall, who wrote verses during his imprisonment in the Tower, the barrister Stewart Kyd, and six others. Members of the Sheffield Society for Constitutional Information, with whom they corresponded, were also arrested. The excuse for the arrest was the plan with which they had been involved for the organisation of a "British Convention", a large public assembly to press for Parliamentary reform.

The Times newspaper led the way in whipping up public opinion into a frenzy of hatred against the arrested men. On 1 June, 1794, Admiral Lord Howe defeated the French navy at a battle in the mid-Atlantic which became known in England as the Battle of the Glorious First of June. In the celebrations that followed in London, a mob, determined to "revenge" themselves on the "traitor" Thomas Hardy, broke into Hardy's house. They frightened his pregnant wife into a miscarriage from which she died. Her death was thought to have been hastened by her worry about her husband in the Tower and her last words were reported to have been "I die a martyr to my husband's suffering." Thelwall's wife was also attacked, and there were brutal attacks on pacifist Quakers who refused to light up their windows to celebrate Lord Howe's victory.

In July 1794, while the London Corresponding Society's leading members were still in prison awaiting trial, the Society attempted to rebut the accusation that it supported violent revolution, or violence of any kind, by publishing a pamphlet, entitled "Reformers No Rioters". Its price was one penny, or seven shillings for a hundred. The pamphlet referred to misrepresentations of its position and drew attention to its founding resolution, which stated that, *"This society do express their abhorrence of tumult and violence, aiming at reform, not anarchy; reason, firmness and unanimity, are the only arms they themselves will employ, or persuade their fellow citizens to exert against ABUSE OF POWER!"*

The pamphlet certainly had an impact on the public, but did not deter the government from its intended course. In October 1794, Hardy and Horne Tooke were tried for treason in two separate trials, both prosecuted by the Attorney-General, Sir John Scott (later Lord Eldon), and defended by the leading barrister of the day, Thomas Erskine. The prosecutors tried to argue that the plan for a "British Convention" had been a plan for a French-style revolutionary assembly which would usurp the power of Parliament. The defence argued that citizens were entitled to meet together to debate Parliamentary Reform, and that neither Hardy nor Horne Tooke had ever advocated or condoned violence.

Both Hardy and Horne Tooke were acquitted by the jury trying them. The government nevertheless went ahead with a prosecution against John Thelwall, believing that the case against him was stronger. Thelwall was an able and passionate lecturer, who had been observed using a knife to sweep a frothy head off a pint of beer with the words "So should all tyrants be served". However, Thelwall's case, again with Scott prosecuting and Erskine defending, also resulted in an acquittal. The trials turned largely on the legal issue of the definition of treason, and the outcome was a reaffirmation of the principle, traceable to King Edward III's Statute of Treasons of 1352, that peaceful advocacy of change to the system of government could not amount to treason. The three cases are regarded as one of the great triumphs of the jury system. The pressure on the juries to convict was immense and, in Hardy's case, the foreman of the jury fainted after giving his verdict. After Thelwall's acquittal, all of the other Corresponding Society members who had been arrested but not yet tried, were released.

The immediate outcome of the trials was therefore a triumph for the London Corresponding Society. Nevertheless, the Society lost some of its momentum afterwards. Those who had been arrested for treason had spent five months contemplating the prospect of being hung, drawn (i.e. their intestines pulled out and burned while they were still alive) and quartered, and the experience caused some of them to withdraw from public life or became less active. Only Thelwall remained as prominent as before.

However the Society revived in mid-1795. It was a famine year, with bread riots in the countryside and severe economic hardship in London. The Society seized the opportunity which this presented to renew its call for Parliamentary Reform. It was at this point that it organised the 29th June meeting at St George's Fields.

There was a centuries-old tradition in England of county meetings at which issues of general concern would be debated. However, such meetings were usually convened by leading local figures in the county, often aristocrats or landed gentry. A small private group of people, with no official status, organising a large peaceful public meeting was a complete novelty. Nothing like it had happened since the Levellers had organised the Putney Debates during the English Civil War. The London Corresponding Society meeting, attended by over fifty thousand people, was something quite unprecedented in its combination of huge scale, private organisation, and peaceful aims and methods.

The Society had previously held its meetings in London pubs, such as the Crown and Anchor in the Strand, the Bell in Exeter Street, and the Unicorn in Henrietta Street, Covent Garden. It decided to hold an open-air meeting partly because government pressure on pub owners and landlords was making it harder and harder for the Society to obtain indoor venues. Precedents for open-air meetings, on a much smaller scale, had been created by the Society two years earlier, when it held an open-air meeting in a field off Hackney Road on 24 October, 1793. It had held another open-air meeting at Chalk Farm bowling green on 14 April, 1794, but there had been nothing before on the scale of 29 June, 1795. The St George's Fields meeting was a conscious attempt, for the first time, to bring pressure to bear on the government, by demonstrating the huge scale of popular support for reform, by way of the vast numbers attending.

The "Address to the King" delivered at the meeting showed that the Society was not Republican, although many of its members inclined to Republican sympathies. It also showed that the Society was seeking peaceful constitutional change, not revolution. This did not prevent its enemies continuing to portray it as a group of traitorous revolutionaries. Hardy, Horne Tooke and Thelwall were referred to in Parliament after their acquittal as "acquitted felons". In response to these pressures, the Parliamentary Reformers took to referring to themselves as "Patriots". Conservatives in the 1790s described themselves as "Church and King" people. Reformers were often anti-Church and frequently anti-King, but they were emphatically pro-country, seeking its improved welfare through constitutional change.

The Society received no response from the king or the government to its address. When none had come by the autumn, it organised a second open-air meeting, on 26 October 1795. This was held on the opposite, northern, edge of London, at Copenhagen Fields, not far from where King's Cross station now stands.

According to the Society's minutes, *precautions were taken to frustrate the efforts of persons hired to promote disorder at the meeting, for which purpose several thousand hand-bills were circulated in the numerous avenues leading to the place of meeting, and on the Ground, recommending orderly and peaceful behaviour".*

15

The minutes record an attendance of over 150,000 persons "according to the concurring calculations of several persons". The meeting was so large that the Society arranged three separate rostrums, so that persons too far away to hear the speeches from the main rostrum could still be spoken to. The meeting was opened by Citizen John Gale Jones and then chaired by Citizen John Binns. Binns read an "Address to the nation" and a "Royal Address". A lengthy address was made by Thelwall. Fifteen resolutions were then put and "unanimously carried", about the need to replace the corrupt system of Parliamentary representation with universal suffrage and annual parliaments. According to the *Morning Post*, "About 5.00 pm this large mass of people separated without the most trifling incident or the least disorder".

Unfortunately for the Society, three days later, at the state opening of Parliament, persons unknown and hostile to the monarchy pelted the Royal Coach, with King George III inside it, with mud. This incident scandalised the establishment, and although there was no evidence to connect it with the Society or the meeting at Copenhagen Fields, Pitt seized on it as a pretext to introduce two bills into Parliament, again aimed at breaking the Society, or any other organisation like it.

The Society organised a protest meeting against what were known as "the Two Bills". This third large open-air meeting took place on 7 December, 1795, in a field next to the Jew's Harp pub, near present day Paddington Station.

Conflicting reports of this meeting can be found in the pages of the liberal inclined *Morning Post* and the conservative *Times*. *The Times* records the number present as being "about five or six thousand … many of them in a truly ragged state, more HOLY than righteous", the *Morning Post* as forty or fifty thousand "among whom we noted Lord Mulgrave, and a party of Treasury friends, in high spirits; and many other members of Parliament, supporters of the administration, were present".

According to the *Morning Post* "Mr Thelwall, from a small stage, addressed a part of the meeting for a considerable time and occasionally used a speaking trumpet to call order. He commented on and condemned the Bills, and said they should not prevent him from meeting his fellow citizens, for the purpose of endeavouring to obtain a redress of grievances… Mr Jones, at another small stage at a distance of 100 yards from Mr Thelwall, addressed another part of the meeting in much the same strain. He said the contest now lay between the Rights of the People and the ambition of Ministers, between the London Corresponding Society and William Pitt… Our blessed Minister (a loud laugh) had every year taken away a part of the constitution to preserve the whole".

The *Post* describes the atmosphere some distance away from the speakers as having been like a fair. *"The persons who could not get close enough to hear the speakers were saluted by Hucksters of all sorts, as well as those who sold literary works, those who sold refreshments... One man cried "Who wants a glass of good Democratic gin or a slice of Free Gingerbread? ... "Here's pig meat for the "swinish multitude"* (Edmund Burke's offensive phrase) *"or grunting cured by the "Two Bills". And others were roaring out, "Here's Treason and Sedition, no more than a penny piece". We say it was <u>amazing</u> to see the scene – for these publications, and their cries, were evidently made only for the purpose of teasing certain of our legislators who attach too much dread to them."*

The *Times* in contrast was wholly mocking and contemptuous in its much shorter and deliberately distorting report. *"The grand rostrum was filled by Citizen Thelwall ... the second by Citizen Jones and the third by Citizen Hodson. Libels of every kind were retailed in profusion, as well as sin; there were Pennyworths of Treason, and Food for the Swinish Multitude. Never was seen such a motley group, composed of all the blackguards and bunters in town, for there were several of the Drury Lane ladies there decked out in their best clothes".* Thelwall was also mocked in a cartoon by James Gillray, which shows him gesticulating above a member of the audience who has a large hole in his trouser bottom. Horne Tooke stands next to him, while another supporter on the platform holds a green umbrella above his head.

The meeting did not stop the passage of the "Two Bills" into law as the "Two Acts" in December 1795. The Treasonable Practices Act extended the law of treason to include putting pressure on the king "to change his measures or counsels". This change meant that, if Horne Tooke and the other London Corresponding Society members were ever to be tried again under the new law, the defence of peaceful advocacy of change, which had resulted in their acquittal in 1794, would no longer be available to them. The Seditious Meetings Act prohibited all meetings of over 50 persons without official permission. The Acts were both temporary. The Treasonable Practices Act was to lapse on the death of King George III, and the Seditious Meetings Act was for three years only.

The Acts were successful in bringing to an end the Corresponding Society's series of meetings. However, they could not end the new tradition which the Society had inaugurated. From 1795 onward, the idea of a peaceful mass meeting, as a means of organising to campaign for political change, was there to stay. The scale and impact of the 1795 meetings would not be forgotten. The word "demonstration" was not yet used to describe them, but the demonstration as we know it today had arrived.

Why did it happen then, and not earlier or later? Why did it happen in England, and not in France or Germany or Holland or anywhere else? And why, despite Pitt's attempt to snuff out the idea, did it revive and spread? To answer those questions we need to delve much further back into English history.

CHAPTER 2

THE ORIGINS

The reason peaceful demonstrations first emerged in England, and not in France or elsewhere in Europe, was because of deep historical differences going back to the Middle Ages.

In France hundreds of years of authoritarian monarchy were followed by the violent uprising which became the French Revolution. When King Louis XVI called the French Parliament, the Estates-General, to meet in 1789, it had not met for 150 years. During that time France had been an absolute monarchy, in other words, in modern terms, a monarchical dictatorship. The Bastille and "lettres de cachet" were part of a system where any subject, high or low, could be destroyed by the king, at his pleasure, without any hope of redress. That system of control and repression was so oppressive and rigid that it could only break and not bend.

Eighteenth-century France, in this respect, was little different from most other continental European states. Spain, Prussia, Austria, and Russia had similar systems of absolute monarchical government.

In England, in contrast, struggles over the centuries had created a system where most educated people believed that they had legal rights, even against the king, and that there were limits to what he was allowed to do to his subjects. This belief was linked to the idea of the rule of law, which did not just mean that people had to obey the law, but that every single person had to do so, up to and including the king.

Why, for so many centuries, did this basic and obvious idea only triumph in England, and not in continental Europe, despite the many links and cultural similarities between England and its continental neighbours? This is a much debated subject, on which libraries have been written. Ultimately, however, it seems to have come down to chance, in particular the unexpected death of England's King John in 1216.

In the time of King John, the thirteenth and fourteenth centuries, a long slow struggle was taking place across medieval Europe, between kings, who wanted to centralise power and control their subjects as much as possible, and the stronger and more powerful subjects, who wanted to retain control over their own destinies. In England those more powerful subjects were "the barons", earls, knights and other landowners, who had most to lose from the arbitrary power of a king. Their demands on the king were framed in terms of the barons seeking to protect their "ancient rights and liberties".

When medieval kings were weak, they tried to buy time and influence by offering guarantees of protection of these "rights and liberties" to their subjects, often in the form of special charters, with a status higher than that of ordinary laws. As soon as the kings became strong again, they tried to repudiate the charters, which they had granted during their weakness. On other occasions a weak king who had granted a charter would be overthrown by a strong successor, who would then refuse to honour his predecessor's promises. For these reasons, although promises to protect rights and liberties were made by medieval kings to the citizens of Germany, Hungary, Italy and Spain, none of those countries ended up with such protection. These promises included those made to the Germans and Italians by the Emperor Frederick Barbarossa by the Treaty of Constance in 1183 and by Emperor Frederick II in 1220; by King Alfonso IX of Leon[1] to his Spanish subjects in 1188 and by King Andrew II of Hungary in the Golden Bull in 1222. All of these rulers were near contemporaries of John of England.

John's comparable promise of protection of ancient liberties to his subjects was Magna Carta – the "Great Charter" – signed in 1215. John, like the other kings, had no plans to keep his promises. Like his European counterparts, he would surely have fought back and destroyed the rights in Magna Carta, but for his sudden death in 1216, less than a year after signing it. When John died, he was succeeded by his son, Henry III, who was still a boy and quite unable to withstand the barons' continuing pressure. Henry was forced by the barons to re-swear Magna Carta, as a condition of agreement to his coronation. He was then obliged to swear allegiance to the Charter again several times in later years, when his own difficulties with the barons got out of hand. By that time, Magna

---

[1]   A despised king contemptuously nicknamed "El baboso" – " the slobberer"

Carta had acquired a momentum of its own, and no later king was able to get rid of it.

The most important provision of Magna Carta was Article 40, which declared "To no man shall justice be delayed or denied". Delaying and denying justice was what King John had been notorious for. Several years before 1215, he had closed all the king's regular courts, which had been administering justice according to laws formally laid down by successive kings. John only kept open his private Court of Exchequer, where he could make up the rules, and decide whatever he wanted. By doing so, John had been able to favour some people, and persecute, ruin or execute others, at his personal pleasure. This was a sharp break with the legal tradition of the earlier Plantagenet kings going back to the reign of Henry 1, a hundred years earlier, and it was bitterly resented. More than anything else, it was John's manipulation of the legal system which caused the barons to rise against him.

Once John's era was over, and in reaction to it, the belief became widespread that kings had to obey the law. This idea became a legal doctrine, propagated by the great fourteenth century English lawyer and scholar, Henry Bracton, who coined the Latin phrase "Rex non est sub homine, sed sub Deo et sub lege" – "The king is not beneath man, but beneath God and the law". This was what lawyers were taught for the next three hundred years, so that by the time of Queen Elizabeth 1 it was an accepted aspect of life in England. By then Magna Carta had acquired a hallowed, sacred status, as the basis of the relationship between the monarch and the people, handed down from ancient times.

This acceptance that the monarch was bound by the law was an aspect of life in England and Wales, but not in Scotland. The kingdom of Scotland had never had a Magna Carta, and had followed the continental European model of absolute monarchy. This difference resulted in a jarring shock when King James VI of Scotland became James I of England, on Elizabeth's 1's death in 1603. James scandalised people on his way down from Scotland to take the throne, by having a man who was caught stealing from his camp hanged on the spot, without first giving him a trial in a court.

As well as establishing the idea of the rule of law, Magna Carta had another effect, which led, centuries later, to the emergence of the first demonstrations. This was the special status which it gave to the right to petition the king for the redress of grievances.

The medieval English courts had developed out of the practice of petitioning the king to right wrongs. That practice is of ancient origin, and occurs all over the world. From imperial Rome to imperial China, to medieval Europe, the idea of beseeching the king to right wrongs or to bestow favours was almost inseparable from the idea of monarchy. In England, by the time of King John, as already explained, there was a highly developed system of courts to right wrong. Because of this, it was recognised that petitions which were based on a claim to a right, such as an entitlement to property, were of a different nature from petitions which simply asked for a favour. The first kind of petition, based on a "claim of right" would be referred by king to the judges, or, later brought directly to the judges rather than to the king himself. For this reason, medieval court cases began by way of a petition. This medieval origin can still be seen in twenty-first century English law, where applications for bankruptcy or to wind up a company are still begun by a document called a petition.

For this reason, when King John agreed, in Article 40 of Magna Carta, that "To no man shall justice be delayed or denied", he in effect agreed that no man should be denied the right to start a case in the king's courts by lodging a petition there. In later centuries a clearer distinction was drawn between "petitions of right", which were court cases, and "petitions of grace", which were requests for a favour and still matters for the king to deal with personally. However this distinction did not affect people's general understanding, based on Magna Carta, that petitioning the king was the guaranteed right of every subject.

The importance of this right to petition became a key issue in the constitutional struggles between the Stuart kings and Parliament in the seventeenth century, along with the more fundamental issue of whether the king was indeed "beneath God and the law" as Bracton had written. James I and his successors did not accept that they were beneath the law. They believed that they had a Divine Right to do as they pleased, according to the doctrine of the Divine Rights of Kings developed in Germany by Martin Luther. When James 1's Chief Justice, Sir Edward Coke, first quoted Bracton's famous maxim in conversation with the king, James exploded in a rage, accusing Coke of treason, and physically threatening him with his fist. That was the start of the cultural clash which culminated in the English Civil War.

The English Civil War was a kind of revolution. Established authority was comprehensively overthrown and replaced, at a cost of some 100,000 lives. Many far-reaching social changes happened while it was in progress. Possibly the most important of these was the ending for several years of all censorship. Under the rule of James 1 and his son, Charles 1, censorship was strictly enforced by the Court of Star Chamber, just as it had always been enforced by European kings, as well as by the Catholic Church. However English royal censorship ended with the collapse of Royal authority in London in 1640. This led to the rapid spread of a host of previously suppressed ideas, democratic, republican, utopian, and religious heresies of every kind. The modern idea of human rights can be traced to a pamphlet by an otherwise unknown author, John Warr, printed in London during the Civil War.

The end of censorship brought an explosion in political activity and debate, and with it the first ever printed newspapers. There also emerged two new forms of petitioning. The first was the circulation of petitions printed for signature on broadsheets, which rapidly became common practice. The second was the delivery of petitions (which no longer went to the king who had fled London, but to Parliament) by way of processions in which large numbers of people, sometimes noisy and rowdy, carried the petition through the streets to Westminster. Nehemiah Wallington, a contemporary observer, wrote that "high and low, rich and poor, of both sexes, go up to Westminster with their petitions", and he himself recorded a hundred petitions to Parliament between 1640 and 1642.

The Civil War Parliament (the "Long Parliament") became impatient with the volume of petitioners, and considered proposals to place restrictions on the number of petitions which could be received. However these proposals aroused strong opposition. The right to petition was described as "the indisputable right of the meanest subject", and references in Parliamentary speeches to Magna Carta were sufficient to stall the proposals. All petitions continued to be received, even from persistent repeat petitioners, some probably insane.

A petition was also the focus of the final constitutional crisis of the Stuart era. The Seven Bishops' Petition in 1688 called on James II to reverse his Declaration of Indulgence of 1687, which under the pretext of granting general religious toleration, was intended to pave the way for a change of the official religion to Roman Catholicism. The petitioners were led by the Archbishop of Canterbury. The reaction of James II was to put them all on trial for treason. The bishops were predictably acquitted, on the well-known ground that peacefully petitioning the king could never amount to treason, being something guaranteed to all subjects ever since Magna Carta. That acquittal caused the immediate collapse of James II's regime, and his flight to France. James was replaced on the throne by the Dutch Protestant William of Orange, who, as a condition of being crowned, was required to enact a Bill of Rights, prepared and passed by Parliament. The 1688 Bill of Rights, among the other rights which it guaranteed, stated that, "It is the right of subjects to petition the king, and all commitments and prosecutions for such petitioning are illegal". The Bill of Rights has never been repealed or replaced and remains part of English law today.

Just over 100 years went by between the Bill of Rights in 1688 and the meetings of the London Corresponding Society in the 1790s. During that century there were still many conservative people who believed in absolute obedience to the queen or king, and there were two notable attempts to restore the absolutist Stuart kings in the 1715 and 1745 rebellions. However the Whigs, who formed the government for much of the period, saw themselves as the guardians of the 1688 settlement, and of its fundamental guiding principle that the king was subject to the law of the land. Their Tory opponents did not have the strength, or necessarily the inclination, to challenge the settlement which had become the established system of government.

The system of government of eighteenth century England thus already differed greatly from that found anywhere in continental Europe. The subjection of the king to the power of Parliament, the independence of the courts, and the requirement for the king's first minister to be a person who could command the support of a majority of the House of Commons, were a unique combination. This system attracted much admiration from reform-minded people in Europe, who saw it as the answer to the absolute monarchies to which they were subjected. The most influential of these reformers was the French writer Montesquieu, whose *L'esprit des Lois* (*The Spirit of the Laws*), published in 1748, contains an idealised account of the English system of government which was highly influential in eventually precipitating the French Revolution.

One of the major beneficial effects of this English system was that important political issues would generally be decided by argument, influence and negotiation in Parliament, leading up to a possible change in the law of the land, rather than by court intrigue on the one hand, or by trying to topple the king on the other, which were the only options for bringing about change in a despotism. This system was conducive to the rise of demonstrations, for the same reason that the tumultuous street petitions of the Civil War period had arisen. There were several hundred Members of Parliament, and a noticeable public gathering was an effective way of drawing an issue to the attention of many of the Members simultaneously. A petition without a public gathering to accompany it was much less able to attract attention, although petitions of all kinds continued to flow in to the government and to Parliament throughout the eighteenth century.

The existence of what was by now an unquestioned right to petition the authorities remained an important background to eighteenth century politics and part of the national consciousness. However, until the very end of the eighteenth century, when peaceful demonstrations emerged for the first time, the commonest form of political public gathering in London was not the petition, but the political riot. The frequency of such riots in London was a direct result of Britain's particular political system, and was a feature of London life that was also noted by overseas visitors. Some major riots, such as the Gordon Riots of 1780, were associated with presentation of a petition, but this was exceptional. Generally the riot was itself the political act rather than being connected with a petition or other event.

Riots had always happened all over England and other European countries. Desperate people who had little to lose, and who had no peaceful means of obtaining redress for their grievances, had always vented their anger at their situation by outbreaks of violence. However, by the eighteenth century, the kind of riot which had become common in London was something quite different from such traditional outbursts. It was also quite different from contemporary riots elsewhere in Britain.

Outside London, eighteenth-century riots were still strictly practical matters, arising from immediate day to day concerns of the working population. The great majority of these riots were "bread riots", triggered by the high price of bread. They often took the form of seizing corn from millers or wholesalers who were believed to be hoarding it to sell at higher prices. There was a good deal of sympathy for impoverished bread rioters among the local dignitaries responsible for enforcing the law and, as a consequence, a degree of rioting was in effect tolerated. This in turn affected the ease with which riots, which were unrelated to livelihood issues, could also be started with impunity.

Apart from bread riots, the main causes of rioting in eighteenth century rural England were protests against enclosure of common land, also a livelihood issue, and rioting against the raising of a militia (i.e. conscription) during the Seven Years War. Rioting against conscription led to a tragedy at Hexham in Northumberland in 1761, where rioting miners killed members of the militia, and were then fired on by the troops, resulting in 42 people being killed. This riot was exceptional on account of the high loss of life. Generally speaking, eighteenth-century riots involved little loss of life, but much destruction of property.

In London, in contrast to rural England, there were no bread riots, and most riots were related to the political issues of the day. London was the home of Britain's political class, and the best way to put pressure on members of that class was a riot. The people who provided the numbers to put on that pressure were not generally people at the bottom of society, but came from the large proportion of the population who did not themselves have a vote, but were politically aware. Less than 10% of the British population had the right to vote in Parliament in the beginning of the eighteenth century, and the proportion steadily fell with the development of large cities like Birmingham and Manchester, and large new London suburbs, which did not send a Member to Parliament. For those who had political views but no vote, a London riot offered a good way of getting their views across to the people who mattered.

Behind the rank and file London political rioters, there were often hidden hands of politicians, manipulating what appeared to be a spontaneous popular outburst in the interest of a particular faction in Parliament. This manipulation had to be secret. As a result it is hard to know exactly how it was done, but it is certain that many of the most important riots of the period were orchestrated in this way. Eye-witness reports describe better-dressed men standing at strategic locations and giving directions to the rioters, while buildings targeted for destruction by the seemingly out of control rioters were often chosen precisely to coincide with the theme of the riot. Thus, in the largest riot of the first half of the eighteenth century, the Sacheverell riots of 1710, which were riots supposedly in defence of the Church of England[2], several Non-Conformist meeting houses were systematically demolished, with their furniture and contents carried into the street and burned, while adjoining properties were untouched, or even protected by the mob[3]. The same happened in relation to Catholic-owned properties in the largest riots of the second half of the century, the anti-Catholic Gordon riots of 1780.

The colonial American envoy in London, Benjamin Franklin, wrote in 1769: *"I have seen within a year riots in the country about corn; riots about elections; riots about workhouses; riots of colliers; riots of weavers; riots of coalheavers; riots of sawyers; riots of Wilkites; riots of government chairmen; riots of smugglers, in which custom house officers and excisemen have been murdered and the king's armed vessels and troops fired on."*

As well as the riots mentioned by Franklin, other notable eighteenth-century riots occurred against Presbyterian meeting houses in 1715 and 1716; against Prime Minister Sir Robert Walpole's Excise Bill in 1733, and against his Gin Act in 1736; against Irish immigrant workers in Spitalfields and Shoreditch in the same year; the French playhouse riots of 1749, provoked by a proposal to open a branch

---

[2]   The riots occurred after the Whig Government, committed to the 1688 settlement, prosecuted Dr Henry Sacheverell, fellow of Magdalen College, Oxford, for sedition, because he had preached a sermon about the necessity of absolute obedience to authority. Sacheverell and his supporters misrepresented the prosecution as an attack on his right to preach and on the Church of England. The riots, which were spectacular, were eventually suppressed by Queen Anne's Life Guards, with remarkably little loss of life, but for generations afterwards politicians were wary of any measure which might be misconstrued as an attack on the Church of England.

[3]   The word "mob" – derived from the Latin "mobile", meaning "moving"- itself first came into general use in eighteenth-century England.

of Paris's Comedie Francaise in London; the Jewish Emancipation riots of 1753, against naturalisation of foreign-born Jews; and several riots against "crimping houses", where men were held against their will to be press-ganged into the Army, in 1794. There were riots against the impeachment of politicians, against public whippings, against press gangs, against the imprisonment of London's chief magistrates, against French footmen, against the gibbets in Edgware Road (where the bodies of those hung at nearby Tyburn were left to hang), and against the high price of theatre tickets.

The fact that several riots involved issues connected with the theatre gives a further clue to the nature of London political rioting. Although the issues involved were always serious for some of those involved, there was also often an element of political theatre. Both the government and the opposition leaders lived in London. By the eighteenth century London had a well-developed range of newspapers and periodicals which might report on events such as riots. Rioters therefore had an audience of a kind which they could not have in rural areas. Political slogans, which would have had no resonance in a small market town in Dorset or Northumberland, could generate strong feelings, both sympathetic and hostile, among the coffee houses, and the varied enterprises of the capital. With luck, rioters might hope to directly influence government policy, especially if they were able to put a few members of the government in fear of being beaten up, or having their houses burned down. On the fringes of the riots would be poorer people, hoping for a chance to steal in the confusion, but generally the passion of the rioters was destruction, rather than theft. Whatever the cause espoused, eighteenth-century London riots were marked by the tinkle of glass window panes being broken by showers of stones.

The government only passed one law about rioting in the whole of the eighteenth century. This was the Riot Act of 1715, which laid down that if twelve or more people, who were unlawfully or riotously assembled, and had been ordered by a magistrate making a proclamation of riot in the king's name to disperse – "reading the Riot Act" –had not done so within one hour, they would be liable to be hanged. However the Riot Act was little used. It was widely misunderstood as meaning that rioters could not be committing any offences until the Riot Act had been read, and it was not often read. Out of 41 riots in Devon in the 1790s, the Riot Act was read only once. The timing of the 1715 Act and its wording make it clear that it was not in fact concerned with ordinary rioting, or even with huge riots like the Sacheverell Riots five years earlier, but with armed rebellions aimed at overthrowing the government, such as that of James Edward Stuart, "the Old Pretender", that year.

In the second half of the eighteenth century, there began to be signs of a different kind of protest emerging, still known as a riot, but which combined presentation of demands, sometimes by way of a petition, with an organised procession. A key figure in the development of this kind of protest was John Wilkes.

From about 1761, Wilkes, a political reformer and aspiring politician, became identified with opposition to King George III and his ministers through his editorship of a satirical newspaper, the *North Briton*[4]. The government's heavy-handed attempt to suppress Wilkes and his newspaper brought Wilkes enormous public popularity, and led to repeated riots in his support, known as the "Wilkite" riots.

Despite the rowdiness of his supporters[5], Wilkes himself was a determined upholder of the rule of law. He successfully used the courts to challenge the procedure by which the government had searched buildings for copies of the *North Briton*. When Wilkes was ordered to be committed to the King's Bench prison, for a supposed contempt of court, his supporters freed him from the court officials, and pulled him through the streets of London in a carriage. However Wilkes insisted that the carriage be pulled to the King's Bench prison, and, on arrival there, he presented himself to the jailer to serve his sentence.

On 10 May, 1768, while Wilkes was imprisoned in the King's Bench prison, a crowd gathered outside demanding his release. Soldiers, provoked by the throwing of a stone, fired into the crowd and killed at least six people. They also shot a completely innocent man, unconnected with the crowd, William Allen, whom they found in a barn into which they had chased someone else. Another fatality occurred later that year at an election riot, where a supporter of Wilkes, John Glynn, stood for Parliament in Middlesex. On this occasion another totally innocent bystander, George Clarke, was killed by bullies hired by Glynn's opponent, Sir William Beauchamp Proctor.

The following year, 1769, Wilkes, whose imagination and creativity come through in accounts of his life, organised an event which marked a definite stage in the emergence of the street demonstration. The event arose because Wilkes was elected an alderman of the City of London. This split the council of the City of London between Wilkes' supporters, and the supporters of the king, who wished to confront Wilkes and reverse his growing influence in the City. In order to

---

[4] The name was taken in mockery of a government-sponsored paper *The Briton*. "North Britain" was a term sometimes used for Scotland, so it was also aimed at the king's Scottish first minister, the Earl of Bute.

[5] One supporter, William Beckford, is suspected of having been a secret manipulator of mobs.

create difficulties for Wilkes, the City supporters of the king decided to march to St James' Palace, to present a petition to the king complaining about Wilkes' alleged licentiousness, profanity, and stirring up of sedition.

Wilkes responded by organising a counter-procession, which joined the route of the first procession in the Strand. The main feature of the counter-procession was a hearse, with a picture of the murder of William Allen on one side, and another picture of the murder of George Clarke on the other side. This counter-procession was almost a modern demonstration. The Wilkites in the procession were neither delivering a petition, nor rioting. They were marching through the streets in procession to make a political point, using a powerful symbol, the hearse, to do so. All that was missing was the conscious commitment to peaceful behaviour which came twenty five years later with the London Corresponding Society.

When both processions arrived together at St James' Palace, accompanied by a large crowd of Wilkite supporters, the Riot Act was read, but the Wilkites failed to disperse. They stood their ground when threatened with shooting by the Foot Guards, and only retired when threatened with a cavalry charge by the Horse Guards. Seventeen Wilkites were arrested, and five sent for trial, but all were discharged by what King George III called the "factious and partial conduct of the grand jury".

Wilkes's counter-procession was thus a great success. He had wrong-footed the pompous royal faction on the City Council, kept his own cause in the public eye, attracted attention and supporters, and ensured, by the popularity he had generated, that the king's attempts to punish his supporters would fail. The counter-procession was an early example of the kind of success which well-planned demonstrations would achieve in future.

There were close personal links between Wilkes, with his emphasis on the rule of law, and the London Corresponding Society, which, twenty-five years later, aimed to carry on Wilkes' reforming agenda. One of Wilkes' strongest supporters in the 1760s was John Horne Tooke, who later became a leading member of the Corresponding Society, and was tried for treason with Hardy and Thelwall.

However, it was the French Revolution, and the Revolutionary Terror which followed it, which, for the first time, made it overwhelmingly important, for large sections of the reform movement in Britain, to take active steps to show that they were peaceful people. The peaceful mass meetings of 1795 were the tipping point, when trends, which had been developing over the years since the Wilkite riots, were transformed, for the first time, into the idea of deliberate, peaceful mass protest. Those first demonstrations were therefore both the result of centuries of political development in Britain which had not occurred elsewhere, and of the particular circumstances which arose in the 1790s. The Corresponding Society's decision, at its St George's Fields meeting, to deliver an "Address to the King", was a natural development of the tradition of petitioning the king. Public protest gatherings on political issues were well-established through the technique of political riots. The novelty of making such gatherings deliberately and demonstratively peaceful was forced on the Society in response to the pressures of the times, as a result of the French Revolution.

This new technique used by the Corresponding Society aroused instant controversy, which has continued ever since. There were many protesters who saw no need to be peaceful, and many persons in authority who regarded peaceful protesters as just as much of a threat to public order as violent protesters. Both these attitudes have always remained common, even as the idea of the peaceful demonstration has grown and spread, and the prevalence of both attitudes is an issue to which this book will repeatedly return.

Having seen where the idea of the peaceful demonstration came from, we can now go on to consider where it went next, after the London Corresponding Society was suppressed. In order to do that, it is necessary to look more closely at the idea of deliberately non-violence protest, and the difficult relationship between non-violent protest and violent protest.

CHAPTER 3

SPA FIELDS

As soon as the London Corresponding Society organised its first mass meetings, they raised an issue which still troubles people concerned with demonstrating today. What exactly is the relationship between the peaceful demonstration and the use of force?

Almost everyone agrees that there comes a point when a ruler becomes so bad that use of violence to remove that ruler is justified. Resistance to the Nazis in occupied Europe is a classic example of justified use of violence against tyranny. This use of violent resistance has been recognized as legitimate for millennia. The debate about when it was justified was already intense in ancient Greece, when Sophocles wrote *Antigone*, where the heroine appeals to the laws of heaven to justify her defiance of the tyrant king Creon to bury her dead brother Polynices. The ancient Chinese philosopher Mencius approved the use of force to overthrow an unjust ruler, and the Hindu Mahabharata states that an unjust king should be killed like a mad dog. In ancient Rome, Seneca wrote *"There can be slain/No sacrifice to God more acceptable/ Than an unjust and wicked king"*.

Those lines by Seneca were known to educated people in seventeenth-century England, including some of those who supported the execution of Charles 1. The 1688 Bill of Rights expressly recognised the right of the subjects to defend themselves against an unjust king who did not abide by the constitutional settlement of which the Bill of Rights was part. While many eighteenth-century English Tories still believed in absolute obedience to authority, all those on the Whig side of eighteenth-century politics were committed, at least in theory to this right of resistance[6]. Thus at least half of the eighteenth-century English political establishment, and probably considerably more, believed that at some point violent resistance to authority was both morally and legally justified. The logic of this belief is the logic recognized since the time of Sophocles and of Mencius. However the question of when the point is reached when violence is justified has always been intensely difficult.

The French Revolution created a dilemma for English believers in the constitutional right of resistance. It was welcomed at first as just resistance against continental despotism. Then, as it degenerated into murderous terror, it became a source of fear for the aristocracy and the better-off. For political reformers, the issue of whether or when revolution on the French model might be justified in England, given England's much less oppressive, but nevertheless flawed and corrupt, system of government, led to heated debate and disagreement. The great majority of reformers opposed a French-style revolution, particularly after Napoleon emerged as dictator of France. However a small but energetic minority of activists continued to support it. Some straddled an uneasy boundary, with their exact position on the issue of revolution unclear. Once the idea of mass meetings for reformist causes took off, there was a real risk that a meeting organised for peaceful purposes could be hijacked by would-be revolutionaries. William Pitt's government was not therefore being entirely paranoid in fearing that the London Corresponding Society meetings could lead to violent unrest, although paranoia undoubtedly played a big part in its reaction.

The London Corresponding Society did not give up without a struggle, but as England's war with France became more dangerous, its task got progressively harder. In 1797, the Society made a deliberate attempt to defy the Seditious Meetings Act, by calling a public meeting in St Pancras in London. Its previous meetings had been deliberately lawful, so this was a change of policy forced on it by Pitt's determination to suppress it. A considerable crowd gathered, but the meeting was then dispersed by magistrates, with Citizen John Binns and five others being arrested. Following this attempt at defiance, the Society ceased to be active. In 1799, the government passed the Corresponding Societies Act, which outlawed such societies and made their members liable to arrest and detention without trial. Many leading Radicals were then detained under the new law for several months, until their scandalous conditions of detention in Coldbath Prison

---

[6]   Dr Sacheverell's prosecution for sedition, referred to in the previous chapter, happened because he refused to recognize this right of resistance to authority, which was the justification for the overthrow of James II.

led to a partially successful campaign for their release, spearheaded by Sir Francis Burdett, whose supporters' slogan was "Burdett and No Bastille".

From 1797, the Pitt government had more substance than previously for its fear of political turmoil weakening Britain in the face of the enemy. There were naval mutinies that year at Spithead (Portsmouth) and the Nore (Medway). The Spithead mutiny was concerned with conditions of service and was settled peacefully. However, the mutiny at the Nore, whose leaders were hanged, had political overtones. Then, in 1798, Ireland rose in rebellion under the leadership of the United Irishmen, who wanted a French Revolution in the British Isles and looked to France for military support. In the event this did not materialise, and the rebellion was savagely crushed.

The United Englishmen was a shadowy organisation suspected of links to the United Irishmen. It seems to have grown up in the late 1790s just as the London Corresponding Society became inactive. Its members included John Binns, formerly of the Corresponding Society, and a distinguished former soldier, Colonel Edward Despard. In the winter of 1797/98, an Irish priest, Father O'Coigly, travelled between Ireland, Lancashire and France, and made contact with the United Englishmen. While John Binns was trying, in January 1798, to find a smuggler to smuggle O'Coigly to France, both were arrested. O'Coigly was found to be carrying a paper with a proclamation to be read if France invaded England. He was tried for treason and hanged, but went to his death without naming his associates. Binns was also tried and was lucky to be acquitted. Colonel Despard was tried and executed in 1803 for plotting an armed rebellion against the government. He went to his death without naming his co-conspirators, and some historians have believed that he was framed, but the usual modern view is that there was some substance to the prosecution case[7].

Because of the war and the threat of invasion, as well as the widespread fear of treason and rebellion, the campaign for Parliamentary Reform became very muted as the Napoleonic Wars continued. Those were the years when Martello towers were being built around the coast to repel French invasion, and when English mothers first started telling their small children that if they did not keep quiet "Boney" (Bonaparte) would come to get them. It was not a good time for radical innovators.

However in 1814, with Napoleon imprisoned on Elba, the campaign for reform of Parliament was revived by Parliament's passage of an extremely unpopular

---

[7] A notable feature of Despard's trial was the appearance on his behalf of Admiral Horatio Nelson as a character witness. They had commanded British forces together in Central America.

measure, the Corn Law which prohibited the import of foreign corn until the price of corn had reached 80 shillings a quarter. It was certain to result in higher bread prices, and so be harmful to the great majority of the British population. It would however mean better profits for British arable farmers, and so higher incomes for the rural landowners who made up a large proportion of Members of Parliament. The law was so unpopular that troops with fixed bayonets were placed around Parliament while it was being passed. As a result of its passage in the face of overwhelming national opposition, the arguments for a reform of Parliament to make it more representative of the country were given new life.

Following Napoleon's final defeat at Waterloo in 1815, campaigning for British Parliamentary reform resumed with renewed energy. By this time, the pace of the Industrial Revolution was accelerating. The Reform campaign overlapped with campaigns against urban poverty, particularly in the Lancashire cotton districts; with machine-breaking riots, such as those of the Luddites; with a huge increase in basic literacy; and with emergence of the first mass circulation daily newspaper. This was William Cobbett's *Political Register*, which was strongly committed to the Reform cause. The combination of these factors caused a tremendous groundswell in popular support for Reform.

Mass meetings for Parliamentary Reform, on the model of the meetings of the London Corresponding Society, were held twice in late 1816 at Spa Fields, Islington, in London. The Seditious Meetings Act had by then lapsed, so mass meetings were legal again.

The organisation of these two meetings was closely monitored by police informers, whose reports have survived. They show a clear divergence between constitutional reformers, who wished to continue the non-violent methods of the London Corresponding Society, and Jacobin-inspired revolutionaries. It is also clear that the revolutionaries made a determined attempt to hijack the Spa Fields meetings to start a French-style revolution. Although this attempt failed, it did lasting damage to the Reform cause, by further associating it with Revolution. It also reduced official tolerance for mass meetings, and gave much support to those who said that such meetings should all be banned because of the risk that they would be taken over by violent revolutionaries.

The small group behind this attempt at Revolution were the Spenceans. They took their names from their founder, Thomas Spence, a bookseller, who had been arrested and charged with treason in 1794 at the same time as Hardy, Horne Tooke and Thelwall, but released without trial after their acquittal. Spence and his followers were committed to the public ownership of land and the abolition of the aristocracy, as well as to universal suffrage. Thomas Spence died in 1814, and by 1816 the most active Spenceans were Dr James Watson, his son, also called James, and Arthur Thistlewood.

The Spenceans were well aware that their own committed following was tiny, and that if they organised a meeting on their own, without collaboration with other activists, it would not be well-attended. Their plan was therefore to share a platform with a popular speaker who would draw in the crowds, and then try to take control of the meeting themselves, and use the big crowd to start their revolution. In retrospect the plan seems fanciful, but this is to underestimate the potential of the technique the Spenceans planned to use. There are many instances in history of small groups of determined people successfully manipulating a situation to generate great events, which would not otherwise have happened. A classic example is that of Lenin and the Bolsheviks in Russia in 1917. While the Spenceans looked foolish and ineffectual with hindsight, it is by no means clear that their plan was doomed to failure. It was exactly their kind of plan that Pitt had feared, when he outlawed the Corresponding Societies in the 1790s, and that his successor as Prime Minister, Lord Liverpool, feared when the Reform movement revived in 1816.

The speaker the Spenceans wanted, to bring the crowds to their meetings, was Henry Hunt, known as "Orator Hunt". Hunt was a Wiltshire farmer who had gradually become radicalised, partly because of being imprisoned as a result of a feud with spiteful neighbouring landowners. He emerged as the most accomplished platform speaker of his generation, able to draw crowds like no-one else.

Hunt was a tall, handsome, vain man, who often spoke wearing a white hat as a symbol of the purity of his motives, setting a fashion which was copied by other Radicals. Hunt, in contrast to the Spenceans, was emphatically a reformer, not a revolutionary. In his speeches he explicitly recognised the existence and importance of the constitutional right of resistance, as laid down in the Bill of Rights, as did everyone on the progressive or Whig side of politics. However he always went on to emphasise that all possible peaceful methods of trying to obtain reform had to be attempted first, and to fail, before it became permissible to consider revolution. By presenting his arguments in this way, Hunt was achieving two goals. He was in practice strongly encouraging a law-abiding approach to the Parliamentary Reform campaign. He was also at the same time conveying a threat and a sense of menace to the authorities, by sending out a message that they should respond to just and peaceful demands, or be faced with something much worse. However Hunt was always careful not to cross the line at his public meetings by saying anything which could be construed as calling for violence.

The first Spa Fields meeting was organised by Dr Watson and Thistlewood for 15 November, 1816. Four well-known reformers were invited to speak – Hunt, Sir Francis Burdett, William Cobbett and Major John Cartwright – but only Hunt accepted. Up to 20,000 people attended. Some speakers at the meeting called for a march on the Prince Regent's[8] residence in Carlton House. That was not itself a call to violence but it came close. With memories of the French Revolution, and the attack on the Bastille, twenty seven years previously, still very much in the minds of many people, it would have been treated by the authorities as an attack on the monarchy, and would have been broken up by troops. Hunt successfully urged the large crowd not to follow that course, but instead to seek their ends by a petition, and to adjourn peacefully. This the crowd did, although there was a small incident of breaking of food shop windows as the meeting ended.

Hunt was due to address a second meeting, on 2 December, 1816, but, before he arrived it degenerated into a riot. A gunsmith's shop was robbed of guns, and a mob set off for the Tower of London with a vague plan to storm it in the manner of the storming of the Bastille. A pedestrian was later killed by the mob.

What seems to have happened, on 2 December, 1816, is that Dr Watson and Thistlewood, excited by the huge attendance at the previous meeting on 15 November, decided to attempt a revolution that day, starting with the second meeting in Spa Fields. They knew that Hunt would not take part in any such scheme, but they needed him to draw in the crowd. Thistlewood therefore deliberately gave Hunt a wrong time of 1.00 pm for the start of the meeting, while Thistlewood himself and the other Spenceans assembled earlier, at 12.00. Before Hunt arrived, Thistlewood had called on the crowd, which already numbered some 2000 people, to head for the Tower of London, and had set off with part of the crowd following him. When Hunt was on his way to the meeting, he heard what had happened, turned back and did not attend.

The Spa Fields meetings thus showed the difficulties involved in keeping a peaceful demonstration peaceful, which have continued to trouble other demonstration organisers ever since. A peaceful demonstration is always potentially at risk of being hijacked by violent people who want to use it for their own purposes. The organisers of any peaceful demonstration therefore have to have arrangements in place to prevent this happening, since otherwise their own cause, however peaceful, is liable to be discredited, as a result of the violence perpetrated by those who attend with their own, different, agenda. Well-organised modern

---

8 King George III was mentally incapacitated from 1811 until his death in 1820. His son, later King George IV, was official Regent on behalf of his father during those years.

demonstrations often involve the use of stewards, recruited by the demonstration organisers, wearing identification such as armbands or badges. One of the uses of such stewards is to maintain order among the demonstrators, and to nip in the bud any attempt to hijack the demonstration for violent or unintended purposes. This practice had not yet developed at Spa Fields in 1816, although it began to emerge soon afterwards[9], possibly because demonstration organisers over the next few years were aware of what had gone wrong at Spa Fields, and wanted to avoid it happening again.

Another way that organisers of modern peaceful demonstrations can reduce the risk of a hijacking is liaison with the police at planning stage. This carries its own risks, which are considered later in this book in the context of demonstrations and the police, but in 1816 it was not an option for anyone, as a modern police force was not introduced in London until 1829.

The aftermath of Spa Fields also revealed another issue which has continued to trouble demonstrators ever since. This is the use by the authorities of agents provocateurs, infiltrated into the demonstrators' ranks to provoke illegal conduct and so enable the authorities to make arrests.

This problem received much publicity just as this book was being written, following the revelations of former British Metropolitan policeman Mark Kennedy, about his infiltration into the Climate Change Camp demonstration movement as a long-term spy, playing an active part in organising demonstrations, some of which led to arrests. Kennedy's revelations caused a lot of shock among people not familiar with the history of demonstrations. In fact his behaviour followed a very old, widespread, and familiar tradition going back to the first emergence of demonstrations.

The organisers of the second Spa Fields meeting, including Dr Watson and Arthur Thistlewood, were arrested afterwards and charged with high treason. Their conviction at first seemed likely, and probably uncontroversial, as they had undeniably organised, and in Thistlewood's case, led a march on the Tower of London, with an armed mob following them, with the intention of starting a revolution.

Dr Watson was put on trial first. However in the course of his trial it emerged that one of the other organisers of the plot for a revolution, John Castle, was a government spy, who had been present at key points in the planning of the attempted revolution, and acted as an agent provocateur, urging on the

---

[9] It was already well-established in Lancashire three years later at the time of the Peterloo Massacre – see Chapter 4.

revolutionary plan. Castle was called by the prosecution as a witness, but the provocative nature of his role emerged when he was cross-examined. In the light of this evidence the jury acquitted Dr Watson. The judge in the trial of Thistlewood and the other organisers then ordered the acquittal of all the defendants, all of whom were also charged on the basis of Castle's evidence[10].

This was the first of several similar exposures of the use of government agents to try to incriminate the Parliamentary reformers. In a sad sequel, Thistlewood, who was undoubtedly a committed revolutionary, was to be hanged only three years later for his part in the Cato Street conspiracy. The conspirators planned to assassinate the leading members of the government at a dinner party they were due to attend. However much doubt remains about Thistlewood's guilt in that case also. The prosecution relied on the evidence of a plotter, John Edwards, who also turned out to have been acting as an agent provocateur, actively plotting with Thistlewood, while keeping the Home Office informed of what was going on.

Despite the fiasco of the second Spa Fields meeting, the Parliamentary Reform movement continued its momentum. As a result, it was through the marches and meetings in support of Parliamentary Reform that the tradition of holding demonstrations grew and spread.

On 28 January 1817, the day of the State Opening of Parliament, a mass petition for Parliamentary reform signed by over a million people was carried through London to Parliament by a crowd of 20,000, led by Lord Cochrane, the popular naval hero, who had been radicalised by his dismissal from the Navy over fraud allegations of which he was probably innocent. However attention was distracted from this petition by a report of an assassination attempt on the Prince Regent, believed by many Radicals to have been a deliberate fabrication by the government to discredit the cause of reform.

The reports of this attempted assassination led to a hysterical outcry against the Parliamentary Reformers, which took its most dramatic form when Lord Cochrane and William Cobbett, the editor of the *Political Register*, were attacked and beaten up by an group of angry Church of England vicars, at a meeting in Winchester[11]. Shortly afterwards Cobbett, fearing imminent arrest on a charge of seditious libel (an offence for which he had already served two years in prison

---

[10] In doing so he was following the established rule in English criminal trials that if the prosecution evidence is such that no sensible jury could convict on the basis of it, the judge must order an acquittal.

[11] Vicars were targets for the Reform movement, and staunch upholders of the status quo, as they lived off compulsory taxes - tithes - payable by villagers, and so were in a position analogous to government officials whose salaries were paid by taxes levied by the unrepresentative Parliament.

from 1810 to 1812), fled England for the United States. He continued to edit the *Political Register* from there, but, given the limitations placed on news by the speed of sailing ships, it was no longer so topical or influential during his exile.

The government responded to the Spa Fields riot and the January Reform petition by suspending habeas corpus, and by preparing a new sedition law. Its failure to distinguish between legitimate demands for reform, and the activities of revolutionaries like Thistlewood, showed narrow-minded intolerance, and made it likely that a violent confrontation would eventually occur between Reformers and the forces of order.

However, after the beginning of 1817, the focus of likely confrontation, and the development of demonstrations as a technique, shifted away from London, and moved to the north-west of England, where both the confrontation and the wider use of demonstrations were propelled forward by the pressures at the heart of the Industrial Revolution.

CHAPTER 4

PETERLOO

In the second decade of the nineteenth century, Manchester was the second city of England in terms of population, and yet was not allowed to send an MP to Parliament. It had sent one in the seventeenth century, but its right to do so had been taken away by Charles II, because of Manchester's strong support for the Commonwealth during the English Civil War. Many contemporaries saw a linkage between the dire poverty among the area's cotton spinners and weavers, and the area's lack of representation in Parliament. For that reason support for Parliamentary Reform became very strong in and around Manchester at the same time as the Spa Fields meetings in London. Large peaceful open air Reform meetings were held at Blackburn, Oldham and Rochdale in 1816 and 1817.

The emergence of these political mass meetings in Lancashire was probably linked to the development of modern trade unions, which were very active in the area, frequently disguised as workers' mutual benefit societies to avoid laws against workers' combinations. Some also attribute the growth in support for Reform to the prevalent influence of Methodism in the area, with its teaching that a man was as good as his master. It is a certainly a matter of record that one of the Lancashire Radical leaders of the period, Samuel Bamford of Middleton, did propose that participants in Reform meetings should boost their spirits by singing uplifting songs, including some of his own composition, in the same way that the Methodists sang hymns. The idea of songs was rejected when Bamford put it forward, but caught on some years later.

In the years after Waterloo, the pressures of the Industrial Revolution, and the poverty and upheaval it generated, led to increasing confrontation between

Radical political activists and the authorities in the Manchester area. As well as not having a Member of Parliament, Manchester had no charter and so was not a corporation. It therefore did not have city councillors or a mayor. The local authorities were justices of the peace, local magistrates who were intensely fearful of an uprising by the huge numbers of poor workers surrounding them.

In 1817 an ambitious attempt to hold a new kind of demonstration led to a violent clampdown by the authorities on the demonstrators. The demonstrators' cause this time was not Parliamentary Reform, but alleviation of poverty in the cotton industry, although many Radicals were active in both causes, which they considered to be linked. Two Manchester-based Radicals, John Bagguley and Samuel Drummond, conceived the idea of the first ever peaceful political march on London, as a way of drawing national attention to the continuing desperate economic conditions of the unemployed spinners and weavers in Lancashire.

The plan was for the spinners and weavers to take a petition to the Prince Regent, by marching with it from Manchester to London, holding meetings on the way to gain the support of other textile workers. The organisers hoped that by the time the march arrived in London there would be over 100,000 marchers willing to tell the Royal Family about the distress being caused by the growth of the new factory system in the industry.

The organisers decided that each man should carry a blanket, rolled and worn over the shoulder like a shoulder belt. This would serve two purposes. It would keep them warm at night, and would show people who saw them on the march that they were weavers. Because of these blankets the march has always been known as the "March of the Blanketeers".

Moderate reformers in Manchester opposed the march, fearing, correctly as it turned out, that it would so alarm the government as to be counter-productive. Samuel Bamford claims in his autobiography, *Passages from the life of a Radical*, that he opposed the march because he feared it would be infiltrated by agents provocateurs, who would be used to discredit the movement. Bamford is an unreliable source, as he went from being a Radical activist at the time to being a man who, in later life, was anxious to make his peace with the authorities. Whether Bamford really suspected infiltration by agents provocateurs at the time of the preparations for the march, or imagined his supposed misgivings years later, is therefore unclear. However, it is certain that there was indeed an agent provocateur, one William Oliver, involved with the organisation of the march.

Bagguley and Drummond called a meeting which was to be the start of the march. This took place in St Peter's Fields in Manchester, and was attended by at least 10,000 people (some reports claim up to 30,000). It was thought to have been the largest meeting ever held until then in Manchester.

Unfortunately for the marchers, the Manchester magistrates had received reports from spies that violence was likely to be used on the march. This was unlikely to have been true, as the march organisers were known supporters of peaceful campaigning, and violence would have been counter-productive to their cause. However, alarmed by the reports, the magistrates decided to stop the march from happening. It is not clear whether the information as to alleged plans for violence came from Oliver, who would have been reporting to the Home Office in London, or was unreliable local information given to the magistrates. Whatever the source, the result was that, as the leaders were addressing the meeting in the square, the magistrates declared it illegal by the traditional method of reading the Riot Act, notwithstanding the fact that there was no riot going on. Cavalry of the King's Dragoon Guards then arrived and arrested twenty men, including Bagguley and Drummond.

A large number of Blanketeers remained determined to march to London, and set off despite the arrest of their leaders. They were followed by the cavalry, who attacked them a mile from the city centre. The cavalry then again attacked the marchers at Stockport, where several marchers received sabre wounds. The soldiers also shot dead a local man who was not a marcher, but who happened to be standing nearby when a stone was thrown at the troops. Further attacks at Macclesfield, and at Ashbourne in Derbyshire, brought the march to an end.

The Blanketeers were doing nothing unlawful by attempting to march to London with a petition. The violent suppression of the march was simply unlawful repression. Undoubtedly behind it was the fear that such a large march would be taken over by leaders like the Spenceans, as the second Spa Fields meeting had been, and would then turn into the forerunner of a revolution like that in France. The March of the Blanketeers appears to have been the first time that people tried to deliver a petition by marching most of the length of England with it before delivering it, and the numbers of marchers expected was very large.

In later years, long distance marches became an established and effective form of demonstration around the world, used most famously by Gandhi, but also by many other campaigners, such as the Hunger Marchers in the 1930s, and the many "marchers on Washington" in the USA. The reason the Blanketeers failed was that in 1817 their idea was simply too novel and the authorities were too frightened to tolerate it. The distinction between peaceful political action and violent revolution was then only just becoming established, and was viewed with scepticism by those in power.

A typical reaction to the large Reform meetings which began to occur in Manchester at that time was that of Sir John Byng, in charge of the army in the north-west of England, who commented, "*The peaceable demeanour of so many thousand unemployed men is not natural: their regular meeting and again dispersing shows a system of organisation of their actions which has some appearance of previous tuition*". To Byng this was not a sign of those attending having been warned not to be violent, but a sign that they were being drilled for some sinister purpose, such as a military attack on the authorities, by people like the Spenceans, who at the right moment would order the crowd to use violence.

Some of the arrested Blanketeers were put on trial, and it was then that the role of William Oliver came to light. The case for the prosecution was that the Blanketeers were part of a general plot to overthrow the government. The government intended to put on trial together with the leaders of the Blanketeers a group of Radicals who had been arrested, shortly before the March, at a house at Thornhill Lees in West Yorkshire. These Radicals were said to have been the ringleaders of the revolutionary conspiracy. However, on 14 June 1817, the *Leeds Mercury* reported that one of the group of men arrested at Thornhill Lees, Oliver, had been allowed to escape, and that according to sworn testimony of several of the local leaders of the Parliamentary Reform movement, Oliver had been the leader of any conspiracy, having been known as the leader of the "physical force party" from London. Once Oliver was suspected of being an agent provocateur, his movements were reviewed, and it became apparent that he had been present at the key meetings where the conspiracy was organised. He had first entered Radical circles on the basis of a letter of introduction from Sir Francis Burdett, which turned out to be forged. It thus became clear, despite the government's efforts, that the conspiracy was the work of an agent provocateur, and not an inherent part of the plan for the Blanket March.

Oliver's aim had been to encourage sufficient violent action to permit prosecution of all the Lancashire Radical leadership for treason or other very serious offences. The plan failed, because the Manchester magistrates, unaware that Oliver was a spy, were panic-stricken at the very idea of a weavers' march to London, and intervened to arrest the marchers and their leaders, too soon from Oliver's point of view.

The revelations about Oliver caused disgust among people of different political persuasions. As a result, most of those arrested on the Blanket March, and others who were also tried at the same time for such offences as sedition and unlawful assembly, were acquitted by juries.

It was at this point that Lord Liverpool's government, realising its actions in breaking up the Manchester meeting and prosecuting the organisers, were legally on shaky ground, introduced a new bill to restrict the right to hold public meetings. Passed into law as the Seditious Meetings Act 1817, it was colloquially known as "Sidmouth's Gagging Act", after the Home Secretary, Viscount Sidmouth.

The Gagging Act prohibited any meeting of more than 50 persons, anywhere, unless it was held in the parish where those calling the meeting lived, and was also the subject of a notice given to justices of the peace (magistrates) by seven householders. The magistrates had power to change the time and place of the meeting at their complete discretion, provided that they gave two days' notice of the change. Adjournments of meetings were not allowed, this prohibition being designed to prevent a meeting from being adjourned and then reassembling at a place other than that originally accepted by the magistrates. Knowingly and wilfully attending any illegal meeting, which included any meeting of over 50 persons, was a crime punishable with up to 12 months imprisonment. Persons attending any unlawful assembly could be required to depart within 15 minutes of the reading of a proclamation, or they would be committing a felony and liable to transportation to Australia for seven years.

Once the Gagging Act was law, it criminalised numerous meetings which had previously been both legal and trouble-free. It gave free rein to magistrates to exercise their personal prejudices in refusing permission for meetings of which they did not approve, and in arbitrarily adjourning meetings to times or places which were impractical for the would-be organisers.

However neither the suppression of the Blanketeers March nor the Gagging Act ended Radical campaigning in the Manchester area. This continued and grew stronger during 1818 and the first eight months of 1819. In January 1819 Henry Hunt, the great orator of the Spa Fields meetings, travelled outside the south of England for the first time, when he accepted an invitation to address a Reform meeting in St Peter's Square, Manchester. This meeting was attended by about 10,000 people, and a novel feature was the way many of those attending arrived in organised contingents with bands playing and banners fluttering.

Hunt, in his speech, invited the assembled audience to draw up and send a Remonstrance to the Prince Regent, setting out the Radical programme for repeal of the Corn Laws, relief of destitution, and Parliamentary Reform. Hunt's choice of the term "Remonstrance" was significant for two reasons. The word is little used in modern British politics, but from the seventeenth to the nineteenth centuries it was a common description of a formal statement of grievances and demands for redress. The term had constitutional resonance, as the most famous

"Remonstrance" was the "Grand Remonstrance" delivered to King Charles 1 by the Long Parliament in December, 1641. Charles 1's rejection of the demands in the "Grand Remonstrance" led directly to the English Civil War. By choosing to call for a Remonstrance, Hunt was showing his commitment to proper constitutional forms and precedents, rather than revolution. At the same the choice would have reminded people with historical knowledge of the "Grand Remonstrance", and the violent consequences which followed when its demands were ignored.

The meeting took place and dispersed peacefully, though Hunt himself was attacked by Loyalists later in the evening when he attended the theatre, and attacked again at his inn. Its success generated further momentum for the Radical campaign in the Manchester area and elsewhere, which carried on for several months. Unfortunately, this very success caused a rise in fear and hostility towards the Radicals on the part of the Manchester magistrates.

The January meeting was followed by one held at nearby Stockport in February. Unlike the January meeting, this one was attended by soldiers summoned by the authorities, and again unlike in January, scuffles broke out as the meeting was breaking up, and the Riot Act was read three times before the crowd fully dispersed.

In June another Reform meeting was held at Stockport, attended by no less than 20,000 people, which this time passed off entirely peacefully. A further large open-air meeting of distressed weavers was held in Manchester in July.

During 1819 the organisers of Reform meetings started to encourage would-be participants to attend drill lessons on the moors, outside the towns where they worked. At these drill meetings, attendees were taught to walk in step, and to assemble at pre-arranged assembly points so as to arrive in organised contingents. Those attending were also encouraged to dress as well as possible, in order to create a good impression on bystanders. For most people, who did not possess good clothes, this just meant making themselves neat and tidy. These meetings were first reported in July, but may have begun earlier.

This drilling was seen as deeply sinister by the magistrates, who began a panicky search of locations suspected of holding concealed weapons. As far as anyone has ever been able to establish, either at the time or later, there were no concealed weapons anywhere connected with the people who were drilling or with the Radical movement. The Manchester Radical leaders, the most prominent of whom were John Knight and Joseph Johnson, were committed to peaceful protest, and their drilling was simply intended to ensure that the very large crowds now assembling to support their cause were orderly and did not bring the cause into disrepute.

Also in July 1819, the national Radical movement intensified the pressure for Reform by planning a series of four huge open-air public meetings, like those which had already been held in London and the North-West, in a bid to make the moment for Reform unstoppable. Meetings were planned in Birmingham, London, Leeds and Manchester. Some 30,000 people attended a meeting at Newhall Hill in Birmingham, a city which, like Manchester, had no Member of Parliament. The speakers were Major John Cartwright and the journalist T.J. Wooler, editor of the Radical newspaper *Black Dwarf.* Those present were invited to vote for a "legislatorial attorney" to represent Birmingham, a sort of tribune elected by demonstrators, purportedly representing the people of Birmingham in substitution for the city's non-existent M.P. Sir Charles Wolseley, a Radical who prided himself on having personally taken part in the storming of the Paris Bastille in 1789, was duly elected to the post by the meeting. This election caused great concern to the government, which asked the law officers for advice on whether such a procedure was legal.

The second of the four meetings was held on Hunslet Moor, Leeds, on 19 July. This one was a failure, with low attendance, probably due to poor organisation. The third meeting was held in Smithfield, London, on 21 July, with Henry Hunt as the principal speaker. The fourth meeting was announced for 9 August in Manchester, again with Hunt due to speak. The Manchester meeting was therefore to be the climax of the campaign.

At this point, events occurred which showed the deep commitment of the Manchester Radicals to acting within the law, contrary to what was later alleged against them by their enemies. These events are worth dwelling on, because up to the present day there is confusion as to whether the meeting which eventually took place in Manchester was intended by the organisers to be legal, or was an act of deliberate civil disobedience. Representatives of twenty-first century British "direct action" groups such as Plane Stupid have attempted to justify their deliberately illegal actions by claiming that early campaigners for democracy in Britain also favoured illegal action to further their cause, and that without direct action there would have been no democracy in Britain. Such claims are in fact quite untrue.

The original plan for the 9 August meeting in Manchester was that, just as in Birmingham, those present should be invited to elect a legislatorial attorney. The advice given by the Government law officers, when the action of the meeting in Birmingham was referred to them by the government, was that it was illegal to hold a meeting for such a purpose, as it constituted a criminal conspiracy to elect a Member of Parliament without the king's writ. However the law officers later changed their opinion, and advised that it was not a criminal conspiracy to organise such a meeting, and that a crime was only committed if the election of the legislatorial attorney actually took place. Until that moment, they considered, such a meeting would remain legal.

Acting on information about the first law officer's opinion, the Manchester magistrates announced that the meeting to be held on 9 August, 1819 was illegal and was banned. The magistrates then received the second law officer's opinion and were faced with the embarrassing possibility of having to rescind their announcement. However they did not need to do this, because the Radicals had themselves gone to the trouble of obtaining a barrister's opinion on the same question. Their barrister, a Mr Ranecock from Liverpool, had taken a more cautious view than the government law officers, and advised that convening a meeting for the purpose of electing a legislatorial attorney would be illegal, the same view as the first law officer's opinion. In the light of this opinion, the Radicals decided not to go ahead with the planned meeting on 9 August, or with the plan to elect a legislatorial attorney. Instead they sent a requisition to the Borough Reeve of Manchester to hold a different meeting on 16 August, signed by 700 people.

The Radicals had thus made strenuous efforts to ensure that their activities stayed within the law. They did not proceed with the meeting planned for 9 August, even though the revised government view was that it would be legal so long as no election of a legislatorial attorney took place. They abandoned the idea to elect a legislatorial attorney. They also applied to the authorities to hold their new 16 August meeting, using the correct procedure laid down in the Gagging Act, by way of notice being given to the magistrates by at least seven householders in the district where the meeting was to be held. These actions show their complete commitment to acting within the law, as frequently expressed by their leaders.

Samuel Bamford describes the preparations for the 16 August, 1819 meeting as follows:-

> *"It was deemed expedient that this meeting should be as morally effective as possible, and that it should exhibit a spectacle such as had never before been witnessed in England. We had frequently been taunted in the press with our ragged, dirty appearance... and the confusion of our proceedings, and the mob-like crowds in which our members were mustered."*

The watchwords for the meeting were "Cleanliness", "Sobriety", "Order" and "Peace". It assembled as planned in St Peter's Square in an entirely peaceful manner, and was attended by at least 60,000 men, women and children from Manchester and the mill towns around it, many of whom had marched into Manchester for the meeting. The atmosphere was described as festive.

Bamford describes heading the contingent from the mill town of Middleton. It was arranged with a group of youths in front wearing laurels "as a token of amity and peace", then some of the men marching five abreast, then the band and the banners inscribed with the slogans "Unity and Strength", "Liberty and Fraternity", "Parliaments Annual" and "Suffrage Universal", and then finally the rest of the men – again five abreast. Every hundred men had a leader distinguished by a sprig of laurel in his hat, and controlling the whole was Bamford himself, who headed the column with a bugleman to sound his orders.

Bamford records, in *Passages from the life of a Radical*, his speech at Middleton before the march started: -

> *"I reminded them that they were going to attend the most important meeting that had ever been held for Parliamentary Reform, and I hoped their conduct would be marked by a steadfastness and seriousness befitting the occasion… They were not to offer any insult or provocation by word or deed… If peace officers should come to arrest myself or any other person, they were not to offer resistance, but suffer them to execute their office peaceably… I also said, that in conformity with a rule of the committee no sticks, nor weapons of any description, would be allowed to be carried in the ranks; and those who had such were requested to put them aside."*

Bamford's contingent met and joined another from Rochdale before continuing on to Manchester. Another contingent came from Oldham, where it had joined groups from Crompton, Royton, Chadderton, Saddleworth, Lees and Mossley. The Saddleworth, Lees and Mossley contingent carried a black banner, inscribed with the slogans "Equal representation or death", "Unite and be free", "No boroughmongering", "Taxation without representation is unjust and tyrannical", "No corn laws", and "Universal Suffrage". This banner, with its reference to equal representation or death, was later used by the prosecution at the trial of the organisers of the meeting, to suggest that the meeting was seditious and intended violence. However the extensive available evidence is overwhelmingly to the contrary. There were large women's contingents from Manchester and Oldham, dressed for the occasion in white. One observer from a window in Manchester, Archibald Prentice, recorded that he had never seen "a gayer spectacle". Another observer, J.B. Smith, wrote: -

> *"It seemed to be a gala day with the country people who were mostly dressed in their best and brought with them their wives, and when I saw boys and girls taking their father's hand in the procession, I observed to my aunt 'Those are the guarantors of their peaceable intentions – we need have no fears'."*

Hunt arrived slightly late for the meeting. As he approached he had shown his instinct for eye-catching showmanship by asking for the white-clad leader of the Manchester Women's contingent, Elizabeth Fildes, whom he passed carrying a banner reading "Manchester Female Reformers", to be lifted up to sit next to him as he made his entrance. In describing this decision later, he referred to Mrs Fildes' "remarkably good figure". Hunt was not just enjoying female company. He appreciated, as many successful demonstration organisers have done since, the critical importance of catching the attention of the crowd by a striking display.

Hunt began speaking at about 1.40 pm, by which time the entire square was full. Both regular troops and mounted Manchester Yeomanry had been posted around the square at the request of the magistrates, and there were special constables sworn in by the magistrates standing around the platform, which was made up of two wagons drawn up together. The Manchester Yeomanry were local volunteers hostile to the Radicals, and by the time Hunt began to speak many of them were drunk.

Unknown to Hunt, just as he got to the platform, the Manchester magistrates, terrified by the huge numbers at the meeting, and by their orderly demeanour, which they found sinister, had decided that Hunt was to be arrested for organising a seditious meeting, and the meeting dispersed. The Yeomanry galloped through the streets to carry out the order and, in doing so, knocked down and killed a two-year-old child, William Fildes (no relation of Elizabeth Fildes). They then plunged into the crowd in the square to attempt to reach Hunt on the platform.

Meanwhile the magistrates had the Riot Act read in Mount Street, near St Peter's Square, but inaudible to most of the 60,000 people in the square. As a matter of law, the reading of the Riot Act was a meaningless gesture, since if the meeting was genuinely a riotous assembly, the law permitted it to be dispersed without a reading of the Riot Act. In addition, the Riot Act itself provided an hour for persons to disperse after it had been read, a provision which the Manchester magistrates ignored, when they proceeded to order the troops to disperse the meeting immediately.

What Hunt said at the meeting, in the few minutes he was allowed to speak before being arrested, was later the subject of much controversy. However, he was a frequent speaker at public meetings about reform, and it seems likely that he made remarks very similar to those he had made on numerous previous occasions, which did not bear any sinister interpretation. He appears to have said that he hoped that, if any person would not be quiet, that they would put him down and keep him quiet, referring to drunken interruptions. *The Times* however reported this remark as a coded exhortation to put down anyone who opposed the marchers' aims.

At this point in his speech, the Yeomanry appeared moving towards the platform, and alarmed cries of "the soldiers, the soldiers", were heard from the crowd. Hunt called out "Stand firm, my friends! You see they are in disorder already. This is a trick. Give them three cheers." The crowd responded with a loud cheer, which temporarily restored their confidence. The Yeomanry then began to move into the crowd making arrests, according to another eye-witness "with the zeal and ardour which might naturally be expected from men acting with delegated power against a foe by whom … they had long been insulted with taunts of cowardice". The crowd attempted to flee, but flight was extremely difficult in the dense crush with soldiers with drawn sabres riding at them from different directions.

When the soldiers reached the hustings, a scene of "dreadful confusion" ensued. The speakers were forced off the platform, and the soldiers then began dashing at the various banners held by the crowd to cut them down. A complete melee followed in which the Yeomanry lost all cohesion and were enveloped by the crowd. Seeing this, a magistrate, Hulton, ordered the commander of the professional soldiers present, Colonel Lestrange, to clear the whole square with a charge of the mounted 15th Hussars. The Hussars charged with sabres drawn, and although they generally attacked the crowd with the flats of their sabres to drive them away, inevitably some were struck by the sharp edges. Many more were crushed by the horses or by the mass of the crowd. The scene was described by a local clergyman who was observing:-

> "[The 15th Hussars] *then pressed forward, crossing over the avenue of constables, which opened to let them through, and bent their course towards the Manchester Yeomanry. The people were now in a state of utter rout and confusion, leaving the ground strewn with hats and*

shoes, and hundreds were thrown down in the attempt to escape. The cavalry were hurrying about in all directions, completing the work of dispersion, which ... was effected in so short a space of time to appear as if done "by magic"... During the whole of this confusion, heightened at its close by the rattle of some artillery crossing the square, shrieks were heard in all directions, and as the crowd of people dispersed the effects of the conflict became visible. Some were seen bleeding on the ground and unable to rise; others, less seriously injured but faint with loss of blood, were retiring slowly or leaning upon others for support... The whole of this extraordinary scene was the work of a few minutes".

Bamford noticed "several mounds of human beings remaining where they had fallen crushed down and smothered". Another observer wrote:-

"The charge of the Hussars swept this mingled mass of human beings before it; people, yeomen, and constables, in their confused attempts to escape, ran one over the other; so that by the time we had arrived at end of the field, the fugitives were literally piled up to a considerable elevation above the level of the ground".

Subsequent investigations indicated that at least 11 people had been killed and at least 400 wounded, many seriously. The 15th Hussars, who carried out much of the atrocity, had fought for their country four years earlier at Waterloo, as had many men in the crowd, including at least one who died of injuries received in the Square. In the circumstances the drawing of ironic contrasts was inevitable, and the local Manchester Radical newspaper, the *Manchester Observer*, reported the break-up of the meeting under the headline "Peter Loo Massacre". The event has been known as the Peterloo Massacre ever since.

There was only one reporter from a national newspaper present at the St Peter's Fields meeting, John Tyas of *The Times*. As the massacre took place, Tyas, who had been on the platform with the speakers, was arrested and imprisoned with them. This appears to have been a deliberate attempt to prevent news of the massacre being reported. As such it foreshadowed a feature of many later violent repressions of demonstrations, when the authorities, having killed and wounded demonstrators, had gone to extreme lengths to suppress the truth of what they had done[12]. However, two Manchester men who had been present at the scene, Archibald Prentice and John Taylor, sent reports to *The Times*. The extensive reports which *The Times* printed are thought to be theirs. Prentice and Taylor, radicalised by what they had seen, went on to found the *Manchester Guardian* in 1821, which in due course became today's *Guardian* newspaper.

The Peterloo Massacre shocked Britain, and has remained in the national memory as a by-word for tyranny and arbitrary use of state violence. In the short term, however, the effect of the massacre was not, as might have been expected, to strengthen the Radical or Reform movement, but to break its power. This phenomenon, which occurred for the first time after Peterloo, recurs repeatedly in the history of demonstrations. When demonstrations have been completely crushed by a massacre, the responsible powers try to justify themselves by putting the organisers on trial and imprisoning them for long periods, while the general population are terrorised into quiescence lasting for years. Something similar happened in France in 1892, and there are parallels with the Tiananmen Square massacre in China in 1989. This does not always happen. Sometimes the atrocity causes large numbers of previously peaceful people to turn towards violent revolution, as happened after the "Bloody Sunday" massacre of demonstrators in St Petersburg in 1905. However such cases are less common than those of successful repression.

Liverpool's government claimed that the meeting had been illegal and seditious, as it had not dispersed following the reading of the Riot Act, and in view of the alleged contents, or planned contents, of Hunt's speech. Hunt and other speakers were arrested and tried for unlawful and seditious assembly. Hunt was convicted and sentenced to two-and-a-half years' imprisonment, Joseph Johnson and Samuel Bamford, to one year each. John Knight was sentenced to two years for his attendance at a meeting at Burnley on November 15, 1815. The case was thought to be finely balanced, with the judge, Mr Justice Bayley, summing up for an acquittal, but an ill-judged defiant courtroom speech by Hunt before the jury retired may well have swung the jury to convicting. Sir Francis Burdett was sentenced to three months' imprisonment for publishing an address to the electors of Westminster condemning the massacre. Major Cartwright and T.J. Wooler were tried and sentenced for the Birmingham "legislatorial attorney" election, Wooler receiving 15 months' imprisonment. The magistrates who had brought about the massacre through their panicked reaction to the meeting were

---

[12] A notable twentieth century example of this phenomenon was the total French news blackout of the massacre of Algerian demonstrators in Paris in 1961, described in Chapter 14.

not punished, and one of them, a clergyman, was shortly afterwards appointed to a lucrative rectorship.

The Liverpool government was determined to prevent similar large meetings happening in future, and to achieve this aim it passed "The Six Acts" at the end of 1819. These did much to restrict pre-existing liberties. They included the Seditious Meetings Prevention Act, which went even further than the 1817 Seditious Meetings Act in restricting meetings. It prohibited any assembly with flags, arms, drums or other music, or in military array. It also provided that places at which lectures were given or debates held were deemed to be disorderly houses, unless they had been licensed by two justices of the peace, and the licence was to be forfeited if seditious or immoral lectures were given. Special regulations were made further restricting any meetings within a mile of Parliament. It was made illegal at any meeting to "express or purport that any Matter or Thing by Law established may be altered otherwise than by the Authority of the King, Lords and Commons in Parliament assembled", and if any such sentiments were expressed by any speaker, the meeting became an unlawful assembly, even if it had previously been lawful. This draconian provision exposed to criminal penalties anyone who happened to be present at a meeting where such views were expressed and who did not leave within 15 minutes of being told to do so. The Six Acts were immediately enforced by Viscount Sidmouth, who was still Home Secretary. The multiple restrictions they imposed, which also included a heavy stamp duty on newspapers to put them beyond the reach of the poor, caused the Radical and Parliamentary Reform movements to collapse temporarily.

An observer in England in 1820 might have been forgiven for concluding that the idea of reform of Parliament was dead, and that the idea of public mass meetings or marches for political causes was also finished. The government held all the cards, and had been willing to engage in a massacre to break up a peaceful meeting, organised by a man who had built his career and reputation on peaceful campaigning and rejection of violence. It looked as if repressive rule with tight restrictions on free speech and assembly would continue for a long time. But such a conclusion would have been wrong. In fact, 1820 was the darkness before the dawn. Within a few years the situation would be transformed, and the demonstrating habit would revive with a vengeance.

CHAPTER 5

DEMONSTRATIONS COME OF AGE: THE REFORM ACT CRISIS OF 1832

Among the politicians in Parliament at the time of Peterloo, the leading supporter of Reform was the Whig leader, Earl Grey. Grey had made Reform the main issue of his career and, as a result, had spent long years in opposition. In 1820, he wrote, to his son- in-law, John Lambton, that he saw little chance of reform "being carried in my lifetime or even in yours". Today Grey's statute stands at the top of Grey Street in Newcastle upon Tyne, commemorating his success, at the age of 68, in piloting into law the Reform Act of 1832.

Peterloo caused deep and long-lasting revulsion and horror among the British population. Because of this, the massacre, which was never planned by the government, but happened because of incompetence and panic on the part of local officials, was an own goal for those who wanted to preserve the existing system of government. If Hunt had been able to hold his big meeting undisturbed, without it being broken up by the troops, it would have done little harm to the government, and little to advance the Reform cause, given the intransigence of the landed interests who stood to lose by Reform. Instead, the government had succeeding in making itself widely hated.

This hatred was not reflected in Parliament, because of Parliament's unrepresentative composition. However among the great majority of people, who did not have the vote, Lord Liverpool's government remained intensely unpopular as a result of Peterloo, and this unpopularity did not wear off even after the economy improved in 1820. It attached itself to Liverpool himself, to

Sidmouth as Home Secretary, and to the Foreign Secretary, Lord Castlereagh. Castlereagh was not implicated in the massacre, but was detested because of his support for government repression and his exceptionally arrogant manner. When Castlereagh committed suicide in 1823, and was given a formal state funeral, a crowd of thousands broke into continuous vindictive cheers around his coffin as it was carried into Westminster Abbey.

There was no public acceptance following Peterloo of the idea that public meetings for political causes might be a thing of the past. Indeed, the fact that meetings were generally expected to continue as a feature of public life was reflected in the partial repeal, in 1824, of the 1819 Seditious Meetings Prevention Act, so that magistrates no longer had the power to change the time and place of a meeting. That repealed provision had probably been the most damaging part of the Act in terms of its effect on those who wished to organise a meeting.

The Parliamentary Reform cause remained dormant for a few years, but was revived by a chance series of events at the end of the 1820s, beginning with events in Ireland. Those events involved mass political organisation of a new kind, and the emergence of an orator capable of galvanizing it, Daniel O'Connell.

A generation earlier, during the crisis of the war with Revolutionary France, Ireland had risen in revolt, seeking independence, with help from France, led by Wolfe Tone and the United Irishmen. French help had not arrived in time, and the revolt had been crushed, and Ireland subjugated with great brutality by General Gerard Lake. A few years later, in 1807, Irish subjugation to Britain had been deepened with the abolition of the Irish Parliament, and its replacement by Irish seats created instead in the British Parliament.

Daniel O'Connell was a lawyer, an inspiring speaker and an able organiser. In contrast to the United Irishmen (whom he had briefly joined as a very young man), but like the London Corresponding Society, Henry Hunt and the Manchester Radicals, O'Connell was a constitutionalist who believed in the rule of law. Like them, he believed in achieving his aims by operating peacefully within the constitution, however much he disliked aspects of it. O'Connell had been a student in London at the time of the London Corresponding Society meetings. There is no evidence that he was involved with them or took any particular notice of them at the time. However his subsequent career suggests that he appreciated at an early stage the power of peaceful mass meetings.

In 1820s Ireland, Roman Catholics, who were over 80% of the Irish population, were allowed to vote, but were not allowed to sit in Parliament. O'Connell, a Roman Catholic, set out to get himself elected to Parliament by an overwhelming majority, hoping that, if he succeeded, the Government would change the law and permit him to take his seat, rather than triggering another revolt in Ireland by refusing to do so. His strategy worked. In 1829, as a result of massive electoral organisation through the Catholic Association, O'Connell was elected by a huge majority to be the Member of Parliament for County Clare.

Lord Liverpool died in 1827, and the British Prime Minister at the time of O'Connell's election in 1829 was the Duke of Wellington, the victor of Waterloo. Wellington, like Liverpool, was an extreme political conservative on most matters, but he happened to be sympathetic to Catholic emancipation. This was because he himself, as a Northern Irishman, was aware of the alienating effects of anti-Catholic discrimination in Ireland, and the way it was pushing the Catholic majority in Ireland towards open revolt. As a result of Wellington's views, his government passed into law the Catholic Emancipation Act of 1829, which enabled O'Connell to take his seat in Parliament after his election.

This huge success by O'Connell showed people throughout the British Isles, and indeed throughout Europe (where O'Connell became much better known than he did in England), that it was possible to achieve fundamental change by peaceful political mass mobilisation and campaigning. It therefore naturally reawakened ideas of such mobilisation among the supporters of British parliamentary reform, particularly as O'Connell's triumph was also over an issue involving parliamentary reform. This led a veteran Radical activist, Francis Place, to form the London Radical Reform Association for the reform of Parliament, in July 1829.

By winning Catholic emancipation, O'Connell removed that issue from the political agenda in England. This meant that general Parliamentary reform became a correspondingly bigger issue. It also disarmed one group of centrist politicians, who had supported Catholic emancipation, but opposed Parliamentary Reform precisely because they believed that a more democratic Parliament would reflect more strongly popular prejudice against Catholics, and so be more hostile to Catholic emancipation. With this issue out of the way, some of these politicians, including Lord Melbourne who eventually became Prime Minister, moved towards support for Reform.

In January 1830, Thomas Attwood, a prominent Birmingham banker, arranged for a public meeting to be held at a vast covered building in Birmingham called Beardsworth's Repository. Between 10,000 and 15,000 people attended the meeting. With Attwood in the chair, the meeting agreed to the foundation of a new organisation, the Birmingham Political Union. This Union was described as a "General Political Union between the lower and middle classes of the people" (both classes being excluded in most places from voting for Parliament). It was consciously modelled as an organising body on O'Connell's Catholic Association, which had been so successful in getting the election law changed in Ireland. The Union's first resolution was to *"obtain by every just and legal means such a reform in the Commons' House of Parliament as may ensure a real and effectual representation of the lower and middle classes of the people in that House."* The Union was emphatically committed to "Peace, Law, Order", reflecting Attwood's determined strategy of promoting reform by peaceful and responsible shows of popular support for the Reform cause. Because of his success in pursuing this strategy, Attwood played a key role in the spread of peaceful demonstrations as a form of political activity. Attwood's brother Charles set up a Political Union in Newcastle upon Tyne, and other Political Unions followed in many other towns.

The meeting at Beardsworth's Repository was comparable in size to the pro-Reform meetings in the period leading up to Peterloo, although not as large as the largest of them. However it generated less alarm and controversy among the Establishment than the meetings eleven years earlier. The main reason for this was the nature of those organising the meeting, with the much larger involvement of the middle-classes, as reflected in the description of the Birmingham Political Union. Attwood, the banker, was a much less threatening figure than Hunt, the demagogue swaying the working classes with his oratory. In addition, the campaign which Attwood launched was for Reform. He was not specific as to how much. The earlier campaigners had fought for universal manhood suffrage, an idea regarded as so radical as to be madness by many conservatives. Some of Attwood's followers also wanted universal manhood suffrage, but many were content with an extension of the franchise to more of the middle class, abolition of the tiny rotten boroughs that could be bought and sold, and provision of seats to the huge cities like Birmingham and Manchester which did not have them. This was a very widely supported programme in the country.

In May 1830, Daniel O'Connell proposed to the House of Commons a Bill for Universal Suffrage. This was lost by 306 votes. In contrast, a non-committal resolution by Lord John Russell in favour of Reform in principle was lost by 91 votes. The matter might have rested there for a considerable time, but for events unconnected with demonstrations.

Instead, the political situation was transformed, on 26 June, 1830, by the death of King George IV, who had been a rigid opponent of any kind of Parliamentary reform. The new King, his brother William IV, also disliked Reform, but was a more easy-going personality, and also more respectful of the limitations placed on a constitutional monarch. William's less hostile attitude encouraged the Reformers to campaign more vigorously. Constitutional convention required an immediate dissolution of Parliament following the death of the king, and in the election campaign following the death of George IV reform became a central issue.

During that election campaign, the situation was transformed again by unexpected dramatic events in France. King Charles X, the last of the restored Bourbon kings of France (of whom it was famously said by the French politician Talleyrand that "they learned nothing and they forgot nothing"), had attempted to rule without Parliament, to suppress the press, and to make himself an absolute ruler, in clear breach of the 1815 French constitution. In response, the French people rose up and overthrew him in a matter of days in July 1830, in an extremely quick and relatively painless revolution involving only minor bloodshed. At its conclusion Charles X's cousin, Louis-Philippe (the "Citizen-King") was installed as a constitutional monarch.

In Britain, these events in France laid the ghost of the Paris massacres in the first French Revolution. Revolution was no longer synonymous with bloodshed, and it was much harder for anyone to argue that moderate reforms would end with the guillotine. The fact that the French had thrown off the yoke of monarchical oppression so easily gave hope to reformers of all kinds in England. The *Edinburgh Review* went so far as to write that "The battle of English liberty has been fought and won at Paris".

The result of the general election, fought on the Reform issue, was a much reduced majority for Wellington and the Tories, with pro-Reform opposition Whigs successful in many places. There was a widespread expectation that the new government would embark on some kind of reform of Parliament, in order to remove the worst excesses and faults of the existing system. However, in a speech to the House of Commons on 2 November, 1830, Wellington stunned the nation by announcing that there would be no moves of any kind towards reform of Parliament while he was Prime Minister. It was obvious, even to his own Ministerial colleagues, whom he had surprised with this impromptu announcement, that he had gone much too far, had completely failed to read the public mood, and could probably not survive long as Prime Minister. Outside Parliament, rumours of revolution began to sweep the country. Wellington had to advise William IV not to attend dinner at the Guildhall in the City of London for fear for his safety. Petitions for reform poured into Parliament from all over the country. Then, on 15th November, Wellington's government was defeated in the House of Commons by 233 votes to 204. He resigned, and the king sent for Earl Grey, who became the first Whig Prime Minister for over 25 years.

Grey made it clear from the first moment that Parliamentary Reform would be the main concern of his administration, as the country expected. He had been written off many times by younger reformers as too cautious, too hesitant, and too unwilling to commit himself to action. However, when his Reform Bill was published early in 1831, it amazed everyone by its radical and sweeping nature.

Grey's Bill provided for complete abolition of the rotten boroughs. Sixty two-member seats were to be completely abolished, and a further 47 were reduced from two members to one, to reflect their small population. The seats so released were redistributed to the large, new, industrial towns and the outer regions of London, as well as to provide additional seats in some counties. The franchise was increased in all borough (town) seats, by giving the vote to everyone owning property rated at ten pounds a year, and the franchise was also extended in the counties.

In terms of simple numbers of new voters, Grey's proposals looked less dramatic than they actually were. Although the numbers are disputed, it seems likely that the Bill as eventually passed into law (very similar in form to when it was first introduced) gave votes to about half a million more people than before. This was an increase in the proportion of the population who could vote from 4% to about 7%. However, the revolutionary aspect of the Bill was the near complete eradication of the tiny seats which could be bought up and controlled by rich people. It was this change which meant that any post-Reform Parliament would be much more sensitive to public opinion.

In Parliamentary circles, the proposals were seen as so outrageously and foolishly Radical that the smart talk was that Grey's Ministry must fall very soon. However a tidal wave of public expressions of support for the reform proposals from the voteless millions quickly changed the situation. A seven-day debate was held on the Bill, and then the vote was taken on its Second Reading. This was a critical moment. Everyone knew that if the Bill was defeated the Government would fall, Grey would be written off as a failure, and the Duke of Wellington would probably be back as Prime Minister. However, if the Bill was carried at Second Reading, even if it failed later, there was a chance of enough momentum by then for Grey to win another election, fought on the single issue of reform, and to carry on.

By the end of the debate, it was known that the vote would be very close. Something of the electric atmosphere and the intense national interest in the result are captured in the memoirs of Thomas Macauley (remembered as a famous historian, but then a young Whig member who had just made his name with a notable pro-Reform speech in the debate). Macauley describes the result, at 3.00 am on 23 March, 1831 as follows: *"It was like seeing Caesar stabbed in the Senate House, or seeing Oliver* [Cromwell] *take the mace from the table; a sight to be seen only once, and never to be forgotten.…As the vote was counted, it was clear that it was extremely close, so close that the result was unclear to all except the tellers (the counters) even after the last Member had been counted. Then a teller read out the numbers. The Bill had been carried by one vote. We shook hands and clapped each other on the back, and went out, laughing, crying and huzzaing into the lobby. And no sooner were the outer doors opened than another shout answered that within the House. All the passages, and the stairs into the waiting-rooms were thronged by people who had waited until four in the morning to know the issue. We passed through a narrow lane between two thick masses of them; and all the way down they were shouting and waving their hats, till we got into the open air."*

This was a first crucial victory in a painfully long-drawn out, uncertain and tense process. The following month the Bill was defeated in the Committee stage. However, as it had passed its Second Reading, the general view of most people, including the king, was that it was appropriate for Parliament to be dissolved and a new general election held in which Parliamentary Reform would be the main issue. William IV behaved with constitutional propriety in quickly granting Grey his request for a dissolution of Parliament, rather than trying to call Wellington back to form an anti-Reform government.

The 1831 election, even though held under the old unreformed system, resulted in a greatly increased majority for Grey's government. Seats which had not been contested in living memory were contested, and sitting members defeated by pro-Reform newcomers. The government itself entered into the market of borough mongers and bought up some of the most corrupt seats for pro-Reform candidates. Elsewhere, seats which had been thought safely in the pockets of Tory landlords surprised observers by returning someone other than the landlord's choice, reflecting the strong wave of popular feeling in support of Reform.

Grey's government introduced a second Reform Bill in the new Parliament, which passed all its stages in the House of Commons by September 1831.

The scene was now set for a constitutional crisis between the House of Commons and House of Lords. Grey knew that defeat in the House of Lords was a strong possibility. However, he hoped to get the bill through by encouraging enough of the Lords to take a broader view of the national interest, rather than following their traditional allegiances.

In order to achieve this, he took the unusual step of quietly telling the leaders of the Birmingham Political Union and the other Political Unions that they should now mount big shows of popular feeling, through demonstrations and public meetings.

A huge pro-Reform demonstration of 50,000 people had already taken place in Scotland, where the feeling for reform was even more urgent and desperate than in England, because of the extreme corruption and lack of popular representation in the Scottish Parliamentary seats. (In Scotland the Reform Bill increased the number of eligible voters to about fifteen times the pre-Reform number).

On 22 September, 1831, the day the Bill passed all its stages in the Commons, Grey met Thomas Attwood and four other Radical leaders privately in London. The meeting had been requested by Attwood to discuss both political reform and his other interest of currency reform. However, Grey made it clear to Attwood that he was concerned specifically with political reform, and that he felt that the time had come for public opinion on the subject to make itself felt.

The leaders of the Political Unions responded to Grey's message. A few days later, on 3 October, 1831, church bells were rung in Birmingham at 10.00 am, and about 100,000 people assembled, from leading merchants and bankers to a large contingent of miners. They marched in procession through the streets, while being entertained by street performers and the Political Union's own band. The march terminated at Newhall Hill, where speeches were made and a petition for Parliament approved, calling for Parliamentary reform. The crowd then dispersed peacefully. With this event, Attwood showed himself a master of the new form of political protest by street demonstration. As the words of the Political Union's own marching song put it:

> "See, see we come! No swords we draw
> We kindle not war's battle fires;
> By union, justice, reason, law,
> We'll gain the birthright of our sires.
> And thus we raise from sea to sea
> Our sacred watchword, Liberty!"

The meeting was twice the size of Henry Hunt's meeting in St Peter's Fields, Manchester, which became Peterloo, and it passed off without any intervention by the authorities, or any violent incidents. It was widely reported, and gave enormous additional momentum to the Reform cause. As such it was probably the first large demonstration in England which could be classed as an unqualified success.

However, despite Attwood's and Grey's efforts, the Reform Bill was still defeated in the House of Lords, by 41 votes, on 8 October, 1831. Grey had attempted to persuade the Lords by two spectacular speeches, which were thought by contemporaries to make him the greatest public speaker in the country. In his second speech, he subtly, while denying any intention of frightening the Lords with fear of revolution if the Reform Bill was not passed, tried to do precisely that. However, his oratory did not sway the intransigence of the Duke of Wellington and his supporters.

The House of Commons then passed a motion of confidence in Grey's government, and the king asked Grey and his ministers to continue in office. Grey proceeded to introduce a third Reform Bill into the Commons, which again easily passed all its Commons stages.

Massive public demonstrations in support of the Bill continued during the preparation for the final showdown with the House of Lords. On Wednesday, 12 October, 1831, a "monster procession" of the London metropolitan parishes took place, for the purpose of carrying a pro-Reform address to the king.

This was the first big demonstration for reform in London. It was organised by two young Radicals, John Powell and Thomas Bowker, based in Bloomsbury, who visited different London parishes in turn to persuade each parish association to take part. As well as encountering a lot of scepticism as to whether a peaceful demonstration could make any difference, they also – unlike Attwood in Birmingham – had to contend with opposition from a significant number of people who opposed the Reform Bill because it did not go far enough. These were supporters of the Rotunda group, forerunners of the later Chartist movement. The Rotunda group, who were regarded by most people, including many within the Reform movement, as dangerous extremists, refused to show support for Grey because he was not introducing universal manhood suffrage. Rotunda supporters opposed Powell and Bowker when they visited Bethnal Green to gather support there.

Despite these difficulties, the "monster procession" was another dramatic success for the street demonstration as a form of political activity. At least 70,000 people took part, and the organisation was impressive. Each parish association fell in behind the next as the procession moved southwards towards St James's Palace, with order maintained by the demonstrators marching in a row of six or eight, with the "flankman" at the end of each row being responsible for its behaviour. At St James's Palace, the Home Secretary, Lord Melbourne, received the petition. All the shops were shut, and a vast crowd of spectators assembled in the streets, much to the alarm of the wealthy. Some Rotunda supporters did after all take part, and their distinctive white scarves caused particular alarm, although none of their leaders was present. However, the procession, which was described as consisting mainly of "shopkeepers and artisans", behaved in a completely orderly way, with no disturbances or breaches of the peace.

The procession made a great impression, as it showed that many serious minded people, who were not usually active in politics, cared enough about the Bill to take part. As Powell later wrote to Francis Place about his and Bowker's achievement, "For young soldiers we were not bad generals". The success of the procession, in turn, showed that any anti-Reform government, whether led by the Duke of Wellington or anyone else, would have a very difficult time governing. In the House of Commons the debate the evening after the procession was mainly about the procession, with the opposition accusing the government of taking the part of "rioters" against the law, as well as attacking it for corresponding with the Birmingham Political Union. The opposition had correctly identified a source of the government's strength and their own weakness, for events had now brought Grey's Whig Party and the Radicals outside Parliament together, and they continued to work together for the remainder of the crisis.

As well as the monster procession in London, there were pro-Reform rallies attended by over 10,000 people in Liverpool and in Manchester, and similar meetings in Rochdale, Oldham, Bolton, Preston, Newcastle, Edinburgh and numerous other places.

Particular public disgust was felt at the conduct of twenty-one Church of England bishops with seats in the House of Lords, who had joined the Duke of Wellington in voting against the Reform Bill. If they had voted the other way, the Bill would have been carried. Public hatred against the bishops made it impossible for them to appear in public. At Worcester the cathedral was decorated with a huge slogan "Judas Iscariot, Bishop of Worcester". On 5 November, Guy Fawkes Night, across England the traditional guy on the bonfire was replaced by a different figure. What happened in one town, Huddersfield, is described by Henry Hetherington in the *Poor Man's Guardian* newspaper:-

> *"Between 15,000 and 20,000 persons paraded the street with an effigy of the bishop (as natural as life!) and no funeral was ever conducted with greater order and solemnity. When the procession reached the spacious and open square in the Market Place, all formed around the Right Reverend Father in God and a person in priestly habiliments delivered, in an audible and impressive manner, the following funeral oration:-*
>
> *"Ho, all ye people of Huddersfield! For lo and behold, here is a great, fat, bloated, blundering bishop, whom we have bartered*

for the poor, deluded, murdered Guy Faux. This is the last 5th of November which shall constitute the anniversary of a bloody church and state conspiracy...

…. We hereby commit his infernal body to the flames... in the certain belief that eternal damnation will be his portion, and that he will never inherit a glorious resurrection".

During the delivery of the oration, a most solemn silence was observed by the assembled multitude... they consigned him to the flames about 10.00 at night, after which the "mob" ... quietly dispersed, and in less than fifteen minutes the streets were as clear as though nothing of an alarming nature had occurred."

However, despite the peaceful nature of most demonstrations, Grey's warning of the risk of revolution was not far-fetched. In parts of England where constitutional reformers were less well-organised, violence broke out, There were riots at Blandford, Sherborne and Yeovil, and serious violence at Derby, where rioters, after attacking the houses of known anti-Reformers, broke into the Borough Gaol and released the prisoners, and were only stopped from storming the County Gaol after three of them were killed. Next day, while troops from nearby Nottingham were restoring order in Derby, Nottingham erupted into riots.

There was particular hatred in the Nottingham area for the owner of Nottingham Castle, the Duke of Newcastle. One of the surprise upsets of the 1831 general election had been at nearby Newark-on-Trent, previously regarded as a "pocket borough" under the Duke's control, where the Duke's candidate unexpectedly lost to a pro-Reform candidate. In revenge, the Duke evicted some of his tenants who were known to have voted for the winner (the secret ballot was not introduced until 1872). This was the Duke's habit after elections, and when he was criticised on a previous occasion for his harshness in evicting them, the Duke had responded with the words "May I not do what I will with mine own?"

In Nottingham, the crowd first attacked other buildings, and then, while troops in the town were fully committed defending them, attacked Nottingham Castle, which was set on fire and burned to the ground. A dramatic painting by an unknown artist of the burning castle silhouetted against the flames and the night sky is the most famous image of the Reform crisis.

Even more serious riots occurred in Bristol, where large parts of the city centre were burned down, and many rioters were killed by troops restoring order.

It was a point of principle for Attwood, Place and most of the constitutional reformers to avoid violence. However, even the constitutional reformers took the view, justified by Whig constitutional theory, that they would, if necessary, use force to resist the imposition of tyranny. During October 1831, the Birmingham Political Union made preparations to adopt a plan for a military organisation, to make such resistance easier if it became necessary. The government, aware of the plans, sent a confidential message to the Union, through a Reformist Birmingham lawyer, Joseph Parkes, that such a plan was illegal and would result in steps being taken to suppress the Union. On receiving the message, the Union abandoned the plan and merely continued instead with its peaceful protests.

Grey's third Reform Bill contained minor amendments designed to sway enough votes in the Lords to ensure its passage, while he secretly obtained a pledge from William IV that, if necessary, new peers (new members of the House of Lords) could be created to ensure the Bill's passage. Grey was reluctant to use the weapon of creation of new peers, for fear that doing so would alienate some lords who had previously supported the Bill. He played his cards close to his chest, and during the early months of 1832, when morale among the Reformers was low, his continued failure to ask the king to create new peers, disappointing the expectations of his supporters, led to debate as to whether he was really a strong leader with a definite strategy, or simply timid and uncertain how to proceed. These doubts were misplaced.

Grey's third Bill passed the Commons easily and came for its Second Reading in the Lords, without any new peers having been created. Again Grey spoke powerfully for the Bill, speaking for an hour-and-a-half from 5.00 am as the sun rose over a chamber still full with over 300 peers in attendance. This time, the second reading was passed by a majority of nine, 184 votes to 175, early in the morning of 14 April, 1832.

However, this was still not the end of the battle. The Bill still had to go through its committee stage in the House of Lords, where any peer could propose an amendment, including one which would have the effect of wrecking the Bill by voting down or fundamentally changing one of its central proposals. On 7 May, the government was defeated on a Tory-wrecking amendment proposed in committee stage. Grey then asked the king to create 50 new peers to ensure the Bill's passage. At this point, William IV, having previously promised to create new peers, stabbed Grey in the back by refusing to do so. Grey and his government resigned, and the king accepted their resignations. It was widely believed that his German wife, Adelaide, had influenced him to do so. For a few days, the fate of Reform again hung in the balance.

Those few days, which were later referred to as the "Days of May", were marked by a completely unique outbreak of pro-Reform public demonstrations.

These happened in almost every town in England. Work and business stopped, and everyone came out to demonstrate. As well as the now traditional marches in large towns, a great variety of demonstrations were also held in smaller places. William Cobbett printed this description of a demonstration at Godalming in Surrey: -

> *"The people of this quiet little town got a cart drawn by a horse and seated in it the representative of a MILITARY CHIEF [i.e. the Duke of Wellington] ; at his side the representative of a FROW* [i.e. a German woman, such as Queen Adelaide, from "Frau", the German word for "woman"]. *The cart appeared to be accompanied during the procession by every creature in the town and also by numerous persons from the villages round about. The personages in the cart were a living man and woman! There was an erection, resembling a gallows, fixed to the cart, with a swing rail going over the heads of the culprits. The procession started from the bridge at the bottom of the town, going on slowly towards the market place at the upper end of the town. At about every fifty yards of the progress the executioner, armed with a pistol and powder, shot the military chief, who fell down backward in the cart, the frow hanging about his neck and screaming. At last the ceremony was concluded, by regularly putting ropes about their necks, white caps on their heads, and these being drawn down over their faces, the offending parties expiated their sins in a very becoming manner, first, listening attentively, with great apparent penitence, to a prayer of considerable length that was read to them, and then committing their souls in due form, to the devil, hanging the legal length of time, and, being cut down, fell apparently dead into the bottom of the cart. The performers of this affair collected a good parcel of money, which they expended in drinking "success to the Reform Bill". The church-bells rang from morning to night, except when the offenders were hanging, when, as a matter of course, the knell tolled ... The FROW appeared singularly fond of the COMMANDER and kissed him, very affectionately, previous to their finally taking leave of this miserable reforming world."*

William IV, having accepted Grey's resignation, asked the Duke of Wellington to try to form a government. The Duke's role at this stage was sinister. He made remarks suggesting that he would like to have the chance to crush the Reform movement by force. These remarks finally led the Birmingham Political Union to start building barricades across the city streets to stop the expected assault by soldiers. A soldier at barracks near Birmingham recorded that his unit (many of them sympathetic to Reform) had been given orders to "rough sharpen" their swords. "Rough sharpening" involved alternatively sharpening and leaving blunt sections of a sword blade, and was done with the deliberate intention that the dirty wounds so inflicted would be more likely to cause death from blood poisoning. The order to "rough sharpen" had previously last been given on the eve of the Battle of Waterloo.

However, Wellington was unable to form a government. He had no chance of a majority in the House of Commons, and the other leading Tory figure, Sir Robert Peel, refused to join him. The final death-knell of his hopes came as a result of a brilliant campaign by Francis Place to organise runs on all the banks by all supporters of Reform, under the slogan "Stop the Duke, Go for Gold!" Two days later, supporters of the Duke let it be known that he was willing to take office to enact a Reform Bill. The proposal was met with derision from all sides of the House of Commons, including both Reformers and anti-Reformers, and at that point Wellington informed the king that he could not form a government.

The tension throughout Britain at this point was unbearable. The day after Wellington abandoned his attempt to form a government, more vast pro-Reform demonstrations were held in Glasgow and in Edinburgh, where 30,000 people assembled outside the walls of Holyrood Castle. The scene was described by Henry Cockburn:-

> "I never before actually felt the immediate presence of a great popular crisis. I advise nobody to create it. The fearful part was the absence of riot. There was nothing to distract the attention, or to break the terrible silence – nothing but grave looks and orderly public proceedings, unconquerable resolution and the absolute certainty that if any accident had made resistance begin anywhere, it would have run like an electric shock through the moment."

After a few days of ever-larger public meetings, stoppages of work and trade, fear and uncertainty, the king reluctantly backed down and agreed that, if necessary, he would create sufficient peers for the Bill to be passed. Once this was known, the tensions subsided. Aware of the unwelcome possibility of creation of new peers, a significant number of peers changed their position, and the Duke and his supporters decided there was no point in provoking such a special creation. The Third Reading of the Reform Bill was therefore easily passed by 106 votes to 22 and the Reform Act became law with William IV's Royal Assent on 7 June, 1832.

The Reform Act created a new kind of Parliament which had to be responsive to public opinion. Among the many huge changes which this brought about in life in Britain, it meant that there was a continuing role for the type of peaceful demonstration which had been critical to the Act's passage. The combination of a responsive Parliament, well-developed newspapers to report on events, and a politically educated and organised population, meant that all the necessary ingredients for future successful demonstrations were now in existence. Even the introduction of a police force in 1829 meant that police were available for when demonstrations got out of hand, as at Spa Fields, or were attacked by other members of the public, a far better situation than when the only means of maintaining public order was with soldiers.

How critical were demonstrations in bringing about the passage of the Reform Act? Are there lessons for demonstrators generally from the use of demonstrations in the Reform campaign?

The short answer to these questions is that the Reform Act would not have been passed when it was, but for the organised national demonstrations which kept up the momentum for Reform. In an age without universal suffrage or opinion polls, the demonstrations, by their scale and geographical spread, convincingly expressed the popular view, in a way which could not otherwise have been achieved.

At the same time, Reform would also not have happened but for other essential success factors. These included the overwhelming dissatisfaction with the existing Parliamentary system; the mood of change brought about by Catholic emancipation; the political skill of Earl Grey; the lack of political skill of the Duke of Wellington and the chance influence of the July 1830 Revolution in France. Despite all these factors which favoured the Reform Act, it was still a very close-run thing.

Demonstrations were indeed an essential part of the process. However they were not on their own sufficient to achieve the desired result. The Reform demonstrations disprove the defeatists who argue that demonstrations can never achieve much. They support the view that demonstrations can usually only achieve their objectives as part of a wider campaign, also using a variety of other political methods, including, of course, elections, in those countries where elections exist.

One of the limitations of demonstrations as a political technique, as will be seen in later chapters, is that, no matter how large or well-planned they are, they can rarely, if ever, succeed, against a totally intransigent government prepared to use force to oppose them. It should be borne in mind, in assessing the success of the Reform demonstrators of the 1830s, that they did not face a government of that kind. Unlike Henry Hunt, they faced a government in power, for all except a short period of their campaign, which actually supported their objectives and tacitly encouraged their activities. Had this not been the case, their campaign could not have succeeded and would probably have been suppressed. This can be seen from what happened during the short period in 1832 when Grey was out of power. The order to "rough-sharpen" swords given to soldiers while Wellington was trying to form a government, showed that Wellington was prepared to use massive force to crush the Reform movement. Such use of force would either have crushed the movement, as it had been crushed thirteen years earlier, or would have provoked the outbreak of violent national revolution. Ultimately it was a matter of luck that, by the time Wellington was prepared to consider such an expedient, he had so little support, even in conservative circles, that he was unable to form a government.

Demonstrations were recognized throughout the British Isles as having played a large and honourable part in bringing about Reform. This applied particularly to Attwood's Birmingham Political Union and the demonstrations in Birmingham. As a consequence, the tradition of protesting about political events, or issues of concern, by peaceful marches and meetings, by reason and law and not by rioting or the sword, had become deeply rooted and widely respected by the time the Reform Act became law. From 1832 onward, the political demonstration was there to stay, as an established part of British national life.

So far, however, this tradition was established only in Britain. It remained to be seen whether it would just be a peculiar British tradition, like burning the guy on Guy Fawkes Night, or would turn into a durable export, like railways, cricket, or the common law.

CHAPTER 6

THE DEMONSTRATING HABIT
BEGINS TO SPREAD

The first people to copy the idea of the British pro-Reform Bill demonstrations were reformers in Germany.

In May 1832, while the "Days of May" were happening in England, Philip Siebenpfeiffer and Johann Wirth issued invitations to a festival, to be held on 27 May, at the ruined castle of Hambach, above the small Rhineland town of Neustadt an der Weinstrasse.

A driving force behind this festival plan were the "Press Vereine", the press unions, of which Wirth was a member, which had been campaigning for a free press. Wirth was the editor of a newspaper, the *Tribune*, whose presses had been destroyed by political opponents earlier in the year. Siebenpfeiffer was a civil servant and writer.

The Hambach festival had twin aims, to promote the cause of liberty generally, and to promote the cause of a free and united Germany, no longer to be under the control of either foreign forces or reactionary local despots.

The "festival" took the form of a huge organised procession from Neustadt an der Weinstrasse up to the castle at Hambach, accompanied by bands and banners, including a huge, red, yellow and black flag to represent a united Germany. The modern (post-1945) German flag originates from the flag flown on that occasion. Between twenty and thirty thousand people took part. Speeches were made by Wirth, Siebenpfeiffer and others, all emphasising the call for "Einheit und Freiheit" – unity and freedom – for Germany, which was then divided into numerous petty principalities. The Hambach festival is recognized in Germany as the first political demonstration in modern German history.

Unfortunately for Germany, the reaction of its rulers to the festival, particular that of the influential Austrian First Minister, Prince Metternich, was implacably hostile, immediate and crushing. Just over a month later, on 28 June, 1832, the German princes met at Frankfurt and agreed on the "Six Articles", confirming that the government of Germany was government by monarchical authority. These "Six Articles" were followed on 5 July by the "Ten Articles", which were a code of restrictions on freedom, specifically including a ban on unauthorised assemblies. Active in promoting these Articles was Britain's King William IV, in his capacity as King of the German state of Hannover. The incipient German demonstration movement was nipped in the bud and did not recover. This had grave consequences for Germany, as described in Chapter 8. Wirth and Siebenpfeiffer were both arrested and sentenced to two years' imprisonment for organising the festival. They did not attempt to organise another.

The first big demonstration in England after the passage of the Reform Act was in support of the Tolpuddle Martyrs, six farm labourers from Tolpuddle in Dorset, who were sentenced to transportation to Australia merely for forming a trade union. On 21 April, 1834, 40,000 people, most of them trade unionists, marched peacefully and in good order from Copenhagen Fields – the same venue where the London Corresponding Society had met in October 1795 – to the Home Office in Whitehall, to hand in to the Home Secretary a petition against the transportation. The Home Secretary was still Lord Melbourne, who in 1831 had accepted the huge petition organised by John Powell and Thomas Bowyer in favour of Parliamentary Reform. This time, however, Melbourne refused to accept the petition, or to commute the sentence. Melbourne tried to justify refusing to accept the petition because the huge procession accompanying it meant that it was not "properly presented", although the procession was not as big as that which accompanied the Reform petition. However the Tolpuddle Martyrs demonstration was not a complete failure. It kept the issue of the transportation in the public eye, showed the strength of public feeling, and helped to ensure that the six were eventually pardoned and given the option of returning to England.

These demonstrations of the 1830s were still not called "demonstrations" but were referred to just as "marches", "processions" or "public meetings". The use of the word "demonstration" to describe them was unknown, until used for the first time in 1839. That first use was for an event on 21 April, 1839, reported by *The Times* under the headline "Demonstration of teetotallers".

The New British and Foreign Temperance Society that year marked its tenth anniversary by organising the Metropolitan Total Abstinence Procession. The idea was copied from American Temperance Societies, which had several times tried to attach a Temperance contingent to American Fourth of July Independence Parades. The idea was controversial with the membership of the Society, some of whom doubted whether such a public procession and meeting was entirely respectable – a kind of reservation about street demonstrations which has remained in existence in some conservative circles up to the present day.

In order to overcome these reservations, the Society chose Kennington Common for the destination of the procession. Kennington Common had respectable religious connotations, being adjacent to the spot where the Methodist preacher, George Whitfield, had preached to an open-air congregation in 1759.

The Times's article described several thousand orderly temperance marchers assembling at Lincoln's Inn Fields, and marching to Kennington Common, wearing white and blue rosettes, and carrying banners with slogans such as "Intemperance is the curse of Britain", "We agree to abstain from all intoxicating liquors, save for medicinal purposes or in a religious ordinance", and "Down with the tyrants" (this banner having a painting of two bottles overflowing with spirits as "the tyrants").

The article also described how the aim of the temperance organisers, which was to conclude the demonstration with rousing temperance speeches, was frustrated, because Kennington Common turned out to be already in use by another demonstration when the temperance demonstration arrived there. The other demonstration was an early demonstration by the Chartists, the supporters of the "Great Charter" who took up the campaign for universal suffrage, where the Political Unions of 1832 left off on the passage of the Reform Act.

At Kennington Common, on this occasion, the Temperance and Chartist speakers were within easy shouting distance of each other, and each tried to drown the other out. The resulting chaos was increased by the fact that each demonstration had up to four speakers addressing the audience at one time from different platforms. This arrangement was necessary with large crowds in the days before electronic voice amplification, and had also been used forty-four years earlier at the London Corresponding Society meetings. As a result of the closeness of the various platforms, moving entreaties to turn away from the evils of drink were interrupted by roars of applause as a Chartist speaker urged his listeners to stand up for their right to vote, and Chartist speakers in turn were interrupted by applause responding to the Temperance speakers.

In due course the temperance marchers adjourned to a further meeting at the Horns Tavern, where, according to *The Times*, they were "refreshed with large cans of water".

Despite the clash of venues with the Chartists, the temperance procession was considered to have been a triumph. The *Temperance Journal* recorded that it was a resounding success "as a demonstration of the strength of our principles". The Society went on to organise many other similar events, which the *Journal* from then onwards invariably referred to as "demonstrations". Within a month of its report on the Metropolitan Total Abstinence Procession, it was describing the "Great Teetotal Demonstration at Penzance", as having been the most striking procession ever seen in the history of the county of Cornwall. The term "demonstration" then rapidly spread into general popular usage from its first use by the Temperance movement.

Unlike Temperance campaigners, who were viewed as highly respectable by the authorities, the Chartists were extremely controversial. Their proposed new "Great Charter", drafted by William Lovett and Francis Place, called for a series of Parliamentary Reform demands, including universal manhood suffrage, annual Parliaments, no property qualification for Members of Parliament, and a secret ballot. Chartists were divided between a large constitutional movement, which wanted to follow the same techniques as the Political Unions had followed in 1832, and a small contingent, the spiritual successors to Thistlewood, Watson, and the militants of the Rotunda, which still believed in violent revolution on the French model.

Lovett, the first Chartist leader, was a constitutionalist, but ironically was harshly punished by the authorities for supposed unconstitutional action for which he was not personally responsible. In July 1839, the Chartists held a national convention. This opened in London, but then moved to Birmingham's Bull Ring. However the Bull Ring gathering was banned by the authorities, and was broken up by the police. Chartist posters were printed describing the police action as illegal. Lovett was prosecuted for seditious libel for the content of the posters, and sentenced to a year's imprisonment. This led to his replacement as leader by Feargus O'Connor, a demagogue with an ambivalent attitude to the rule of law.

Particular controversy surrounds the actions of Chartists in Newport, South Wales, in November 1839. Feelings in South Wales had been aroused by the sentencing of a Chartist supporter, Henry Vincent, to 12 months imprisonment in August 1839, for making inflammatory speeches. On 4 November, some 3,000 Chartists marched to Newport to protest about Vincent's treatment. On arrival, they discovered that several local Chartists had been arrested by the magistrates, and were being held in the Westgate Hotel. The marchers attempted to storm the hotel, using staves, clubs and other weapons. There were already soldiers placed in the hotel to guard the prisoners, and eventually these soldiers fired into the attacking crowd, killing at least 20 and wounding over 50. John Frost, the organiser of the march, was tried and condemned to death, but the sentence was commuted to transportation to Australia.

The extent to which events at Newport were part of a concerted attempt by revolutionary Chartists to overthrow the government has always been contested. Frost claimed that he attempted to dissuade others from violence, but this is disputed, and other Chartists later claimed that freeing the prisoners at Newport was intended to be the first step in a wider uprising.

The demands set out in the Chartists' "Great Charter" were not unreasonable. Save for annual Parliaments, all were eventually met by changes in the law. However, from its outset, the Chartist movement attracted the suspicion and hostility of the Establishment. This was for several reasons.

Firstly there was widespread fear of another revolutionary crisis like 1832. The fear was that this time constitutional Chartism would ally with elements intent on violent revolution in such strength as to be able to bring down the government. This fear was then exacerbated by the mainly working-class character of the Chartist movement, unlike the Political Unions, which had been alliances of the middle classes and the working classes. It was also further increased by the unattractive strategy and personality of Feargus O'Connor, and his apparent hostility to the rule of law.

Only a minority of the middle-class reformers who gained the vote in 1832 were active in the continuing campaign for universal suffrage. Although Attwood supported the Charter, his vocal commitment to the rule of law was no longer a dominant voice. Instead, the tone was set by O'Connor, whose speeches, to his predominantly working class audiences, usually contained veiled threats of revolution if the legitimate peaceful demands of Chartism were not met. Where Henry Hunt had emphasised that the resistance to tyranny by force was a last resort, to be used only where all other strategies had failed, O'Connor reversed this message and proclaimed that forceful resistance would come if the Chartist demands were not met. O'Connor seems to have combined notable violence of language with a marked tendency to avoid personal trouble with the authorities, by at once giving way if finding himself in a confrontation with them. This character trait played a key part in the failure of the Chartist movement, through the failure of its most important street demonstration in 1848.

English fears of Revolution, which had temporarily been reduced after the bloodless second French Revolution of 1830, revived in response to events in continental Europe in 1848, the European "Year of Revolution", which saw revolutionary movements in France, Germany, Italy and Hungary.

An insight into these fears is given by a surviving memo written in June 1848 by General Sir John Burgoyne, the general commanding the Metropolitan Region, who was responsible for public order in London if called on to assist the civil government in time of crisis.

"London", Burgoyne wrote, *"is peculiarly liable to danger from internal commotions. The population is enormous, and among them are to be found many thousands, out of work, suffering, and discontented, with numbers of political enthusiasts ready for the most violent attacks on the powers that be... we have a formidable association under the denomination of Chartists only waiting its opportunity and ready to connect themselves with any malcontents of high and low station, hints having already been thrown out of a combination of efforts between them and the advocates of a renewed Reform agitation."*

Such was the fear that trouble might spread to England from the 1848 continental revolutions, that, when a major Chartist "Grand National Demonstration" and petition of Parliament was announced for 10 April, 1848, Queen Victoria and her family deliberately left London, to avoid possible revolutionary danger, and took refuge at their additional home at Osborne on the Isle of Wight.

The Chartist Grand National Demonstration of 10 April, 1848 seems to have been the first occasion that the Metropolitan Police (founded in 1829) managed to trick a demonstration organiser into agreeing to a condition which deprived his demonstration of much of its power and impact. This police technique has since been refined, and is regularly used by the Met and other police forces in places where demonstrations are legally permitted. In the run-up up to the Grand National Demonstration, the police suggested to Feargus O'Connor that the place at which the demonstrators should assemble, prior to presentation of their petition to Parliament in Westminster, should be Kennington Common. O'Connor agreed to this seemingly sensible suggestion for use of this by now traditional venue. He appears not to have realised that the effect of assembling at Kennington Common would be to keep the demonstrators away from central London for much of the day. After some 50,000 Chartists had assembled at Kennington Common on the day, the police for the first time told O'Connor that no mass march to Parliament would be permitted. The Chartists would only be allowed to hold their meeting at Kennington and then disperse. This police condition was of doubtful legality, but the police made it clear to O'Connor that if he did not agree to it he would immediately be arrested. A more intelligent planner would have foreseen this situation in advance and not agreed to hold the meeting in Kennington. Instead O'Connor was trapped in a situation where he either had to agree to this unexpected police condition, or face immediate arrest for defying it. A more courageous or imaginative man might have announced that he would walk alone from Kennington to Parliament to present his petition, something which he was guaranteed the right to do by Magna Carta. Alternatively he might have invited the police to arrest him on the grounds that he believed that he was within his rights in marching to Parliament with his followers. That might have called the police bluff, as the arrest of O'Connor, simply for wishing to lead his march, while hundreds of thousands were assembled to support him would surely have generated unrest, which the authorities wanted to avoid. Instead O'Connor accepted the police ultimatum, and got into a taxicab to deliver his petition, returning later to his meeting at Kennington[13].

O'Connor's action in delivering the petition by cab, against a background of his past threats of revolutionary violence, invited ridicule and was a public relations disaster. In addition, the effect of the "Grand National Demonstration" being confined to Kennington was to make it very much less visible and so less effective than it would have been if it had taken place in the centre of London. These two factors led to a widespread feeling that the "Grand National Demonstration" had been a damp squib and a failure. Because expectations had been very high beforehand, this anti-climax led to disillusionment so severe that it broke the Chartist movement. Active support for Chartism dwindled sharply over the following months, and 1848 marked the end of the movement as a significant political force.

The failure of the Chartist demonstration movement illustrates key limitations of the mass public demonstration as a force for change. These are highlighted by the contrasts with the successful demonstrating campaigns of 1830 to 1832. Firstly, the Chartist movement did not have nearly as wide support as the demonstrators of 1832. Much of its support was based on the circulation of the *Northern Star* working man's newspaper which was controlled by O'Connor. Middle class support, was very limited. Without overwhelming public support, a

---

[13] This was an option for delivery of petitions which had only become available a few years earlier. Hansom cabs had been introduced for the first time in London in 1834. They were horse-drawn two-wheeled cabs, with enclosed seating for passengers, a driver sitting behind, and a taximeter to record the distance covered and the fare due.

street demonstration movement could not overwhelm the views of the legislature, which in 1839, although still based on a limited franchise, had far more democratic legitimacy than the pre-Reform Parliament of 1832. In addition, the movement was dominated by O'Connor, who was both a poor strategist and an unconvincing leader. O'Connor effectively abandoned the strategy pursued by earlier Reformers, like the London Corresponding Society, Hunt, Attwood and Place, of emphasising the respectability, and worthiness of being granted the right to vote, of those excluded from the franchise. Instead he simply held out a threat of turmoil and unrest if the Charter was not granted. This flawed strategy was bound sooner or later to force him either into a situation of violent confrontation or, as happened, one of anti-climax. O'Connor's poor leadership was compounded by his exaggerated claim that the petition presented to Parliament had five million signatures. Scrutiny by Parliament showed under two million signatures, still an impressive total even allowing for a significant number of obviously bogus signatures such as "Victoria R" and "Duke of Wellington". However, instead of emphasising this still very high number, O'Connor was foolish enough to challenge one of the Parliamentary scrutineers to a duel, and was then arrested for his disorderly conduct by the Parliamentary Sergeant at Arms.

In view of the fact that there was a further huge increase in the British Parliamentary franchise by the Second Reform Act in 1867, just nineteen years later, it is hard to resist the conclusion that the Chartist movement might have achieved much more in 1848 under a better leader. However it would have done so not by demonstrations alone, but by effective use of demonstrations as part of a wider, more broadly based, and better organised long term campaign. That indeed has to be the role of demonstrations in a democracy. Anything else is a revolution from the streets, which may be profoundly undemocratic.

While the Chartists were demonstrating in England, Daniel O'Connell, the Irish leader, who had amazed Europe in 1829 with his success in achieving the repeal of the laws preventing Catholics from sitting in Parliament, was attempting to use giant demonstrations as a technique to achieve more Parliamentary reform in Ireland. O'Connell's dream, having got into the Westminster Parliament, was to bring about the repeal of the Irish Act of Union of 1807, which had replaced the Irish Parliament in Dublin with Irish representation at Westminster, and to have the previous Irish Parliament restored. For much of the 1830s O'Connell attempted to promote this cause in the House of Commons, but found himself isolated, with no significant support in either of the two main parties, Whigs and Tories.

When it became clear to O'Connell that he would not be able to get a Repeal Bill passed by the Westminster Parliament through the traditional method of political alliances there, he decided to try to follow the example of the political unions in 1832, and to put pressure on the government through massive demonstrations. This was an imaginative idea. One of the great advantages of demonstrations is that they can draw attention to an issue which is of little interest to the majority of the population but intense importance to a minority. Most British MPs from parts of the United Kingdom other than Ireland had only a limited interest in Ireland, and were either hostile to the idea of restoring the Irish Parliament or had no strong views on the issue. In Ireland, in contrast, the issue was of obvious importance and O'Connell's aims enjoyed great support. O'Connell's mass meeting campaign of the 1840s, as a consequence, became one of the major events of nineteenth century Irish history. It ultimately failed because of the intransigence and lack of imagination of the members of the British Government responsible for policy towards Ireland.

O'Connell, like the London Corresponding Society and the political unions, and unlike the ambivalent O'Connor, was explicitly committed to peaceful protest and the rule of the law. At the same time his campaigns were intended to revive Irish nationalism and to raise passions, as far as could be done without crossing the line away from non-violence. He often appeared dressed in green as the Irish national colour, and his emblem, carried on banners at his meetings was the Irish harp. His stature gave credibility to his plan to pressure the British Government to grant repeal by a series of huge public speaker meetings, described as "Monster meetings". Like Henry Hunt, he relied on the threat implied by vast peaceful meetings, which was that those peaceful meetings could be followed by something worse, if their peaceful demands were not met. At the same time O'Connell always avoided making the explicit threats of force so frequently uttered by O'Connor.

On 15 April, 1840, O'Connell founded the Repeal Association. The next year it changed its name to the "Loyal National Repeal Association" to emphasise that O'Connell was not seeking Irish independence but an Irish Parliament under the British Crown. O'Connell designated 1843 "The year of Repeal", and began travelling through Ireland addressing audiences at huge, well-publicised open-air meetings. He was then in his late sixties, and the combination of organising, travelling and speaking was an impressive burden for a man of his age to carry. There were a total of 40 meetings, 31 of which were addressed by O'Connell personally. Unlike the English 1832 demonstrations, which were organised by a wide variety of local organisations, in Ireland it was very largely O'Connell's overwhelming personality and organising ability which made these monster meetings happen, with only limited local assistance.

The campaign began to gather momentum with a "Monster meeting" at Mullingar, County Westmeath, said to have been attended by 150,000 people, followed by an even larger one at Mallow, County Cork, said to have been attended by 400,000. Other huge meetings took place at the Curragh and at Cashel.

These figures for attendance at Mullingar and Mallow were probably overestimates. Ever since the first demonstrations, demonstration organisers have seen the value of giving the highest credible estimate of numbers attending. The bigger the numbers, the more resounding the success, and the greater the strength of the demonstrator's cause. Figures from the authorities, conversely, often underestimate numbers, as the authorities often wish to downplay the extent of support for a policy they oppose. It is actually very difficult to make an accurate count of the number of people at a large demonstration. Nearly all rounded figures which appear in the historical records for attendance numbers at demonstrations are therefore both approximate and liable to have been either inflated, if they come from the organisers, or deflated, if they come from the authorities. O'Connell certainly understood the value of overestimating attendances for propaganda purposes. However there is no doubt that the meetings he convened were enormous, and completely unprecedented in the numbers who appeared.

A third giant meeting was held at Lismore, County Waterford, again with an estimated attendance of 400,000. Unfortunately, while the size of the meetings was seriously alarming the British administration in Ireland, the Prime Minister in London, Sir Robert Peel, was a committed opponent of an Irish Parliament, and a personal enemy of O'Connell's. The effect of the monster meetings was therefore to raise tensions dramatically in Ireland, while at the same time failing to generate any realistic prospect of success in London. The contrast with 1832, when the political unions had a tacit ally in the Prime Minister, showed the limitations of the demonstration as a political weapon, when faced with completely intransigent opposition from the authorities.

A German traveller, Jacob Veneday, recorded this description of another Monster meeting, held at Athlone on 15 June, 1843:

> *"Now there arose a cry such as never before greeted my ears: now all hats were raised in the air, and there burst forth the unanimous shouts "Hurrah! hurrah! hurrah! Long live O'Connell! Long live the Liberator! A hundred thousand voices sent forth these salutations to the man whose magic power had circled them round him. He sat*

*on the box seat of a carriage drawn by four horses, and answered
the salutation with head, hand and cap… How he made his way
I do not even to this day comprehend, for there was no room for a
person to fall, much less to walk. "Make way for the Liberator!" was
the charm word which accomplished the wonder that otherwise had
been an impossibility."*

Like the meetings of the English Parliamentary Reformers, O'Connell's meetings
were carefully regulated to ensure peace and order. Stewards, some of whom were
priests, checked people to ensure that no-one was armed, or drunk or behaving in
a disorderly manner. The meetings were dominated by O'Connell's oratory, and
because of his reputation as "the Liberator", they took on something of the fervour
of a religious revival meeting. The poet Bulwer Lytton (Lord Lytton) attended one
meeting and described it in verse, which while rather stilted and unoriginal, does
convey something of the atmosphere:

> *"Walled by wide air and roofed by boundless heaven;*
> *Beneath his feet the human ocean lay,*
> *And wave on wave flowed into space away.*
> *Methought no clarion could have sent its sound*
> *E'en to the centre of the hosts around.*
> *And, as I thought, rose a sonorous swell …*
> *To the last verge of that vast audience sent,*
> *It played with each wild passion as it went:*
> *Now stirred the uproar, now the murmurs stilled,*
> *And sobs and laughter answered as it willed…"*

On 15 August, 1843, the biggest of all the Monster meetings was held on the
ancient hill of Tara, north-west of Dublin. Tara is a place of deep significance in
Irish history. Inhabited since pre-historic times, it was where the ancient kings
of Ireland were crowned, and was the place where the Irish broke the power of
the Viking invaders of Ireland in battle, in 980 AD. The symbolic location and
its proximity to Dublin resulted in an attendance which O'Connell estimated at
over a million, and even his most committed disparagers accepted was in excess of
100,000. O'Connell travelled to the meeting in a procession a mile long, which
included a trumpeter on horseback, a harpist in an open carriage drawn by six
grey horses playing " The Harp that once through Tara's Halls", horsemen four
deep, men on foot six abreast, and flags and banners carrying harps and the word

"Repeal". O'Connell had enlisted the support of the Church, with two altars on the Hill of Tara, and Masses celebrated on the hill by two bishops and 35 priests before the meeting began. Appointed officials were in place to relay O'Connell's words as he spoke to those in the vast crowd who were out of earshot.

"We are standing", said O'Connell as the climax of his speech, *"upon Tara of the Kings, the spot where the monarchs of Ireland were elected, and where the chieftains of Ireland bound themselves by the solemn pledge of honour to protect their native land against Dane and every stranger... This was emphatically the spot from which emanated every social power and legal authority by which the force of the entire country was concentrated for national defence. On this important spot I have an important duty to perform. I here protest in the face of my country and my God against the continuance of the Union."*

A hostile local magistrate sent a report to the authorities in Dublin and London about the meeting. *"No one could contemplate,"* he wrote, *"the display made on this occasion without having the conviction forced on his mind that the very excitement caused by such a meeting must, in all human probability, eventuate in some attempt at a subversion of government of the country – which will involve us in all the horrors of either a civil or a religious war."*

This was one of the reports the authorities had before them when they decided on their response to the next Monster meeting to be held in the Dublin area, which was scheduled to held at Clontarf, just outside Dublin, on 8 October, 1843. The day before, the Dublin authorities announced that the meeting had been banned. This faced O'Connell, the committed constitutionalist, with the impossible choice of either proceeding with the meeting, which the authorities would then have attempted to suppress with force, or abandoning his Monster meeting programme and effectively abandoning the Repeal campaign. Proceeding with the meeting might well have resulted in a Peterloo Massacre on a much larger scale, or even initiated a violent revolt or civil war. For this reason O'Connell chose to end his campaign. This principled decision proved to be an irreversible humiliation, which ended his power over public opinion.

The sad sequel was that O'Connell was then arrested and charged with sedition. He was convicted and spent several months in prison, before his conviction was quashed on appeal to the House of Lords. Despite this, he emerged from prison a discredited and broken man, and achieved little in the remaining three years before his death in 1847. Until Clontarf, he had had an aura of invincibility. Afterwards he was a mere mortal, and other younger reformers were no longer inclined to accept his authority. The horror of the Irish Potato Famine and the mass emigration which accompanied it also meant that far fewer people had time for issues of Parliamentary reform. An eventual effect of this diminution of O'Connell's stature was that important principles he stood for, of non-violence and protest within the law, also lost ground among Irish nationalists, and gave way to a more militant nationalism sympathetic to the idea of violent revolt. To that extent, later British governments paid a heavy price for not responding to O'Connell's peaceful mass activism.

O'Connell's Monster meetings were not forgotten. An account of them appeared in German, written by Jacob Veneday, the German traveller quoted above. As a consequence, when Czech nationalists in the 1860s wished to campaign for greater rights against the Austro-Hungarian Empire under which they lived, they were aware of O'Connell's campaign, and consciously attempted to follow his lead with huge open-air meetings. These were referred to in Czech by a newly invented word, derived from English, "Mitingy". Unfortunately their campaign was also unsuccessful.

However in the 1850s an unanticipated major victory was achieved very largely by use of peaceful demonstrations. This was the first unqualified victory achieved by demonstrations since 1832, and the first to be achieved outside the United Kingdom.

In the aftermath of the collapse of Chartism in 1848, many committed Chartists, disillusioned with the failure of the movement in the United Kingdom, emigrated to Australia, particularly to the new colony of Victoria, founded in 1851. The Ballarat Gold Rush, which occurred there in the 1850s, attracted people from all over the world. It created a labour shortage in the new capital, Melbourne, which made it an unusually favourable environment for labour organisers and activists.

Melbourne (named after the Prime Minister who as Home Secretary had been responsible for transporting the Tolpuddle Martyrs to Australia's shores), was in the 1850s a wild, frontier town, with muddy streets and rough living conditions. Among the town's ex-convicts and fortune seekers were political refugees and activists of many persuasions, as described in a memoir of the time written for Australia's centenary in 1889:

> "The years I speak of were years of political excitement and turbulence. Among the newcomers were combatant Chartists from Glasgow, Clerkenwell and Chelsea, brimful with schemes for the reformation of mankind and the people of Victoria in particular; and the Eastern Market was their forum. There were not many amusements in those days for the crowd of people which sauntered

along the south side of Bourke Street East, after nightfall, and any political adventurer who wanted to bring himself before the public had only to mount an empty hay-van, illuminated by cotton-wicks burning in tin dishes of tallow, and to commence a noisy harangue on the wrongs of the people, accompanied by suitable violence of gesture, in order to gather round him an amused and amusing crowd, some of whom would reward him with cheers and with cries of "Go on, old man ! Give it 'em hot"; while others would banter with the speaker and interrupt him by sarcastic interjections… Many of them had been … in the revolutionary movements which had agitated Europe in 1848. You met men who had fought in the streets of Paris, political refugees from Frankfort, Berlin, Vienna and Buda Pesth, and Carbonari from Italy. Mostly young, ardent, enthusiastic, and animated by more or less Utopian visions of reconstructing the political and social institutions of civilised mankind so as to bring about an era of universal peace and prosperity, these heterogenous exiles flung themselves heartily into the popular movements of the day."

Two notable Chartist immigrants to Melbourne were James Stephens and James Galloway. Both were stone masons. James Stephens came from Newport, South Wales, and had taken part in the violent Newport uprising in 1839. He had been badly beaten in the fighting, but had escaped to London without being arrested, and worked there as a mason on the new Houses of Parliament, then being built to replace the old Houses of Parliament, which had burned down in 1834. Stephens became a prominent trades union organiser, with a particular concern with working hours.

In the height of the Victoria gold rush interest in trade union activity declined, as everyone tried to make their fortune in the goldfields. However when Stephens and Galloway arrived, both in 1855, the most extreme gold fever had passed, and the time was right for a union revival. Because of the labour shortage in Australia, wages were significantly higher than in England. The main issue between workers and employers was therefore not pay, but hours of work. As well as labour pressure for shorter hours, support came from middle-class reformers such as Thomas Embling, who argued that a shorter working day would leave workers with more time for self-improvement and so help build a better society.

On 11 January, 1856, a public meeting was called in Melbourne, at which a campaign was launched to reduce the ten-hour working day to eight hours, to take account of the much greater heat in Australia, and to allow workers, less tired after eight hours, to have some time to devote to mental improvement.

Less than a month later, on 4 February, 1856, Stephens and Galloway formed a local branch of the Operative Masons' Society, a stonemason's trade union. Other ex-Chartists were also involved. This foundation meeting is usually seen as the start of the eight-hour day movement, which later became world-wide, although in fact most stonemasons in Sydney had already obtained an eight-hour day through strike action the previous October. What made the eight-hour day movement in Melbourne different was the greater militancy of the workforce, encouraged and helped to organise by the ex-Chartists, and their use of Chartist style demonstrations as a weapon.

On 25 March, 1856, a mass meeting of employers and workers agreed that the eight-hour day in the industry should be introduced on 21 April. Most employers readily agreed to this demand, the exception being the employer whose masons were building the new Victoria Parliament House. A public meeting was called for 11 April, of "all trades, professions or occupations whatever, to fully and fairly discuss the expediency and practicability of abridging the hours of labour to eight hours per day". A packed meeting was held in the Queen's Theatre, with the Mayor of Melbourne in the chair. Leading Melbourne Radicals put the case for shorter hours, stating that "the old idea that prevailed at home, that one class was born to labour, and another to direct that labour, ought not to find a place here." An organisation to advance the eight-hour day, particularly in trades not yet organised, was proposed, and, swept away by the spirit of the meeting, the Mayor closed the proceedings by offering a prize of ten guineas for the best address on the subject of shorter working hours.

On what was later referred to as "the Glorious 21st of April", James Stephens led a major street demonstration for the eight-hour day, starting from the half-built Old Quadrangle Building of Melbourne University, under banners bearing the words "Eight hours labour, eight hours recreation, eight hours rest." As the demonstration proceeded through the city centre, it was gradually joined by more and more workmen from the building sites which it passed. The march finished at Parliament Hill, where the workers on the Parliament House downed tools to join in, and was then followed by a banquet. From that day on, the eight-hour day was generally recognized by most trades in Australia. Nineteenth century Australian trade union buildings were often decorated with the numbers "888" (meaning eight hours of work, eight hours recreation, and eight hours rest) worked into the stonework to commemorate the stonemasons' achievement. For the remainder of the nineteenth century, commemorative parades were held across Australia on 21 April each year, with each trade represented by elaborate banners, floats and costumes. In Victoria, until 1951, 21 April each year was the "Eight Hour Day" public holiday.

The news that Australian workers had achieved an eight hour day galvanized workers and their representatives around the world. Because of the eight-hour day, Australia was sometimes described, by nineteenth century workers' representatives elsewhere, as "the workers' paradise". New Zealand achieved an eight-hour day the following year, 1857, and demands for an eight-hour day became an important part of labour campaigns in both the United States and Europe from the 1860s onwards. These campaigns invariably involved marching through the streets with banners calling for an eight-hour day, as the successful Australian workers had done. One of the incidental effects of the Australian eight-hour day movement was therefore to spread the practice of peaceful demonstrations far beyond the British Empire.

Why did the Eight-Hour Day demonstrators succeed? Undoubtedly because there was very widespread support for the cause they were promoting. With the Mayor of Melbourne supporting their cause, the stonemasons had the support of the leading authorities in Melbourne. The only people they were opposing were a minority of employers, who had the bulk of the population firmly arrayed against them. The Eight Hour Day movement, opposing recalcitrant building firms, was comparable in that respect with the Political Unions opposing the tiny number of recalcitrant peers who were against Parliamentary reform in 1832. It is usually only in this situation of overwhelming popular support that demonstrators can expect to bring about their desired result solely through demonstrating.

This is not to downplay the Eight-Hour Day campaign's achievements. What it gained for Australia was at the time unprecedented in the world. However very few other demonstration campaigns since then have been as trouble-free, as we shall see when we turn to the arrival of demonstrations in the United States.

CHAPTER 7

Demonstrations Come to the United States

Today most people who think about why we should be allowed to go out and hold a demonstration would say that it is because it is part of our right of freedom of assembly. However when the idea of freedom of assembly was first used, it did not have anything to do with demonstrations, and it was a long time before demonstrations and freedom of assembly were seen to have any connection. The expression "freedom of assembly" became well-known because it was used in the constitution of the United States of America, but what it originally meant there was simply the freedom of citizens to assemble to debate issues in the official meetings of the national or state legislature.

The United States was the first country to have a written constitution. The idea of having one derived from the individual pre-independence American colonies which came together to form the United States. One hundred and fifty years before the American War of Independence, the first small English colonies on the coast of North America had to decide how to govern themselves. They generally did so by adopting a written governing charter or fundamental law. The first to do so was Connecticut in 1639. The first to include a list of citizens' rights in its charter was Rhode Island in 1647. This background made it natural for the Continental Congress, which approved the United States Declaration of Independence in 1779, to prepare a fundamental law, or constitution, for the newly created nation.

It was not until 1789, ten years after independence, that citizens' rights were made part of the constitution by adding to the constitution the series of ten amendments called the Bill of Rights. However it was not until 1804 that the United States Supreme Court, in the landmark case of <u>Marbury v Madison</u>, confirmed the idea that breaches of the constitution were "justiciable".

"Justiciable" meant that a person could go to court and obtain a court order that a law, or an executive decision, need not be obeyed, because it was inconsistent with the constitution. This was a fundamentally important decision for the future of the United States and indeed the world. Had the decision in <u>Marbury v Madison</u> gone the other way, the United States Constitution would have been no more than a statement of aspirations, a set of ideals which would have been impossible to enforce in practice, because they lacked any direct legal effect. <u>Marbury v Madison</u> brought into being the subject of constitutional law, as it confirmed that laws or government actions which were inconsistent with the wording of the constitution, might be declared unlawful by the courts. This idea has now spread from the United States to many other countries, although there are still some countries, such as China, which have a list of rights set out in their constitution which are not enforceable and remain no more than an aspiration.

The wording of the First Amendment to the United States constitution (the first of the original ten Bill of Rights amendments) is well-known, although its historical origins are often overlooked. *"The freedom of speech and of the press",* it reads, *"and the right of the people peaceably to assemble and consult for their common good, and to apply to the Government for the redress of grievances, shall not be infringed."*

Today this article protects the right to demonstrate in the United States. However this has only been clearly established since the Supreme Court cases arising out of Martin Luther King's civil rights campaigns in the 1960s. For most of the history of the United States, freedom of assembly did not include the right to demonstrate.

The reason that freedom of assembly was protected by the Bill of Rights in 1789 was to protect the national legislature, Congress, and the state legislatures of each state, from outside interference. This was important, because it was the colonial assembly of Massachusetts which had organised resistance to King George III of England, in the period before the War of Independence. Samuel Adams, who organised the Boston Tea Party, had his power base there. General Thomas Gage, sent by George III to be military governor of Massachusetts, banned the Massachusetts assembly, and declared that it would be treason for it to meet. That declaration was fundamentally illegal, as it breached the English

Statute of Treasons of 1352, which gave treason a narrow and precise meaning relating to killing the king or violently overthrowing his government. This action by Gage outraged public opinion in the American colonies, and was one of the events which precipitated the independence struggle. Protecting the right of the national and state law-making bodies to meet without interference was therefore an obvious priority in the new United States.

There was opposition to enactment of the First Amendment from one member from Massachusetts. Although not expressly stated, this seems to have been due precisely to a fear that the Amendment would protect undesirable unauthorised assemblies, which might be hostile to the government. This fear reflected the fact that three years earlier, in 1786, post-independence Massachusetts had experienced Shay's Rebellion, a full-scale revolt against the state government, when courthouses were burnt by farmers, to prevent mortgagees getting foreclosure orders on their farms. The concern from Massachusetts was that protection for unauthorised assemblies would encourage more rebellions like Shay's. However the First Amendment was enacted with the support of the great majority of the members of Congress.

The new United States Congress not only failed to take steps to protect the right of assembly as understood today. In 1798 it also abolished the ancient English right of petition derived from Magna Carta. It did this because members of Congress were irritated by interruptions to their deliberations by delegations of former soldiers from the Revolutionary War presenting petitions for pensions or compensation. This was six years before Marbury v Madison, and no one seems to have thought to challenge this abolition of an ancient right in the Supreme Court, on the grounds that it was in breach of the First Amendment right to apply to the government for the redress of grievances. As a result, from 1798 to 1939, a period of 141 years, there was no legal protection at all anywhere in the United States for the right to hold either a public meeting or a procession.

This did not of course mean that meetings and processions did not happen. On the contrary, parades and processions were very popular, and were traditional on important dates like 4 July (Independence Day). Unlike in France or Germany, there was no law against use of a procession for a protest. However any procession which was intended as a protest was liable to be suppressed by the authorities, if they chose, with virtually no prospect of any successful legal challenge by the organisers, or of any form of redress. The right of the people peaceably to assemble did not extend to protests.

There was also deep opposition in the early United States to the idea of a protest march on the capital city. The United States became independent of

Britain a few years before the London Corresponding Society organised the world's first deliberately peaceful demonstrations in London. While such events became widely accepted in Britain from 1832, in the United States for a long time a protest march continued to be viewed as a warlike act. This was shown by events after the presidential election of 1877, when the Republican candidate, Rutherford B. Hayes, was declared elected following large scale vote-rigging in his favour in several states. A Democrat Congressman, Henry Watterson, called for a march on Washington to protest at the rigged election. However the defeated Democratic candidate, Samuel Tilden, publicly rebuked Watterson, although Watterson was his supporter, stating that Watterson's call for such a march was treason.

The idea that the First Amendment might protect unauthorised public meetings was eventually raised in the Supreme Court of Massachusetts, and then in the United States Supreme Court, in 1896, in the case of <u>Commonwealth of Massachusetts v Davis</u>, only to be emphatically rejected.

Boston Common was a traditional place for open-air public gatherings and speakers, like St George's Fields in eighteenth century London. Prior to 1862, anyone could make a speech there. However, in that year, a local law had been enacted which required permission to be obtained from local officials for any "sermon, lecture, address or discourse on the common or other public grounds" of the city. Opponents of the new law claimed that it was adopted at the bidding of the rum sellers of Boston, to silence local temperance campaigners.

William F Davis, known as "Brother Davis", was a street preacher who was repeatedly fined during the 1880s for violating the Boston Common permit law. In 1885 he unsuccessfully challenged the law, on the grounds that, by preventing his preaching, it violated the freedom of religion provision of the Bill of Rights[14]. After this he continued preaching on the Common and continued being fined. In 1894 he appealed his conviction on the ground that the permit law violated the freedom of assembly provision of the First Amendment. The case came before one of the most respected jurists in United States legal history, Oliver Wendell Holmes, which made the court's rejection of Davis's argument all the more devastating. Holmes held that a public body such as the State of Massachusetts had just as much right to restrict or terminate access to public land, such as a common, as a private landowner had to restrict or stop access to private land. He was endorsed by the US Supreme Court on further appeal. Holmes said nothing

---

[14]   This is the first part of the First Amendment "Congress shall make no law respecting an establishment of religion or prohibiting the free exercise thereof".

about the point that such a rule, taken to its logical conclusion, could completely prevent any public meetings anywhere.

This was the United States into which the idea of workers' demonstrations for better pay and conditions spread, as a result of the success of the Australian workers in obtaining the eight-hour day, and the impetus that gave to workers everywhere, including in the United States, to hold organised marches to achieve their objectives.

Following the successes of the eight-hour day movement in Australia and New Zealand in the 1850s, the movement rapidly developed momentum in the United States. A strike in support of an eight-hour day was held in Chicago in 1867, beginning on May Day and continuing for a week. May Day was a traditional European celebration of spring, derived from the ancient festival of Beltane, but that strike in Chicago led to it being chosen for other workers' protests, notably on the working hours issue.

The end of the American Civil War in 1865 saw the beginning of industrial revolution in the United States. Conditions for workers were often harsh, particularly for new immigrants, who included many embittered German Radicals who emigrated in the 1850s following the repression of the German 1848 Revolution. It was said that by the end of the 1850s there were more German anarchists in the United States than in Germany. It was among such immigrants that workers' movements developed their strongest support.

The eight-hour day movement brought together the main traditional American labour organisation, the Knights of Labour, and the more radical, Marxist-influenced, Federation of Organized Trades Unions and Labour Unions of the United States and Canada. The Knights of Labour constitution, adopted in 1878, called for an eight-hour day, and the Knights passed resolutions in favour of the eight-hour day in 1883 and 1884. However it was the Federation which favoured militant action to bring the eight-hour day about.

The Federation's 1884 resolution, proposed by George Edmonston, founder and first president of the Brotherhood of Carpenters and Joiners, was that *"eight hours shall constitute a legal day's labour from and after May 1, 1886, and that we recommend to labour organisations throughout this district that they so direct their laws as to conform to this resolution by the time named."*

The Federation went on to organise a nationwide stoppage on 1 May, 1886, in support of its campaign, involving both strikes and street demonstrations. Across the USA, at least 400,000 people, and possibly up to 500,000, either struck or demonstrated or both. There were strikes and demonstrations in most of the large cities, including Chicago, New York, Boston, Detroit, Milwaukee, St

Louis, Cincinnati and Baltimore, and in smaller cities and towns such as Duluth, Minnesota; Mobile, Alabama, and Galveston, Texas.

In Chicago, between 60,000 and 90,000 are said to have demonstrated, and 30,000 to 40,000 gone on strike. The world's first May Day Parade was a procession of 80,000 workers up Chicago's Michigan Avenue. A separate parade was held by about 10,000 German, Polish and Czech immigrants working in the lumber yards. The Knights of Labour meatpacking unions closed down the stockyards, and, winning their strike, gained an eight-hour day without a pay reduction.

Unfortunately, this initial success was followed almost immediately by a tragic setback with far-reaching consequences.

On 3 May, 1886, as part of the continuing campaign for the eight-hour day, an afternoon rally was held outside the McCormick Harvester Plant, where much of the workforce was on strike, but strike-breakers had been employed to keep the plant working. About 6,000 people attended. The audience included strikers from the plant, and, when the strike-breakers were due to come off duty, some strikers broke away from the meeting to attack them. During the confrontation which followed, the police fired into the crowd, killing four people and wounding many more.

August Spies, an immigrant from Germany, and a well-known anarchist speaker and organiser in Chicago, was present when the police fired on the crowd. Spies immediately wrote a leaflet calling on workers to strike back at the forces of authority, and calling a protest meeting for the next day. This took place in Haymarket Square, Chicago. The meeting was addressed by Spies and two other leading Chicago anarchists, Samuel Fielden and Albert Parsons. The main subjects of the speeches were the eight-hour day and the need for the workers to resist the oppressive behaviour of the McCormick company and the police. However, significantly, in view of what came later, there was no call for violence by any of the platform speakers.

The protest meeting was within a few minutes of its end, and many of those who attended had already left because of a sudden rainstorm, when a contingent of 180 police under a Captain Ward and a Captain Bonfield arrived, and ordered the meeting to disperse. Bonfield was an aggressive and brutal individual, who had been looking for a chance to teach the anarchists a lesson. He had decided to break up the meeting after receiving a report that Fielden had uttered a remark that "the law deserves to be throttled".

As Fielden was protesting to the police at the scene about their order to the meeting to disperse, an unknown person threw a bomb at the police line, killing one policeman and wounding over 70. The police responded by firing their revolvers into the crowd, killing at least one person and wounding many. A total of six more policemen eventually died of wounds. At least seven or eight members of the public died, and thirty to forty were wounded.

The thrower of the bomb was never identified. There was no evidence to link the bomb to those who spoke at the meeting. However the bomb throwing generated a wave of anti-anarchist hysteria both in Chicago and across the country. The atmosphere after the bombing is described in the autobiographical novel *Memoirs of an American* by Robert Herrick:-

> *"The morning after the fourth of May the city was sizzling with excitement. From what the papers said you might think there was an anarchist or two skulking in every alley in Chicago with a basket of bombs under his arm. The men on the street seemed to rub their eyes and stare up at the buildings in surprise to find them still standing. There was every kind of rumour floating about... It was all a parcel of lies, of course, but the people were crazy to be lied to, and the police, having nothing better, fed them lies".*

Police Captain Michael Schaak, in charge of the investigation into the bombing, fed the panic by announcing to the newspapers a continuous stream of discoveries of anarchist plots. It was said of him that:-

> *"He saw more anarchists than vast hell could hold. Bombs, dynamite, daggers and pistols seemed ever before him; in the end there was no society, however innocent or laudable, among the foreign born population that was not to his mind an object of great suspicion."*

The press, fed by Schaak's fantastic stories, and only too willing to embroider them further, created a belief that the Haymarket bomb had been the signal for a violent revolutionary conspiracy to overthrow the entire government of the USA. The American public, terrified by tales of the anarchist conspiracy, was desperate for strong action against anarchists. Every major newspaper in the USA called for the anarchist movement to be destroyed by force.

Much anarchist and revolutionary socialist propaganda did call for revolution. Anarchist publications regularly called on their supporters to go armed, although in the USA, where the right to bear arms is written into the constitution, this was not illegal. However some anarchists actually promoted the use of dynamite (then a novelty) by workers against their oppressors, and some anarchist magazines contained instructions as to how to make it. An extreme example is the following extract from the anarchist magazine, Alarm:-

> *"Dynamite! Of all the good stuff, this is the stuff. Stuff several pounds of this sublime stuff into an inch pipe, plug up both ends, insert a cap with a fuse attached, place this in the immediate neighbourhood of a lot of rich loafers who live by the sweat of other people's brows, and light the fuse. A most cheerful and gratifying result will follow… A pound of this good stuff beats a bushel of ballots hollow, and don't you forget it."*

Most Americans were understandably alarmed at such sentiments. At the same time it had some attraction to a few desperate immigrants, working in conditions of great exploitation, and coming from societies where the ballot did not exist.

It seems to have been the combination of the feared anarchists coming to prominence in the leadership of the popular and reasonable eight-hour movement, the unprecedented huge demonstrations on May Day, and then the equally unprecedented attack on police with a bomb just afterwards, which caused Chicago and the country to go mad. A contemporary letter from Chicago describes the atmosphere: *"One week ago freedom of speech and of the press was a right unquestioned by the bitterest anti-socialist… Today all this is changed… Socialists are hunted like wolves… The Chicago papers are loud and unceasing in their demand for the lives of all prominent socialists. To proclaim oneself a socialist now in Chicago is to invite immediate arrest".*

The outcome of this frenzy was that eight men were charged and tried for murder. They were Spies, Fielden, Parsons, George Engel, Adolph Fischer, Louis Lingg, Michael Schwab and Oscar Niebe. A ninth man, Rupert Schnaubel, was named by the prosecution as the bomb thrower, but had fled and was never caught. Schnaubel was almost certainly not the bomb-thrower, despite being so characterised in the popular novel *The Bomb*, by Frank Harris, published in 1908.

One of the eight defendants, Louis Lingg, a German, was an authentic anarchist bomb-maker. Lingg had been operating a bomb factory in his flat, and eventually committed suicide by blowing himself up in prison with a self-made bomb. It is likely that the bomb thrown at the police was one of Lingg's bombs, although there was no evidence that he had planned, or been involved in, the throwing.

However there was absolutely no evidence to link Lingg with Spies, or with any of the others on trial. Spies's evidence was that he had only seen Lingg once, and never spoken to him. They certainly did not move in the same circles, or share the same philosophy. None of the others on trial had any record of violence. One police witness claimed that Spies had been next to the bomb thrower and told him to throw the bomb. This witness was contradicted by numerous witnesses who said that Spies had never left the platform until after the bomb had been thrown. The witness who claimed Spies had ordered the bomb thrown was shown under cross-examination to be unreliable and untruthful.

In a normal trial the lack of evidence against the accused would have led to their acquittal. The Haymarket trial was a mockery of justice, in which both judge and jury showed themselves determined to convict, irrespective of the evidence. Many of the jurors, when challenged by the defence at the start of the trial before the jury was chosen, freely admitted that they were prejudiced against the accused. Despite this, the judge, Joseph E. Gary, overruled the challenges and allowed a heavily biased jury to be empanelled. The officer responsible for issuing the calls to jury service openly boasted that he had deliberately picked people on the list whom he was certain would be bound to convict the defendants.

The prosecution advanced, and Judge Gary upheld, the contention that as Spies, Fielden and others of the accused had called in speeches for the overthrow of American institutions, they were guilty of aiding and abetting the bomb thrower by encouraging him to do what he did. This interpretation of the law was said to apply irrespective of the fact that the accused men did not know the bomb thrower, did not know that a bomb was to be thrown, and had never called for a bomb to be thrown. Based on this interpretation, the judge permitted the prosecutor to put in as evidence against the accused the wildest anarchist articles he could find – including the article about dynamite quoted above – even though they had not been written by any of the accused.

Despite the preposterous nature of the evidence, the atmosphere in Chicago was such that the very fact that the group of defendants included Lingg, who was a bomb maker, made it virtually certain that all the defendants would be convicted, even if the jury had not been packed. Moves to split the trial, so that Lingg was tried separately, as well as to delay it until passions had cooled (the last injured policeman to die had died a week before it opened) were both rejected by Judge Gary.

The prosecutor, State Attorney-General Julius Grinnell, concluded his address to the jury with the words:-

"Law is on trial. Anarchy is on trial. These men have been selected, picked out by the grand jury, and indicted because they are the leaders. They are no more guilty than those thousands who follow them. Gentlemen of the jury; convict these men, make examples of them, hang them, and you can save our institutions, our society."

All were convicted. An appeal to the Illinois Supreme Court was dismissed, and the US Supreme Court refused to intervene. Despite an international campaign to save them, four of the eight, Spies, Parsons, Engel and Fischer, were executed on 11 November, 1887. Lingg would have been executed but cheated the gallows by suicide. Fielden and Schwab were sentenced to death but their sentences were commuted to life imprisonment. Oscar Niebe, who had not been at the meeting, and against whom there was no evidence at all except that he was an anarchist, was given 15 years.

Seven years later, on 26 June, 1893, a new governor of Illinois, John Peter Altgeld, issued a governor's pardon to all eight of the convicted men. In his message of pardon, Altgeld publicly acknowledged that "the defendants were not proven to be guilty of the crime", that they were completely innocent, were the victims of packed juries and a biased judge, and had not received a fair trial. Altgeld was execrated for his action, and partly as a result was not re-elected as governor, but history today entirely concurs with his assessment.

Spies's final words before he was executed were, "There will come a time when our silence will be more powerful than the voices you strangle today". The words are carved on Chicago's Haymarket Monument, which commemorates the execution.

Spies' predictions proved accurate, for outrage at the judicial murder of the Haymarket defendants, extending far beyond anarchists and their sympathisers, gave worldwide impetus to the eight-hour day campaign and to the use of May Day as the worker's day, when workers demonstrated for their cause by parading through the streets. After Haymarket, workers' May Day demonstrations were established as regular annual events in many countries around the world. It was these May Day demonstrations which brought the demonstrating tradition to much of Europe, as well as parts of Latin America.

CHAPTER 8

DEMONSTRATIONS COME TO EUROPE

In 1889, two years after the execution of Spies, Parsons, Engel and Fischer, the International Working Men's Association, meeting in Paris, ("the Second International") declared May Day an international working class holiday. The declaration was proposed by a French delegate, Raymond Lavigne, but a proposal to the same effect is thought to have been sent to the International by Samuel Gompers of the American Federation of Labour. On the same occasion the red flag of the Paris Commune, originally the flag of the city of Paris, was adopted as a symbol.

As a result of Haymarket, and of the resolution of the Second International, the practice of May Day workers' processions and parades became established in the UK, the USA, Australia, Belgium, Switzerland, Denmark, Sweden, Austro-Hungary, Spain and Portugal[15], and, with some difficulty, in France and Germany. The practice never ceased to be controversial. In the United States it was supported by militant and revolutionary workers' groups such as the International Workers of the World, while more conservative Labour groups, such as the American Federation of Labour, tended to prefer Labour Day, in September. Australia and New Zealand also celebrated Labour Days in September and October. In some European countries the appeal of May Day was more widespread, but it was everywhere dear to the heart of the revolutionary Left, and usually regarded with dislike by conservatives. Workers' rights, strikes, revolutionary socialism and

---

[15] The first May Day demonstrations outside the United States were held in these countries in 1890, and May Day demonstrations were also held that year in Cuba, Chile and Peru.

May Day were linked, both in the minds of the revolutionary socialists and in those of their enemies.

Because demonstrations came to continental Europe with May Day, as a tradition of the Revolutionary Left and of militant workers' organisations, they had a very different image in most European countries from their image in the British Isles, Australia and New Zealand. There were not, for a long time, European equivalents of such respectable British demonstrating figures as Thomas Attwood, the Birmingham banker, or the ladies and gentlemen of the British and Foreign Temperance Society. It is true that the Establishment in Britain shared with their counterparts in continental Europe a fear of violent workers' demonstrations which might lead to revolution. The fear in England was of the militant wing of the Chartist movement, while in Europe it was from anarchists or Revolutionary Socialists. However, in Britain there was also general recognition at all levels of society that many demonstrations were non-revolutionary, peaceful and even respectable. There was no such recognition in much of Europe for a long time.

The ultimate respectable Victorian English demonstration was also the world's first environmental demonstration, organised to protest at plans to demolish the Crystal Palace. The Crystal Palace was built for the Great Exhibition of 1851, to the design of Joseph Paxman. It was the first building to use glass to create a light and airy structure with a graceful appearance. In 1852, the year after the Great Exhibition, the government announced plans to demolish this eye-catching wonder. This announcement of the intended demolition generated a movement for the preservation of the Palace, supported by many leading figures in society. Eventually this campaign led to a full-scale organised street demonstration, advertised in *The Times* as a "Grand Promenade".

The "Grand Promenade" was attended by some 80,000 people who marched, peacefully and in good order, seven miles from central London to the location of the Crystal Palace, on what were then London's southern outskirts at Norwood. As might be expected with a demonstration advertised in *The Times*, some of those taking part were prominent in society. In reporting on the event *The Times* described it as "almost an emeute (riot) of the fashionables". The demonstration was accompanied by seven military bands, including that of the Life Guards. The fact that the demonstration included serving soldiers was remarkable, as it was entirely private, unofficial, and hostile to the government of the day. The government announced in response to the demonstration that it would not be "intimidated", but its plan to demolish the Crystal Palace was shelved. The Palace survived until accidentally burned down in 1936.

This kind of middle and upper class protest march was a natural culmination of the tradition of peaceful protest which started with the London Corresponding Society trying to show itself to be peaceful and respectable, so that its members would be judged worthy of being allowed to vote for Parliament. By 1852 this tradition was already over seventy five years old.

In this respect the situation in the British Isles contrasted dramatically with neighbouring France. In France, the idea of peaceful demonstrations on the English model did not catch on at all for most of the nineteenth century, despite the proximity of the two countries. In *Les Miserables*, Victor Hugo's great historical novel of early nineteenth century Paris, published in 1862 but set in the 1820s and 1830s, Hugo devotes a whole chapter to analysing the supposed difference between a riot and an insurrection, but he never mentions the idea of a peaceful demonstration. Hugo was a well-informed writer whose books are full of allusions to events in European, including English, history. Events in nineteenth century England, like the Reform Act demonstrations, must have been known to him. The reason that he never mentions peaceful demonstrations in Paris was because they never happened there in his time.

At the heart of this difference was the fact that in nineteenth century France control of the street was seen as a legitimate route to power, in a way which it could never be seen in England. The French Revolution had come from the street in 1789 when the Paris mob stormed the Bastille. The Restoration Bourbon monarchy had been swept away by a peaceful revolution from the streets in 1830. Again in 1848, Louis Philippe, the Citizen King, was swept away by street revolution which ushered in the short-lived Second Republic. Then in 1871, with the German defeat of France in the Franco-Prussian war and the collapse of the Second Empire of Napoleon III, came the occupation of the streets of Paris by its inhabitants, in the short-lived Paris Commune.

Given this remarkable history of seizure of power from the streets, the French Third Republic, established after the crushing of the Commune, was extremely wary of any kind of street political activity. Those who supported the Republic saw it as fragile and vulnerable, and wished to ensure that street protest did not cause it to go the way of previous overthrown regimes. Moreover, France remained bitterly divided by the crushing of the Commune. Many Socialists venerated the fighters of the Commune, and wished to keep their memory green and their traditions alive. The political Right, in contrast, was afraid of a resurgence or repetition of the Commune, and lukewarm at best in its adherence to democracy. Both the Right and the Bonapartist elements of the Left were attracted by authoritarian military leaders who might seize power from the street, such as General Boulanger, who seemed to be threatening a coup in 1890. In this environment, the leading democratic figures of the Third Republic, like Leon Gambetta, understandably saw a commitment to reaching decisions in the legislature, rather than the street, as fundamental to democracy, and were hostile to street demonstrations on principle.

In what was possibly the first attempt at a peaceful demonstration in Paris, the Socialist Jules Guesde organised a commemorative march to the "Mur des Federes", the Communards' Wall, in the Pere Lachaise cemetery on 23 May, 1880. The Communards' Wall was where one hundred and forty seven Communard fighters, including women and children, had been shot and buried in an open pit by French Government troops at the end of the fighting in May 1871. Guesde led some 25,000 people, most wearing symbolic red roses in their buttonholes, overwhelming police cordons designed to prevent the march, but apart from that marching peacefully. The march was regarded as successful, strengthening the campaign for an amnesty for the many surviving Communards, who had been deported to exile in the French Pacific colony of New Caledonia. A full amnesty law was passed two months later, leading to the return of thousands of Communard exiles.

However this march also added to the government's fear of losing control of the streets. As a result it contributed to the government's decision to enact two measures designed to ensure that it would not lose control. One of these was the passing of the Law of 30 June 1881, which criminalised any unauthorised meeting ("reunion") on the public highway. This law meant that from that date onward any spontaneous demonstration was by definition illegal, whether it was a "cortege" (procession), defile (parade) or attroupement (gathering).

The other measure was the organisation by the government, on 14 July, 1880, of the first "14 July "parade. This event, held on the date of the storming of the Bastille in 1789, marked the government's stance as the heir to the liberal first phase of the French Revolution, and at the same time reinforced its symbolic control of the streets of France. The 14 July parades have continued to be held in France every year since 1880.

However the French revolutionary Socialist Left was determined to claim back the use of the street by organising its own national day for street parades and this was part of the domestic French background to the proposal by the Paris delegate to the Second International, Raymond Lavigne, for May Day as an annual workers' procession day.

From 1889 onwards, sections of the French workers' movement attempted each year to demonstrate on May Day. However permits were rarely issued for such demonstrations and May Day demonstrations in France generally remained illegal. As such, they were regarded as unacceptable by centrist political opinion, while also being opposed by the political Right which detested what they stood for. The demonstrators themselves were drawn to the tradition of revolutionary rhetoric going back to the First French Revolution, and had no particular commitment to non-violence or abiding by the law. In this volatile situation there was always a high risk that confrontations between demonstrators and the forces of law and order would become violent, and this happened very frequently. Year after year, May Day demonstrations were broken up by the police, often with casualties on both sides.

The year 1891 was a high point of May Day-related violence, including what could be regarded as France's equivalent of England's Peterloo massacre. May Day demonstrations across the country were violently suppressed. At Lyon, Roanne and St Quentin crowds of demonstrators were charged by police and arrests made. An organiser of the demonstration at Charleville was condemned to two years' imprisonment. However the most extreme violence was at Fourmies, in north-east France, a centre of the weaving and spinning industries.

Early on 1 May, 1891, at the request of the town mayor, mounted gendarmes with drawn sabres charged a crowd of about 1,500 demonstrating strikers outside the Sans Pareille spinning works. Three of the demonstrators were arrested and kept in custody. This led to increasingly angry responses by the demonstrators who remained at liberty. They gathered in the main square chanting slogans demanding the eight-hour day – "C'est huit heures, huit heures, huit heures. C'est huit heures qu'il nous faut[16] "– alternating with chants for the release of the prisoners – "C'est nos hommes, nos hommes, nos hommes. C'est nos hommes qu'il nous faut[17]." Then at about 3.00 pm a group of about 150 demonstrators attempted to break through a line of troops with a view to freeing the prisoners. The troops responded by opening fire on the crowd without any warning, with powerful new Lebel rifles with which they had recently been equipped. The troops killed nine people and seriously wounded over 30. Many of the casualties, who included women and children, had not even been demonstrators, but were people who happened to be in shops or cafes surrounding the square. An eleven- year-old girl was shot dead inside a café. Two other girls were killed inside a bar.

The massacre had a powerful but polarising effect on public opinion in France. It strengthened the Socialists, and brought into their camp the gifted politician

---

[16]   "It's eight hours, eight hours, eight hours. It's eight hours that we need"

[17]   "It's our men, our men, our men. It's our men that we need".

Jean Jaures, who became their leader for 20 years until his assassination on the outbreak of World War One. However the majority of the National Assembly voted by 339 to 156 against holding any inquiry into the shootings. The French authorities reacted in a manner strangely reminiscent of the reaction of the British government in 1819 to the Peterloo Massacre. They did not prosecute or discipline any of the troops involved, but instead tried the local strikers' leader, Hippolyte Culine, for "inciting an unlawful assembly", for which he was convicted and sentenced to six years' imprisonment. The Communist politician Paul Lafargue (son-in-law of Karl Marx), who had made an arguably inflammatory speech in Lille two weeks earlier, was also tried on a similar charge and sentenced to one year's imprisonment. Lafargue then stood for the National Assembly while in prison, in a by-election in Lille, and, such was the local feeling about the Fourmies massacre, that he was elected for a seat which had not previously returned a candidate of the Left. The National Assembly recognized his election, which brought about his immediate release from prison. Culine then followed Lafargue's example, and stood and was elected to the National Assembly four times, only to have his election declared invalid each time. Culine was however released from prison in 1892.

The Socialist reaction to Fourmies included the composition of the *Workers' Marseillaise*, a variant on the French national anthem, which called on the workers to rise up and hold demonstrations:-

"Allons forcats des filatures,	"Let's go, galley slaves of the
Le Premier Mai vient de sonner	spinning factories
Levons nous pour manifester (bis)	The First of May has just sounded
Las enfin tant de tortures	Let's get up to demonstrate (twice)
Des exploiteurs, la race infame	So leave such tortures
Vient de conclure un pacte	The infamous race of exploiteurs
odieux,	Has just concluded an odious pact
Affament nos enfants, nos	Making our women and children
femmes	famished
Nous reduisent au sort des gueux	Reducing us to the fate of beggars"

Demonstrations, however, still remained unacceptable to all except the Socialist Left. It was only in 1899 that the (non-Socialist Radical) Prime Minister, Georges Clemenceau, stated in the National Assembly that not all demonstrations were wrong, and only on 17 October, 1909 that the first peaceful street demonstration, of the kind that had developed in London in the 1790s, was held in Paris. The occasion was a protest, which proved to be unsuccessful, led by Jaures, against the intended execution in Barcelona of a former long-time resident of Paris, the Catalan anarchist scholar and educator Francisco Ferrer. As late as 1911, the annual May Day demonstration was broken up and the organisers prosecuted. Demonstrations, now so characteristic of Paris, did not become common there until after the First World War, when street demonstrations had been given huge momentum worldwide as a result of their successful use by the Bolsheviks in the Russian Revolution.

Turning from France to other European countries, it is perhaps surprising that autocratic and intolerant Tsarist Russia should have seen the start of a demonstrating tradition as soon as France, and much sooner than Germany.

The first political demonstration in Russian history took place on 6 December, 1876, in front of the Kazan Cathedral in St Petersburg. It was organised by members of Zemlya i volya ("Land and Liberty"), and workers associations, and was attended by some 400 people. A powerful speech attacking the Tsarist autocracy was given by Georgi Plekhanov. The police moved to break up the gathering, and 31 demonstrators were arrested, 18 of whom were later sentenced to varying terms of imprisonment or exile. This repression did not stop the spread of the practice of holding demonstrations. By the 1880s student demonstrations were occurring, and the designation of May Day as the International Workers Day in 1889 was at once recognized by a May Day strike of 10,000 workers in Warsaw, and by a demonstration in Helsinki (both then part of the Russian empire) on May Day, 1890, and the following year by a May Day workers' meeting in St Petersburg, organised by M.I. Brusnev. In 1892 to 1894 there were May Day meetings and demonstrations in St Petersburg, Tula, Warsaw, Lodz, Vilnius, Kazan, Kiev, and Nizhni-Novgorod. On May Day, 1900, there were demonstrations in Kiev, Warsaw, Vilnius, Helsinki and Kharkov. Lenin was an early and enthusiastic supporter of demonstrations as a political weapon, and wrote to the organiser of the 1900 Kharkov demonstration several months before it was due to take place, emphasizing its importance.

Some of these demonstrations – for example in Warsaw and Helsinki – were in areas where Russia was an alien occupying power, and whatever their stated cause will also have been a reflection of anti-Russian feeling. However it is hard to explain the fact that holding demonstrations as a form of political action seems quickly to have caught the imagination of many Russians. It is tempting to see a cultural connection with the ancient Russian practice of Easter parades carrying icons of saints, to which walking in procession behind banners with slogans bears some superficial similarities, but there seems to be no direct evidence to support this. It is also possible that the complete lack of democratic institutions in the Russian Empire left more people feeling that they had few alternatives to street demonstrations, as a way of making their feelings known. A much more detailed study is needed to establish the reason why demonstrations in Russia caught on so fast.

In January 1905, a workers' demonstration was held in Russia which was larger than any previous ones. It resulted from the climate of increasing discontent which developed because of Russia's unpopular war with Japan, and which led to a wave of strikes in St Petersburg's factories. At this point a complex and controversial figure, Father Grigory Gapon, became involved in articulating the workers' demands and seeking to mediate with the authorities. Gapon was not a person of the political Left. He was loyal to the Tsar, and accepted a regular and publicly known payment from the police, while at the same time organising something approximating to a workers' trade union. His reformist approach was hated by the Revolutionary Left, and eventually led to his murder by Social Revolutionaries in 1906. His relationship with the police led Soviet Russian historians to stigmatise him as an agent provocateur. However independent research suggests that he was a genuine and idealistic supporter of better conditions for workers, if somewhat naïve and confused.

Gapon organised a petition to the Tsar asking for improved conditions for workers, as well as for political freedom, including freedom of speech, and for an eight-hour working day. On Sunday, 9 January, 1905, between 50,000 and 100,000 people marched with Gapon towards the Winter Palace to deliver the petition to the Tsar. They were deliberately and demonstratively peaceful, many demonstrators walking with their pockets turned inside out to show that they were not carrying any weapons. Many women and children took part, some carrying holy icons or portraits of the Tsar, and singing hymns as they marched. The Social Democrats, who were committed to overthrowing the Tsar, played no part in organising Gapon's march, because they did not approve of his monarchism, but many workers with Social Democratic sympathies came out to march out of general sympathy for the marchers' aims.

The singing marchers approached the Winter Palace from different directions. No-one was expecting violence, but without warning, near the Narva Gate, a bugle was sounded, as a signal for soldiers to open fire on the crowd. Some 40 people were immediately killed or wounded. Soldiers then also opened fire on the crowd at several other locations. The official figures, probably an underestimate, were that 130 marchers were killed and 299 seriously wounded. Gapon was not killed, and escaped after being hidden in the houses of several sympathisers. At the time of the shooting he is said to have exclaimed "There is no God any longer! There is no Tsar!"

The day of the demonstration immediately became known as "Bloody Sunday". The fury it provoked, both in St Petersburg and in the provinces, started the 1905 Russian revolution. That lasted a year, and culminated in the Tsar being forced to give some concessions to the revolutionaries, in the form of a constitution, Parliament, and more accountable government.

The revolution generated particularly acute tension in Poland. Immediately after Bloody Sunday, peaceful protest demonstrations began in Warsaw. As the demonstrations continued, and a general strike was declared on 14 January, clashes began between demonstrators and Russian troops. Over the three day period, 14 to 16 January, 1905, Russian troops fired 60,000 cartridges at civilian demonstrators in Warsaw, killing 64 people and wounding 69.

This terror did not quell the unrest but instead turned people to increasing violence, with terrorist bands raiding armourers' shops and attacking public buildings. Polish public opinion rejoiced in Russian defeats in the Far East, notably the dramatic Japanese naval victory at Tsushima in May. Students joined in the street demonstrations in an example that was copied by students in Russia proper. The Russian government attempted to recapture the initiative by organising a patriotic fake demonstration, but this was a fiasco. A further popular counter-demonstration on 8 February ended with workers and students chanting pro-British and pro-Japanese slogans outside the British Consulate. The response of the Russian Governor of Warsaw was to ban all demonstrations. But they continued. A large one on 1 March, organised by the Socialist Party, proclaimed the slogans "Down with tsarism", "Long Live an independent Socialist Poland", " Down with the war", and "Long live Japan".

On May Day 1905, Warsaw was shut down by another general strike. The authorities prohibited marches and demonstrations that day but a workers' May Day demonstration nevertheless went ahead, carrying red flags and singing revolutionary songs. It was entirely peaceful and orderly. When the demonstration reached Jerusalem Street, then as now one of the main streets of central Warsaw, a column of Cossacks rode up to the procession, which peacefully made way for the horsemen to pass. Once the Cossacks had passed the procession, they drew up blocking its path. A troop of infantry then marched up to the demonstrators and without warning began firing indiscriminately into the crowd of demonstrators, while at the same moment the Cossacks charged back into the demonstrators from the opposite side with their swords drawn. Troop continued firing at the demonstrators as they broke and ran away. Thirty-one demonstrators were killed and over 200 wounded in this completely unprovoked massacre. The government then added insult to injury by announcing a week later that a special secret commission had concluded, incredibly, that the shooting had started when the demonstrators fired on the police.

The massacre in Poland did nothing to restore peace, and by May the government was forced to make major concessions by agreeing to set up local councils to replace rule by appointed officials, and by permitting much wider use of the Polish language. These concessions were too little and too late, and Poland continued to simmer until the end of the revolutionary crisis at the end of the year.

In 1917 those events of the 1905 revolution were only 12 years in the past and were engraved in the minds of those taking part in that year's Russian Revolution . This earth-changing event began with a peaceful demonstration to mark International Women's Day on 8 March, 1917 (23 February in the Western calendar), which gradually turned into a series of growing and spreading demonstrations against the tsarist regime.

On May Day 1917, Communists and revolutionary socialists used the day as an occasion for enormous demonstrations by revolutionary workers. These demonstrations acted as a focus for discontent with the Kerensky regime which had replaced the tsarist monarchy, and intensified the revolutionary atmosphere. On 3 and 4 July, 1917, armed and violent demonstrations by crowds of Bolshevik--supporting workers and soldiers on the streets of Petrograd caused numerous casualties. Kerensky's government accused the Bolshevik leaders of attempting a coup, and the two most prominent Bolsheviks, Lenin and Zinoviev, went into hiding to avoid arrest. Those armed demonstrations were probably not a coup attempt, but merely a show of force designed to intimidate the government. However they illustrate how important demonstrations were to the growth of the Bolshevik movement, leading up to the Bolshevik seizure of power from the Kerensky government in October.

Within a few months of the Bolsheviks gaining power, they were themselves suppressing demonstrations by force, and imposing their own iron system of repression. However demonstrations continued to hold an honoured place in Bolshevik propaganda and mythology, reflecting the reality that they had played a big part in making the Bolshevik revolution happen. For this reason, Article 15 of the First Constitution of the Soviet Union, promulgated in July 1918, read as follows:-

"In order to ensure for the toilers real freedom of assembly, the Russian Socialist Federated Soviet Republic, recognizing the right of the citizens of the Soviet Republic freely to organise assemblies, meetings, processions, etc, shall place at the disposal of the working class and the poor peasantry all premises suitable for public gatherings, together with furnishing, lighting and heating".

Two and a half years after this constitution was promulgated, the last vestiges of freedom in Soviet Russia were destroyed with the crushing by the Red Army of the Kronstadt Naval revolt of January 1921. Well before that, anyone organising an unauthorised demonstration would have been at greater risk of being shot than under the tsars. This remained the position in Russia for most of the Soviet era, at least until well after the death of Stalin in 1953.

The right to organise assemblies, meetings and processions was deleted from the second Soviet constitution of 1924. However in a bizarre mockery of the aspirations of the pre-Revolutionary demonstrators, it was included in the third Soviet constitution, known as the "Stalin Constitution", promulgated in 1935. That constitution bore no relationship to how the Soviet Union was actually governed, but was a form of propaganda, aimed at public opinion in foreign countries. Article 125 of the Stalin constitution provided that:

"In conformity with the interests of the working people, and in order to strengthen the socialist system, the citizens of the Union of Soviet Socialist Republics are guaranteed by law: (c) freedom of assembly, including the hold of mass meetings; (d) freedom of street processions and demonstrations. These civil rights are ensured by placing at the disposal of the working people and their organisations printing presses, stocks of paper, public buildings, the streets, communication facilities and material requisites for the exercise of these rights."

Anyone who attempted a demonstration in Stalin's Russia would have faced certain death. However that did not mean that Article 125 was nothing more than a meaningless lie. Because the Soviet Union was very influential in the world for a long time, the constitutions of many other countries copied the Stalin constitution and included protection of the right to demonstrate in their constitutions. Examples are the constitutions of China, Portugal, South Africa, and present day post-Soviet Russia. In some of these countries, over time, the constitutional right to demonstrate has acquired real meaning and effectiveness.

A particularly unusual example of the seamless web of history, which this "right to demonstrate" provision illustrates, is provided by the Chinese constitution.

As is well-known, and as described in Chapter 19, freedom to demonstrate does not yet exist in China. However this did not prevent the Chinese side of the negotiating team for the return of British Hong Kong to China, in 1985, from asking for the right to demonstrate to be included in the new constitution for Hong Kong, to be known as the Basic Law of the Hong Kong Special Administrative Region of the People's Republic of China. Why this was done is unknown. It may just have been a wish, out of national pride, to put into the Basic Law a freedom which was in the Chinese constitution but not already being proposed by Britain, as a way of having more Chinese input into it. Whatever the reason it was suggested, the British readily agreed to what was for them an uncontroversial proposal, as Hong Kong already had a highly developed tradition of peaceful street demonstrations. Since Hong Kong's return to China in 1997, this tradition has continued. The importance of the constitutional protection for the right to demonstrate has been recognized by the courts of the Hong Kong Special Administrative Region. By this roundabout route even Stalin's mockery of the right to demonstrate has ended up being transformed into a reality in at least one place. The struggles of the workers in pre-Revolutionary Russia have ended up guaranteeing this important right a hundred years later in modern Hong Kong.

In Germany, in contrast to Russia, the attitude to May Day demonstrations was even more hostile than the attitude in France. As a result of the German princes' reaction to the Hambach Festival, described in Chapter 6, unauthorised demonstrations of all kinds were officially banned by law from the 1830s onwards. In addition, Bismarck's anti-Socialist law banned socialist organisations of any kind. Because of the anti-Socialist law, the German Social Democrats, who represented a powerful section of German public opinion, were organised clandestinely from Zurich in Switzerland, with all their candidates standing officially as independents. On account of this precarious position, the Social Democrats, probably also reflecting German cultural attitudes to authority, had become punctilious in complying with laws and regulations, in order that the government would have no excuse to take action against them or any of their party officials or candidates. Their vote in elections to the Reichstag increased steadily in the later decades of the nineteenth century, and there was every indication that they might in due course hope to capture power through the ballot box. For this reason their leaders, first Wilhelm Liebknecht and then August Bebel, were not at all attracted to the street demonstration as a political weapon. Bebel, the leader in 1890, was strongly opposed to the declaration of May Day as the workers' day to be marked by annual demonstrations. "The best demonstration there is of our strength", he wrote, "is our result at the last election". As a result of Bebel's stance, German support for May Day demonstrations was much less than it might otherwise have been. The Social Democrats, tried to make sure that their members would not feel left out of May Day, because of the absence of demonstrations, by instead organising May Day picnics. These were convivial open air meals, usually accompanied by a few speeches and sometimes a brass band, which had nothing in common with street demonstrations.

This lack of Social Democrat support for May Day demonstrations in turn meant that right up to the twentieth century no tradition of street demonstrations developed in Germany. This had profound political effects on Germany. The first significant German political campaign which involved deliberately peaceful demonstrations on the English model was the 1911 campaign for widening the franchise for election to the Prussian Parliament. On this occasion, campaigners for a wider franchise, no doubt aware of English history, did organise peaceful demonstrations across Germany. However this one-off campaign was not enough to create a demonstrating tradition. There were also anti-war demonstrations in Berlin in 1914 and 1916, but these again were rare events which did not create a tradition.

It was no coincidence that after World War 1 the German streets, in which peaceful demonstrators were virtually unknown, became the home of large gangs of violent thugs formed into private armies, who fought pitched battles for political power. These armies emerged from gangs of demobilised soldiers, but were soon formally organised into paramilitary organisations known as Political Combat Leagues. The political right was first represented by the Stahlhelm ("steel helmet") Combat League, in due course supplanted by the Nazi Party and its Sturmabteilung ("assault division"), the SA. Communist street fighters were grouped in the Red Flag Fighting Front, and even the Social Democrats set up a paramilitary organisation, the Reichsbanner.

Demonstrations were used in Germany in the aftermath of World War 1, not as a means of peaceful protest but as a method of deliberately provoking violence with a view to destabilising the state, and creating either Left-wing or Right-wing revolution. How this happened is vividly described by James Diehl in his book *Paramilitary politics in the Weimar Republic*. "*Demonstrations and counter-demonstrations in connection with political issues under discussion in the Reichstag were also a familiar part of the agitated political life of the Weimar Republic and an abundant source of political violence. The massive demonstrations occasioned by the Dawes Plan, Locarno Treaties, and Flag Ordinance of 1926, as well as the various referenda that were promoted in later years, inflamed political passions and were a constant invitation to violence. Writing in 1926, supposedly a calm year in the political life of the Republic, the Reichskommissar complained that the "contesting of political differences in the street, the linking of political demands with demonstrations of well-ordered, disciplined mass organisations, the play with putsch rumours, and the threat of violence, which have gradually become commonplace, unquestionably create great dangers for public order and the security of the Reich".* Demonstrations were organised and scheduled by Political Combat Leagues so as to be deliberately provocative to their opponents, in the hope of starting a battle. *"The announcement of an organisation's intention to hold a meeting or a demonstration led to immediate counter-measures by the opposing organisations. First, violence was threatened in the hope that authorities would prohibit the meeting. If this failed, counter-demonstrations were called either simultaneously, or if that was not allowed, shortly thereafter, in order to regain "honour".* In 1926 for example, Bavarian Rightist organisations, following a Reichsbanner meeting in Bavaria, organised an enormous memorial celebration in honour of the army and navy, a demonstration which its organisers admitted would not have been held "if the attack of the Reichsbanner had not forced us to.""

By 1926 deaths in street fighting between demonstrating Political Combat Leagues had become commonplace. The culture of the Leagues was one in which proving oneself in street fighting played an ever more important role[18]. In 1929 the Reich Minister of the Interior, Carl Severing, wrote, "Hardly a day goes by in which somewhere in Germany, usually in many places, political opponents are not shot at, beaten or stabbed". This culture was deeply de-stabilising to the institutions of the Weimar Republic, and it was from the witches' brew on the German streets that the Hitler and the Nazi Party were able to spread out and to seize the state.

These events in Weimar Germany could not have been further removed from the peaceful principles of Thomas Attwood and the pioneers of demonstrations in Britain. They explain why until the end of the twentieth century attitudes to street demonstrations in much of continental Europe, and particularly in Germany, remained much less tolerant and accepting than in Britain.

The history of the first peaceful demonstrations in other European countries is hard to piece together. Broadly speaking, they started early in Belgium, which was strongly British influenced in the mid-nineteenth century. By the later

---

[18]   A by-product of this endemic street violence was the development of water cannon for riot control, first used in 1930 in Weimar Germany.

nineteenth century they were also common in the Swiss city of Zurich, which was a stronghold of socialist political activity. The idea of demonstrations was accepted rather later in Holland, with attempted demonstrations still being broken up by the Amsterdam police in the 1880s. Sweden had May Day parades, but there seems to be no record of any other demonstration there until the movement to end the powers of the monarchy and move to Parliamentary government in 1917. Demonstrations occurred in parts of the Austro-Hungarian empire from the 1860s, with the attitude of the authorities fluctuating between tolerance and repression. May Day demonstrations became common in Italy and Spain from the start of the May Day movement, but there was no general acceptance of the idea of peaceful demonstrations. In Italy the role of street demonstrations was exploited by the explicitly violent Fascists, notably in Mussolini's "March on Rome" in 1922. In much of Spain in the nineteenth and early twentieth century the rule of law scarcely existed[19], so that the concept of a British-style demonstration, that deliberately kept within the law, would have been hard for people to comprehend.

Having considered how demonstrations spread to Europe, it is time to return to their further development in Victorian and Edwardian Britain.

---

[19]   Much of nineteenth-century rural Spain was controlled by local strongmen, known as "caciques", who in practice had virtually absolute power in the areas they dominated.

CHAPTER 9

DEMONSTRATIONS AND VOTES FOR WOMEN

By mid-Victorian times, demonstrations in Britain were so well-established as a national habit that the Annual Register, the yearly almanac of events published throughout the nineteenth century, contains no less than 50 references to demonstrations between 1842 and 1880.

As well as the Chartists, there were many other demonstrations in favour of Parliamentary reform. There were also demonstrations for, and against, free trade. An anti-free trade demonstration in 1848 took the innovative form of a large procession of demonstrating boats, decorated with banners, proceeding up the Thames to Parliament to present a petition. There were anti-Papal demonstrations on Guy Fawkes Day in 1850. There were demonstrations by Irish Fenians in 1869 and 1874, demonstrations by matchmakers against a proposed tax on matches in 1871, demonstrations against the high price of meat in 1872, demonstrations in favour of bank holidays in 1876, and even a demonstration in 1875 by supporters of the false claimant to the Titchborne inheritance, the self-styled "Sir Roger", demanding his release from prison.

There were also a series of huge demonstrations, on a succession of Sundays in June and July 1855, against Lord Robert Grosvenor's Beer Bill to ban Sunday sales of beer. Karl Marx was one of those taking part on 25 June, and left a vivid account of the event, which he estimates to have been attended by about 200,000 people. The demonstration was organised by remnants of the Chartist movement, to protest against the hypocrisy of preventing working people from drinking their usual drink on their day off. The police attempted to require the demonstration to disperse, on the grounds that Hyde Park was private property, but were unable to prevent a Chartist speaker, Finlan, from addressing the crowd surrounded by a mass of people so dense that the police were unable to approach him. Rich people traditionally rode in Hyde Park on Sunday afternoon in their carriages, and on this occasion were surrounded and mocked by huge crowds of demonstrators in what the *Morning Post* later described as "a scene in the highest degree disgraceful and dangerous".

While the first two anti-Beer Bill demonstrations were largely peaceful, the third one generated into an old-fashioned riot, with hundreds of windows broken in the West End. After this Lord Robert Grosvenor withdrew his Bill. The Beer Bill had faced strong opposition throughout from a combination of working class, secular and brewing interests, but there is no doubt that it was the series of demonstrations which led Grosvenor to withdraw, showing that the extent of popular opposition was much greater than he had realised.

The fact that 200,000 people were willing to gather in Hyde Park in 1855, on that June Sunday afternoon, despite the much weakened support by then for the Chartists, showed that it was relatively easy to gather a huge crowd to a demonstration in Victorian London. It is true that stopping people drinking beer on Sunday was a highly emotive issue. Nevertheless, the ease with which vast numbers were assembled showed that scope remained for equally large demonstrations on other issues as they arose. Grosvenor's subsequent withdrawal of his Beer Bill also showed that such demonstrations might succeed in their objectives, if only they could muster enough support.

Inevitably, when extending the right to vote once more became a live issue again a few years after the Beer Bill riots, huge demonstrations were again a feature of the campaign to extend the franchise.

An attempt by Lord John Russell's government to widen the franchise in 1860 was voted down, but five years later pressure for reform began mounting again, probably influenced by the success of the democratic Union forces in the American Civil War. Two organisations were formed to campaign for reform, the Reform Union, mostly made up of members of the Liberal Party, and the much more broadly based Reform League, which specifically aimed to repeat the success of 1832 by exerting pressure through mass demonstrations. One of the key organisers of the Reform League was a former Chartist and poet, John Bedford Leno.

The League's first big demonstration was held on 29 June, 1866, and involved a march from Clerkenwell Green to Trafalgar Square, followed by speeches. A second meeting was held on 2 July, 1866, and on 23 July, 1866 a giant meeting was planned in Hyde Park. This meeting was declared to be illegal and banned by the Conservative Home Secretary, Spencer Walpole. Many were doubtful about Walpole's interpretation of the law and believed that he had no power to ban it. For this reason the Reform League decided that the meeting should go ahead.

The demonstration began with a procession, led by John Leno, starting from the Reform League's headquarters near the Strand. When the head of the procession reached Marble Arch, they found the gates to Hyde Park chained shut, and 1,600 police, on foot and mounted, guarding the entrance. Leno and the other leaders demanded to be let through and threatened to break in, but were simply laughed at by the police. However, while they were arguing, someone noticed that the railings surrounding the park were very insecurely fixed into the ground. After being pushed backwards and forwards a few times, the railings collapsed, allowing people to enter the park in large numbers at any point they wished, despite police efforts to stop them. While Leno and his companions were breaking in at Marble Arch, similar railing collapses and break-ins occurred along Park Lane and at Knightsbridge, where the demonstrators were led by the famous atheist and Radical campaigner Charles Bradlaugh, himself a veteran of the Beer Bill demonstrations eleven years earlier. The police were described as being overwhelmed "like flies before a waiter's napkin", as an estimated 200,000 people swept into the park. The police called for military support, but when the Horse Guards arrived they declined to try to enter the park, and simply manoeuvred at a distance. The Reform meeting in the Park then took place as planned. The event is commemorated today by the "Reformers' Tree", memorial set into the paving in Hyde Park, which replaced the stump of an actual tree used for many years for posting notices about political meetings[20].

The success of the Hyde Park meeting, with the collapse of the railings. gave an enormous boost to the Reform League. The League greatly expanded the number of its branches, and organised demonstrations around the country, holding huge meetings in Birmingham, Manchester, Leeds, Glasgow and Dublin.

Just like its predecessors, the Political Unions, in 1832, the Reform League saw it as critical to its credibility to avoid violence. This meant avoiding any further even arguably illegitimate actions, like the pushing over of the Hyde Park railings. To prevent this, the League therefore organised what was referred to as "close stewarding" of its meetings, to prevent disorder. That meant having many official stewards, ready to intervene at the first sign of unauthorised activity

---

[20] In the aftermath of the Hyde Park riot the Commissioner of Works, in 1872, designated the north-east section of Hyde Park as a location for political meetings. This is the origin of Speakers' Corner which continues in use today.

by the demonstrators, so that the chances of spontaneous direct action were greatly reduced.

For the same reason, the League stopped holding central London meetings in late 1866. The number of venues for a large central London meeting was limited. Hyde Park was the only place which could accommodate really large numbers, and another meeting planned in Hyde Park might have given the government a further opportunity to impose a ban on meetings there, perhaps with worse results for the League than the outcome on 23 July, 1866. There was also the risk that a Hyde Park meeting might degenerate into an orgy of window breaking, as had happened with the third anti-Beer Bill demonstration in 1855.

Instead of another Hyde Park meeting, therefore, the League held a march, on 3 December, 1866, in pouring rain, from central London to Beaufort House, Chiswick for a meeting there. However by April 1867, by which time the League had over 100 branches nationwide, the pressure for another central London meeting was irresistible. A meeting was organised for Good Friday, but postponed in order not to alienate religious segments of public opinion who might disapprove of a demonstration held on that day. The postponed meeting was then rescheduled for Hyde Park on 6 May, 1867. Spencer Walpole, still Home Secretary, announced that he was banning it, as he had banned the meeting the previous year. The Reform League responded by announcing that the ban itself was illegal, and posting posters to this effect calling on people to attend. The government made plans for forcible suppression of the meeting, but at the last minute gave way and allowed it to proceed. Again some 200,000 people are thought to have attended, with speakers addressing them from ten different platforms.

Spencer Walpole then resigned as Home Secretary over his responsibility for the confusion as to the legality of the Hyde Park meeting. Shortly afterwards, the Derby-Disraeli government passed the 1867 Reform Act, doubling the size of the electorate, by extending it to most working men in towns, so that the principal objective of the Reform League was achieved. The Reform League continued in existence, but moved its principal activity to campaigning for the secret ballot for elections, which was in due course introduced in 1872.

The Reform League thus joined the ranks of those organisations which had achieved outstanding success by the use of demonstrations. As with their predecessors in 1832, their strict commitment to non-violence and legality were an essential part of their success, which was also helped by the tight discipline and self-discipline of their supporters. Although their Hyde Park meetings are sometimes loosely and inaccurately referred to as "the Hyde Park riots", the only aspect that could be regarded as in a sense riotous was the knocking over of the railings after access was banned, probably illegally, for the first meeting. In all other respects the meetings were conspicuously peaceful and orderly. These meetings, particularly the huge second Hyde Park meeting in 1867, added enormous momentum to a campaign whose time had come. It was probably the vast public support shown by the demonstrations, in support of a traditional Liberal cause, that led the Conservative leader, Disraeli, to "steal the Liberals' clothes" by doing what the demonstrators, and much of the public, wanted, even though he and his party had voted down a Liberal attempt to do the same thing the previous year.

With the examples of the two successful Reform campaigns of 1832 and 1867, demonstrations were an obvious method for anyone else to copy who wanted to bring about changes to the British voting system. In some ways, it is surprising, against this background, that demonstrations for votes for women did not start sooner than they did.

Women were active in demonstrations from the very start. Old prints show women in the audience at the first public meeting of the London Corresponding Society in 1795, in demonstrations for the First Reform Bill in the 1830s, and at the Hyde Park demonstrations in 1866, although admittedly in small numbers. There were women among those killed while attending the Peterloo meeting in 1819, and there were women Chartists[21]. However demonstrations for votes for women did not start until nearly forty years after the passage of the Second Reform Act in 1867.

The reason for this was partly connected with the general situation of women in Victorian Britain, and partly to do with women's attitudes to street demonstrations.

The major upheavals which led to voting Reform each generated modest accompanying movements for women's suffrage. During the 1832 Reform Bill crisis, Mary Smith from Yorkshire petitioned Parliament for women such as herself, who met the property qualifications for voting, to be allowed to vote, and Henry Hunt raised the issue on her behalf in Parliament. In June 1866, while the Reform League campaign was at its height, a petition was handed in to Parliament by Elizabeth Garrett Anderson, the first British woman doctor, and Emily Davies, signed by 1,499 women, calling for votes for women. However for most women the most pressing political issue in 1866 was not the right to vote but the legal inability of married women to own property.

---

[21]   Three leading women Chartists were Elizabeth Pease, Jane Smeal and Anne Knight, all Quakers. There was a National Female Charter Association. The Birmingham Charter Association had over 2,000 women members.

Until the late nineteenth century, a married woman's property automatically became that of her husband on her marriage. This unjust and oppressive situation was only ended, after lengthy campaigning, by the Married Women's Property Act, 1882. It was only once that issue relating to married women's property had been finally resolved that women's inability to vote became a more important political issue. Once that happened, after 1882, Women's Suffrage Societies began to grow in numbers and activism.

Until the end of the nineteenth century, the Women's Suffrage campaign proceeded by way of indoor public meetings, meetings with politicians, letters to newspapers, speeches and other forms of conventional middle-class political activity. It was only when these activities failed to bring results that support slowly began to grow among women's suffrage campaigners for bolder tactics, such as demonstrations. This was so particularly after a Women's Suffrage petition to Parliament with nearly 250,000 signatures, presented to Parliament in 1896, failed to generate any response. However, even then, there was much resistance to the idea of women campaigning by way of street demonstrations, which were felt by some to be unladylike, undignified, and potentially dangerous.

The leading women's suffrage campaigning organisation from 1897 onward was the National Association of Women's Suffrage Societies ("NUWSS"), formed that year by the merger of two earlier organisations. Its most prominent figure was Millicent Garrett Fawcett, the sister of Elizabeth Garrett Anderson. The NUWSS was committed to obtaining reform by organising speaker meetings and presenting bills in Parliament. Its style was once described by Millicent Fawcett herself as "like a glacier, slow but unstoppable".

This glacial pace was intolerable for some campaigners, and resulted in 1903 in the formation of the Women's Social and Political Union ("WSPU"), under the leadership of Mrs Emmeline Pankhurst. Mrs Pankhurst's background virtually guaranteed that under her leadership street demonstrations would become important in the Women's Suffrage Movement.

Emmeline Pankhurst was a Mancunian who was proud to be descended from a grandfather who had narrowly escaped death at Peterloo. She had been the wife of a liberal lawyer, Richard Pankhurst. who was closely involved with the drafting of the Married Women's Property Act, 1882. Richard Pankhurst died young in 1898, leaving his widow to raise four children on a small income. By then Mrs Pankhurst already had a notable record of campaigning on many issues, including two particularly related to free speech and the right to meet in public, namely the right to hold meetings in Trafalgar Square, London, and the right to hold them at Boggart Hole Clough in Manchester.

The origin of the Trafalgar Square campaign of 1887 was a demonstration in the Square which got out of hand on 8 February, 1886. It was organised by the Social Democratic Federation (SDF) an early Socialist group whose leading figure was Henry Myers Hyndman. The SDF speakers called for radical redistribution of wealth, and criticised idle aristocrats who lived off the poor. The oratory went to the heads of the audience, who moved off down adjacent Pall Mall, and, after being taunted by some clubmen, broke the windows of most of the London clubs. Hyndman and others were tried for their part in organising a meeting which turned into a riot, but were acquitted. However as a result of this riot, the Metropolitan Police Commissioner, Charles Warren, decided to impose a permanent ban on all public meetings in Trafalgar Square, from 7 November, 1887. This closure was controversial, as Trafalgar Square was the obvious large open space in central London, apart from Hyde Park, for holding a public meeting. Warren's ban was also of doubtful legality, being just an administrative instruction to the police by the police commissioner, and not a law. Opinion about the merits of the ban was divided, with *The Times* describing it as a justifiable minor restriction on the right to meet, in the interest of public order, while the Liberal *Pall Mall Gazette* described the imposition of the ban as a crisis, and called for resistance to it as an encroachment on popular liberties.

A mass demonstration in protest at the ban was organised, to be held in Trafalgar Square on 13 November, 1887. It was promoted as "a peaceful meeting to test the legality of the ban". However the crowd of several thousand demonstrators who converged on the Square that Sunday was attacked and forcibly broken up, with extreme brutality, by large numbers of mounted police, aided by Grenadier Guards with fixed bayonets. Two hundred injured demonstrators were treated in local hospitals, and two, a Mr Corner and a Mr Harrison, died of their injuries. Notable figures who took part in that demonstration, as well as the Pankhursts, included William Morris, the pioneer socialist and writer, Annie Besant, the co-founder of the Indian Congress Party, and the editor of the *Pall Mall Gazette*, W.T. Stead. The demonstration leaders, Robert Cunningham-Graham[22] and John

---

[22]   Robert Cunningham-Graham was at the time Liberal and Radical M.P. for North-west Lanark. Before entering politics he had spent 14 years working as a gaucho in Argentina, trying to reclaim the lost colonial fortune of his Spanish grandmother. Elected as a Liberal, he later declared himself a Socialist, and as such was the first Socialist M.P. in the U.K. Parliament. He was a founding member of the Labour Party and then in later life founded the Scottish National Party. He was a writer and a friend of the novelist Joseph Conrad, and is the model for the character of Charles Gould in Conrad's *Nostromo.*.

Burns[23], were both severely beaten in public by the police, and were then charged with riot. Both were acquitted after trial, although convicted of the lesser offence of unlawful assembly, for which they were sentenced to six weeks' imprisonment. The trial was notable for the evidence which emerged of police brutality, and the way the police were shown to have lied by claiming that they had been attacked by Cunningham-Graham and Burns. A further "indignation meeting" to protest at police behaviour on 13 November, was held on 20 November. That meeting was also forcibly broken up by mounted police, with the death of a further demonstrator, Alfred Linnell.

The events in and around Trafalgar Square on 13 November, 1887 became known as "Bloody Sunday", a name later also applied to Father Gapon's demonstration in St Petersburg (Chapter 8 above); to the massacre of spectators at a football match in Dublin in November 1920 by the "Black and Tan" [24] auxiliary police; and to the shooting of unarmed demonstrators by soldiers in Londonderry in 1972 (Chapter 17 below). Opinion about the 1887 "Bloody Sunday" divided on political lines, with the opposition Liberals denouncing police conduct as an outrage, while the governing Conservatives tried to justify it on public order grounds. The government won a vote in the House of Commons, and then enacted the Trafalgar Square Regulation Act, 1888, which gave legal effect to Commissioner Warren's[25] previous legally dubious ban. However, after the Liberals were returned to power in 1892, the regulations made under that Act to govern meetings in Trafalgar Square were greatly relaxed by the new Home Secretary, Henry Asquith (who, coincidentally, had been the barrister who successfully defended Cunningham-Graham at his riot trial). Asquith's revised regulations allowed demonstrations on Saturday afternoons, Sundays and bank holidays, provided that advance notice had been given to the police. This change took the heat out of the controversy, and ensured that from 1892 onwards demonstrations could be held in Trafalgar Square at most times when organisers wanted to hold them.

---

[23]   The dock worker's leader, one of the founders of the ILP, and later Labour MP for Battersea.

[24]   The Black and Tans were auxiliary police recruited by the British authorities in Ireland to attempt to restore British control, as it collapsed in the years leading up to Irish independence in 1922. They became a by-word for murderous brutality. Their name came from the colour of their uniform…

[25]   Charles Warren was a former soldier who had spent much time in southern Africa, and was known in some circles as "the saviour of Bechuanaland". He had little or no understanding of British domestic politics and this seems to have been the explanation for the abnormal rigidity and savagery of his response to demonstrations.

Boggart Hole Clough was a traditional open-air public meeting place on the northern edge of Manchester. It was bought by Manchester City Council in 1895, specifically with a view to stopping meetings of the newly-formed Independent Labour Party (ILP)[26] being held there. The Council passed a by-law prohibiting meetings on the Clough, and when the ILP leader Keir Hardie addressed a meeting of some 50,000 people there in 1896, he was arrested, though later released without charge, following the intervention of the Home Secretary. However Manchester City Council proceeded to prosecute a large number of other people for breaking the by-law by meeting on the Clough. Those prosecuted included Mrs Pankhurst and her husband, who had set up the Manchester branch of the ILP shortly after the party's foundation. The local prosecutor bringing the cases to court happened to be one Cobbett, grandson of the Radical journalist William Cobbett of the Peterloo era (described in Chapter 4). Knowing this, Mrs Pankhurst courted arrest, and maximised publicity for her cause, by organising and speaking at a meeting at Boggart Hole Clough entitled "The Life and Times of William Cobbett". Eventually the Home Secretary persuaded Manchester City Council to stop the prosecutions, and to give a public undertaking that the by-law against meetings would not be enforced, although it remained on the statute book.

Mrs Pankhurst was thus already an experienced campaign organiser when she founded the WSPU. Her plan with the WSPU was to embark deliberately on acts designed to shock, as a way of forcing attention on to the Women's Suffrage cause. This led within a year to a split between the WSPU and Millicent Fawcett's NUWSS, which remained strongly committed to its traditional activities. However the NUWSS was gradually forced into greater militancy by the need to compete for supporters with the militants of the WSPU.

To understand Mrs Pankhurst's strategy, it is important to understand social attitudes to the role of women in society at the start of the twentieth century. The unquestioned assumption of the majority of society was that a woman's place was in the home, unless she was required by economic necessity to go out to work. In addition, the ideal woman was expected to be gracious, gentle, and domestic in her pre-occupations. Although fifty years had passed since Dickens' novels appeared, the character of Dickens' female heroines still encapsulated the feminine ideal of many Edwardian men and women. For this reason there were

---

[26] The Independent Labour Party was founded in Bradford in 1893, to secure working men's representation in Parliament independent of the Liberal Party. It was a forerunner and member of the Labour Representative Committee formed in 1903 and of the Labour Party, founded in 1906.

women, such as the novelist Mrs Humphry Ward[27], president of the Women's National Anti-Suffrage League, who campaigned actively against giving the vote to women, because they believed women should not seek to compete with men but should remain in their own separate sphere within the home, or they would compromise their dignity and femininity.

Because of these prevailing social attitudes, Mrs Pankhurst faced an almost diametrically opposite problem to that which had faced the London Corresponding Society and the Parliamentary Reformers of the early nineteenth century. Those earlier campaigners had to convince others that they were respectable people who deserved the vote, rather than a disreputable rabble. Mrs Pankhurst's problem, in contrast, was that many people believed that women should be above the fray of politics, and should not demean themselves with its sordid confrontations.

Mrs Pankhurst quite correctly understood that these attitudes would have to be broken down, at least partly, if the women's suffrage campaign was to be taken seriously by those in power. This involved showing that women could be every bit as assertive and determined as men in pursuing their suffrage demand. Inevitably, this meant that there would need to be street demonstrations by women, despite the reservations held by many women about demonstrating[28]. It also meant that the WSPU would need to take other steps to publicise their cause and their determination, some of which would shock traditional people. However the initial acts of WSPU "militancy", although they shocked contemporaries, were mild by modern standards. It was only after the WSPU's very well-organised peaceful campaigns had failed, for reasons which were not the fault of the organisers, that the WSPU abandoned the rule of law and undertook the acts of serious violence which characterised the later part of its campaign.

The first act of WSPU militancy was very mild, but generated a disproportionately violent reaction. Two WSPU members, Emmeline Pankhurst's daughter Christabel, and Annie Kenney, attended a Liberal Party political meeting in the Free Trade Hall in Manchester in October 1905, at which the main platform speaker was Edward Grey, later Liberal Foreign Secretary. Annie Kenney took advantage of question time to ask the speaker if a Liberal Government (the Conservatives were then in office) would grant votes to women, while Christabel

---

[27] Born Mary Arnold, she was the niece of the poet Matthew Arnold, and the aunt of the novelist Aldous Huxley.

[28] There is a similarity between those reservations held by women in the 1890s, and the reservations initially held by temperance campaigners about the respectability of demonstrations, which were dissipated by the success of the Grand Metropolitan Temperance Demonstration of 1839 (Chapter 6).

Pankhurst unfurled a banner reading "Votes for women". Annie Kenney repeated her question but got no answer. When the meeting broke up she stood up again and shouted "Will the Liberal Government give votes to women?" At this point both women were violently attacked by the audience and ejected bleeding from the meeting. Outside the hall they refused to depart. After Christabel Pankhurst slapped and spat on a man whom she believed to be a Liberal supporter, but who was in fact a plain clothes police inspector, both were arrested for assault and obstruction. They refused to pay their fines and were sent to prison. This incident set a pattern for progressively more militant action by the WSPU. During 1905 this consisted of nothing more threatening than heckling politicians at meetings, which seems insignificant today, but had the power to shock then, because it was so different from the behaviour expected of respectable women.

On 23 October, 1906, WSPU militancy went a little further, with a demonstration by ten women in the lobby of the House of Commons, for which they were arrested, and sentenced to two months' imprisonment.

These militant actions attracted supporters. The WSPU grew from having just three branches at the beginning of 1906 to 47 branches at the end of the year.

In February 1907, the WSPU organised a "Women's Parliament" in Caxton Hall, Westminster. At its conclusion, Mrs Pankhurst led a procession of 400 women who tried to enter Parliament. The police blocked their path and then attempted to disperse the demonstration by force. The scene was described by *The Times*:

> "[The women campaigners] *retreated as far as Dean's Yard, followed by the police. More scuffles ensued, and more arrests were made. The mounted police came up and galloped their horses into the procession, which was dispersed, Several women were knocked down and injured. Still the women collected again and again, and linking arms, according to instructions, endeavoured to force their way through. After a time the women got separated into groups of a dozen or more, and these from time to time tried to get past the police; then the police charged, and the women, followed by constables and mounted men, ran back to Dean's Yard. These tactics continued for about an hour, and arrests were made from time to time.*"

By the end of the evening 52 women and two men had been arrested and charged with disorderly behaviour. Most were convicted and were sentenced to short periods of imprisonment, as an alternative to fines, which they refused on principle to pay. A second march on Parliament by the WSPU a month later had similar consequences.

These attempts to force an entry to Parliament were militancy of a different order from heckling at meetings. From a democratic point of view they were hard to justify, as interrupting the legislature is interfering with its legitimate operation. They followed the disreputable tradition of Lord George Gordon, who had led a march to Parliament to hand in a petition in 1780, and then intimidated Parliament with a huge crowd of his supporters while the petition was debated, leaning out of a window of the Parliament chamber to inform the mob (who shortly afterwards began the worst riots of the eighteenth century) which members speaking were their friends or their enemies. While presenting a petition to Parliament was legal, attempting to force entry en masse was not, so that this procession crossed a line from legal to extra legal action.

At the same time, the action was probably successful in its main aim of concentrating public attention on the Suffrage issue. The sight of women resisting a police charge, as described in *The Times*, demonstrated the campaigners' determination, and the heavy-handed and excessive police action to disperse the procession also generated sympathy for the WSPU cause. It was only after WSPU acts of militancy started that the NUWSS, responding to the WSPU challenge, finally organised its first large street demonstration, which also took place in February 1907. This was an entirely peaceful march from Hyde Park Corner to Exeter Hall off the Strand, attended by between 3,000 and 4,000 women, with banners and bands. It passed off without incident and was generally felt to have been a success, despite bad weather. Because of the bad condition of the London streets through which the protesters marched, the demonstration became known as "the Mud March", a name adopted from an incident in the American Civil War[29]. Other similar large peaceful NUWSS demonstrations followed, including a two-mile march from the Embankment to the Albert Hall in the summer of 1908, attended by about 10,000 marchers.

These relatively modest marches were eclipsed by the WSPU's own demonstration in Hyde Park, held on the summer solstice, June 21, 1908, which was on an entirely different scale. The WSPU demonstration was inspired in part

---

[29] The original "Mud March" was General Ambrose Burnside's unsuccessful winter offensive for the Union Army of the Potomac in January 1863. The American anti-slavery struggle was an inspiration to the Women's Suffrage Movement. Mrs Pankhurst's followers attempting to storm Parliament in February, 1907, sang, to the tune of "John Brown's Body", "Rise up, women, for the fight is hard and long; Rise up in thousands singing loud a battle song; Right is might, and in strength we shall be strong; And the cause goes marching on."

by a statement in Parliament on 28 February, 1908 by the Liberal Home Secretary of the day, Herbert Gladstone, as to why the government had not yet granted the vote to women. Gladstone said:-

> *"There comes a time when political dynamics are far more important than political argument… Looking back at the great political crises in the thirties, the sixties… it will be found that people assembled in their tens of thousands all over the country … Of course it cannot be expected that women can assemble in such masses, but power belongs to the masses, and through this power a Government can be influenced into more effective action than a Government will be likely to take under present conditions".*

The 21 June 2008 demonstration was the Suffragette[30] response to this challenge by Herbert Gladstone. It was certainly the biggest demonstration held in Britain up to that date. It attracted somewhere between 250,000 and 500,000 participants, and was described at the time as "the largest political meeting in the history of the world". There were over 700 banners in the Suffragette colours of white, green and purple[31]. Thirty special trains from all over England brought participants to London, and from the London stations 30,000 marchers paraded through the streets with their banners, carrying thousands of flags, and led by a total of 40 musical bands. Hyde Park was completely submerged by a sea of people.

Mrs Pankhurst described the event in her autobiography:-

> *"What a day was Sunday, June 21ˢᵗ – clear, radiant and filled with golden sunshine… it seemed to me that all London had turned out to witness our demonstration. And a goodly part of London followed the processions. When I mounted my platform in Hyde Park and surveyed the mighty throng there waiting and the endless crowds that were still pouring into the park from all directions, I was filled with amazement not unmixed with awe. Never had I imagined that so many people could be gathered together to share in a political demonstration. It was a gay and beautiful as well as an*

---

[30] The term "Suffragette" was originally a derisory term coined by the hostile Daily Mail, which later spread into general use.

[31] WSPU demonstrations were notable for their imaginative use of colour and design. This owed much to Emmeline Pethick-Lawrence, a close collaborator of Emmeline Pankhurst until 1912.

*awe-inspiring spectacle for the white gowns and flower trimmed hats
of the women, against the background of ancient trees, gave the park
the appearance of a vast garden in full bloom".*

Within the park there were twenty platforms for speeches, and at the end of the afternoon a resolution was carried at each of them calling for votes for women. A WSPU launch called on Members of Parliament as they sat on the river terrace of the House of Commons and invited them to attend. Male literary figures who took part included George Bernard Shaw, Thomas Hardy, Israel Zangwill and H.G. Wells. After the passage of the resolutions, bugles sounded and the demonstration ended with the crowds shouting "One, two, three – votes for women", before dispersing. The meeting was considered a great success and copied by smaller meetings around the country.

This giant demonstration was very much Mrs Pankhurst's personal achievement. She was both an exceptionally able organiser and the unchallenged sole leader of the WPSU. However, internally the WSPU was not a democratic organisation. Mrs Pankhurst frankly described herself as a general commanding an army. This autocratic style, in which she was closely supported by her equally autocratic daughter Christabel, brought impressive results like the 21 June, 1908 demonstration, but also understandably generated a lot of opposition. As early as 1907 the WSPU split, with a group of some 70 members, led by Charlotte Despard[32] and Teresa Billington-Greig, leaving it to set up an alternative organisation, the Women's Freedom League (WFL), on the grounds of the lack of democracy within the WSPU. The trigger for their departure was the preparation by Teresa Billington-Greig of a constitution for WSPU, which Mrs Pankhurst then ostentatiously tore up at a meeting, announcing that the WSPU was an army under military discipline. The WFL campaigned using similar tactics to those of the WSPU, but aimed to have democratic internal procedures. This aim was not completely successful. Charlotte Despard's personality came to dominate the WFL, whose telegraphic address was "Despard. London". However the WFL was democratic compared with the WSPU.

The 21 June, 1908 demonstration was bigger than any which had been held in the 1830s or 1860s, so the Suffragettes had more than met Herbert Gladstone's challenge to demonstrate the power of mass support. They could reasonably

---

[32] Charlotte Despard was the widow of the great nephew of Colonel Edward Despard, hanged for treason in 1803 (Chapter 3). Born Charlotte French, she was the sister, and political opponent, of Sir John French, who commanded the British Army for much of World War One.

have expected, as a consequence, some progress towards achieving their goals. However the giant peaceful demonstration did not bring any immediate results. This unexpected failure had profound effects on the direction of the women's suffrage movement. It increasingly turned it away from peaceful protests such as demonstrations, towards a policy of deliberate and steadily increasing violence. Both the failure of the demonstration to achieve results, and the consequent upsurge in violence, lie squarely at the door of the then Liberal Prime Minister, Henry Asquith.

Asquith's unyielding and destructive opposition to women's suffrage is a source of much puzzlement to historians. Asquith was a proud adherent to Liberal principles of tolerance and rationality. He had shown these in 1892 in the context of meetings in Trafalgar Square, with his revision of the by-laws to permit demonstrations there. However his hostility to women's suffrage was utterly implacable, despite the fact that the majority of the Liberal MPs in Parliament while he was Prime Minister were women's suffrage supporters.

Some have attributed Asquith's hostility to Women's Suffrage to his experiences with his own wife, Margot. Others believe that Margot herself was behind the opposition. One member of a Women's Suffrage delegation to Downing Street records hostile silent stares through an open door from Margot Asquith, while waiting in an ante-room as part of the delegation to meet her husband. However the most likely explanation for Asquith's hostility was political calculation that the granting of votes to women would favour his Conservative opponents, particularly if votes were initially only granted to wealthier women, on a limited property franchise, in line with some compromise proposals. If this was the reasoning, it backfired spectacularly. Asquith's total opposition to an obviously reasonable reform, which was being enacted in other countries in the years when he was Prime Minister, was a major factor in the weakening of the Liberal Party, and its replacement by the Labour Party, in the 1920s, as the main vehicle for progressive politics in Britain. As Millicent Fawcett put it in 1911, "If it had been the Prime Minister's intention to enrage every woman suffragist to the point of frenzy, he could not have acted with greater perspicacity."

After the 1908 demonstration, Asquith marked his opposition by refusing even to receive a women's suffrage delegation. As a result the WSPU, disillusioned by the complete failure of their attempts at peaceful persuasion, gradually moved on to increasingly violent protest.

One of the first major examples of the new WSPU militancy was the heckling of the Chancellor of the Exchequer, Lloyd George, by WSPU members at a meeting in the Albert Hall in December, 1908. Not only did the hecklers completely prevent Lloyd George from speaking for half an hour, but some of them also carried whips, which they used on anyone who tried to eject a Women's Suffrage heckler, with such effectiveness that no hecklers were removed. The alarm caused by this new tactic was sufficient to cause the government to enact a new Act of Parliament, the Public Meetings Act 1908, specifically to criminalise disorderly conduct at meetings such as would prevent the transaction of the business for which the meeting was called. This led to the arrest and imprisonment of numerous Suffragettes.

On 29 June, 1909, Mrs Pankhurst and eight other women went to Parliament to present a petition to the Prime Minister. Asquith had instructed the Chief Inspector of Police on duty to inform the deputation that he would not see them. The inspector passed on Asquith's letter to Mrs Pankhurst, who threw it on the ground and slapped the inspector twice in the face. Following behind her was a vast crowd of supporters who engaged in fierce struggles with the police, requiring the deployment of 3,000 police to hold them back. The Suffragettes threw stones through nearby windows, with messages wrapped round them including "Grant the tax-paying women of Britain the vote", and "Taxation without representation is tyranny". By the end of the day 107 women and eight men had been arrested. These events came to be known as the "Women's Suffrage riot".

At her subsequent trial on a charge of obstructing the police in the execution of their duty, Mrs Pankhurst justified her conduct by relying on her right to petition Parliament under the 1688 Bill of Rights. However the courts held that she had not just been presenting a petition, but had been trying to require an MP to receive a deputation, which she did not have the right to do.

This was one of the last occasions on which the WSPU tried to use the law to advance its cause, as opposed to deliberately breaking it. From then on its policy was one of violent confrontation and deliberate lawbreaking, including damage to property on a very large scale[33], under the slogan "Deeds, not words". A favourite tactic was pouring paraffin into post boxes and setting fire to the mail. Another was breaking windows, including those of the Prime Minister's residence at 10, Downing Street. As the aim was to shock, the WSPU needed to become increasingly violent to achieve its aim, as the shock of merely moderately violent acts gradually wore off. Peaceful mass demonstrations, as used in 1907 and 1908, became less of a focus of activity, although a 40,000-strong Women's Suffrage

---

[33] A single incident of organised window smashing in the West End in March 1912 did some £5,000 worth of damage.

march was still held in London on 17 June, 1911 to mark the coronation of King George V.

The year 1909 was also the time when the WSPU adopted the tactic of hunger strikes in prison to protest against its activists being denied the status of political prisoners. This in turn led to the force-feeding of prisoners, which was declared by the courts to be legal in a test case brought by the Suffragette Mary Leigh. Force-feeding, involving forcing a tube down the struggling prisoner's throat, was painful and humiliating. However, despite this, many imprisoned Suffragettes maintained their hunger strikes except when they were being force-fed, until the government eventually hit on the idea of legislation permitting their release while weak from hunger, but also their rearrest and detention as soon as they had recovered. This was the Prisoner's (Temporary Discharge for Ill-health) Act, 1913, commonly known as the "Cat and Mouse Act".

In September 1909, Asquith was twice physically attacked by Suffragettes. However in 1910 there was a "truce" between the militant Suffragettes and the Liberal government, while Asquith faced the Parliament Bill crisis over the powers of the House of Lords. An attempt was made to agree a "Conciliation Bill", which would grant some women the vote on the basis of a limited franchise based on a property qualification. Asquith then appeared to deliberately insult the Suffragettes, when he announced a Suffrage Bill which extended the vote to all working men, but did not include any provision for women's suffrage. This was in fact probably not a deliberate insult, but a short-sighted political calculation. Extending the vote to women on a limited franchise was liable to favour the Conservatives. Extending the vote to the poorest men, in contrast, was likely to favour the Liberals.

The effect of this further setback to the Suffragette cause was to encourage still more violent Suffragette militancy. Lloyd George's home was blown up by a Suffragette bomb, and the Home Secretary, Winston Churchill, was publicly horsewhipped. Church services were interrupted, buildings set on fire, and paintings slashed in museums. Suffragette militants were further inflamed in 1912 by a bizarre and widely publicised statement at an anti-women's suffrage meeting in Bristol, by a Cabinet Minister, Charles Hobhouse. Hobhouse asserted that in the case of women's suffrage there had not been the kind of popular feeling which accounted for the burning of Nottingham Castle in 1832, or the pulling down of the railings in Hyde Park in 1866. Mrs Pankhurst described this speech as "like a match to a fuse"[34]. Emmeline Pethick-Lawrence of the WSPU commented that Hobhouse took "the very grave responsibility of inciting them to serious forms of violence in comparison with which Mrs Pankhurst's exhortation is mildness itself." A few weeks later, in July 1912, a group of Suffragettes, led by the former hunger-striker Mary Leigh, attempted to set fire to the Theatre Royal, Dublin, while Asquith and an audience were inside. Mary Leigh also threw a hatchet at Asquith, which missed him, but wounded the Irish leader John Redmond, who was travelling with him.

The WFL was generally less violent than the WSPU, reflecting Charlotte Despard's preference for passive, or "spiritual" resistance. Between summer and November of 1909 the WFL responded to Asquith's refusal to meet women's suffrage demonstrations by holding a non-stop all-weather demonstration vigil for Women's Suffrage outside Parliament, entitled the "Great Watch", said to have involved 14,000 woman-hours of watching. It was however the WFL which adopted the technique of protesting against women not having the vote by pouring chemicals into ballot boxes at a polling station in Bermondsey, to destroy the ballot papers. This was thought to be a non-violent protest but in fact caused injury to an official who tried to rescue the papers. As a result the perpetrators, Alison Neilans and a Mrs Chapin, were sentenced to several months in prison.

The immediate effect of the post-1908 militancy was to damage the Suffragette cause. After acts of Suffragette violence began, Suffragettes and Suffragette gatherings, which had previously not been unpopular with the general public, had to be protected by the police from attacks from hostile crowds. This was particularly so after Mrs Pankhurst's decision in 1912 to step up the level of violent activity, a decision opposed by other leading members of the WSPU, including Emmeline Pethick-Lawrence, whom she then expelled.

Public hostility did not extend however to the most famous act of Suffragette militancy, which was Emily Davidson's action in throwing herself at the reins of the king's horse during the 1913 Epsom Derby, pulling down the horse and killing herself in the process.

Emily Davidson was one of the WSPUs most committed militants, and had served a sentence of six months' imprisonment in 1912 for placing "noxious matter" in the letter box of an opponent of women's suffrage. She probably did not intend to kill herself at the Derby, but her action there clearly carried

---

[34] Christabel Pankhurst responded to this challenge by ordering her sister Silvia to set fire to the rebuilt Nottingham Castle. Silvia's refusal to do so caused a breakdown of relations between the sisters.

a very high risk of death. Her willingness to sacrifice her life for the cause had a powerful impact across the country on people who had not previously taken the suffrage issue seriously. There had been many, including the future Labour Prime Minister, Ramsay Macdonald, who had dismissed the Suffragettes as frivolous, but who changed their minds after Davidson's death. The impact of the incident was dramatically increased because the whole incident was captured on the new medium of cinema film, and broadcast on cinema newsreels across the country. Vast, largely silent, crowds lined the London streets for Davidson's funeral procession.

Suffragette tactics were still involved in a pattern of escalating violence in 1914, including the bombing of a railway station and the slashing of the Velazquez painting known as the *Rokeby Venus* in the National Gallery[35], when the outbreak of World War 1 brought the movement to a sudden end. Mrs Pankhurst realised that it would be disastrous to continue campaigning during the war, while men were dying on active service, and suspended the WSPU's campaign. She then astutely combined strong patriotic support for the war with a campaign for women to be allowed to help the war effort by taking up traditional male occupations, so as to release men for the fighting. The success of this campaign, combined with the resignation of Asquith as Prime Minister and his replacement by the much more sympathetic Lloyd George in 1916, led to the belated decision in 1917 to grant the vote to all women aged over 30. This change was combined with abolition of the £10 property qualification for voting, so that the one third of men who had until then been excluded from voting also gained the vote. Women were able to cast their vote for the first time in the post war election of 1918. Those who did so included the octogenarian Emily Davies, who had handed in the first women's suffrage petition with Elizabeth Garrett Anderson in 1866.

There has been much debate as to whether the WSPU militant tactics helped or hindered the Suffrage cause. There is no doubt that the WSPU's initial focus on demonstrations, which the NUWSS had previously avoided, was successful in raising the profile of the women's suffrage issue and recruiting many new supporters. In 1903, when the WSPU was founded, few would have thought that it would ever be possible to hold a demonstration on the vast scale of 21 June 1908. Had a person other than Asquith been Prime Minister at that point it seems reasonable to speculate that there would have been some form of women's suffrage granted in response. However, although there were no opinion polls

---

[35] Both carried out by Mary Richardson, who eventually abandoned her commitment to votes, and became the organiser of the Women's Section of Oswald Mosley's British Union of Fascists.

at the time, common-sense suggests that the later WSPU tactics of breaking windows, burning letter boxes, horsewhipping politicians, and planting bombs, were counter-productive, as shown by the crowd hostility which developed.

This debate about effectiveness of tactics obscures the fact that an upsurge in violence was inevitable after the unprecedented huge peaceful demonstration of 21 July, 1908 failed to produce any results. It seems likely that a militant movement would have emerged alongside the constitutional Suffrage movement in any event, just as smaller violent movements had accompanied the peaceful campaigns for Parliamentary reform in the 1830s (the riots in Nottingham, Bristol and elsewhere), the 1840s (linked to the "Newport rising" in 1839) and the 1860s. However once Asquith's intransigent opposition meant that the road of moderation and dialogue was obviously closed, the attractions of militancy were greatly increased. This resulted in violence by women on a much larger scale than would otherwise have been the case. As a letter to *The Times* pointed out in November 1911, *"nothing that has yet been reported in the press can give any idea of the impulse of blind rage which the announcement of* [Asquith's] *Manhood Suffrage Bill has given to the suffrage movement"*.

This is an important illustration of a general feature of demonstrations, which is that they represent an outpouring of strong popular emotion through a peaceful outlet. If that outlet is effectively blocked, by refusal of all the demonstrators' demands, however reasonable, it is very likely that the frustrated emotions will be channelled instead into more destructive channels, involving violence and crime, as happened with the Women's Suffrage issue between 1908 and 1914. Wise authorities will not repeat Asquith's mistake of believing that a powerful, popular demonstration movement can simply be ignored, in the hope that the demonstrators will eventually just get tired and go away. The usual response to that kind of deliberate unresponsiveness will not be that the issue goes away, but that it goes violent. Perhaps the only surprising thing about the Women's Suffrage militancy is that, apart from Emily Davidson, it seems to have killed no-one – despite the bombs, and despite Mary Leigh's actions in Dublin in July 1912.

An interesting comparison with the campaigns of the Suffragettes is provided by the campaigns of American Women's Suffragists at the same period. These are best considered in the context of the new demonstration techniques which developed in the USA at the end of the nineteenth century and the start of the twentieth.

CHAPTER 10

MARCHING ON WASHINGTON

This chapter describes two linked features of the development of street demonstrations as we know them today. The first is how the capital of the United States, which (unlike London), was not a place for demonstrations in the nineteenth century, became a popular and traditional demonstration venue. The second is how the tradition of long-distance marches on the capital city developed, as an effective form of demonstration, now used in many countries, as a result of successive "marches on Washington", by different American demonstrating campaigns. This tradition began at just about the same time as the US Supreme Court ruling in <u>Commonwealth of Massachusetts v Davis</u>, which held that there was no right to hold a public meeting anywhere in the United States (described in Chapter 7 above).

The "marching on Washington" tradition began with the march to Washington by "Coxey's Army" of the unemployed in 1894. It was enormously developed, and made mainstream, by the American Suffragists from 1913 to 1919. It was used on a large scale by the Bonus Marchers in the 1930s, and from then on was an established form of protest. Then in the 1940s the intention to hold a march was used by African-Americans simply as an effective threat of adverse publicity, without a march actually taking place. The restrictive Supreme Court decision in <u>Commonwealth of Massachusetts v Davis</u> was eventually reversed, after the right to demonstrate had become more widely accepted.

The idea of a peaceful protest march on the capital city to draw attention to grievances is in many ways such an obvious one that it is hard to say who first thought of it. The first recorded attempt at organising such a march as a deliberately peaceful event seems to have been the unsuccessful March of the Blanketeers in England in 1817, which was forcibly broken up as it left Manchester for London[36]. Long distance marches on London do not seem to have been used by other nineteenth-century demonstrators in Britain, so that it was in the United States that this form of demonstration first became important.

The great advantage of a long-distance march on the capital, from the point of view of a campaign organiser, is the massive publicity which it is likely to generate. Unlike a one- day event in a particular location, the publicity can be sustained over many days, or even weeks, as the marchers progress towards the capital. The climate of raised expectations so generated may also increase the chance of a conciliatory gesture by the authorities when the marchers reach the capital.

However the first march on Washington was something of a flash in the pan. It was organised by Jacob Coxey and Carl Browne in May 1894. The march by "Coxey's Army", who were mostly unemployed people desperate for jobs, was intended to promote a public works job-creation programme. Coxey and Browne were both rather unattractive self-publicists, and their unsuccessful campaign left their followers, many of whom genuinely expected something to be done for the unemployed as a result, largely disillusioned. However the march broke the mould by taking place at all, and by ending essentially peacefully. It thus showed that a march on Washington did not need to be an act of armed rebellion, or treason against the United States, as ex-presidential candidate Samuel Tilden had believed, when he publicly rebuked his supporter, Henry Watterson, for proposing a march on Washington after the 1877 election[37].

Coxey "marched" to Washington from his home town of Massilon, Ohio, in a horse-drawn carriage, with his wife and new-born son, but accompanied by some 500 marchers on foot. The march got a hostile reception from the press, being referred to as "the Army of Tramps". In response, the marchers made strenuous efforts to be disciplined and appear respectable. The march itself was lawful, although many "marchers" travelled on trains from the western United States – where depression was hitting hardest – without paying, while marchers from Montana hijacked an entire train, leading to the most dramatic rail chase in American history. A train carrying the sheriff chased the hijacked "wild train" hundreds of miles along the Northern Pacific Railroad from Butte through Billings to Forsyth, where it was finally stopped.

---

36 See Chapter 4.
37 Chapter 7 .

Coxey shared William F Davis's view that the constitution guaranteed his right to hold an outdoor public meeting. He believed that it entitled him to hold one outside Congress in Washington, despite an 1882 law prohibiting the use of the Capitol Grounds for political action. However, when he and Browne attempted to address a meeting there, they were arrested, for breaking the Capitol Grounds law, and spent twenty days in jail. His followers camped around Washington for some weeks, but eventually left, after threats of arrest, with their demands unmet. President Grover Cleveland refused to meet the marchers or to give them any assistance or recognition. The first march on Washington thus fizzled out like a damp squib.

It was 19 years before the next march on Washington, which was completely different in style, aims, and methods. The organiser was an American campaigner for Women's Suffrage, Alice Paul, who had worked in England for Mrs Pankhurst's WSPU, served a jail term in England as a Suffragette, and been force-fed there as a hunger-striker in 1909. Alice Paul has not been commemorated in the same way as the nineteenth-century founder of the women's movement in the United States, Susan B Anthony, who appears on American stamps and banknotes. However Paul played a critical part in obtaining the vote for American women, due to her combination of single-mindedness and of clever calculation to obtain maximum publicity for her cause. Part of her campaign involved inventive new forms of demonstration.

Paul was appointed in 1913 as the Congressional representative of the National American Women's Suffrage Association (NAWSA) and rapidly developed this position into her own organisation, the Congressional Union. In order to make a powerful impact for women's suffrage, Paul decided to organise a giant march for women suffragists in Washington, as part of the parades and processions for the inauguration of the new President, Woodrow Wilson, on 4 March, 1913. The plan was to place women's suffrage squarely on the agenda of the new presidency, by focussing attention on the issue during the presidential inauguration. This approach meant that the march was not necessarily antagonistic to the authorities or the incoming Wilson administration. On the contrary, part of the plan for the march involved conciliating the authorities as much as possible, and persuading them that the march was a legitimate and respectable part of the inauguration celebrations, provided this could be done without destroying the march's effectiveness. Paul therefore made maximum use of her contacts within the administration to ensure that the march was permitted to take place.

Paul's technique was to maximise the positive impact of the march, and to overcome reservations about women taking part in street marches, by conveying an image of respectability, and at the same time to convince waverers that granting women the vote would not somehow make them less feminine. This was similar thinking to that of the English Suffragettes in their earlier, pre-1909, phase. For these reasons, the theme of the march was beauty and dignity, and it was tightly organised, like a military parade. Alice Paul engaged a professional pageant organiser to design and prepare floats for the march, and instructed the marchers to dress so as to present an array of colours. Businesswomen and librarians were to march together and all dress in blue. Artists and musicians were to march together and all dress in pink. The march eventually included 26 floats, six golden chariots, ten bands, 45 captains, 200 marshals, six mounted heralds and six mounted brigades. The march was led by a deliberately chosen beautiful woman, Inez Milholland, dressed in white, riding on a white horse, wearing a blue cloak with a gold Maltese cross, designed to convey an impression of Joan of Arc. The slogan on the demonstration banners was *We demand an amendment to the constitution of the United States enfranchising the women of the country*. Sadly, Alice Paul was a racist, and attempted to limit numbers of black women taking part in the march, and to minimize their presence, on the ground that they would make the march appear less respectable.

The police chief of Washington DC initially announced his intention to ban the march, relying on a law which required permission for parades along Pennsylvania Avenue. However, at the request of outgoing President William Howard Taft, the police chief backed down and allowed the march to proceed.

The march on the day was initially in danger of being overwhelmed by the huge crowds lining Pennsylvania Avenue, consisting mainly of tourists in Washington for the inauguration, who had heard that there was a march to see. Some of the crowd were aggressively hostile men. Sufficient police had not been provided to keep the march route open, and the march was unable to proceed until Alice Paul telephoned an aide to President Taft, who called out members of the US Cavalry to clear a route. This the cavalry succeeded in doing, so that the march was then able to proceed, albeit very slowly, and managed to reach its destination.

However Alice Paul knowingly distorted her account of what had occurred by reporting that the march had been prevented from proceeding, and that women had been insulted and manhandled by passers-by, because of the deliberate failure of the police to assist them. The fact that the US Cavalry had then assisted effectively, and that the march had been able to reach its destination, was glossed over. Accounts of the police standing by while defenceless women were attacked by hostile men made excellent copy for the newspapers, and generated much additional publicity for the Suffrage cause.

At the date of the demonstration, nine US states, including California, had already granted the vote to women. The cause was therefore one which was making progress, and the Suffragists' march and resulting publicity added momentum. Three months after the march, the important state of Illinois, including the city of Chicago, became the first state east of the Mississippi river to pass a law extending the franchise to women.

The march was followed, on 25 July, 1913, by delivery to Congress of a petition for Women's Suffrage, signed by 250,000 people. However, towards the end of the year, Alice Paul was expelled by the National American Women's Suffrage Association, because her approach was considered too radical.

Alice Paul was often compared with the Pankhursts, and there are obvious similarities in the break between the NAWSA and her own organisation, the Congressional Union for Women Suffrage, and the break between the NAWSS and the WSPU in the UK. However there were important differences. Alice Paul was a strict Quaker, deeply committed to non-violence. Unlike major figures in the development of peaceful demonstrations in the British Isles, such as Hunt or Attwood, Paul was perfectly willing to break the law, if it would advance the Women's Suffrage cause. However, unlike the Pankhursts, she was not willing to commit or encourage violence. She would never have condoned the horsewhipping of a politician or the planting of a bomb. She also faced, in President Woodrow Wilson, an adversary who, unlike Asquith, was not actually opposed to women's suffrage, but would not take positive steps to bring it about unless he could do so without upsetting the powerful Southern conservative Democrats in his party. Alice Paul very nearly succeeded in obtaining women's suffrage by peaceful and legal means in 1913 and 1914, and it was only when these means narrowly failed that she deliberately turned to increasingly controversial actions, as a way of gaining continuing publicity and keeping the suffrage issue in the public eye. However those actions remained non-violent. As such they could be regarded as an early example of the technique of passive resistance, which is considered further in the next chapter.

On 2 May, 1914, the Congressional Union orchestrated demonstrations in cities across the USA, including one attended by 5,000 women in Chicago. On 9 May, 1914, it held a further demonstration in Washington. This was smaller than the great demonstration of the previous year, and on this occasion was well-policed without controversy. The fact that it did not generate controversy showed that the previous year's demonstration had really broken the mould, and made demonstrations in Washington something which the authorities and the public accepted as normal. At the same time, the lack of controversy had the practical disadvantage that it meant less publicity for the cause, making the demonstration a less effective campaigning weapon.

Shortly afterwards, Congress voted on a women's suffrage Amendment to the US constitution. This failed by just one vote to obtain the required two-thirds majority. Had there been one more vote, the majority of American women (outside the states which already permitted voting) would have obtained the vote six years earlier than they did, and Alice Paul would be remembered simply as an effective organiser of large, lawful demonstrations.

Instead, Alice Paul moved on from peaceful marches, and embarked on a series of new publicity-raising ventures, determined to ensure that the issue of women's suffrage remained continuously in the public eye. First, there was a Women's Suffrage Drive Across America, with the women motorists who had driven from the West Coast met by a parade as they reached Washington. Then Alice Paul organised a highly controversial boycott of Democratic Party candidates in the mid-term elections of 1914, designed to punish President Wilson for his inaction on Women's Suffrage. This was an abandonment of the previous bipartisan approach which had involved both Republicans and Democrats in campaigning for Women's Suffrage, and naturally angered the many Democrat Suffragists. The campaign was alleged to have resulted in the failure of some Democrat candidates in Western states. Two further states granted women the vote in 1914, Montana and Nevada, but this was modest progress and not necessarily a result of the national campaigns. When a second electoral boycott of the Democratic Party brought no clear result in 1916, and President Wilson announced that he would not receive any further Women's Suffrage deputations, Alice Paul decided to move on to a new technique. This was use of continuous silent demonstrations, by small groups of women, in all weathers, outside the White House, who were given the name "Silent Sentinels". Wilson invited the first group to come in for tea and biscuits but the offer was refused.

The start of the campaign by the Silent Sentinels coincided with the growth of the threat of war between the United States and Germany. Some members of the public felt that distracting the President with Women's Suffrage when war threatened was irresponsible, and great controversy ensued at the outbreak of war in April 1917, when Alice Paul, unlike Emmeline Pankhurst in the UK, did not call off her campaign. That decision cost her organisation some 10,000 members, but the "Silent Sentinel" demonstrations continued month by month. As Woodrow Wilson presented the war as a war for democracy, the Sentinels took to demonstrating holding banners with quotations from Wilson's speeches about democracy. This reached a climax just after the Russian Revolution of February 1917, when the Sentinels held up a banner outside the White House for the press to see, addressed to the new post-Revolutionary Russian leader, Alexei Kerensky, reading: *"We, the women of America tell you that America is not a democracy. 20 million American women are denied the right to vote. President Wilson is the chief opponent of their national enfranchisement. Help us make this nation really free. Tell our government it must liberate its people before it can claim Free Russia as an ally."*

The treatment of the Sentinels deteriorated dramatically in response to this banner, which was seen as damaging the United States internationally while it was fighting a war. A government order prohibited picketing outside the White House, and numerous Sentinels were arrested. There were further arrests when mass pickets were organised by the Suffragists on Independence Day and Bastille Day, and many of those arrested were sentenced to 60 days' imprisonment in the workhouse. Alice Paul, with her talent for publicity, ensured that graphic accounts of the worst aspects of the workhouse prison were soon publicised worldwide. Embarrassed by the publicity, Wilson issued presidential pardons to most of the imprisoned demonstrators. After the Silent Sentinels resumed operations on 23 July, 1917, there were further arrests, and some of those arrested were sentenced to much longer periods of imprisonment as repeat offenders, usually six months. Their response, like the English Suffragettes, was hunger strikes, to which the US Government, like the British Government, responded by forced feeding. A well-publicised brutal beating of Suffrage prisoners by the guards at the workhouse, in response to a demand that they be granted political prisoner status, resulted in a sudden release of most of the Suffragist prisoners in November 1917. This coincided with the granting of the vote to women in New York following a state-wide vote by New York's male electorate. Shortly afterwards, on 9 December, 1917, the House of Representatives announced that it would set a date for a vote on the Women's Suffrage Amendment. This passed the House in January 1918 but in June was filibustered out in the Senate.

In response to this further disappointment, Alice Paul, who had already organised a Sentinel picket outside the White House by women workers from the war munitions factories, chose a new technique of regular demonstrations at the statue of Lafayette, in Lafayette Square, Washington. The location was chosen because Lafayette, the French general who had given critical help to George Washington in the American War of Independence, was a symbol both of American democracy and of idealistic sacrifice, and particularly relevant while Americans were fighting in France.

At this point Woodrow Wilson spoke out in support of the Women's Suffrage amendment before Congress, but on 30 September, 1918 the amendment failed by two votes to obtain the required two thirds majority in the Senate. The demonstrators at Lafayette Square then began publicly burning the speeches of anti-Suffrage senators. In December Paul resumed her campaign against Wilson, and announced plans to keep a perpetual flame burning in Lafayette Square, fuelled only by Wilson's speeches about democracy, until the Women's Suffrage Amendment was carried. This was followed by a decision to burn Wilson's effigy in Lafayette Square on 9 February, 1919. Twenty Suffragists were given short sentences of imprisonment for fire setting. On 24 February, 1919, Wilson was due to speak at the New York Opera House, and Suffrage demonstrators burned his speeches outside the building while he was speaking inside. The campaign finally came to an end when the Senate passed the Women's Suffrage Amendment with the required two thirds majority on 21 May, 1919. The amendment became law when ratified by 36 states on 18 August, 1920.

The US Women's Suffrage campaign thus achieved success two years after the British campaign, which had been called off during Britain's war with Germany. However this was probably due to the laborious and haphazard process of constitutional amendment in the USA, as compared with the relatively simple procedure of a Parliamentary Bill in the UK. Probably both Emmeline Pankhurst's decision to call off her campaign during the war, and Alice Paul's decision to continue hers, were correct, in terms of the best policy to advance their cause in the prevailing national conditions. If Alice Paul had stopped, it is hard to see how Women's Suffrage could have remained on the crowded American political agenda, near enough to the forefront to be acted on. Probably her ruthless single-mindedness brought about Women's Suffrage some years sooner than would otherwise have been the case.

Almost incidentally, as part of her campaign, Paul also permanently changed national attitudes to marches to or through Washington. From 1913 onward, following the 1913 Women's Suffrage March, a variety of different groups held demonstration marches there. A few months after that first Suffrage March, temperance campaigners marched through the city, and received good newspaper coverage for the event. In 1922 there was a small silent march by African Americans protesting against lynchings in the American South, a similar event to a larger march held in New York in 1917. In 1925 and 1926 the powerful racist secret society, the Ku Klux Klan, was freely allowed to parade through Washington, along Pennsylvania Avenue, subject only to the police stipulation that while the Klansmen could wear their white uniform gowns, they should not wear their pointed, mask-like hoods. Some 25,000 Klan members took part in each of those marches, which seem to have passed off without incident.

The first major controversy relating to marches on Washington, after that surrounding the Womens' Suffrage marches, arose not with the Klan, but in connection with the unemployed or destitute ex-soldiers who took part in the "Bonus March" of 1932

Much had changed in the USA and the world between the successful end of the Women's Suffrage campaign in 1920 and the 1932 Bonus March, in ways that directly affected demonstrations.

Firstly, fear of Communism had become a permanent feature of American political life. The Bolshevik commitment to world revolution, the significant number of supporters the Russian revolution gained in the USA, the revulsion at the murder of Tsar Nicholas II and his family, and the explicit Communist contempt for American democratic institutions, combined to bring about an intense hatred and fear of Communism on the part of much of the American political and business establishment. In the early 1920s a campaign of massive arrests against suspected Communist sympathisers was carried out by the new director of the Federal Bureau of Investigation (FBI), J. Edgar Hoover, involving much oppressive and illegal police action, such as widespread use of agents provocateurs. Communism was not regarded as a serious threat in the later 1920s, but with the economic catastrophe of the Great Depression, many of those in positions of responsibility, including both President Herbert Hoover and the US Chief of General Staff, General Douglas MacArthur[38], were convinced that there was a real threat of a Communist-inspired revolution. This threat seemed particularly real, since in 1929 the Communist International, the Comintern, had issued a call for Communists in the Western democracies to attempt to seize power by means of street demonstrations. The widespread resulting fear of Communist demonstrators fomenting revolution powerfully affected the attitude of the authorities to the Bonus Marchers, although the overwhelming majority of the Marchers had no connection at all with Communism and were as opposed to it as the government was.

Secondly, the rise of Fascism in Europe, with Mussolini's march on Rome in 1922, and the advances of the Nazis in Germany, also alarmed American democrats. Fascism probably had a wider appeal in the United States than Communism, and represented an equal threat to democracy. Fear of Fascist-style

---

[38] The same Douglas MacArthur who later commanded US forces in the Pacific in World War Two.

pressure from the streets was therefore also a factor that led some politicians to oppose the Bonus marchers on principle.

A third change which happened in the 1920s was the invention of tear gas and its introduction as a police method of crowd control. "Tear gas" is a generic name used for various tear-inducing gases. The first recorded use of such a gas by police appears to have been in 1913 in Paris, when police used gas to capture a criminal who had barricaded himself in. Tear gas was then used by the French Army on a small scale in the opening stages of World War One, before the development by the Germans of fatal poison gas for warfare. The idea of use of tear gas for crowd control seems to have come from the United States Chemical Warfare Service, which developed tear gas grenades for use in riot control in 1919. Lieutenant Amos S Fries of the Chemical Warfare Service proposed its use for this purpose in American colonies, the Philippines and the Panama Canal Zone, but also stated that *"the gas will be equally effective in smoking out the desperado, who occasionally in our own country runs amuck and then barricades himself with firearms and ammunition in some house or barn and for days bids defiance to the world."*

Use of tear gas for riot control was initially banned by the US War Department, which meant that such grenades could not be available so long as the US Army was the only source of supply. However it was of great interest to the police after a demonstration trial in Philadelphia in July 1921. That trial showed that a contingent of the strongest policemen were unable, despite three charges, to capture six men armed with a supply of 150 tear gas grenades to throw at their attackers, who were driven back choking each time. An officer who had helped develop the grenades for the U.S. Army then set up his own private company, so that tear gas became available for purchase commercially. It was first used by police at Jackson, Kentucky, on 16 December, 1921, and by the end of 1923 over six hundred U.S. city police forces were equipped with tear gas.

Its availability transformed riot control. It was in some respects beneficial, as rioters could be dispersed with only temporary choking and eye-irritation from the gas, instead of receiving serious injuries from clubs or being shot dead. It therefore probably reduced the number of deaths and serious injuries when a riot was brought under control. At the same time it gave enormous additional power to the police or the army, which was equally capable of being used, or misused, against peaceful demonstrators, by firing gas grenades to force them to disperse. The first occasion when tear gas was used extensively to break up a large peaceful demonstration appears to have been when it was used against the Bonus Marchers in 1932.

Finally, another great change since 1920 was the growth of new forms of mass media. The 1930s were the heyday of radio. For the first time, radio was a source of news and information of at least equal importance to the newspapers. Another important medium, which had appeared before World War One and remained important until television became popular after World War Two, was the film newsreel, shown in cinemas before films. In 1932 between 60 and 75 million movie tickets were sold each week to cinemas which opened their film shows with newsreels, while almost every American listened daily to the radio. This meant that to be truly effective, the organisers of any public campaign, whether or not involving street demonstrations, now had to ensure that their message was reported on newsreels and on radio as well as in the press.

The years 1931 and 1932 were the worst of the Great Depression in the USA, which followed the great stock market crash of 1929. Industrial production fell by 25%. Unemployment rose to 25% of the workforce. In Cleveland, Ohio, the figure was 50% and in Toledo, Ohio, it was 80%. Thirty-four million people lived in families in which there was no regular wage earner. Eleven thousand of the 25,000 banks in the USA failed, taking people's savings with them. One million farm families lost their farms. During these years, for the first time in the history of the United States, more people emigrated than immigrated. Millions of homeless people travelled across the country, searching for subsistence and work, in migrations of the kind immortalised in John Steinbeck's novel *The Grapes of Wrath*. Colonies of shanty town shacks, inhabited by the destitute, grew up around cities, similar to those found today in poor cities of the Third World. They were mockingly named "Hoovervilles" after the luckless President Hoover who presided ineffectually over the economic collapse.

The background to the Bonus March was complex. US soldiers who had fought in World War One had been promised part payment for their war service by an "Adjusted Service Certificate". This was a kind of insurance policy, which, under provisions first enacted in 1924, was to be payable on the veteran's death or in 1945, whichever was sooner. As the Great Depression deepened across America, and many World War One veterans found themselves jobless and destitute, a campaign developed for these war veterans to be paid their Certificates, generally just called "Bonuses", immediately, as a form of poor relief, instead of being forced to wait until 1945. This campaign was opposed by the Republican Hoover administration, which was committed to cutting government expenditure in response to the fall in government revenue caused by the economic slump. It was also opposed by part of the Democrat opposition, on the grounds that unemployed veterans were only a small proportion (13%) of the total number of unemployed, many of whom were every bit as needy as the veterans. For this reason, notable progressive figures in Congress, such as Senator Robert La Follette and Congressman Fiorello Laguardia, were also against payment of the bonus, while some conservative-minded politicians, who felt that veterans should be given priority over others, were inclined to support full early payment. Fear of losing the veteran electoral vote persuaded many Congressmen to support payment of the bonus, irrespective of party. However the pressure to pay the bonus did not come from the official veterans' associations, which had been parties to an agreement with the government in 1924 that the bonuses would not be paid until 1945, but from thousands of ordinary individual veterans who were in need.

The first "Bonus March" on Washington was a parade by 1,000 veterans on 21 January, 1931, bearing a petition, with millions of signatures, asking for the bonuses to be paid immediately in full. The parade and petition took place without incident, but did not persuade Congress to act on the marchers' demand.

In December 1931, and January 1932, there were two hunger marches on Washington involving people who had lost their jobs or their savings as a result of the Depression. The first was organised by the Communists, the second by a Roman Catholic priest, Father Cox. Again, despite the desperate atmosphere of the Depression, both passed off without major incidents. The Communists would have welcomed a harsh crackdown on their demonstration, as it would have provided good propaganda for their cause, but the authorities did not oblige. However while these two marches were trouble- free, the second Bonus March, in mid-1932, turned into a major national crisis.

This second, much larger, march, was in support of a Congressional Bill for early full payment of the bonus, moved by Democrat Congressman Wright Patman of Texas. The idea of the march seems to have come from a group of some 300 men from Portland, Oregon, who decided to march to Washington to give Patman's Bill their support.

Walter Waters, an unemployed former World War One army sergeant from Portland, became the leader of the Portland marchers as they crossed America, after their original leader disappeared with the group's funds. Waters' success in forcing railway officials to let his men travel by train, from East St Louis, Illinois, towards Washington, gained much media publicity, and led to a large number of other contingents of Bonus Marchers setting out from other cities, some of whom arrived in Washington before the Portland contingent. While marchers from the Western states travelled much of the huge distance involved by train, many of those closer to Washington marched the whole way.

After the Portland contingent reached Washington, in June 1932, Waters was chosen as the leader of the majority of the marchers, to whom he gave a quasi-military title, the "Bonus Expeditionary Force". Waters was a strong American patriot and committed supporter of the rule of law. He required all new marchers to swear to abide by the US Constitution, and did not allow Communists in his organisation. Communist Bonus Marchers formed a separate group under their own leaders, Emmanuel Levin and John Pace.

The number of marchers present in Washington eventually numbered over 20,000. On arrival in the city, many of the marchers camped at Camp Anacostia, a tent and shack city they constructed on the south side of the Anacostia river, across a drawbridge from the city centre.

Unlike Coxey's Army or the Women's Suffragists, the Bonus Marchers started with widespread popular legitimacy. They had fought for their country, which entitled them in almost everyone's eyes to some respect. This was reflected in their treatment by President Hoover, who was reluctant for some time to take any action against them. Unlike President Cleveland in 1895, who had refused to give any assistance at all to the men of Coxey's Army, President Hoover discreetly provided substantial federal assistance, through various veterans' agencies, to accommodate and feed the Bonus marchers, and to provide them with medical care[39]. Hoover halted a substantial federal building programme in Washington and permitted the marchers to camp in half-demolished buildings on the sites to be developed. The marchers also received much assistance from the Washington police chief, ex-Brigadier-General Pelham Glassford, who was openly sympathetic to their aims, to the extent of accepting an invitation from the marchers to be the temporary official Treasurer of their organisation, for the purpose of safeguarding and administering the donations which they received.

The marchers capitalised on the public respect for them as war veterans, by a parade along Pennsylvania Avenue on 7 June, 1932. Between 7,000 and 8,000 veterans took part. The men marched in disciplined rows, but in ordinary civilian clothes – a deliberate decision to emphasize that they were ordinary democratic-minded American citizens and not Fascists. Prominent at the front of the procession were 14 decorated war heroes from World War One. Scattered

---

[39] Hoover had made his name running the American Relief Operation in Belgium in World War One, which at one time was feeding over 10 million people. He was therefore more attuned than most people to the needs of large numbers of destitute people and how to meet them. In the 1920s he was seen as a dynamic and effective person, and was wooed by both Republicans and Democrats as a potential president. His later reputation as an ogre stemmed entirely from the events of the Bonus March.

throughout the various companies of veterans were trucks carrying disabled veterans, to remind people how the war was still affecting the lives of those who fought in it.

The Bonus Marchers also emphasised their diversity and inclusiveness, as part of their claim to represent all Americans. Unlike Alice Paul, Waters and his co-organisers were determinedly non-racist, and white and black marchers camped, marched, and campaigned together, a striking contrast with the otherwise racially-segregated conditions of Washington DC. This racial integration was unusual in the United States of the 1930s and may itself have helped to fan opposition to the Marchers, as well as the completely incorrect belief that they were Communist or Communist- controlled. In fact, the great majority of the ex-servicemen were so anti-Communist that, as Walter Waters put it in his memoir, *The B.E.F.*, his chief problem with the Communists was how to prevent his own men from killing them.

The immediate effect of the 7 June parade was to generate additional support for Patman's Bonus Bill, from Republicans as well as Democrats. As the Bill remained under consideration by Congress, the Bonus March leadership decided that the Marchers should remain in Washington and continue to lobby members of Congress.

This lobbying was initially effective. The Bonus Bill was given House time to be debated, and was then passed by the House of Representatives on 15 June. However on 17 June it was defeated in the Senate by 62 votes to 18. This was a bitter disappointment for the Bonus Marchers, and was effectively the end of the legislative process which the Bonus March had been intended to support,

Immediately after the defeat, Walter Waters had to handle a difficult situation with his angry and desperate supporters. When he addressed his supporters his initial references to his disappointment prompted an angry murmur from the audience. Waters then warned them that their opponents would "be justified and excused if you riot", and asked them to prove "the nation's faith" in them by marching back to camp in line. The Marchers then removed their hats and sang the anthem *America,* before marching away.

This display of controlled patriotism reassured those who feared that the Bonus Marchers would react to their disappointment with a riot. However there was confusion and uncertainty as to what should happen next. Logically, as Patman's Bill had failed, the focus of the march no longer existed, and there was no point staying in Washington. However some of the Bonus March leaders wanted to broaden the focus of their campaign from the issue of the Bonuses to the wider issue of poverty, while others wanted to continue campaigning for the Bonus despite the defeat of the Bill. The majority of the marchers, led by Waters, decided to remain in Washington to continue campaigning. Waters went so far as to state that he would remain in Washington if necessary till 1945 when the Bonuses were due to be paid. From then on the "Bonus March" changed from a demonstration related to a particular event, into a protest camp of unlimited duration.

The Bonus March seems to have been the first important modern demonstration involving use of an indefinite protest camp. This form of protest has since become widely used. Examples in Britain include its use by the Greenham Common anti-nuclear demonstrations, by anti-global warming climate camps, and by Brian Haw, who demonstrated against war while camping for an unbroken ten years in Parliament Square outside the U.K Parliament.

Such indefinite camps in public places, unlike demonstrations of limited duration, are not usually regarded by lawyers as being protected by the freedom of assembly and the right to demonstrate, so they still remain controversial today, as they were in 1932. The European Court of Human Rights has specifically held, a case involving a camping protest outside the Norwegian Parliament, that the right of freedom of assembly does not extend to a camp of unlimited duration outside Parliament[40].

There were disturbing signs by July 1932 that power had gone to Waters' head. He first resigned the leadership of the Bonus Marchers, and then permitted himself to be persuaded to resume the leadership, on the express condition, to which the Marchers agreed, that he be given the powers of a dictator. As a former sergeant, Waters was used to being obeyed, and from shortly after arrival in Washington he had organised "military police" to keep the marchers in order, as well as his own bodyguards. However Waters also organised kangaroo courts, one of which "sentenced" a Communist infiltrator to one of the Marchers' camps to be given 15 lashes. He tried to turn the marchers into a semi-military organisation, which he named the "Khaki Shirts", and the newsletter produced by the marchers contained an article in July 1932, noting that "Hilter" (sic) in Germany, and Mussolini in Italy, had started off as unemployed outsiders and were now powerful leaders in their countries.

It is not surprising in these circumstances that the U.S. authorities eventually took action to remove the Bonus Marchers from Washington. In some ways, ironically, it was a sign of Hoover's strong tolerance for demonstrations, and his sympathy for veterans and for the unemployed, that action was not taken

---

[40] "…a demonstration by setting up a tent for several days in an area open to public traffic must necessarily cause disorder" (X v Norway (1984) 6 EHRR 357).

earlier. The manner in which action was taken, however, was to destroy Hoover's reputation forever.

Further demonstrations relating to the general issue of poverty were held on 4 July, although by then Congress was in recess and Congressmen no longer in Washington. Some marchers left Washington, but for a while the numbers of marchers in the city were kept at the same level because of a stream of late arrivals.

As the days of July passed, the authorities became gradually stricter in enforcing the restrictions on demonstrating in the grounds of the Capitol, which had not been enforced during the early period of the Marchers' presence. For the first time, Walter Waters disobeyed a police order, and was arrested for entering the Capitol Grounds. However he was promptly released, as the police knew that without him the Marchers' discipline would sharply deteriorate. At the same time, the Communists tried to expand their influence among the Marchers. They achieved little success, but their efforts caused further alarm to the authorities.

On 28 July President Hoover finally gave way to pressure from his Secretary of State for War, Patrick Hurley, and from General Douglas MacArthur, and agreed that the army should be used to clear the camps of the Bonus Marchers from the centre of Washington. Hoover asked MacArthur not to evict them from their main camp across the Anacostia river at Camp Anacostia, but MacArthur ignored this order, and cleared the camp that night, at one hour's notice.

The catalyst for Hoover's order to clear the camps using the army was the occurrence of a small riot when police tried to evict Bonus Marchers from a city centre camp, at the remains of the Old Armoury Building. A further riot then developed, in which a policeman shot dead two veterans in circumstances which remain hotly disputed. Some veterans threw bricks from the half-demolished building at the police. One policeman, Shinault, who later claimed that he was in fear of his life, drew his revolver and shot dead two Bonus Marchers, William Huska, a holder of the Distinguished Service Cross, and Eric Carlson. The report of the shooting persuaded Hoover that he had to act.

The manner in which MacArthur cleared the camps caused national outrage. He used tear gas grenades, infantry with fixed bayonets, cavalry with drawn sabres, who looked horribly sinister sitting on their horses in gas masks, and a line of tanks. His troops drew no distinction between Bonus Marchers, spectators or reporters, all of whom were attacked. The people evicted from the camps in this operation included several hundred women and children. Many families were separated in the melee and unable to reunite for days. The list of those seriously enough injured to require treatment in hospital was 53 according to the *New York Herald Tribune*, 55 according to *Time*, and 60 according to *The Washington Post*.

Hoover and MacArthur then briefed the press to the effect that the Marchers had been driven out because they were controlled by Communists who intended to stage a violent revolution. It was announced that a full FBI investigation into this Communist plot was under way. These statements received wide publicity, and were initially believed, so that the brutal treatment of the Marchers did not at first attract widespread sympathy. At that point it seemed that the Bonus March had ended in humiliating failure. However it soon became clear that there had been no Communist plot, and that the assertion that there had been one was bogus, and a slander of the jobless veterans. Police Chief Pelham Glassford gravely damaged the administration's credibility, when he delivered a careful point by point refutation of assertions in the first report on the operation, prepared for Hoover by his attorney-general, William Mitchell, showing that most of Mitchell's allegations against the Marchers were false. At this point a public backlash against the clearance operation set in. This became so strong that it played a decisive role in President Hoover's defeat by Franklin Roosevelt in the autumn 1932 Presidential Election.

It was believed for generations that Hoover had deliberately deceived the Marchers, in order to have a chance to use strong arm methods on them. However research in the 1970s, when Hoover's personal papers had become available after his death, showed convincingly that Hoover had himself been lied to, and misled, by MacArthur and by Hurley, and that the brutal way the military operation was carried out was attributable to MacArthur[41], and not to Hoover.

Roosevelt's election victory was an indirect, but very substantial, delayed triumph for the Bonus Marchers. Roosevelt did not favour immediate payment of the Bonuses, but, in sharp contrast to Hoover, he was committed to reflationary economic policies intended to create jobs. His "New Deal", public works-based, economic policies represented a reversal of Hoover's expenditure-cutting austerity policies, which had been behind Hoover's opposition to the payment of the Bonuses. Roosevelt's economic policies brought about a big reduction in unemployment in 1933 and 1934, though it still remained high. Roosevelt also specifically made an executive order giving priority for jobs in his newly set up Civilian Conservation Corps to Bonus Marchers.

---

[41]   MacArthur oversaw the operation mounted on a white horse, assisted by Colonel George S Patton, later famous as "Blood and Guts" General Patton of World War Two. Both MacArthur and Patton had fought in the American campaign in the Argonne in World War One, like many of the men they drove out of Washington. Patton, wounded, had been carried to safety under fire by Joe Angelo, who walked from New Jersey to Washington as a Bonus Marcher and was one of those evicted on 28 July.

Roosevelt also made a point of showing tolerance and even support towards protest demonstrations in Washington. When 3,000 Bonus Marchers again arrived in Washington to petition the administration to pay the Bonus in January 1933, Roosevelt, while still opposing their demand, nevertheless assisted the marchers with camping facilities (though deliberately located outside the city so as to make it harder for them to organise), and even with transport to the White House to deliver their petition. He saw a delegation, where he explained his opposition to immediate payment of the Bonus, while his wife Eleanor paid a visit to their camp, which was filmed by the newsreels. Partly as a result of the sympathetic attitude of the Roosevelt administration, from the 1930s onward demonstrations in Washington became commonplace on innumerable different issues.

In 1936 Congress passed a Bill for payment of the Bonus. Roosevelt vetoed it, but his veto was overruled by Congress. As a result the Bill became law, and one billion one hundred million dollars worth of Bonus payments had been made to veterans by the Roosevelt administration by 31 July, 1936. These huge payments, and the apparent righting of the harsh treatment of the veterans on 28 July, 1932, probably contributed to Roosevelt's re-election in the autumn of 1936.

The tradition of demonstrating in the United States by protest marches and meetings was thus well-established by 1939, when the US Supreme Court at last reversed its previous attitude to the right to hold a public meeting, as set out in Commonwealth of Massachusetts v Davies in 1894. Its 1939 decision involved a city law from Jersey City, New Jersey, just across the Hudson river from New York, which prohibited all public meetings in the city without a permit.

From 1917 to 1947, Jersey City was under the control of Mayor Frank Hague and his political machine. Hague was an unscrupulous, authoritarian, bullying big city boss, typical of the early twentieth century United States, who eventually overreached himself. Hague boasted that industry was safe in his city because he would not allow "Un-American" labour groups like the Committee for Industrial Organisation (CIO) to meet, picket, or pass out literature in the city. Hague believed that the law laid down in Commonwealth of Massachusetts v Davis allowed him to completely prevent any meetings in his city by organisations he disapproved of. He was contemptuous of the idea that he might be infringing constitutional rights. *"We hear about constitutional rights, free speech and a free press. Every time I hear those words I say to myself, "That man is a Red, that man is a Communist". You never hear a real American talk in that manner."*

In November 1937, the CIO decided to do battle with Hague, by organising a membership drive in Jersey City. Hague's response was to have police waiting at CIO headquarters when the organisers arrived, who forcibly put them on lorries, without any legal justification, and drove them out of the city. Shortly after this episode, the American Civil Liberties Union tried to obtain a permit from the director of public safety of Jersey City to hold an open-air meeting there on the subject of civil liberties. The permit was refused, and the refusal was then challenged in the courts, leading eventually to the Supreme Court case of Hague v CIO.

The evidence before the Supreme Court was of massive bias in the issue of permits in Jersey City. It led the Supreme Court to rule that the streets and parks, far from being held in the same way as private property, as Oliver Wendell Holmes had ruled in <u>Commonwealth of Massachusetts v Davies,</u> were in fact held by the city council on trust for the public, for the purpose of assembly. Their use could therefore be regulated in the public interest, but it could not be completely denied.

This new landmark case provided a precedent for use by anyone who suspected that the issue of permits for processions or meetings by a city council was being operated unfairly, whether on grounds of race or otherwise, and it provided a degree of legal underpinning to the later protest marches and meetings of the Civil Rights era of the 1950s and 1960s. The facts which gave rise to it also give a flavour of the kinds of official attitudes and behaviour which civil rights protesters had to face, even without the aggravating issue of race.

Two years later, in 1941, a successful attempt was made to use the idea of the march on Washington to redress specifically African-American issues. The idea came from a trade unionist, Philip Randolph of the Brotherhood of Sleeping Car Porters, who was also founder of the National Negro Congress. He realised that the outbreak of World War Two, as well as generating new grievances for black workers, offered new opportunities for achieving progress in ending racial discrimination. As the United States rearmed, defence industries expanded and hired new labour. However black Americans were the last to benefit from this economic revival, being systematically excluded from many areas of the segregated armed forces and from work in defence industries. Some limited steps were taken to change the situation, with a training programme for black pilots funded by Congress in 1939, and the Selected Service Act in 1940 prohibiting discrimination against drafted men. Some states passed laws prohibiting discrimination by military contractors, but these were not always enforced. These measures made little difference in practice to the pervasive climate of discrimination.

President Franklin Roosevelt was theoretically committed to opposing discrimination, but in practice highly reluctant to do anything which would antagonise a substantial part of the white electorate. For this reason a meeting which he held with Randolph and with Walter White of the National Association for the Advancement of Coloured People in September 1940, on the issue of discrimination, was cordial but led to no changes.

Against this background, on 16 January, 1941, Philip Randolph issued a press release proposing that:-

> *"TEN THOUSAND (10,000) Negroes march on Washington DC, the capital of the nation, with the slogan WE LOYAL AMERICAN CITIZENS DEMAND THE RIGHT TO WORK AND FIGHT FOR OUR COUNTRY."*

Randolph's idea was that a huge demonstration would shake up white America and official Washington. He was sure that *"mass demonstrations against Jim Crow* [segregation laws] *are worth a million editorial orations."* The timing of the march was to be critical to its success. The United States under Roosevelt's leadership was moving towards war with Nazi Germany. President Roosevelt was particularly anxious that the USA should present an image, internationally, of a free and fair society, in contrast with Nazi totalitarianism, brutality and racial hatred. Against this background, the possibility that Washington might see a solemn, dignified march by thousands of black Americans, protesting against discrimination and segregation, was potentially disastrous for Roosevelt's credibility, and that of the USA internationally. This gave Randolph leverage to use the threat of a march to force Roosevelt to take action against discrimination. Roosevelt understood the threat, and became increasingly concerned to stop the march happening, as soon as it became clear in late spring 1941 that it was likely to be big.

Both Randolph and Roosevelt realised that it would be impossible to stop such a march by force, without providing an even worse propaganda victory for the administration's enemies than the march itself, particularly in view of Roosevelt's personal toleration for other demonstrations in Washington up to that point.

The march was scheduled for 1 July, 1941. By May it was clear that Randolph's call for 10,000 participants was going to be vastly exceeded. Organising committees for the march were at work in at least 19 cities. Organisation was taking place through Randolph's members, the sleeping car porters, carrying messages on the Pullman trains; through the support of a 26,000-member black fraternal organisation, the Improved Benevolent Protective Order of Elks of the World; and through numerous distinguished and influential black Americans, including Mary Macleod Bethune, a black member of Roosevelt's administration.

By May the organisers were expecting 50,000 marchers, and by June the figure had grown to 100,000.

At that point, Roosevelt invited the march leaders to the White House, where they presented him with a list of six positive steps to outlaw discrimination, which were their minimum terms for calling off the march. Further negotiations followed, and on 25 June, 1941, less than a week before the date of the march, Roosevelt signed Executive Order 8802, which met some, but not all, of the six demands put to him. It outlawed discrimination in vocational training programmes and prohibited the award of federal contracts to any contractor who discriminated on grounds of race. It also set up a board to monitor and enforce these provisions, entitled the Commission on Fair Employment Practices. In return, Philip Randolph called off the march.

Randolph was criticised by many activists, who felt he could have got much more from Roosevelt by way of concessions. Randolph himself in due course came round to the same view. It must have been a difficult judgement call at the time, when dealing with a notoriously wily and devious president such as Roosevelt.

Randolph remained convinced of the great effectiveness of marches, and co-founded the March on Washington Movement to continue to use marches to campaign against discrimination. In August 1946, the threat of another great black American march on Washington persuaded President Truman to sign an order outlawing discrimination in the US military, one of the key demands from 1941 which until then had not been met. Again the planned march was called off after the presidential order outlawing discrimination was signed. These highly effective campaigns by Randolph later provided inspiration to the American Civil Rights Movement of the 1950s and 1960, which is described in Chapter 12.

Thus by the mid-twentieth century protest marches and other forms of demonstration in Washington DC, which had been completely unknown half a century earlier, had become a popular and accepted form of political activity, which from 1939 even enjoyed a degree of constitutional protection. With the vast extension of the global influence of the United States as a result of World War Two, this American tradition set an example for demonstrators in many other countries.

Before going on to consider how that American tradition developed in the second half of the twentieth century, it is time to consider the very different new technique which Alice Paul began using in the later part of her Suffrage campaign, passive resistance.

CHAPTER 11

Demonstrations and Civil Disobedience—Gandhi

As we have seen in previous chapters, the development of street demonstrations in the British Isles was closely linked to ideas of the rule of law and exercising a peaceful non-violent right to protest. The linkage goes back to John Wilkes insisting that his supporters convey him to prison after his committal there by the court (described in Chapter 2). The London Corresponding Society was committed to the rule of law, as were Henry Hunt and Thomas Attwood and the Reform campaigners of the 1830s. The Hyde Park railings affair of 1866 happened because of uncertainty as to whether or not the law allowed the banning of the Reform meeting in Hyde Park. It was only after the lawful demonstrations of the Suffragettes in support of their reasonable aims failed to get any response from the government that they began to adopt violent tactics. In the United States adherence to the law as embodied in the constitution was important to many early demonstration organisers, notably Walter Waters of the Bonus Marchers.

However a different tradition also contributed to the development of the modern demonstration. This was the idea of peaceful civil disobedience, involving deliberate breaking of laws deemed to be morally repugnant. It is forever associated with the name of Mahatma Gandhi, but Gandhi did not invent it. The tension between the rule of law approach and the civil disobedience approach remains a difficult issue for many demonstrators today.

In 1845 a young American Harvard graduate, Henry David Thoreau, decided to try to live as simply as possible in a log cabin in the woods near his home town of Concord, Massachusetts, obtaining his food from the land, and living as far as possible without money. He lived in his cabin for two years, and wrote up the experience in a book, *Walden*, in which he mocked excessive attachment to material possessions and extolled the virtues of a simple existence close to nature.

Trying to live without money raised special issues in relation to paying taxes. A person without income can expect not to be troubled by income tax, but Massachusetts in 1845 had other taxes which the law would not allow Thoreau to avoid. In particular it had a poll tax of US$9 per head, payable by every citizen. Thoreau refused on principle to pay it, insisting that the government did nothing for him, that he received nothing in return for the poll tax, and that by imposing the poll tax the government was trying to force him to live in a way which he did not want to. He felt that it was impracticable for him to campaign for the repeal of the poll tax in the Massachusetts legislature, as no one else chose to live like him and he would therefore get little support, while wasting much time. He therefore simply refused to pay and was eventually committed to prison by the Massachusetts authorities. Thoreau stayed in prison only one night before someone unknown paid his poll tax, bringing about his immediate release. He later wrote up this experience and its justification in a separate essay entitled *Civil Disobedience*.

Thoreau's position that the state government did nothing for him and therefore he should not pay its tax is open to obvious challenges. Did the state's maintenance of a machinery of law and order really do nothing for him in his log cabin in the woods, or did the mere fact of its existence help him by deterring casual robbers? And although healthy young Thoreau did not need the state's assistance, was there no possibility that he might need it as an old person or a sick person, and that other old or sick persons were needing it at that moment.

However despite the apparent whimsical nature of Thoreau's refusal to pay, and the rather arrogant and flippant tone of his essay, the points he made were serious.

Poll taxes have always been unpopular and controversial, precisely because they treat everyone alike irrespective of their ability to pay. A harsh poll tax caused the English Peasants Revolt of 1382, and the reintroduction of a poll tax in England in the early 1990s (euphemistically renamed the "community charge") caused widespread riots. Moreover, in most of British colonial Africa poll taxes, deeply resented, were used precisely to drive into the money economy people who would otherwise have continued to live without money in agricultural communities, but who were forced to work in mines or on plantations, or as labourers for the government, so that they would have income to pay the tax.

Thoreau was not alone in being a minority objecting to a law which the majority were totally uninterested in changing. A well-supported cause may sometimes increase its support through the ordinary process of democratic debate enough to bring about a change in the law. However there will often be causes of great importance to minorities, but of no interest to the majority, or actively opposed by it, so that change through the democratic process appears impossibly remote. Sometimes the imposition on the minority may be intolerable, and a means of opposing it has to be found. Thoreau's concept of civil disobedience, not to bring about regime change, but simply to bring about a change in the law which would not happen otherwise, may offer an effective means of redressing a legitimate grievance. This is all the more plausible if the government to be disobeyed is not a democratically-elected government, such as that of Massachusetts, but is unelected and unaccountable.

Thoreau's political views were taken seriously by few people in his lifetime (he died in 1862), but their influence, and in particular that of his essay *Civil Disobedience*, increased in the years after his death. One person who acknowledged his influence was Alice Paul. Another was the Russian novelist Tolstoy. However what caused Thoreau's views ultimately to change the world was that they happened to be read by Mohandas Karamchand Gandhi. Gandhi read Thoreau's *Walden* in 1906, when he was already involved in campaigns on behalf of the Indian community in South Africa, and read *Civil Disobedience* while he was serving a jail sentence in Volksrust Prison, Johannesburg, in 1908.

Indians in South Africa in the early twentieth century faced severe and intensifying racial discrimination from white South Africans and from government. Gandhi's involvement with their cause began almost accidentally when he arrived in South Africa from British India as a young London-trained lawyer. Gandhi was travelling from Durban to Johannesburg in connection with a case, when he was thrown off the train at Pietermaritzburg for refusing to leave a whites only first class railway compartment, and was left to spend the night in the station waiting room. Having been awakened to the grievances of the Indian communities in Natal and the Transvaal by this incident, he became their recognised spokesperson and organiser in resisting government moves against them.

Initially Gandhi's aim was to convince the colonial authorities that the Indian community would be good citizens and loyal subjects of the British Empire. In this spirit he organised an Indian ambulance corps in the Boer War, and another in the Zulu rebellion of 1906, holding the rank of sergeant-major in the latter campaign. However this approach completely failed to mitigate the militant racial hostility of the majority of whites.

In 1906, just after the Zulu rebellion, the Transvaal government announced plans to introduce a Bill requiring all Indians over the age of eight to be fingerprinted and to carry with them at all times, and produce on demand, a certificate of registration. Indians who failed or refused to register would automatically forfeit their right to live in the Transvaal, and could be fined, imprisoned or deported. Any police officer could arrest an Indian who failed to produce his certificate, and the police could enter any Indian house without a warrant and demand to see the certificate. It was to be produced for any dealings with public officials, even to obtain a bicycle licence.

A mass protest meeting about the law was called at the Empire Theatre, Johannesburg, on the afternoon of 11 September, 1906. About 1,000 participants were expected, but over 3,000 attended. The meeting was opened by a rich businessman, Abdul Gani, who announced that he would refuse to register under the new law, and called on others to follow him. He was followed by Gandhi, who had worked out the strategy behind the meeting. Gandhi warned those present to prepare for suffering for their cause. He said:-

> *"We may have to go to jail where we may be insulted. We may have to go hungry and suffer extreme heat or cold. We may be flogged by rude warders. We may be fined heavily and our property may be attached and held up to auction if there are only a few resisters left. Opulent today, we may be reduced to abject poverty tomorrow. We may be deported. Suffering from starvation and similar hardships in jail, some of us may fall ill and die. In short, therefore it is not at all impossible that we may have to endure every hardship that we can imagine, and wisdom lies in pledging ourselves on the understanding that we shall suffer all that and worse".*

After Gandhi finished speaking the whole audience rose and pledged themselves by acclamation to go to jail rather than obey the new laws. That was the start of the first modern civil disobedience campaign. The concept was so new that there was no clear word for what Gandhi and his fellow campaigners were doing. A competition to choose a new name was held in *Indian Opinion*, the newspaper Gandhi published and edited. Gandhi chose the name "Satyagraha", meaning "firmness for truth", or "truth-force". People who practised "satyagraha" were to be known as "satyagrahis". The movement was a reaction to a situation where conventional politics would never have yielded results, as the numerically dominant Europeans were determined to oppress the Indians. It was also quite different from a campaign to change a regime. At the end of the Empire Theatre meeting the audience, having pledged themselves to civil disobedience, gave three cheers for the king-Emperor Edward VII and sang *God Save the king.*

The first plan for a registration law was dropped after a lobbying trip to London by Gandhi, as a result of which Royal Assent was refused to the Transvaal Bill, which would have introduced the compulsory registration proposals.

During that trip Gandhi had a meeting with Emmeline Pankhurst, but was later at pains to make it clear that he did not support Mrs Pankhurst's violent approach to campaigning for Women's Suffrage. He acknowledged that Mrs Pankhurst did not want to kill people, but correctly stated that she did want to thrash some people, which, as he made clear, was not an approach that he could accept, being committed to non-violence. He also met Charlotte Despard of the WFL, whom he found "wonderful", writing that he much admired her policy of "spiritual resistance".

A few months later, on 1 January, 1907, "responsible government", approximately equivalent to internal self-government, was granted to the Transvaal, meaning that its laws were no longer subject to approval from London. The Transvaal government at once enacted the previously vetoed Indian registration law, which took effect from 1 July, 1907. The government announced that Indians who had not registered under the law by 31 July, 1907 would be deported at 48 hours' notice. Despite this threat, only about 500 of the 13,000 Indians living in the Transvaal registered by the due date. Posters appeared all over Johannesburg and Pretoria stating:-

> *"Boycott! Boycott permit office! By going to Gaol we do not resist, but suffer for our common good and self-respect. Loyalty to the king demands loyalty to the king of Kings. Indians be free".* Gandhi
> claimed full responsibility for these posters.

The Transvaal government attempted to control the situation by repeatedly postponing the deadline for registration, in the hope that the heat would go out of the protests. However, after three postponements, by 30 November, 1907, only 511 persons had registered, and the government decided to start enforcing the law.

Gandhi was one of the first to be brought before a court, and on 10 January, 1908 he was sentenced to two months' imprisonment without hard labour, despite his request to the magistrate to be given the maximum sentence of six months' imprisonment with hard labour.

After Gandhi had been in prison for about a month he was taken to a secret meeting with General Smuts, Prime Minister of the Transvaal. Smuts offered him concessions. Registration would be optional. Fingerprinting would not be required of persons who had a conscientious objection to it. The law would be repealed and replaced.

Gandhi initially agreed to Smuts's proposals. He was at once released from prison and attempted to persuade the Indian community to accept them. However the government proposals were vague and unsatisfactory and a substantial segment of the community began to regard Gandhi as having sold out to Smuts. This was not true, but Gandhi had trusted Smuts too much and had been outwitted. When Gandhi himself went "voluntarily" to register, he was attacked by angry Indians, and would have been clubbed to death had friends not managed to intervene. He had scarcely recovered from this attack when, travelling to Durban to address a meeting, he was again the subject of an assassination attempt. Both attempts were by the Pathan community, which had decided that he was a traitor.

As it gradually became clear to Gandhi that Smuts was not going to deliver on his promises, he developed new techniques for restoring momentum to the civil disobedience campaign. Educated Indians were sent into the street to court arrest as unlicensed hawkers, and registration cards taken out under the voluntary procedure were ceremonially burned. On 16 August, 1908, Gandhi organised a ceremonial mass burning of registration certificates attended by 3,000 people. He had previously notified the government that the event would happen. About 1,300 certificates were placed in a cauldron on the speakers' platform, doused in kerosene and set on fire. After a second public burning the total number of certificates burned reached 2,300. However the government stood firm in its insistence on enforcing the registration law.

On 7 October, 1908, Gandhi was again arrested, for not carrying a certificate and for refusing to give fingerprints, and was again sentenced to two months, but this time with hard labour. It was during this much more unpleasant imprisonment that he read Thoreau's *Civil Disobedience*. He was imprisoned a third time, for three months, early in 1909. After his release, he travelled to London to represent the South African Indian community in discussions on the future of South Africa. The occasion was the negotiation between the British Imperial Government and the South African leaders, Smuts and Botha, of the treaty to combine Cape Province, Natal, Transvaal and the Orange Free State into the Union of South Africa. Gandhi and his supporters took part in lengthy and ultimately unsuccessful negotiations with the British government about the position of the Indian community, before returning to South Africa.

At this point Gandhi unexpectedly received very large financial donations from rich Indians in India, who had been impressed by his Satyagraha campaign. The industrialist Ratan Jamshed Tata gave 25,000 rupees, and other large donations came from the Maharajah of Mysore, the Maharaja of Bikaner and the Nizam of Hyderabad. At about the same time he received the donation of a farm, which he named Tolstoy Farm, after the Russian novelist, whom he greatly admired and with whom he was in correspondence. The farm and the financial donations enabled him to maintain the momentum of the Satyagraha campaign. In particular he used the farm as a place of refuge for the destitute wives and children of satyagrahis who had been imprisoned for refusing to register under the registration law.

Despite these advantages, the campaign against registration did not achieve any dramatic breakthrough. In 1912 one of the leading Indian nationalist political leaders, Gopal Krishna Gokhale, toured South Africa with Gandhi to inspire the campaign. Gokhale met Smuts and Botha at Pretoria, and received promises that the condition of the Indians would be improved. However, after Gokhale left, no action was taken by the South African government to implement its promises. Instead, the government seems to have attempted to divert attention from the grievances relating to registration by encouraging the emergence of a much bigger grievance. The Supreme Court of the Transvaal ruled that only marriages celebrated according to Christian rites were recognised as valid in Transvaal. It seems likely that this decision was inspired by the government, which certainly took no steps to respond to the wave of outrage and panic which it generated in the Indian community.

These developments led Gandhi to embark on a new and more dangerous stage of the civil disobedience campaign. He decided to stake everything on bringing the confrontation with the government to a head, by marching groups of Indians across the Natal/Transvaal border in both directions, courting arrest and imprisonment by travelling without certificates, and at risk of violent retaliation from border guards. Some groups left from Tolstoy Farm near Johannesburg and marched south. Others started from another similar farm run by Gandhi, Phoenix Farm near Durban, and marched north.

When the Transvaal marchers reached Newcastle in northern Natal, where the mine workers included many Indians, the Indian mine workers came out on strike and joined the Satyagraha movement. Under Gandhi's personal leadership, a huge gathering of over 2,000 men, women and children, including a large contingent of Newcastle miners, crossed the border into the Transvaal on 6 November, 1913. While Gandhi himself distracted the border guards, by engaging them in conversation about crossing through the approved crossing point, the other satyagrahis simply crossed the border en masse at any point where they happened to reach it. Gandhi then crossed himself in the resulting confusion. Over the next few days, as they marched through the Transvaal, numerous arrests took place. Gandhi himself was arrested three times. After being twice released on bail, the third time he was personally arrested by the Principal Immigration Officer of the Transvaal, and sentenced to three months' imprisonment.

At this point Gandhi's strategy began to pay off. Support in India for what he was doing had become so great that it led both the Governor-General of Bombay, Lord Willingdon, and the Viceroy of India, Lord Hardinge, to express concern. Willingdon said that the situation of the Indians in South Africa had become "an imperial question", and Hardinge said that he and all India felt "deep and burning sympathy" for the sufferings undergone by Indian labourers in South Africa. Hardinge sent his own envoy to South Africa, and Gokhale also sent two English missionaries with a deep knowledge of India, Charles Andrews and William Pearson, to assist Gandhi with his campaign, in particular through Andrews' personal contacts with the former Home Secretary Herbert Gladstone (of the provocative speech about women getting the vote, and the force feeding of the Suffragettes, as described in Chapter 9), who had become Governor-General of South Africa.

Smuts initially reacted aggressively to this interference in South Africa's internal affairs, demanding the recall of Hardinge from his post of Viceroy. The British Government did not wish to recall Hardinge, and attempted to defuse the situation by the time-honoured device of setting up a commission of inquiry. However Gandhi refused to co-operate with the commission. By this time, Gandhi's position was much stronger, as a result of the influential support from India, and Smuts was finally forced to back down. The three pound poll tax levied on Indians was abolished, all monogamous marriages of Indians were recognised in law, domicile certificates were to be regarded as sufficient evidence of the right to enter South Africa, and educated Indians were permitted to enter Cape Province from where they had previously been excluded. These concessions amounted to meeting most of Gandhi's demands, and in response the Satyagraha campaign was called off. For a while at least -not wholly, but in large measure – the world's first mass civil disobedience campaign had succeeded.

With this success resounding around the world, it was only a matter of time before the Nationalist movement in India itself began to apply the techniques Gandhi had developed in South Africa.

Gandhi himself returned to India in 1915, after several months in London during which he organised another Indian ambulance corps, this time to help Britain's effort in World War One. He was naturally approached for support on arrival by people with a wide variety of grievances, but did not immediately involve himself in civil disobedience. He took up the cause of the exploited indigo workers of northern Bihar, and helped them with claims for unpaid wages by meticulous collection of evidence. Ultimately Gandhi's private commission of inquiry was so successful it forced the government of India to set up an official inquiry, which resulted in payment of a large indemnity to the workers who had been ill-treated.

Gandhi's first attempt to use civil disobedience in India was three years later, in 1918, in support of a campaign for reduction of taxes for farmers in the Kaira district in Gujarat who had suffered crop failure. He organised the farmers for a mass campaign of withholding of the land tax. After four months, an unsatisfactory compromise was agreed under which the richer peasants paid the full tax, while the poorer peasants paid nothing. Gandhi considered the campaign to have been a failure.

At the time of the Kaira campaign, Gandhi was still a loyal supporter of the British Empire. Like many Indians of his generation, he believed that if Indians showed themselves worthy of equal treatment with white Europeans in the British Empire, they would in due course be given equal treatment. He also held, until that year, considerable respect for the Empire itself as an institution. His attitude was however fundamentally changed, like that of millions of other Indians, by the chain of events in 1919 which culminated in the massacre at Jalianwalla Bagh in Amritsar.

Some two and half million Indians enlisted for overseas service with the British forces during World War One. In 1918 and 1919, as these men returned from overseas, there were widespread hopes, particularly among India's political classes, that their sacrifice for the Empire would be recognised by some improvement of conditions for Indians in India. Tragically, the British authorities in India failed to recognise the strength and legitimacy of this feeling, and were instead preoccupied, in the light of the Russian Revolution, with the spread of Bolshevik-inspired sedition and subversion. They were also concerned about possible renewal of the terrorism which had begun in Calcutta in 1909, in response to the decision to partition Bengal, and which had led to the decision to move the Imperial capital from Calcutta to New Delhi in 1911.

The Imperial Government set up a commission during World War One to inquire into the question of sedition in India, chaired by a high court judge,

Mr Justice Rowlatt. The Rowlatt Commission reported in July 1918, and recommended extreme measures to combat political violence. Anyone engaging in terrorist activity or suspected of engaging in it, would be tried by a special tribunal sitting in camera, without a right of appeal. Reports of the proceedings would not be published. The possession of a seditious document was to be a felony punishable with two years' imprisonment, followed by a further two years in which the prisoner must engage only in those activities which the government permitted, must not make speeches or write anything which could cause a breach of the peace, and must live where the government directed.

In 1919 the Government of India announced that it would legislate the Rowlatt recommendations into law. At the same time it did not announce any measures to meet expectations of political reform. This combination was a crushing blow, particularly as the Secretary of State for India had spoken during the war about the possibility of India receiving self-government within the Empire – "dominion status" similar to Australia, Canada and New Zealand – when the war was over.

Gandhi organised a campaign of non-violent resistance to the Rowlatt Bill, coinciding with its passage into law in April 1919. The campaign was described as a nationwide "general hartal" or general strike. The idea was to bring the whole machinery of government to a standstill. It failed to stop the enactment of the law, and it also failed as a non-violent demonstration, as in many places violence erupted, particularly after crowds became incensed on hearing of Gandhi's arrest, while on his way by train from Bombay to Delhi. The violence was particularly extensive in Ahmedabad, where Gandhi had lived, and was best known. Government buildings were burned down and Europeans murdered in cold blood. Gandhi called off the hartal, describing it as a "Himalayan blunder".

A week later, not directly connected with Gandhi's hartal, came the Jalianwalla Bagh massacre. In Amritsar, the holy Sikh city in the Punjab, Brigadier-General Reginald Dyer, newly arrived to take charge of the garrison, prohibited all public meetings. His order was not properly publicised and did not reach the organiser of a traditional Sikh fair at Jalianwalla Bagh, a piece of open but enclosed ground. About 6,000 unarmed people were listening peacefully to a speaker address the crowd, when Dyer arrived at the scene and ordered soldiers to fire into the crowd without warning. The soldiers fired repeatedly as the crowd tried to flee from the enclosed space. Officially 379 people were killed, and many more wounded. The true numbers will never be known but are probably higher. Some 1,650 rounds of ammunition are known to have been fired, and as the firing was at close range most will have killed or wounded at least one person.

Dyer followed this atrocity with a reign of terror and humiliation for the inhabitants of Amritsar. The day before Dyer's arrival in Amritsar, a European woman, Mrs Sherwood, had been brutally attacked in the city and left for dead. Dyer ordered that all Indians passing the spot where this had happened must do so crawling on all fours.

Dyer was eventually criticised by a Commission of Inquiry and was relieved of his command and not given another. However he was not tried for any crime and vast sums were raised for him by supporters in England, who believed his removal from command was unfair.

Dyer gave conflicting reasons for his actions, which were clearly premeditated. Insofar as they had a rational motive, it seems to have been to make an example of Amritsar because of the attack on Mrs Sherwood. The predictable effect of the massacre was to destroy all trust between the British and vast numbers of Indians who had previously trusted them. Dyer's actions, combined with the lack of proper punishment for them, made eventual Indian independence a certainty.

Against this background, it is arguable that the main achievement of Gandhi's subsequent world-famous campaign of non-violent satyagraha was not to bring about Indian independence, which would have come anyhow. Instead it was to make the progression towards independence (though not independence itself) less bloody and violent than would otherwise have been the case. It also made it less bloody and violent than was the case in other large countries which were part of European empires, such as Indonesia, Algeria and Vietnam. This came about in two ways. Firstly, Gandhi's non-violent teachings attracted a huge Indian following, including the leadership of the main pro-independence party, the Congress Party, and ensured that moves planned by Congress to bring about independence were peaceful. Secondly, the moral power and symbolism of Gandhi's actions converted many British people into his sympathisers, including a significant number in the British administration in India. Eventually a substantial proportion of British public opinion was on Gandhi's side, so that the British Labour government of 1945 came to power committed to granting India independence.

Gandhi did not dare to start another hartal after the Amritsar massacre, because of the likelihood that it would precipitate further outbreaks of mass violence. Indeed the failure of his 1919 "general hartal" and the ensuing violence brought Gandhi face to face with one of the limitations of the form of civil disobedience he had pioneered in South Africa.

A mass movement of peaceful civil disobedience is inevitably at risk of being joined by people who are not peaceful, or who cease to be peaceful after a while, perhaps under provocation. The larger the movement, and the more emotional the issue, the greater the risk that it will not remain peaceful.

Gandhi had a good deal of time to ponder this problem, as he was imprisoned in 1922 for his part in organising hartals, and specifically for his role in relation to events at Chauri Chaura, near Gorakhpur in India's United Provinces (modern Uttar Pradesh). There a group of his supporters, after being attacked by police, had surrounded the police station and murdered the officers inside. Gandhi had no involvement in, or direct responsibility for, this incident, but gladly pleaded guilty. His famous speech from the dock set out the case for ending British rule in India. He was sentenced to six years' imprisonment, of which he served just under two years.

When Gandhi eventually reactivated the Satyagraha movement some years after his release, he tried to avoid incidents like Chauri Chaura by deliberately abandoning mass campaigns, and instead pioneering the technique of civil disobedience by small, well-organised groups, led by himself.

For this method to work it was necessary, firstly, that those carrying out the acts of civil disobedience had moral standing, and secondly that their actions were well-publicised. By the time he embarked on these campaigns, Gandhi's moral authority was already enormous, both on account of his achievements and because of his ascetic lifestyle and modest demeanour. As for publicity, he was so well-known that extensive journalistic coverage of any event he organised was certain. He was therefore in a position to be reasonably confident of success, when he embarked on the most famous demonstration of his career, the salt march to Dandi.

The law in British India was that all salt collected there was to be taxed. Gandhi's plan was to march from his ashram near Ahmedabad to the sea at Dandi, and there, symbolically, to take some salt from the salt pans nearby, and appropriate it, without paying tax. This in turn was to be a signal for the commencement of a more general campaign of civil disobedience.

Gandhi set off on 12 March, 1930, accompanied by 79 volunteers. He was then aged 61, and wore only the simple white dhoti (loincloth), drawn up between the legs, which he had made his trademark. He carried a staff like a pilgrim.

As Gandhi passed through Ahmedabad, the numbers joining his procession increased, until it was two miles long. Crowds lined the road and spread green leaves on the path in front of the marchers. Each night the marchers stopped at a village, where Gandhi would deliver a homily to the villagers about the themes of most concern to him, such as the desirability of spinning to make homespun cloth (to make India self-reliant and not dependent on imported cloth from Britain);

the need to treat untouchables with brotherly affection; to improve sanitation in the villages; to abandon alcohol; to break the government's salt monopoly; and to join the Satyagraha movement. Each day Gandhi walked 10 to 15 miles under the hot sun. A bullock cart was available should he be too tired to continue on foot, but he insisted on marching the whole distance himself. He took frequent short rests, and sometimes the march rested for a day.

During the march, Gandhi made remarks suggesting he was preoccupied with death. Such a preoccupation would have been rational, as his march represented a devastating threat to the stability of the regime. Had he been facing the Russian regime which ordered its soldiers to fire on Father Gapon (Chapter 8 above) his chances of surviving to reach Dandi would have been poor. The same would have applied if the local British military commander had been another Dyer. However there were no Dyers on the route from Ahmedabad to Dandi, and the British Indian government seems to have been either slow to appreciate the significance of Gandhi's move, or unsure how to respond. The Viceroy, Lord Irwin, gave orders that nothing should be done to impede Gandhi's movements, and waited on events.

On 5 April, 1930, after a march of 241 miles in 24 days, Gandhi and the satyagrahis neared Dandi. The satyagrahis prayed through the night, and the following morning Gandhi, accompanied by his followers, walked into the sea for a ritual bath of purification. At 8.30 am he solemnly bent down and picked up a small lump of natural salt, which, strictly, he could not legally remove from the beach without paying tax. There were no police present and there were no arrests.

A sense of anti-climax followed. However the following week, as news of Gandhi's action circulated, India was swept by a wave of salt-making frenzy. Everyone who sympathised with independence looked round for a way of breaking the salt law. Crowds assembled on beaches to watch salt being gathered, and did their best to prevent the police coming near the salt gatherers. Gandhi again ceremonially broke the salt law two days later, on 8 April, at Aat, a small village near Dandi.

For a few days it looked as if the movement initiated by the salt march might fail, because of the lack of British repression in response to it. However incidents occurred which forced the government to act. A group of terrorists in Bengal, wholly unconnected with Gandhi, organised by the Hindu Republican Association, raided the arsenals in Chittagong, and escaped into the jungle after murdering six people. At the other end of the country, the arrest in Peshawar of Khan Abdul Ghaffar Khan, an influential Pathan leader and follower of Gandhi, known as "the Frontier Gandhi", led to demonstrations, which in turn forced the police to retreat from Peshawar, leaving the city in the hands of Ghaffar Khan's followers, the Red Shirts, who released him from the jail. Two platoons of the 18th Royal Garhwali Rifles were sent to establish order, but refused to fire on the crowds and broke ranks. This was a particularly significant defection, as the crowds in Peshawar were overwhelmingly Muslim, and the regiment concerned was exclusively Hindu. Peshawar was then retaken by the Gurkhas, with air support. On 27 April, 1930, press censorship was imposed across India, making it a felony to print anything at all about the civil disobedience movement.

Gandhi responded by deliberately provoking the government to greater repression. He sent a letter informing the Viceroy that he and his companions intended to raid the Dharasana saltworks and take possession of it in the name of the people. He was arrested before he could lead the raid, but it went ahead in his absence, in May 1930, led by Mrs Sarojini Naidu.

The raid was to be non-violent. The idea was that each protester would be arrested in turn, and that the sheer numbers of those coming would overwhelm the forces of authority. About 2,500 members of the Congress Party took part, wearing white dhotis and Gandhi caps. The government, forewarned by Gandhi, had placed 400 policemen armed with steel-tipped lathis (long clubs) within the saltworks compound. The saltworks was on open land, with some waterlogged ditches and a barbed wire fence dividing it from the surrounding coast. As soon as satyagrahis crossed the surrounding ditch they were attacked by the police, and few of them were able to reach the barbed wire fence. The police clubbed unarmed demonstrators on head and body with their lathis, easily knocking them down and often seriously wounding them. As more satyagrahis kept on coming, the police became furious, and lost all semblance of restraint, clubbing them into unconsciousness, gashing them with the steel tips of their lathis, and torturing them by squeezing their testicles, pushing sticks up their anuses and kicking them in the abdomen. The British officers in charge had given orders that under no circumstances was any satyagrahi to be permitted to enter the saltworks, and a line of riflemen was posted nearby, ready to open fire.

The procession of satyagrahis continued for two hours. Eye-witnesses counted 320 wounded satyagrahis in the makeshift field hospital set up by the marchers. The march ended with a police charge terminating in the arrest of Sarojini Naidu and Gandhi's son Manilal. Two satyagrahis died of wounds.

The civil disobedience campaign continued for a further eight months until February 1931, when the government agreed to call a Round Table Conference on the future of India in London. Gandhi went directly from jail to negotiations in London, and a popular tour of England. Although the conference did not resolve any problems, the fact that it had happened at all was a tribute to the forces unleashed by the Satyagraha campaign. To that extent, the campaign was a success. It also advanced the cause of Indian independence by gravely damaging Britain's prestige in India and around the world, as a result of the repression, particularly the police action at the Dharasana saltworks.

Gandhi was probably fortunate that Lord Irwin, the Viceroy of India at the time of Dandi and Dharasana, was a man of peace, with a strong dislike of repression. His love of peace was later to discredit him, when, as Lord Halifax, British Foreign Secretary in Neville Chamberlain's government in 1938, he negotiated with Hitler the infamous Munich agreement for the dismemberment of Czechoslovakia. However in India, in 1931, his unwarlike inclinations meant that he was anxious to talk to Gandhi, to understand him, to meet such aspirations of the Congress Party as might be met by Britain in terms of practical British politics, and above all to avoid violence. Irwin was forced into repression wholly against his nature. Had a less scrupulous person been viceroy, Gandhi might not have been able to reach Dandi, and his 1930 civil disobedience campaign might never have got off the ground.

Gandhi's methods and his personality were peculiarly well-suited to challenging a regime which preferred to play by recognised rules and which contained many people, from its highest levels downwards, who had liberal views which they were reluctant to abandon. Although there were a significant proportion of British people in India who thought like General Dyer, and not like Lord Irwin, no-one ever suggested that Dyer's action was the policy of the government.

Subsequent attempts to use Gandhi's techniques in other countries have shown that they cannot usually prevail, at least in the short term, against dictators who share Dyer's bloodthirstiness and savagery.

Gandhi himself appears not to have realised this. He fundamentally failed to understand the nature of Nazi Germany, suggesting that Jews persecuted by the Nazis should respond by practising satyagraha. In 1938 he wrote a well-meaning letter to President Eduard Benes of Czechoslovakia, advising him how to practise satyagraha against Hitler, by outlining the proper behaviour of a Czech satyagrahi when confronted by the German army. Not until towards the end of World War Two did he acknowledge that the actions of Hitler were of a different order of repression from those of Britain. Only with reluctance did he concede, at the time of the Hindu-Muslim riots in 1946, that violence in self-defence could be legitimate, and he never fully carried through this modification of his thinking.

Even within the confines of the situation in British India, there were other weaknesses in satyagraha, as well as the difficulty, already referred to, of ensuring that it remained peaceful. In 1932 and 1933 Gandhi turned his attention to the issue of discrimination against untouchables and began to organise satyagraha to force temples to open their doors to untouchables, and to get other discrimination against untouchables stopped. This campaign, unlike the popular campaigns against British rule, offended a large proportion of the higher caste Hindu population. Some of those who were offended began to organise their own satyagraha campaigns against those organised by Gandhi. As Gandhi moved around India, he was followed by the supporters of one Pandit Lalnath, who waved black flags and threatened to lie down in front of the temples which Gandhi wished to open to untouchables, to prevent the untouchables from entering. Lalnath had closely studied Gandhi's technique, and was determined to apply exactly the same technique against him, including inspiring his own followers to suffer in their cause. On some occasions, one group of non-violent resisters fought the other group to a standstill. "We want to be hurt by the police or your volunteers," Lalnath once said to Gandhi. Gandhi never found any simple way to oppose Lalnath. When Lalnath's men lay down in the road in front of Gandhi's car he could abandon his car and walk, but when they formed a human wall in front of the temples and would not let him through there was little he could do.

Nor did Gandhi find a way of dealing with untouchables who themselves applied satyagraha to him, when they felt he was not going far enough to meet their demands. In August 1938, when Gandhi was living at Sevagram, the model village he founded near Wardha in central India, the village was invaded by a small army of untouchables, who announced that they would not leave until their demands were satisfied.

By this time, limited internal self-government for India had been introduced, in 1936, and there was an Indian Cabinet. Before the new system was introduced, Gandhi had started a fast to the death, in opposition to a plan to have a separate electoral roll for the untouchables, which would have been a move towards a sort of segregation. This new technique was dramatically successful, and the plan was dropped in response. However, the untouchables who invaded Sevagram demanded that Gandhi should get an untouchable appointed to the Indian Cabinet, and then copied Gandhi by announcing that they too would start a fast to death, and would continue until Gandhi met their demands.

The untouchables at Sevagram insisted that Gandhi set aside for them rooms in the village, which they had already selected and which the occupants were forced to vacate, and that he provide them with attendants. Gandhi had to give way to their demands. The group stayed for a few days, mocking him with high-sounding speeches and insistent demands, and then vanished. Gandhi was deeply shaken by the experience. Fortunately for him he did not have to undergo a repetition.

Both Pandit Lalnath and the untouchables of Sevagram showed that the civil disobedience campaign ran up against an insurmountable barrier where others used that same civil disobedience technique against the original disobeyer. To this extent, any civil disobedience campaign is liable to fail, if faced with an effective opposing civil disobedience campaign.

Perhaps the essence of Gandhi's success was not the use of civil disobedience in itself, but the use of novel techniques of protest to catch the public imagination. He was himself a novel and unusual figure and when he started civil disobedience in South Africa it was a novel idea. However, in India, by 1930, the novelty was not in civil disobedience, but in the image of the frail-looking old man defying the might of the British Empire by the simple gesture of picking up a lump of sea salt on a beach. It was that dramatic image, more than anything else, which led to his techniques being copied all over the world, in a wide variety of circumstances, some more amenable than others to his kind of demonstration.

Just five months after India achieved independence in August 1947, Gandhi was tragically assassinated in Delhi by a Hindu chauvinist militant, Nathuram Godse, on 30 January, 1948. His martyr's death enhanced even further, if that were possible, his world stature, and helped to ensure that future generations around the world would look to his example, including many would-be organisers of demonstration campaigns.

In the following chapters I consider the successes and failures of some of the attempts which have been made, since Gandhi's death, to use his civil disobedience techniques as the basis of campaigns around the world, particularly in South Africa, in the United States, in Northern Ireland, and on the high seas.

CHAPTER 12

GANDHI'S LEGACY

Some Gandhians today still do not accept that Gandhi was misguided in advising President Benes of Czechoslovakia on how to practise satyagraha against the Nazi armies. They believe that it could have been done, and that if more people had attempted to do that the Nazis would have been stopped.

This dangerous fallacy sometimes draws on a misunderstanding about a successful demonstration against the Nazis, which occurred in Berlin in the middle of World War Two. That demonstration in fact had nothing to do with Gandhi or his teachings, but before turning to Gandhi's conscious imitators, it is important to look at what actually did happen in Rosenstrasse, Berlin, in the early weeks of 1943.

The building in Rosenstrasse, outside which the demonstrators demonstrated, was the Berlin headquarters of the Gestapo, and the demonstrators were the non-Jewish wives of Jewish men, who had been arrested for deportation to the Nazi death camps.

The Nazi policy of extermination of the Jews was decided on at a conference held at Wannsee in Berlin in December 1941 and began on a gigantic scale in 1942. Jews were deported to the death camps from all over Nazi-occupied Europe. Jews in Berlin were subject to the same regime as Jews elsewhere. However, Berlin, although the capital of Germany, was a city where support for the Nazis had always been weaker than elsewhere in the country. There had also been better relations between Jews and non-Jews in Berlin than in much of Germany, and much more inter-marriage.

From early 1943, non-Jewish Berliners began gathering openly in the Rosenstrasse to demonstrate against the deportation of their family members who were Jewish. The vast majority were non-Jewish women married to Jewish men. The demonstrations continued day and night, with individuals coming and going from the demonstration in order to make time for other commitments. At times the number present in the street rose to about 600 people, and an estimated 6,000 people had taken part in the protest by the time it came to an end.

The predictable reaction of the Gestapo was to threaten repeatedly to shoot the demonstrators if they did not disperse. However, after a week, Goebbels, the Nazi Party leader for Berlin, ordered the release of between 1,700 and 2,000 Jews who were married to non-Jews. The individuals were able to return to their jobs, were never deported, and mostly survived World War Two.

The Rosenstrasse protesters appear not to have been political people, and not to have been motivated by any particular ideology. Nathan Stolzfus, who has written about the protests, has described them as "resisters of the heart", meaning that they were non-political people who in many cases did not even oppose Nazism until it affected their loved ones. Their protest was not against the Nazi regime, or even against the deportation of the Jews, but limited to opposing the deportation of the individuals to whom they were married. This does not lessen the immense courage of the demonstrators in taking an action which, during much of the existence of the Nazi Third Reich, would have resulted in their immediate deaths. However it does illustrate the very limited extent to which the demonstration was a challenge to the regime.

The reason that the demonstration succeeded, and was not followed by the mass executions of demonstrators which might normally have been expected, was due to an accident of timing. The Rosenstrasse protest occurred just after the massive defeat of the German Army at Stalingrad. The German surrender at Stalingrad occurred at the very end of January and beginning of February 1943 and knowledge of the surrender reached Germany at about the same time. The surrender for the first time destroyed the carefully maintained myth of Nazi invincibility. February 1943 was therefore a time of unprecedented insecurity for the Nazi regime. The Rosenstrasse protest was well-publicised, even being reported by the BBC from London. A key element of the Nazi extermination plan for the Jews was secrecy, which was placed at risk by the continuation of the public protests in the centre of Berlin. It appears that for this reason, in particular, Goebbels initially decided to postpone the deportation of the intermarried Jews for a few weeks, in the expectation that the protest would lose its momentum and deportation could then be carried out more easily. In the event the order to resume the deportations was never given.

The Rosenstrasse protest thus came at a critical moment very favourable to achieving its objectives. The complete ruthlessness of the Nazis in murdering anyone who opposed them would probably have meant that the protesters would have been killed if their protest had been either earlier or later. The fate of the White Rose Group, Catholic schoolchildren in Munich who distributed leaflets attacking the Nazis, and who were all promptly executed by the Gestapo, is an example of the usual fate of protesters under the Nazis.

It is possible that if there had been more protests like the Rosenstrasse protest more lives of Jews and others facing deportation and death would have been saved. However it is at least equally possible, and probably more likely, that it would have resulted in a Nazi massacre of protesters to set a deterrent example to the population. There was nothing about the protest to suggest that it pointed to a viable Gandhian passive resistance solution to Nazi terror.

Turning from the non-political Rosenstrasse protest to protests which deliberately set out to apply Gandhi's teachings, the record is not encouraging. This applies particularly to the continued attempts in the course of the twentieth century to apply Gandhian methods in South Africa, where they had first been invented.

The name of Robert Sobukwe is today best known to historians specialising in mid- twentieth century southern Africa. However if his Gandhian ideas had succeeded, it would be Sobukwe, and not Nelson Mandela, whom we would remember today as the father of free South Africa and the man who defeated the white apartheid regime. Of the many would-be followers of Gandhi in South Africa, it was Sobukwe who had the clearest and most ambitious vision of what he wanted to achieve using Gandhian techniques.

Gandhi had worked with the South African Indian community, but his teachings and his success were noticed by the majority black African community. The South African Native National Congress (later called the African National Congress, the ANC), in its first constitution, adopted in 1919, listed its intended activities at Article 13, including among them "passive action". There were attempts in 1919 to use Gandhian passive resistance in a campaign against the laws requiring Africans to carry passes, which was organised by Horatio Mbelle, J.W. Dunjwa and P.J. Motsoake. The organisers stated that their object in initiating passive resistance was not to challenge the government in any way, that there was no disloyalty on their part, and that they owed absolute allegiance to the king and the British constitution. They collected a sackful of passes and exemption papers and delivered them to the pass office, stating that they had resolved to resist the Pass Law, as it was no more nor less than a system of slavery. The campaign ended with violent attacks on peaceful anti-pass law protesters by police and white vigilantes, and a commission of enquiry consisting of government officials. The commission recommended some relaxation of the pass laws but its recommendations were not implemented.

An ANC call for a passive resistance campaign in June 1931 met with little response, and the ANC and its allies were unable to oppose effectively, by any means, repressive legislation in 1935, which ended the common voting roll for whites and blacks in Cape Province, and limited black participation in national public life to election of a small number of white MPs from a special roll.

After World War Two, Indian passive resistance revived in 1946 for the first time since Gandhi, with unsuccessful passive resistance against an Asiatic Land Tenure and Indian Representation Act passed by the Smuts government. The Indians were by then in a weak position, as they faced both implacable white opposition and hostility from blacks. In January 1949, a violent anti-Indian race riot by Zulus in Durban left 142 Indians dead. The Indians no longer had a Gandhi to lead them. Some of their leaders remained committed to Gandhian principles of non-violent civil disobedience, but could not find an effective way of putting them into practice so as to achieve results. "Non-violence has not failed us. We have failed non-violence," said J.D. Singh, a leader of the South African Indian Congress, some years later when the Congress was reviewing its policy of non-violence. This was however a difficult view to maintain when faced with the apparent complete intransigence of the bulk of the white population.

In 1948, Smuts' pro-British United Party was voted out of office, and the strongly Afrikaner National Party of Dr Malan took power. Malan was committed to the Afrikaner doctrine of apartheid, meaning total separation of races with power concentrated in the hands of the whites. This change of power coincided with a change of generation within the ANC, with older people such as Dr Alfred Xuma, who were at home with the politics of deputations and resolutions, being replaced by younger people such as Oliver Tambo, who saw more merit in direct action.

In 1952, the ANC organised the Defiance Campaign, a carefully prepared movement of non-violent passive resistance, under the leadership of Nelson Mandela and Oliver Tambo. Eight thousand five hundred demonstrators were imprisoned, and the action inspired widespread international sympathy for black South Africans, but it did not lead to any slowing of the pace of apartheid. On the contrary, Malan's government passed new restrictive legislation, the Criminal Law

Amendment Act 1953, prohibiting meetings of more than 10 Africans without a permit, and providing that any African who committed any offence "by way of protest or in support of any campaign against any law" could be sentenced to a whipping of 10 strokes, a £300 fine, three years in jail, or a combination of any two of those penalties. For a person whose words were calculated to incite others to commit an offence as a means of protest, those maximum penalties were increased by an additional £200 or two years.

The Defiance Campaign seems to have been regarded by many black South Africans as a failure. The ANC went into steep decline in the following two years, evidenced by a sharp fall in membership, and deep rifts in strategy were exposed between those who felt that the campaign was a mistake, because it had abandoned the previous tradition of working within the system, and those who felt that it failed because it had not gone far enough or been sustained for long enough. Although, with the passing of the years, the second point of view became the generally accepted one, the ANC did not initiate a similar campaign again. In 1958, the ANC's perceived lack of action led Robert Sobukwe to break away from the ANC, and set up his own alternative organisation, the Pan Africanist Congress (PAC).

Sobukwe was determined to put Gandhian techniques into practice against apartheid. He planned to do so by breaking one of its main weapons of control of the black population, the pass.

Black Africans had been required for decades before the 1950s to carry passes when travelling away from their home areas. However the pass system was made more intensive and humiliating under apartheid, with continual arrests for minor breaches of the law. The pass laws were linked to laws such as the Group Areas Act, which prohibited black people from residing outside designated "native areas" except with permission. As such they were a key structure underpinning the apartheid state. The pass laws were deeply hated, and a demonstration focussed on them was certain to attract a lot of support. They were therefore an appropriate target for mass protest action.

Sobukwe's idea was very simple. At a given signal, black Africans would go to police stations and symbolically tear up or destroy their pass cards in the presence of the police officers there. Destroying a pass card was itself an offence, so such action in the precincts of a police station would normally mean immediate arrest. Sobukwe's vision was that the number of arrests would be so great that the state would not be able to cope. Police stations and prisons would be full to overflowing, and essential workers would be missing from the economy in huge numbers because they were under arrest. This would force the repressive authorities to negotiate and to accept change. This idea was similar to the ANC's unsuccessful Defiance campaign of 1952, but Sobukwe hoped to ensure success by organising on a much larger scale than the Defiance campaign. For his campaign to work this time, a much larger number of arrests would be needed than happened in 1952.

The vision was inspiring, but Sobukwe was playing for high stakes with a weak hand. Apart from facing the ruthless repression of the apartheid state, the PAC was a minority movement among the black population, which did not have general support. Although the PAC was growing, most politically-conscious Africans supported its rival, the ANC. The ANC was unfortunately not prepared to co-operate with the PAC in what it foresaw as being a possible repeat of its 1952 failure. This meant that Sobukwe had to go it alone. When he decided to do so at the end of 1959, large areas of the country had few PAC members, and could not be involved in the campaign. This alone probably doomed his civil disobedience campaign before it had even started.

The PAC resolved in December 1959 to start its planned mass anti-pass law demonstration on "D-Day", which was secretly fixed as 21 March, 1960. A series of three pamphlets calling for the demonstration were circulated early in 1960, but did not specify the date on which it was to take place. This was to prevent the South African police from knowing and preparing in advance. This aspect of the plan appears to have been successful, despite the regime's network of police informers.

21 March was a Monday. The intention was that as well as the pass law protest there would be a mass stay away from work, accompanied by demonstrations. Three days beforehand, Sobukwe announced the date. However on 21 March the hoped-for nation-wide campaign did not materialise. In Johannesburg, where Sobukwe presented himself for arrest with a group of PAC supporters, the day of action was largely ignored. The same happened in the important industrial centre of Port Elizabeth. In Cape Town, about 1,500 people marched from the township of Langa to the police station at Philippi, and presented themselves for arrest not carrying a pass. However instead of arresting them on the spot, the police took their names, and told them to come back later. After some hours the police baton charged the crowd and killed two demonstrators. A riot then broke out, in which one bystander was killed. What happened in Cape Town amounted to a failure both for civil disobedience and for non-violence.

Apart from Langa, the only area where the day of action was well-supported was in the towns of the Vaal triangle – the heavily industrialised area south of Johannesburg. By Sunday night groups of residents were converging on police stations in the area, and a particular crisis developed at Sharpeville, near Vereeniging.

Sharpeville police station was repeatedly surrounded by local PAC activists, as part of a strategy of tiring out the police before the big demonstration the next day. This had the effect of making the police both tired and frightened. Their fear was increased when the only telephone line to the police station malfunctioned. Police reinforcements with Saracen armoured cars arrived early on the Monday morning to protect the police station. Armoured cars were not a common sight, and their arrival dramatically heightened tensions on both sides. During the morning a large crowd took up position around the police station, waiting for something to happen. The crowd was too large, and the situation too tense, for the police to be able to disperse the demonstrators peacefully. Nor could the police arrest more than a small proportion of those present, whatever legal basis there might be for the arrests, as the police station did not have holding capacity for more than a few prisoners. By 1.00 pm, 294 police, in and near the police station, were surrounded by a crowd of many thousands. The police estimate was 15,000. The true number will never be known and was probably less, but was high enough to prevent any sort of crowd control. The huge crowd intimidated the police, who did not know anything about the nature of the planned civil disobedience campaign, and believed they were about to be attacked. The police station was surrounded by a security fence, which was bulging inward under the weight of demonstrators pressing against it. The police lacked crowd control equipment or training. However they were not lacking in arms. Later investigations revealed that they had about 4,000 rounds of ammunition, revolvers, rifles, light machine guns (Sten guns), pistols, and heavy machine guns mounted on the armoured cars.

The atmosphere at Sharpeville was inflamed by awareness of recent events near Durban. Cato Manor, a densely populated black area of Durban, had recently been deliberately cleared of its inhabitants by the South African government, as part of its apartheid policy of removing black people from urban areas, and relocating them to so-called "homelands". The previous month, police at Cato Manor had fired on unarmed demonstrators protesting against their forced evictions. The crowds had fought back against their attackers, and a mob had attacked a police station and killed nine policemen. This had been the first time that demonstrators had fought back on such a scale when shot at by the police. The police at Sharpeville were well aware of the Cato Manor incident, as were some members of the crowd who taunted them by referring to it.

At 1.29 pm, a man known only by a nickname, Geelbooi, arrived at the police station. He was a petty thief with no connection to the PAC, and no standing in the community. One of the police officers on duty outside the station was a Sergeant De Bruin, who some months earlier had brutally beaten Geelbooi.

When Geelbooi, who was drunk, saw De Bruin, he fired two shots at him with a pistol. Geelbooi did this on his own initiative. His action was wholly against the intentions of the demonstration organisers and had not been foreseen by them.

Geelbooi's action was immediately followed by a mass discharge of over 1,000 rounds of ammunition by the police, firing directly into the crowd. As the crowd turned and fled, the police continued firing into their backs as they ran. Within a few minutes the crowd was gone except for the bodies of the dead and wounded.

The number killed at the Sharpeville massacre remains disputed. It is widely believed that some bodies were secretly disposed of by the police to reduce the official tally of dead, which was put at 69. The number of wounded is also uncertain but was not much less than 200. The immediate aftermath of the massacre was witnessed by journalists, who had already arrived in the vicinity, and news about it was rapidly broadcast round the world.

Sharpeville polarised attitudes. It made the world outside South Africa start the first moves towards economic sanctions and isolating South Africa. It made the apartheid regime more determined than ever to use brute force to resist the will of the majority, and it made black activists increasingly certain that only the path of armed conflict would offer any hope of change. Although the ANC president, Albert Luthuli, ceremonially burned his pass-book after Sharpeville, in a gesture of solidarity with the murdered demonstrators, everyone knew that the massacre had shown that dismantling apartheid through non-violent civil disobedience was not a realistic strategy in South Africa at that time. Robert Sobukwe was convicted of incitement, and sentenced to three years' imprisonment. He was held in solitary confinement on Robben Island, and his detention was extended administratively after the end of his sentence, with no release until 1969. After his release he remained banned from political activity, and required to live in internal exile in Kimberley, Cape Province. He died of lung cancer in 1978.

Sharpeville is a striking example of the limitations and failures of peaceful demonstrations as a means of opposing a repressive regime. There are many others. Leaving aside those where demonstrators were seeking the end of the regime, there have been innumerable demonstrations were much more limited demands have been met with a hail of bullets. Where a regime is prepared to use unlimited force against unarmed protesters, neither the law-abiding demonstration, nor the Gandhian route of passive civil disobedience, offers much hope of bringing about change, absent special factors such as international support or a regime which is deeply divided within itself.

For this reason it is not surprising that the greatest triumph of Gandhian principles, since Gandhi, did not occur in a tyrannical regime, but was that of Martin Luther King and the Civil Rights Movement in the United States.

By the 1950s, the United States was a long established democracy, with a deep attachment to the principles set out in its constitution. Although the system of entrenched discrimination which black Americans faced in the Southern states was very similar to apartheid in South Africa, that Southern U.S. system, unlike the system in South Africa, was not supported by the whole machinery of the state. Many people in the north, and elements within the Federal Government, were sympathetic to the Civil Rights Movement. In addition the Civil Rights Movement generally enjoyed overwhelming support among black Americans. Although there were small violent movements which rejected Martin Luther King's non-violence, there was nothing comparable to the split between the ANC and the PAC in South Africa.

In addition, there were other factors which favoured King. He was a dedicated Gandhian, who visited India in the 1950s to learn more about Gandhi's techniques. He often publicly acknowledged his debt to Gandhi, and drew his commitment to civil disobedience and passive resistance directly from him. However King, unlike Gandhi, and also unlike Robert Sobukwe, was working in an environment where it was possible for him to make a credible claim that, if the law was understood in its true meaning, he was not breaking the law by his civil disobedience campaigns, but actually had the law on his side.

King's campaigns involved direct defiance of numerous city and state ordinances in the southern states. However, these campaigns were always based on the premise that the laws in question were unconstitutional, in other words, that those laws themselves broke the United States Constitution, which was a higher norm with which all other laws had to comply. The fact that King was campaigning on a basis of claimed legality gave his campaigns a moral authority in the eyes of uncommitted people, which they would not otherwise have had. Retaining this moral authority was a critical part of King's campaigning strategy. King, unlike Gandhi and Sobukwe, was thus expressly committed to the rule of law, as much so as the nineteenth century Parliamentary reform campaigners in the British Isles.

King was also helped by the fact that, at the time when he started his campaigns, the United States was changing. The structure of discrimination in the southern states had been underpinned for the previous half century by the United States Supreme Court decision in Plessey v Ferguson (163 US 537) in 1896. The court in Plessey v Ferguson had held that it was legitimate for a public authority to segregate its facilities by race, provided that equal facilities were provided for different races. That decision, which concerned the trams in New Orleans, provided a legal basis for discrimination, by which black people were segregated to separate facilities, from buses to restaurants to public toilets, which were in practice anything but equal to those provided to whites. However, in 1954, in <u>Brown v Board of Education of Topeka</u> (347 US 483), the US Supreme Court ruled that the racial segregation of schools in Topeka, Kansas, was unconstitutional, being in breach of the U.S. constitution's equal rights amendment, passed just after the Civil War. In reaching this decision, the Supreme Court consciously overruled its own earlier decision in <u>Plessey v Ferguson.</u>

The decision in <u>Brown</u> meant that it was likely that many other segregation measures would also be struck down as unconstitutional if the Supreme Court had to rule on their legality. This gave King and the civil rights campaigners of the post-1954 era opportunities which had not existed a few years earlier in the 1940s, when Philip Randolph was organising the Negro Marches on Washington. The civil rights campaigners could now challenge state laws and institutions which perpetuated segregation, confident in the knowledge that those laws and institutions would in due course be found to be operating unconstitutionally.

Finally, King was a master tactician and campaigner. Despite the factors which can be seen with hindsight to have operated in favour of the Civil Rights campaign, the odds at the campaign's outset were very much against its success. The system of suppression of black people in the South by means of lynchings, carried out by the Ku Klux Klan, whose masked members included judges, police and other key authority figures, had worked with terrifying effectiveness for many years. It was quite unclear that its power could be successfully challenged. King's success in this respect was due in large measure to his own qualities, which combined inspiring oratory with a very clear sense of how to mobilise his supporters most effectively.

The first big successful campaign organised by King was a boycott of the segregated buses in Montgomery, Alabama, triggered when the civil rights activist Rosa Parkes refused to move from a section of a bus designated for whites. The boycott continued until the bus company, under economic duress as a result of the boycott, agreed to desegregate.

This was followed by a special new kind of demonstration, the "sit-in". Sit-ins had already been used to protest against segregation in parts of the South in the 1940s. However they had never before been used on the scale of the sit-in which started at a lunch counter in Greensboro, North Carolina, on 1 February, 1960.

Across much of the South, lunch counters in stores would only serve whites. In Greensboro, a group of black student civil rights activists occupied the lunch counter in a store, and refused to leave until they were served. The students told the press, "We believe, since we buy books and papers in the other part of the store, we should get served in this part". When they were forced to leave, when the store closed at the end of the day, they had still not been served.

Sit-ins then began across the whole South. The basic sit-in plan was that a group of students would go to a lunch counter and ask to be served. If they were served they would move on to another lunch counter elsewhere. If they were not served they would remain seated, waiting until they were served or until the store closed. If they were arrested a new group would take their place. Those taking part in sit-ins were instructed to be good-humoured and polite. Many students took school books with them and studied while seated waiting to be served. Despite this, in many places, notably Nashville, Tennessee, the sit-in protesters were charged with disorderly conduct and fined.

By August 1961, over 700,000 people had taken part in sit-ins, of whom 3000 had been arrested, and many lunch counters had desegregated under pressure. The sit-in technique was also used to integrate other segregated public facilities such as cinemas. Because of their effectiveness, they continued to be used until the Civil Rights Act 1964 outlawed all segregated public facilities.

While the sit-in campaign was in full swing, a traditional demonstration occurred which in due course led to an important Supreme Court decision about the right to demonstrate. On 2 March, 1961, a group of some 200 black high school and college students met at the Zion Baptist Church in Columbia, South Carolina, and walked in groups of about fifteen to the South Carolina State House grounds, an area of two city blocks open to the general public. Their stated purpose was "to submit a protest to the citizens of South Carolina, along with the Legislative Bodies of South Carolina, our feelings and our dissatisfaction with the present condition of discriminatory actions against Negroes, in general, and to let them know that we were dissatisfied, and we would like for the laws which prohibited Negro privileges in this State to be removed". On arrival at the State House grounds, they walked in single file or two abreast through the grounds in an orderly manner, each group carrying placards bearing messages such as "I am proud to be a Negro", and "Down with segregation". They continued doing so for about forty-five minutes, during which some 200 to 300 onlookers congregated. No violence occurred, and there was no evidence that the onlookers were anything other than curious. There were no insulting remarks or offensive gestures.

After about forty-five minutes, police who were present informed the demonstrators that they would be arrested if they did not disperse within fifteen minutes. The demonstrators did not disperse. After listening to what the record of evidence in the subsequent court case records as a "religious harangue" from one of their leaders, they began singing *The star-spangled banner*, and what were described as "other patriotic and religious songs", while stamping their feet and clapping their hands. A total of 187 students were then arrested, and were later convicted of breach of the peace, thus beginning four years of legal appeals which eventually reached the Supreme Court.

Two months after the demonstration at Columbia, the Civil Rights Movement started a campaign against racially-segregated toilets. A group called the Congress of Racial Equality (CORE) planned a "Freedom Ride" from Washington D.C. to New Orleans. The plan was that the freedom riders would consist of both blacks and whites, and at each rest stop the whites would go to the blacks only toilets and other areas of the rest stations, and the blacks would go to the whites only areas. The ride was to take place between 2 May and 17 May, 1961. This idea was again not completely new. A previous attempt in 1947 had ended with the participants arrested and put to work on a chain gang in North Carolina. On this second occasion, the Freedom Riders made it as far as Alabama, where they split into two groups. The first group's bus was attacked and its tyres slashed, then a few miles further on the bus was firebombed and destroyed. The second group was met by a Ku Klux Klan mob in Birmingham, Alabama, and badly beaten up. There were no police present at the bus depot, and it was later learned that the police had been aware of the planned mob attack, and had deliberately stayed away to allow it to take place. At this point the bus company, afraid of losing another bus, refused to take the Freedom Riders any further. The Freedom Riders attempted to negotiate, but two days later fled Birmingham in fear for their lives.

Shortly after the original Freedom Riders had given up, a group of civil rights activists arrived from Nashville, planning to carry on the ride where the others had left off. At this point the United States Attorney-General, President Kennedy's brother Robert, put pressure on the bus company to carry the new group of Freedom Riders. Kennedy was determined that an existing law which outlawed segregation on inter-state transport should be enforced across the country, instead of being ignored in the South, as it had been until then. In response to this Federal pressure, the Alabama police promised that a private plane would fly over the bus, and that there would be a state patrol car every fifteen or twenty miles along the highway between Birmingham and Montgomery. However all police protection disappeared when the bus entered Montgomery, and as the riders got off the bus they were attacked and severely beaten by another mob. Robert Kennedy responded by sending Federal marshals to police the city. Martin Luther King flew to Montgomery and held a mass meeting in a church in support of the Freedom

Riders. The church was surrounded by Federal marshals holding back a mob of several thousand angry whites. Under pressure from Kennedy, the Governor of Alabama declared martial law and sent in the National Guard to disperse the mob and allow those at the church meeting to leave.

After this incident, Kennedy asked the Freedom Riders for a "cooling-off period". However the Riders refused. As one of them said, *"We'd been cooling off for 350 years and… if we cooled off any more, we'd be in a deep freeze."* The Riders continued as far as Mississippi, where they were all arrested and sentenced to 60 days in jail. Other riders who tried to take up the cause were also arrested and jailed as soon as they crossed the Mississippi state line. Eventually the Riders gave up, none of them having succeeded in making it across Mississippi to Louisiana. However they had not lost. The following year the Supreme Court ruled, in Turner v Memphis (369 US 350 – 1962), that segregation was unlawful in all transportation facilities, including toilets.

In 1963 Martin Luther chose Birmingham as the focus for a major campaign. He did so because of its notoriety as the place where the Freedom Riders had been beaten up, and as "Bombingham", with eighteen unsolved bombings in black neighbourhoods in the previous six years. It was in Birmingham that King perfected the style of demonstration which came to symbolise the Civil Rights Movement. His demonstrations were deliberately and strictly non-violent, and were designed to contrast the dignity and peacefulness of the demonstrators with the behaviour of the undisciplined mobs who attacked them. The demonstrations drew on the religious and choral traditions of African Americans, and singing freedom songs played a big part in them. As well as the famous *We shall overcome*, other popular demonstration songs included *Ain't gonna let nobody turn me round* :-

> *"Ain't gonna let nobody turn me round, turn me round, turn me round. Ain't gonna let nobody turn me round. I'm gonna keep on a talking, keep on a walking, marching up to freedom land".*

King later set out the four principles underlying his demonstrations in an article for the *Saturday Review* magazine:-

> *"1. Non-violent demonstrators go on to the streets to exercise their constitutional rights. 2. Racists resist by unleashing violence against them. 3. Americans of conscience in the name of decency demand federal intervention and legislation. 4. The administration, under*

mass pressure, initiates measures of immediate intervention and remedial legislation".

The criticism has sometimes been made that it was wrong for King deliberately to send his supporters into situations where they were likely to be badly hurt, or even killed, as part of what could be described, accurately if very unfairly, as a policy of provoking violence. The first answer to this is that the civil rights demonstrators were only provoking to fanatics determined to deny them their basic rights. Their dignified marches could not have provoked anyone who did not want to be provoked. The act of holding the march was what triggered the attacks on the marchers, not anything the marchers did. The second answer is that the Civil Rights Movement had no viable alternative strategy. Throughout his leadership of the movement, King needed to maintain the allegiance of angry black people who would otherwise have been tempted to turn to his militant rivals, like Stokely Carmichael, who believed in violent revolution and total rejection of white society. King, for whom a violent revolution would have been against his principles, also never lost sight of the obvious fact that a violent revolutionary uprising by blacks would have been crushed by whites with enormous loss of life. At the same time as fighting the challenge from militant revolutionaries, he was also fighting a bigger challenge from the apathy of many potential supporters. He had to show black people in the South, who had been oppressed without hope for generations, that there was something which his movement could do which could bring results. The non-violent demonstrations offered a way forward. Democratic channels were blocked in the South. Blacks in most areas were prevented from registering to vote by racist white returning officers. King's demonstrations therefore served a classic function of demonstrations, by giving a voice to the voiceless and powerless.

Birmingham was one of the most extreme examples of a city where no black person could ever hope to get a permit for a demonstration. King and the local civil rights organiser, the Reverend Fred Shuttlesworth, head of the Alabama Christian Movement for Human Rights, decided to challenge the system in Birmingham by deliberately organising unlicensed demonstrations, and defying the city authorities to do their worst. The aim was to break segregation in Birmingham, and in particular to force the brutal city police commissioner, Eugene "Bull" Connor, who had been responsible for the beating of the Freedom Riders, to resign. Connor was already in difficulties because of a quarrel within the city leadership between his supporters and a faction which wanted him to go, so the timing was right for a confrontation.

Civil rights demonstrations started in Birmingham on 6 April, 1963, when police arrested 45 protesters marching from 16th Street Baptist Church to the city hall. The purpose of the march was to protest at the denial of civil rights to black people in the city of Birmingham. The next day another demonstration took place and more demonstrators were arrested. One demonstrator, Leroy Allen, was attacked and injured by police dogs. A local judge then issued an injunction, naming King and 133 other civil rights activists and prohibiting them from organising demonstrations.

A further march, planned before the injunction, took place in defiance of the injunction, on the afternoon of Good Friday, 12 April, 1963. It was this march which ultimately led to the second great Supreme Court case of the civil rights era, Shuttlesworth v City of Birmingham. Fifty-two people were led out of a Birmingham church by three ministers, King, Fred Shuttlesworth and Ralph Abernathy. They walked in an orderly fashion two abreast for about four city blocks. The marchers stayed on the pavements, except at street intersections, and did not interfere with other pedestrians. No cars were obstructed, nor were traffic signals disobeyed. As the marchers moved along, a crowd of spectators fell in behind them at a distance. The spectators at some point spilled out into the street, but the street was not blocked and vehicles were not obstructed.

At the end of four blocks the marchers were stopped by the Birmingham police and were arrested for violating a city ordinance which prohibited any procession without written permission from the city police commission. Fred Shuttlesworth was convicted of breaking this law by organising the Good Friday march, and was sentenced to 90 days' imprisonment with hard labour, and 48 days additional hard labour in default of payment of a $75 fine and $24 costs. His case, like that of the South Carolina students, began its journey through the appeal court system. Martin Luther King was detained with Shuttlesworth and others who had been on the Good Friday demonstration, and King remained in jail until 20 April. However the demonstrations in Birmingham went on. Andrew Young, King's assistant, continued with their organisation while King was imprisoned. His description of the Easter Sunday Civil Rights march to the jail, in which some 5,000 people participated, dressed in their best clothes, is memorable:

"We marched from New Pilgrim (Baptist Church) until we arrived at a point about two blocks from the jail, where the police had set up barricades to block us. They were out in force, Bull Connor barking orders with his foghorn voice. Fire trucks blocked the street and firemen were ready with their hoses… Bull Connor shouted at us "Y'all have to disperse this crowd. Turn this group around". But there were five

*thousand people behind us, and up ahead, two blocks away, were our people in jail
who were surely watching what was happening from their tiny cell windows."*

Young's solution and that of his fellow organiser Wyatt Walker was to call on
the entire demonstration to go down on their knees and pray. However after a few
minutes a demonstrator shouted out: "The Lord is with this movement! Off your
knees! We're going to the jail". Young's description continues:-

> *"Everybody in the front rows got up and started walking towards
> the barricades and the amassed police. Stunned at first, Bull Connor
> yelled, "Stop 'em, stop 'em!" But none of the police moved a muscle…
> they all just stood watching us as if they were transfixed. Even the
> police dogs which had been growling and straining at their leashes
> when we first marched up were now perfectly calm. The firemen just
> stood there, holding their hoses. We were walking right past them,
> and Bull Connor was yelling "Turn on the hoses, turn on the hoses!"
> But the firemen didn't move either. I saw one fireman, tears in his
> eyes, just let the hose drop at his feet. Our people marched right
> between the fire trucks.. They were not rushing. It was a very slow,
> serious march. They just marched on to the park across from the jail,
> where we convened to sing to the people in the jail… Bull Connor
> stood there cussing and fussing. All his resources had failed him. His
> policemen had refused to arrest us, his firemen had refused to hose us,
> and his dogs had refused to bite us… I'll never forget one old woman
> who became ecstatic when she marched through the barricades. As
> she passed through she shouted, "Great God Almighty done parted
> the Red Sea one mo' time!".*

King was released on 20 April, and promptly varied the form of the demonstrations
by inviting children to take part in another big demonstration on 2 May, 1963.
The idea was that, while adults had bills to pay, and could often not afford to go
to jail as part of a protest, young people did not have the same responsibilities,
but were just as effective in jail in terms of putting pressure on the city authorities
to change their policies. At the same time their imprisonment did not pose any
economic threat to their families.

On 2 May, children ranging in age from six to eighteen gathered in Kelly
Ingram Park, across the street from 16th Street Baptist Church. At 1.00 pm, about
50 teenagers set off for the city centre, singing *We shall overcome*. They were all
arrested and put in police vans. As soon as this happened another group set off

from the park in the same direction and were also arrested. Then a third group followed, and then a fourth. Soon the police had no more vans in which to put the children and began pushing them into school buses instead. Within three hours, there were 959 children in the jails, which were full to bursting.

The next day more than a thousand children stayed out of school and went to Kelly Ingram Park. Bull Connor was determined not to allow them to pass, but could not arrest them as he had no more jails to put them in. Instead he called out the fire brigade and ordered them to train their fire hoses on the children at maximum pressure. The force of the water was sufficient to break bones and to roll protesters along the road. All this was done in the presence of television cameras, and Connor's treatment of the children shocked the nation, exactly as King had planned. Within a few days, on 10 May, the authorities in Birmingham backed down and agreed to desegregate the city, the white business community insisting on the changes, over the objections of the city officials.

It was after this victory that the Civil Rights Movement organised a new Negro March on Washington, in support of a proposed new Civil Rights Bill to end segregation. Philip Randolph was again involved in the organisation, this time with Martin Luther King. Unlike the planned Negro marches in 1941 and 1946, this march actually happened, on 28 August, 1963. It went ahead despite much pressure being put on the organisers by President Kennedy's nervous government to call it off. At least 250,000 people arrived in Washington in more than 30 special trains and 2,000 chartered buses. The destination of the march was the Lincoln Memorial, and it was there that Martin Luther King made his famous " I have a dream" speech, beginning with the words " I am happy today to join with you in what will go down in history as the greatest demonstration for freedom in the history of our nation."

In 1964, with a presidential election due, the attention of the Civil Rights Movement shifted to voter registration. A campaign to organise blacks to register as voters in Mississippi led to the murder of three civil rights workers by local whites. King and his allies in the Southern Christian Leadership Council decided to target Selma, Alabama, a notorious place where it was virtually impossible for any black person to register to vote. As in Birmingham, the peaceful demonstration technique was used to focus attention on the issue. After several marches within Selma, at one of which King and 250 demonstrators were arrested, Hosea Williams and John Lewis led a march by 600 people who intended to walk the 54 miles from Selma to the state capital, Montgomery. This time the marchers had only marched six blocks when, although entirely peaceful, they were attacked by a massed force of state troopers and police, some mounted, at the Edmund Pettus

Bridge. The soldiers and police, who had orders from Governor George Wallace to block the march, attacked with clubs, tear gas, bull whips, and rubber tubes wrapped in barbed wire, and drove the marchers back into Selma. John Lewis was knocked unconscious. Sixteen other demonstrators were hospitalised. Again the police brutality happened in full view of the television cameras, and had a nationwide impact as television networks interrupted their evening programmes to broadcast live from Selma. ABC TV happened to be showing a documentary about the Nazis that evening called *Judgment at Nuremberg*, with footage of Nazi mobs attacking Jews. When the programme was interrupted by the scenes at Selma some viewers at first did not realise that it was an interruption, and thought they were witnessing another atrocity from the Nazi era, until the unedited nature of the screaming made it clear that they were seeing live news.

King immediately made plans to maintain the pressure for change by means of a second march from Selma to Montgomery. However, because of the fear of violence, a federal judge who had previously often supported the Civil Rights Movement issued an injunction prohibiting the march. King was therefore faced with a tough decision. This was not a decision by a dubious state court but by a federal court. King's commitment to the rule of law had to be weighed against the disappointment to his followers and the possible loss of momentum of the campaign. The Civil Rights Movement decided to cancel the march, and to replace it with a short march to the Edmund Pettus bridge in Selma to lay a wreath, to the confusion of many marchers who had not been told and thought they were marching to Montgomery.

The tense and confused situation at Selma was then further inflamed by the murder by white racists of a visiting white clergyman, James Reeb, who had been taking part in the march. A young black man, Jimmy Jackson, had also been killed a few days earlier, without much notice being taken by the media, and there was some bitterness that it took the death of a white to generate national press coverage. However, whether as a result of the general revulsion at the murders, or by coincidence, another federal judge then ruled that the state had no power to block a march from Selma to Montgomery. On 21 March, 1964 a third march therefore set out from Selma, and this time the marchers reached Montgomery 25,000 strong, led by King and by Rosa Parkes, who had started the Montgomery bus boycott.

King's strategy brought success. The Civil Rights Act, outlawing segregation, reached the statute book in 1964. The Voting Rights Act, making it much easier for blacks to register in the South, was signed into law by Lyndon Johnson in 1965. The structure of segregation and white domination in the South was broken. It seems unlikely that these changes would have happened for many years, if ever, but for the Civil Rights Movement.

The movement's constitutional approach was also vindicated by the courts. Eventually, when the case of the Columbia, South Carolina, demonstrators reached the Supreme Court, under the name Edwards v South Carolina, the Supreme Court found that the offence of breach of the peace, of which the demonstrators had been convicted, was impossibly wide, and that the arrests of the demonstrators infringed their constitutional rights of free speech and freedom of assembly. Likewise in Shuttlesworth v City of Birmingham, the Birmingham city law under which Fred Shuttlesworth had been arrested was found to be an unconstitutional restriction on freedom of assembly. The two cases for the first time made it clear that under United States law everyone is entitled to hold a demonstration in the streets as part of the exercise of their rights of free speech and freedom of assembly. These two decisions thus gave strong constitutional protection to the right to demonstrate, and vindicated the basis of King's constitutionalist strategy. King's combination of passive resistance tactics and a strong rule of law commitment thus brought about one of the greatest achievements ever by a demonstrating movement.

The vindication of King's position about the unconstitutionality of laws and police actions in the Southern states happened because the Supreme Court of the 1960s was a very different court from that of the 1890s, when Plessey v Fergusson and Davis v Commonwealth of Massachusetts were decided. The Civil Rights Movement cases of Edwards v South Carolina and Shuttlesworth v City of Birmingham have stood the test of time and remain important statements of the right to demonstrate in the United States. However these two landmark cases are in many ways an exception to the usual role of the courts in relation to demonstrations, which tends to be negative, over deferential to the authorities, and lacking in understanding of the realities of holding a demonstration. It is to the role of the courts in relation to demonstrations that we now turn.

CHAPTER 13

Demonstrations and the Law

We have seen how the development of a law-based culture in England led to respect for the right to petition the sovereign, and so indirectly to the rise of the law-abiding street demonstration. We have also seen how eventually the right to hold a peaceful demonstration came to be recognised as a constitutional right in the United States. This chapter considers the role of the law in relation to demonstrations in England, since the peaceful demonstration became part of British national culture in the early nineteenth century. It also highlights some areas where English and American law about demonstrations are different.

The role of the law in this area has been generally disappointing to supporters of the right to demonstrate. Only too often, the courts have given no weight at all to any right to protest, and have delivered judgments which have meant that in practice holding demonstrations has been dependent on the arbitrary and easily withdrawn goodwill of the police.

The role of the British courts (Scotland is implicated as well as England) contrasts disappointingly with the attitude of the US Supreme Court as shown in cases such as Edwards v South Carolina and Shuttlesworth v City of Birmingham. This is partly due to the different constitutional arrangements in the UK, as compared with the United States. Since the United Kingdom does not have a written constitution, the courts do not have to consider whether a statute conforms with the constitution, as they do in the United States. Instead, the courts interpret statutes by applying the doctrine of Parliamentary sovereignty. Under that doctrine, Parliament is supreme, and can create law as it sees fit. If the law is clear, the only role of the judges is to apply it. The judges cannot mitigate the effects of the law, however harsh or unreasonable. The right to petition the Crown in Parliament is protected by Magna Carta and by the 1688 Bill of Rights. However any restriction on the right to demonstrate which is enacted by Parliament, and which does not conflict with either of those two rarely cited historical documents, must be applied by the courts using its clear wording, however unjust the result. This constitutional theory has led to repeated narrow-minded legal interpretations, based purely on statute and precedent, with no regard to protection of rights, the very existence of which is often denied. In addition, the judges have often shown themselves to be more executive-minded than the executive, only too willing to devise new restrictive interpretations of the law, which have helped the government or the police in disputes with demonstrators.

There has been some improvement in the attitude of the English courts in the last twenty years. This is probably attributable to the influence of the European Convention on Human Rights. However the European Court of Human Rights, which oversees the European Convention, itself has a highly uneven and unsatisfactory record of decisions in relation to demonstrations. Legal protection for the right to demonstrate in the United Kingdom and in Europe therefore remains partial and flimsy.

A classic example of narrow-minded judge-made law, affecting the holding of demonstrations, was the 1893 decision in <u>Harrison v Duke of Rutland</u>, about whether there was any kind of right to walk on the public highway. Without such a right, there could never be a right to hold a demonstration.

Harrison appears to have been an early predecessor of twenty-first century England's anti-blood sports movement. The Duke of Rutland owned a grouse moor used for shooting. A road crossed the moor, and the subsoil of the road also belonged to the Duke. On a day when the Duke and his friends were out shooting, Harrison, from what the court (in the person of the Master of the Rolls, Lord Esher) later described as "some perverted notion of desiring to interfere with the grouse shooting", went on to the road for the purpose of discouraging the grouse from flying towards the butts where they would be shot. He did so with some apparent success, by waving his handkerchief and opening and shutting his umbrella. He was asked to stop by the Duke's servants but refused. He was then forcibly held down on the road by the servants until the shoot was over, when he was released. He sued the Duke for assault and false imprisonment, and the Duke counterclaimed for trespass.

It was found at trial that the Duke's servants had not used any more force than was necessary to prevent Harrison from interfering with the grouse shoot. The judge directed the jury that Harrison could not be guilty of trespass as a matter of law, as he was on a public highway. The jury then found that the Duke had not committed assault or false imprisonment, but that Harrison had not committed trespass. Both sides appealed to the Court of Appeal, which held that Harrison had after all been guilty of trespass, because his limited right to pass and re-pass along the highway did not extend to using the highway to distract the grouse being shot on the adjacent moor. The court did not go so far as to say that any use of the highway other than passing or re-passing would be a trespass. However it held that anything which was not a "reasonable and usual use" of the highway was a trespass, and that the use of the highway to disturb the grouse shoot was not a reasonable and usual use. The court thus left open the question of whether a demonstration could ever be a reasonable and usual use of the highway, but implied by the terms of its judgment that this would depend on all the circumstances of a particular case.

The decision in <u>Harrison</u> was followed in <u>Hickman v Maisey</u> in 1900. Hickman owned land on the Wiltshire downs which was crossed by a highway. He let the land to a racehorse trainer for training and racehorse trials. Maisey was the publisher of a racing magazine. He took to watching the horses training from the highway in order to judge their form and report on it in his magazine. The racehorse trainer objected, and asked Maisey to stop, but Maisey refused. On the day which gave rise to the court case, Maisey walked backwards and forwards on a portion of the highway about 15 yards in length, the subsoil of which belonged to Hickman. He did so for about an hour and a half, observing the horses through binoculars, and taking notes of the results of the horse trials. Hickman sued for damages for trespass, and for an injunction prohibiting such conduct in future.

At a trial before a jury, the judge, following <u>Harrison</u>, directed the jury to decide the case on the basis of whether or not what Maisey did was a reasonable and usual use of the highway. The jury found that it was not, and awarded Hickman the modest damages of one shilling. The judge granted Hickman an injunction prohibiting Maisey from setting foot on the highway while the horses were being trained. The Court of Appeal held that the judge's direction to the jury was correct, and dismissed Maisey's appeal.

The deference shown by the courts in each of these leading cases to the rights of the owners of the sub-soil suggested that the courts were likely to be unsympathetic to arguments based on a right of meeting or demonstration, as in due course proved to be the case.

For many years, only one English court decision held out some limited encouragement to demonstrators, by recognising, although only implicitly, a right of citizens to form a procession and march through the streets. This was the famous case of <u>Beatty v Gillbanks</u> in 1886. This leading case again involved the Temperance Movement, which had already been responsible in 1839 for the adoption of the term "demonstration" for marches through the street[42].

The Salvation Army was a new organisation in the 1880s, strongly committed to temperance. It was in the habit of organising processions through the streets in many towns, headed by a band, flags and banners. These processions aroused some hostility, encouraged by the brewing interests to which they represented a threat. In the seaside resort of Weston-super-Mare, this hostility took the form of a rival group, calling itself the "Skeleton Army", which assembled at the same time as the Salvation Army processions, and attempted to block the passage of the Salvation Army processions through the streets, causing (according to the facts found proved in court) *"shouting, uproar and noise, to the great terror, disturbance, annoyance and inconvenience of the peaceable inhabitants of the town, and to the endangering of the public peace".* The "Skeleton Army" also carried a banner, decorated with a skull and crossbones. On some occasions there was a general fight between the Skeleton Army and the Salvation Army.

On 23 March, 1882, the Salvation Army parade was accompanied by "a disorderly and riotous mob of over 2,000 persons", in the midst of which there was fighting and stone-throwing. The police were overpowered and unable to cope. The Salvation Army forced their way through several streets to a place called the Railway Parade, where a general fight occurred. William Beatty was the leader of the Salvation Army parade on this occasion, but there was no evidence that he or any member of the parade committed any act of violence. The police were eventually reinforced and the crowd dispersed.

The following day two magistrates issued a notice, which was posted prominently around the town, and which required all persons "to abstain from assembling to the disturbance of the public peace in the public streets".

Despite the notice, on 26 March, a Sunday, the Salvation Army again paraded under William Beatty's leadership. The head of the procession was again surrounded by a mob of about 100 people, which rapidly increased in size. After the procession had proceeded through several streets, it was stopped by the police, and a police sergeant asked Beatty if he had seen the notice. Beatty confirmed that he had. The sergeant then told Beatty that he must obey the notice, desist from leading the procession, and disperse at once. Beatty refused to comply, marched on, and 20 yards further on was arrested. He then shouted to the other marchers

---

42   See Chapter 6 .

to continue. William Mullins and Thomas Bowden took over direction of the procession and led it onward, whereupon they were both also arrested.

The magistrates convicted Beatty, Mullins and Bowden of breach of the peace. The three Salvation Army leaders appealed by case stated to the Divisional Court of Queen's Bench. The Divisional Court upheld their appeal, and ruled that the facts could not support any finding that they had committed a breach of the peace.

Before the Divisional Court the prosecution argued that as the course of action taken by the Salvation Army leaders had on several previous occasions produced riots and disturbances, and that as Beatty and his companions had known that such consequences would happen again when they again assembled that day, they were liable for the breaches of the peace which occurred, as these were a foreseeable consequence of their own acts. However Mr Justice Field held that this could not apply where the disturbances were caused by other people antagonistic to the appellants. He ruled that an unlawful organisation, the Skeleton Army, had assumed the right to prevent the appellants and others from lawfully assembling together, and that the convictions by the magistrates amounted to a finding that a man could be convicted for doing a lawful act if he knew that his lawful act might cause another person to commit an unlawful act, which could not be right.

Mr Justice Field's ruling gave legal protection to peaceful demonstrators at risk from attacks by violent counter-demonstrators. Over the years his ruling came under severe pressure in other cases, with the pendulum swinging sometimes towards cutting down the protection it gave, and at other times swinging back to his original view. However Beatty v Gillbanks remains good law today.

Beatty v Gillbanks contrasted with the position taken by the Irish High Court in the earlier case of Humphries v Connor (1864), which reflected Ireland's history of acute sectarian tension. A Protestant woman, Anne Humphries, had insisted on walking through the streets of a strongly Catholic area of Northern Ireland, wearing in her lapel, as a symbol of the Orange Order and the Protestant cause, an orange lily. She was approached by a policeman, who asked her to remove it. When she refused the policeman gently and without any force removed the lily from her lapel. He did so because he feared that if she continued to parade with the lily a riot would break out. Anne Humphries sued the policeman for assault. The Irish High Court dismissed her action, holding that the policeman's action was legally justified as a means of preventing a breach of the peace.

Beatty v Gillbanks and Humphries v Connor are difficult to reconcile. The decision in each case represents an important principle, on the one hand the protection of people going about lawful activities from violent attack, on the other the need to prevent the outbreak of riots and possible consequent deaths or injuries. A distinction can be drawn between the two, in that Mrs Humphries was acting deliberately provocatively, while the Salvation Army, although in fact provocative, probably did not intend to be. However the English courts have distinguished the cases not on the basis of the intention of the demonstrator, but on the basis of whether a reasonable person in the vicinity of the demonstrator would be provoked to violence by the demonstrator's actions. This is the basis for the decision in Wise v Dunning in 1902.

Mr Wise was a Protestant street preacher in Liverpool, who habitually held meetings in the street, at which he used gestures and language which were highly insulting to Liverpool's large Roman Catholic population. One epithet he used was "red-necks", which according to the case stated by the magistrates was *"intended to annoy and insult the Roman Catholics, and was well calculated to cause a breach of the peace, and a breach of the peace did take place, and a number of stones were thrown, and fights took place between those attending the meeting, and the police had to interfere and separate them."* The magistrates bound Wise over to keep the peace over the next twelve months, with two months' imprisonment in default if he did not do so. Wise challenged this bind-over in the Divisional Court, where he was represented by the famous barrister F.E. Smith.

F.E. Smith relied on Beatty v Gillbanks to argue that his client could not be guilty of a breach of the peace, as he had not himself committed such a breach or incited one. His opponent relied on the Irish cases involving Catholic/Protestant provocation. The court found that the bind-over was justified, because Wise's language and conduct was likely to cause a breach of the peace, since that was a natural consequence of using insulting language towards persons of a particular religion in the public streets. Wise v Dunning determined the approach of the English courts to cases involving use of religious or racial insults in the course of public meetings and demonstrations, which has endured for many years. This essentially sets the limit of free speech at the point where the speech becomes so provocative that it is deemed likely to cause a reasonable person to react with violence.

The United States courts have adopted a different approach on this important issue. The key American decision, the exact equivalent of Wise v Dunning, was Kunz v New York in 1950. Kunz was a Baptist Minister who had in 1946 applied for and obtained a permit to hold public worship meetings in the street, under a New York ordinance which made it unlawful to hold such meetings without first obtaining a permit from the city police commissioner. The same ordinance also made it unlawful to collect any assemblage of persons to ridicule or denounce any form of religious belief. The ordinance made no provision for revocation of permits. In November 1946, Kunz's permit was revoked after a hearing by the police commissioner. The revocation was based on evidence that he had ridiculed and denounced other religious beliefs at his meetings. Kunz publicly denounced the Catholic Church and called the Pope "the Anti-Christ". He called Jews "Christ-killers", and with reference to the burning of Jews by the Nazis stated, *"All the garbage that didn't believe in Christ should have been burned in the incinerators. It's a shame they all weren't."* He admitted that there was disorder when he spoke at his meetings, but said that when a police officer was present there was no trouble. He also stated that he had plans to continue speeches in the same vein.

A majority of the United States Supreme Court held that the withdrawal of Kunz's street worship meeting permit was illegal. Their reasoning was based on the fact that the ordinance under which the police commissioner acted gave him no guidance as to how to exercise his power. It held that it did not matter whether the exercise of the police power by the commissioner had been reasonable on one particular occasion. The way that the ordinance had been framed left it open to arbitrary interpretation by officials, and this was not permissible. The ordinance was therefore unconstitutional.

The United States Supreme Court does recognise that free speech can be restricted to prohibit utterance of what are termed "fighting words". These were defined in <u>Chaplinsky v New Hampshire</u> in 1942 as *"words … which by their very utterance inflict injury or tend to incite an immediate breach of the peace."* The rationale laid down in <u>Chaplinsky</u> for prohibiting such words is that they *"are no essential part of any exposition of ideas and are of such slight social value as a step to truth that any benefit that may be derived from them is clearly outweighed by the social interest in order and morality"*.

In a dissenting judgment in <u>Kunz</u>, Justice Jackson, recently returned from being the United States prosecutor at the Nuremburg trials of the leading Nazi war criminals, argued that some of Kunz's remarks, such as "Catholicism is the religion of the Devil" fell within the definition of fighting words and justified a ban on his speeches. This argument seems strong when Kunz's remarks are compared with the very much milder "fighting words" for which Chaplinsky, a Jehovah's Witness street preacher, had been arrested, which were merely to call the US marshal threatening to arrest him a "damned Fascist" and "a God-damned racketeer". However the long-term effect of the majority decision in <u>Kunz</u>, and of other similar Supreme Court decisions, has been a general acceptance in United States law that racial and religious insults are protected by the free speech right in the First Amendment. For this reason, college codes of behaviour which have outlawed use of racial insults by students have been repeatedly struck down by the US courts, as breaches of the First Amendment rights of those students who might want to utter such insults (see e.g. Doe v University of Michigan, 1989).

Since this is the US law relating to free speech and hate speech, it of course follows that, where the exercise of First Amendment rights takes the form of peaceably assembling in a demonstration, the demonstrators are constitutionally protected if they choose to utter racial or religious insults, whether aimed at the target of their demonstration or at bystanders.

This aspect of United States law led to the bizarre events associated with the Chicago suburb of Skokie, in 1977 and 1978.

In the 1970s about half of the population of Skokie was Jewish, and 10% were survivors of the Nazi Holocaust, probably the highest proportion of such survivors of any community in the world. These were people who, during World War Two, had personally undergone terrible Nazi persecution and seen most of their families killed by the Nazis. The National Socialist Party of America (NSPA), a neo-Nazi party, announced that it would hold a demonstration outside the community hall in Skokie, and wrote to the Skokie Park District authorities asking for a permit.

The NSPA wore uniforms modelled on Hitler's Brownshirts. Their leader, Frank Collin, was a vitriolic Jew-hater, whose own father had been a Jewish refugee from Hitler. Collin senior had been imprisoned in the Dachau concentration camp and on arrival in the USA had changed his name from Cohen to Collin. When Frank Collin announced his plan for the Skokie demonstration, he had told the media that he intended to frighten the Holocaust survivors, stating, *"I hope they're terrified. I hope they're shocked. Because we're coming to get them again. I don't care if someone's mother or father or brother died in the gas chambers. The unfortunate thing is not that there were so many Jews who did not survive but that there were so many Jewish survivors."* However Collin was careful to avoid attracting a "fighting words" ban to his demonstration. He announced that the demonstrators would simply parade with placards bearing the words "White free speech", "Free speech for the white man", and "Free speech for white Americans". He disclaimed any intention of uttering insulting words, and promised to "abide by all town ordinances".

There were at most 2,000 neo-Nazis in the whole of the United States at this time, and Collin had never been able to get more than 50 people to his demonstrations. He could easily be dismissed as a pathetic publicity seeker with a personality problem, but that was not how he appeared to some of Skokie's inhabitants, who remembered that Hitler had begun his career as a misfit on the fringes of society. The people of Skokie organised to stop Collin's march. Skokie Council passed two laws prohibiting a range of demonstrations, including demonstrations in military uniform, while it also obtained a court injunction against the proposed march. On 1 May, 1977, when Collin's neo-Nazis attempted to assemble in Skokie, the injunction was enforced by the police, who stopped their cars at the exit from the Chicago expressway.

At this point, in a move which generated much surprise and indignation, the main American civil liberties organisation, the American Civil Liberties Union (ACLU), went into battle on behalf of Collin's neo-Nazis and their right to hold a demonstration in Skokie. The ACLU assisted Collin with legal representation to challenge both the injunction banning his demonstration and Skokie's new demonstration laws. Collin's wish to exterminate all Jews did not prevent him from accepting representation from a Jewish lawyer working for the ACLU, David Goldenberger. As a result, David Goldenberger became a hate figure to many American Jews.

The ACLU defended its position on the grounds that free speech was absolutely sacred, being the underlying guarantee of all other freedoms, and that it should be maintained at all cost, even though this meant protecting the right to free speech of someone whose views were overwhelmingly regarded with revulsion. It was able to point to the intolerance against Communists and suspected Communists in recent American history (by people like Mayor Frank Hague of Jersey City, as described in Chapter 10 above), and also emphasised the argument, relied on by free speech advocates since John Milton first made the point in the seventeenth century, that in a free battle of ideas truth would always win.

These ideas had much support in American constitutional law. The Supreme Court had repeatedly declared all prior restraints on free speech unconstitutional. In 1921 in <u>Near v Minnesota</u> it had struck down the suppression by the state of Minnesota of a virulently anti-Catholic, anti-Semitic and anti-black newspaper. In <u>Rockwell v Morris,</u> in 1961, it had held that the then leader of the American Nazi party, George Lincoln Rockwell, had a legal right to speak in a New York park and could not be prohibited from doing so. Now that demonstrations were within First Amendment protection, following the civil rights decisions in <u>Edwards v South Carolina</u> and <u>Shuttlesworth v Birmingham</u>, the Collin demonstration at Skokie also appeared to be entitled to First Amendment protection.

The ACLU, on behalf of the neo-Nazis, achieved complete success in court against the lawyers retained by Skokie, on behalf of the Holocaust survivors. The Skokie demonstration laws were struck down as being in breach of the First Amendment, and the injunction against Collin's demonstration was found to be an illegal prior restraint on free speech. These decisions were upheld by the Supreme Court. Collin was free to go ahead with his demonstration in Skokie.

However the demonstration in Skokie did not happen. At a late stage, after winning in court, Collin decided to change the venue to a park in Chicago. His motivation seems to have been fear. It was clear that any demonstration would be met by a massive counter-demonstration by Jewish and anti-Nazi activists, who would be in a very aggressive and hostile mood. A demonstration by Collin and his group at St Louis, Missouri, on 11 March, 1978, was only possible with very heavy police protection against huge crowds of counter-demonstrators. The neo-Nazis were afraid not only of being injured, but also of being arrested and ending up in prison, where their white racist rhetoric meant that they were likely to be attacked by black inmates.

Two NSPA demonstrations eventually took place in Chicago, after attempts by the city of Chicago to get injunctions banning them failed. One was held in the Federal Plaza on 24 June, 1978, and the other in Marquette Park on 9 July, 1978. Both were met with huge counter-demonstrations, to which people came from as far away as Israel. About twenty neo-Nazis appeared on 24 June, protected by hundreds of police, and were met with a hail of missiles. After about ten minutes they abandoned their demonstration, and were helped by police to escape. About a dozen counter-demonstrators were arrested. On 9 July, about twenty-five neo-Nazis appeared but were unable to make themselves heard. Fighting broke out between the Nazis and counter-demonstrators, and 72 people were arrested.

The heat went out of the situation after these two demonstrations. Some months afterwards, Collin was charged with indecency with minors, and in 1980 he was sentenced to five years' imprisonment. On his emergence from prison he stated that he was "no longer into being a neo-Nazi", and instead became a devotee of a cult which believed that it had found the lost continent of Atlantis in the American state of Wisconsin. The ACLU underwent a sharp drop in membership and donations, although within a year it had bounced back to previous levels.

Many ACLU members still regard Skokie as a victory for free speech and human rights values. The ACLU position was summarised by a prominent member, Arieh Neier. *"Once the freedom of one group is abridged, that infringement will be cited to deny the rights of others. The people who most need the ACLU to defend the rights of the* [Ku Klux] *Klan are the blacks. The people who most need the ACLU to defend the rights of the Nazis are the Jews."*

Neier's view was given added credibility by the fact that he was Jewish and had lost three of his four grandparents in the Holocaust. However it overlooks a crucial distinction. The black civil rights marchers and their supporters in

197

the American South were marching in support of their basic right not to be discriminated against. The Ku Klux Klan, in contrast, existed for the purpose of maintaining that discrimination by violence, and for suppressing the rights of others. For this reason the two groups do not have the same legitimacy. Equating their rights ignores this. Moreover, most rights are not absolute, but subject to some reasonable limitations. Most people would agree that there must come a point at which strict observance of free speech must give way to considerations of public safety and public order, along the lines accepted by the Irish High Court in Humphries v Connor. The right of free speech does not include the right to shout "Fire!" in a crowded theatre when there is no fire. Nor, many would agree, should it include freedom to start a race riot through deliberately provocative behaviour. Finally, it is arguable that the American courts have taken a much too narrow view of the exception to the First Amendment protection prohibiting "fighting words". The courts have long accepted that "speech" includes symbolic speech such as waving a banner. It is on that basis that they have upheld the right of Americans to burn the American flag (Texas v Johnson, 1989; Eichman v United States, 1990). Waving a swastika at a concentration camp survivor might be regarded as both symbolic speech and symbolic fighting words, liable to provoke immediate violence. However none of these points appear to have been raised in the Skokie litigation or later American judgments, and at present the law in the USA remains that such conduct is legally protected.

In the United Kingdom, in contrast, the legal assumption ever since Wise v Dunning has been that certain kinds of insulting slogans are liable to lead to a breach of the peace, and may in appropriate circumstances be criminalised or prohibited, if they would provoke a violent reaction in a reasonable person. This subjective approach naturally leads to wide variations in outcome between cases, and has often led to the freedom to demonstrate being unjustifiably curtailed. It does however provide a degree of legal protection to those at risk of being the target of aggressive and provocative marches, such as the marches which Frank Collin was legally permitted to hold at Skokie.

The issue of provocative marches came to a head in the United Kingdom during the period between the two world wars. However before turning to how that issue was handled, it is worth examining more generally the way in which English and Scottish law dealt with demonstrations during the inter-war years.

The 1920s and 1930s saw numerous legal and extra legal restrictions on freedom of assembly in Britain, which did much to erode the traditional practice of holding street demonstrations. Unlike in the United States, where Hague v CIO in 1939 marked a recognition of the special constitutional protection to be given to the right of public meeting, no such right was recognised in the UK. The ability of groups which were not regarded by the authorities as "respectable" to organise meetings or marches was severely curtailed from 1920 onward. Rights which appeared to have been established by hard struggles, in the nineteenth century and earlier, seemed to wither away, with many people neither knowing nor caring that this was happening.

To understand the atmosphere relating to demonstrations in Britain in the 1920s, one has to remember the impact of the Bolshevik Revolution in Russia, which relied very heavily on street demonstrations in its early stages (as described in Chapter 8 above). Conservatives in Britain and Western Europe, like those in the USA, were horrified by the murder of the Tsar of Russia and his family, and terrified of violent overthrow of the established order. They were aware of the Communist commitment to world revolution, and were desperate to prevent Communists and Communist sympathisers from using traditional methods of political campaigning, such as marches and meetings, to gain support. At the same time, the truth about Communist oppression of human rights was only slowly becoming known, and numerous idealist people on the political Left were inclined to support Communist Russia or at least give it the benefit of the doubt. The prospect of substantial growth in Communist support in Britain therefore seemed real, particularly after Lenin himself stated in 1918 that Britain was ready for revolutionary socialism. This prospect created the same sort of panic in Britain that led to J. Edgar Hoover's arrests of Communist sympathisers in the USA (Chapter 10 above), and to the Rowlatt Act in British India (Chapter 11). This fear in turn reinforced the tendency of the police and other authorities in Britain, already evident in the nineteenth century with the Chartists, to give much less toleration to working class political movements than to other groups of demonstrators. Harsh treatment of Communist demonstrators in Britain was part of a wider reaction to Communism, which included the Zinoviev letter forgery in the *Daily Mail* in 1924[43], and the trial of leaders of the British Communist Party for sedition in 1925. This background explains, but does not justify, the authorities' treatment of Communist-linked marches and meetings.

Demonstrations which the authorities disapproved of were commonly prevented through use of local authority by-laws requiring prior consent of

---

[43]   The letter purported to be an instruction to the British Communist Party from Zinoviev to encourage disaffection in the British Armed Forces. Its timing, just before a general election, was designed to embarrass the Labour Government, which had just dropped a prosecution against a leading Communist for inciting disaffection in the armed forces.

magistrates for meetings. This was exactly the type of provision which had attracted such hostility when enacted on a national scale by Sidmouth's Gagging Act in 1817 (see Chapter 4) and which had given rise to the disputes at Boggart Hole Clough in the 1890s (Chapter 9).

In Scotland, Glasgow Green was a place where by-laws required prior approval of magistrates for meetings to take place. An unsuccessful attempt was made to challenge the legality of a conviction for breaching this provision in Aldred v Miller in 1925, on the grounds that the by-law was not being applied consistently or fairly. The Court of Justiciary in Edinburgh deplored the evidence before it of "sporadic enforcement" of the by-law, but nevertheless held that the local authority was legally free to enforce it as it saw fit. In Greenock, near Glasgow, similar by-laws were used in a blatantly selective way, to permit marches by the Boy Scouts, the Boys' Brigade, and the Salvation Army, but to prevent meetings by the Communist Party. A large meeting was held in Greenock by the Communist Party in defiance of this by-law in 1925, and was broken up by the police, with several of those involved being arrested.

On 18 October, 1920 widespread outrage was caused by a police attack on a march up Whitehall in London by 20,000 unemployed people, protesting at their lack of jobs. The march had been organised by the mayors of several London boroughs with high rates of unemployment, including George Lansbury, the mayor of Poplar, who was later leader of the Labour Party. It included a deputation which was received at 10 Downing Street by the Prime Minister, Lloyd George. The prior demonstration plan agreed with the police had been that while the deputation went to Downing Street (which is off Whitehall) the remainder of the demonstration would halt on the Embankment, and would not go into Whitehall. However many demonstrators, possibly unaware of the agreement between the organisers and the police, did go into Whitehall to wait peacefully for the outcome of the deputation. A police order then appears to have been given to clear Whitehall with maximum force. *The Daily Herald* described that episode as follows: *"the manner in which the police in a mad frenzy were ordered to charge up and down Whitehall running down and clubbing men, women and children is only on a par with the sort of outrage committed by the Black and Tans in Ireland."*

There appears to have been no subsequent legal challenge to this police action. However it led to the setting up in 1921 of a Communist-controlled organisation dedicated to fighting for the unemployed, and to using demonstrations as one of its main forms of political activity. This was the National Unemployed Workers' Movement (NUWM). The NUWM was an amalgam of seventy to eighty local committees of unemployed workers which had sprung up after the end of World

War One. It was the creation of Wal Hannington, an unemployed engineer and lifelong Communist, who had been blacklisted for his union work as a shop steward. Hannington was an effective public speaker, and recruited many members to the NUWM by addressing meetings in the street outside Labour Exchanges. The NUWM organised the first national hunger march on London, to protest about unemployment and low levels of unemployment assistance. This took place in autumn 1922, with an estimated crowd of 50,000 taking part by the time it reached London. This march passed off without major incident, despite prior press headlines including "Great Communist plot exposed", "Whitehall riot plan", and "Organised Plan to provoke a riot at dictation of Moscow".

The NUWM's support then gradually declined until the end of the 1920s, when it revived with the rise in unemployment associated with the Great Depression. In 1931, some 900 NUWM supporters assembled in Parliament Square as part of a much larger crowd watching the floodlighting of Parliament to mark its return from the summer recess. As the group were shouting slogans against the newly formed National Government, mounted and foot police moved in and drove them away from the rest of the crowd. There were protests in Parliament at the "wholly unnecessary and most provocative display of force" by the police, to which the Home Secretary unconvincingly responded by citing the Sessional Order for maintaining free access to Parliament while it was in session.

On 23 February, 1932, the NUWM called a "national day of struggle" against unemployment in general and the means test for unemployment benefit in particular. In several places running battles took place between police and demonstrators. During the year there were clashes between demonstrators and police in Merseyside, Manchester, Birmingham, Cardiff, Coventry, Nottingham, Oldham, Porthcawl, Stoke, Wigan, Preston, and Bolton, and in Belfast, where two demonstrators were shot dead by police.

In autumn 1932, the NUWM organised another hunger march on London, planned to start in Glasgow on 26 September, and to arrive in London on 26 October, one day before the State Opening of Parliament, when the marchers were to present a petition against the means test. On 27 October, 1932, as the culmination of the march, a mass meeting to protest about the means test was held in Hyde Park, attended by some 12,000 people. The meeting itself was peaceful, but a running battle developed between police and a procession moving towards the meeting along Edgware Road. Demonstrators accused the police of an unprovoked attack on them. The police claimed that they had first been attacked by individuals with iron bars.

On 1 November, 1932, the hunger marchers attempted to present to Parliament a petition, with one million signatures, against the unemployment benefit means test. The bundles with the petition were brought to Charing Cross Station, from where a deputation of 50 petitioners was to carry them to Parliament. However at Charing Cross Station the entire petition was simply confiscated by the police so that it was never delivered. The breach of the right of petition derived from Magna Carta appears to have been flagrant, but no legal challenge was ever mounted. This confiscation provoked attacks on the police by the demonstrators. A crowd of some 20,000 to 30,000 then assembled in Trafalgar Square, and was forcibly dispersed by mounted police. The organiser of the intended presentation of the petition, Sid Elias of the NUWM, was prosecuted and sentenced to two years' imprisonment for "attempting … to create public disturbance against the peace".

A further large NUWM hunger march to London in 1934 passed off peacefully. So did the very large and famous Jarrow Hunger March of 1936, from the economically devastated north-eastern shipbuilding town of Jarrow, which was not organised by the NUWM, and was deliberately non-party. On the Jarrow marchers' arrival in London, Ellen Wilkinson, MP for Jarrow, handed in a petition with 12,000 signatures to Parliament. The Jarrow march was thus able to proceed without police suppression or harassment, exercising the traditional right to petition Parliament. There is no obvious explanation for this difference in treatment between the Jarrow march and the NUWM marches apart from the fact that the Jarrow march organisers, who were mainstream Labour Party activists, were clearly not associated with the Communist Party. As a consequence the Jarrow march, unlike the NUWM marches, was not seen as representing any threat to established institutions.

Many NUWM meetings and demonstrations were suppressed by the authorities, using tactics which were not likely to generate a test case in the higher courts. The word of the police was invariably accepted in court when they claimed that the unemployed marchers had initiated violence against them. The records and memoirs left by the marchers, in contrast, repeatedly assert that they were subjected to unprovoked violent attacks by the police. As the police also sometimes used agents provocateurs disguised as violent demonstrators, to give them an excuse to suppress a demonstration, working out exactly how violence started on a particular occasion can be impossible. Because the police were invariably believed in court, magistrates considered that they were justified in binding over NUWM leaders to keep the peace. When Wal Hannington refused to be bound over, believing himself not to have committed any breach of the peace, he was imprisoned for a month.

On those rare occasions when police conduct did reach the higher courts, the courts invariably found for the police, in a manner which severely restricted the traditional right to hold a march or a meeting, so that it would have been better for the demonstrators if the case had never reached the higher court at all. Three of these restrictive decisions are considered below.

The first case arose in the aftermath of the 1932 NUWM march when the marchers' petition was confiscated. It concerned the extent to which a search warrant was needed to seize documents found in a building in which a person had been arrested, where those documents related, not to the person arrested, but to someone else. It had previously been thought that such a seizure was not possible without a search warrant. When the police arrested Sid Elias at the NUWM headquarters, they seized and retained many documents relating to the NUWM's organisation. This retention was later justified on the grounds that the documents also revealed incitement offences by Elias's co-organiser, Wal Hannington. On the strength of those documents, Hannington was prosecuted and sentenced to three months' imprisonment. Elias sued the police for seizure of the documents, but in Elias v Passmore (1934), the High Court held that seizure of documents without a search warrant in relation to a possible offence by another person was lawful.

The following year, in Thomas v Sawkins (1935), the High Court held, again contrary to previous understanding of the law, that the organiser of a public meeting held on private premises had no power to require a police officer present to leave, if the officer had reasonable cause to believe that an offence of any kind might be committed while the meeting was in progress. The case arose because the police insisted on attending a meeting being addressed, on private premises, by a Communist speaker, Alun Thomas, at Maesteg in South Wales, and refusing to leave when told that they were trespassers. Fred Thomas, organiser of the meeting, brought an action for trespass against one of the police constables. The police defended the action on the unconvincing basis that there was a risk of breach of the peace because several of the audience had convictions for violence. This assertion was however accepted both by the local magistrates and by the Lord Chief Justice of England, Lord Hewart, when the case reached the Divisional Court.

As well as interference with their demonstrations, the NUWM found itself subject to a secret ban ordered by the Metropolitan Police Commissioner, Lord Trenchard, who directed that *"no meetings are to be held by unemployed or other persons in close proximity to Labour Exchanges, irrespective of whether or not any actual obstruction is caused, on the ground that such meetings have been found liable to lead to breaches of the peace."*

This ban was deliberately aimed at the street meetings which had been the main method of recruitment of members by the NUWM. There appeared to be absolutely no legal basis for the ban, but when it was challenged in the High Court it was upheld, again by, Lord Hewart, in Duncan v Jones in 1936.

Duncan v Jones was a particularly unjust decision, as Mrs Duncan, the NUWM speaker, had deliberately chosen to hold her meeting in a cul-de-sac where there was no possibility of obstruction of the highway, had obstructed no-one and had not caused a breach of the peace or said anything liable to provoke a breach of the peace. However Lord Hewart was prepared to accept that the police might have had reasonable grounds for anticipating a breach of the peace inside the Labour Exchanges, simply on the basis that there had previously been disturbances inside other Labour Exchanges when other speakers spoke outside, and that the police were therefore entitled to stop Mrs Duncan from speaking, on the grounds of a potential risk of a breach of the peace. It was put to him that Mrs Duncan was no more responsible for a breach of the peace by someone else in these circumstances than the Salvation Army was responsible for breaches of the peace by the Skeleton Army in Beatty v Gillbanks. Lord Hewart's response was simply to dismiss Beatty v Gillbanks as "a somewhat unsatisfactory case".

The effect of Duncan v Jones was summarised at the time by the distinguished constitutional lawyer, Professor E.C.S. Wade, who wrote that: *"The net has closed entirely upon those who for lack of resources or for other reasons, desire to hold meetings in public places. The result is that there is now no assurance, unless police permission is secured in advance, that a meeting can be held anywhere in a public place... We venture to think that had the police sought a general power of this nature from the legislature, no House of Commons in the twentieth century would have been willing to grant it."*

Such was the concern among people on the moderate political Left at the manner in which the NUWM hunger marchers were being treated by the police, that the National Council for Civil Liberties was set up, a few days before the arrival of the 1934 NUWM hunger march in London, specifically to monitor police behaviour at the scene of the marches. Its founder members included the future Prime Minister Clement Attlee, and the writers Vera Brittain, A.P. Herbert and H.G. Wells. Their concerns were well-justified. The NCCL founders might have guessed, but could not then have known for sure, that Lord Trenchard, the Metropolitan Police Commissioner, was then campaigning within Whitehall for demonstrations to be banned entirely from central London, as being "an anachronism" in the modern age.

In 1932 demonstrations were started by the Radical Right as well as the Radical Left, with the foundation of Sir Oswald Mosley's British Union of Fascists (BUF). Mosley, a former Labour MP, hoped to make himself dictator of Britain using the methods of Mussolini and Hitler, including stirring up hatred against Jews. After Mosley visited Mussolini in Rome, and was presented by him with a black shirt, Mosley's followers began wearing the black shirts which gave them their name, and marching in army style military formation.

The attitude of the police to the Fascist Blackshirts was at first much more sympathetic than to the Communists, with police efforts made to protect Blackshirts from having their meetings broken up by their political opponents. This was partly because the Fascists, instead of calling for revolution, liked to pose as the friends of the police and guardians of order. The pattern of the early Fascist meetings was that they would invariably be targeted by hecklers, often Communist, who attended in quite large numbers. Fascists present in the audience would respond by attacking the hecklers with extreme violence. The violence was orchestrated by the organisers of the meetings, with the hecklers first being picked out, after they had spoken, by spotlights trained on them as they stood in the audience. This was done even to the most mild of hecklers, often attacking them with weapons such as knuckledusters. There was an obvious inspiration from Nazi tactics in Weimar Germany. Hundreds were injured in this way at Mosley's rally at Olympia in June 1934, and revulsion at the episode did much to reduce support for him. In March 1936, after Thomas v Sawkins had made it clear that the law permitted the police to enter a public meeting on private premises to prevent an anticipated offence, Mosley was allowed to proceed with a rally at the Albert Hall, but the police banned all other meetings within half a mile, and violently dispersed an anti-Fascist rally in Thurloe Place, Kensington, which was within the half mile radius, with many injured among the demonstrators. This lack of police even-handedness attracted increasing criticism from the public and politicians.

The high point of Mosley's movement, and the start of its downfall, was his attempt to hold a march through Jewish areas of the East End of London on 4 October, 1936. This generated such public outrage that many thousands of people turned out and effectively blocked the roads into the East End, determined to fight if necessary to prevent the Fascists from getting through. The police initially attempted to clear a way for the Fascists, but became involved in a series of running battles with anti-Fascist protesters. Some streets were cleared, but at Cable Street, in Wapping, the crowd held its ground, and withstood the maximum aggressive efforts of both mounted and foot police patrols. A lorry was commandeered by the crowd, and sticks and stones rained on the police. At this point the new

Metropolitan Police Commissioner who had succeed Lord Trenchard, Sir Philip Game, required Mosley and his supporters to disperse. This victory for the anti-Fascists in the "Battle of Cable Street" was an enormous psychological and political blow to Mosley's movement, and a triumph for his opponents.

Following the battle of Cable Street, there was a consensus in Parliament that a new law was required to regulate demonstrations. A Bill was introduced on 9 November, 1936, which was the day before the 1936 NUWM hunger march was due to reach London, and it was quickly enacted, with all-party support, as the Public Order Act 1936. Conservatives anxious to give the police more power to deal with far-Left demonstrators allied with Labour and Liberal MPs anxious to put a stop to Mosley's Blackshirts.

The Public Order Act 1936 banned marching in uniform, and possession of an offensive weapon at a public meeting. Military style drilling *"for the use or display of physical force in promoting any political object, or in such manner as to arouse reasonable apprehension that they are organised and trained or equipped for that purpose"*, was made a criminal offence. It gave the police a controversial power to ban all demonstrations in a particular town or district if they believed that a demonstration or demonstrations were likely to cause serious public disturbance in the area. It also created a new criminal offence of *"using threatening, abusive or insulting words or behaviour in a public place with intent to provoke a breach of the peace or whereby a breach of the peace was likely to be occasioned"*.

Mosley's British Union of Fascists was badly hit by the Public Order Act, and never recovered the momentum it had before Cable Street. The ban on marching in uniform in particular had a serious effect on it. Another attempt in 1937 to march into the Jewish East End was met by use of the police power to ban all processions in the area concerned for a period of six weeks, thus ending the problem of provocative Fascist marching in Jewish areas. After a humiliating performance in local elections in East London in 1937, the BUF split into rival factions, and ceased to be a significant political force.

The scholars, Gearty and Ewing have accurately summed up the effect of the Public Order Act 1936: *"Undeterred by any ideological commitment to free speech at any cost, British law was able to rise, however belatedly, to a challenge to its very basis, the full seriousness of which was to be made profoundly obvious in the years of war that were to follow. That the legislation should have been so slow in coming, and that the final acts that broke the executive's commitment to inaction should have been those of the Left rather than the Right, should not be allowed … to obscure the Act's overall effectiveness"*.

All of the provisions in the Public Order Act 1936 introduced to deal with Mosley remain part of English law today, having been re-enacted as part of the Public Order Act 1986, including the offence relating to threatening, insulting or abusive words likely to create a breach of the peace. English law has therefore been based, since 1936, on the earlier principle from Wise v Dunning, that abusive racial or religious epithets are liable to cause a breach of the peace, and are therefore not permitted.

These Public Order Act provisions have stood the test of time, in a country where demonstrations remain everyday events, because they have not in practice interfered much with the holding of peaceful demonstrations. Having said that, there is no doubt that the power to ban all meetings in a particular area has been occasionally been abused by the police, notably in 1977, when a new wave of Fascist marches and anti-Fascist counter-marches led the Metropolitan Police Commissioner to ban all demonstrations throughout Greater London for a period of two months. A challenge to that banning order in the European Court of Human Rights was rejected (Christians Against Racism and Fascism v United Kingdom (1984)).

In the last quarter of the twentieth century, English law moved, with extreme slowness, to recognise that reasonable use of the highway might, after all, include using it for a demonstration. The first move in this direction was Lord Denning's dissenting judgment in Hubbard v Pitt (1975).

Pitt and the other defendants in the case were a group of social workers who had organised a campaign on behalf of tenants in the Islington area of London. The object of the campaign was to protest against social problems caused by the redevelopment of property known as "gentrification", and to prevent further redevelopment. The campaign focussed on an estate agent, Prebble & Co, which was involved in the redevelopment, and involved assembling outside Prebble's offices on Saturday mornings, with placards and leaflets which stated that picketing would continue until the protesters' demands were complied with. The protesters did not obstruct the pavement, and left ample room for people to walk past them into the estate agent's offices.

The estate agents applied for an injunction to prohibit the protesters from "besetting" the premises. The protesters claimed that they were doing nothing unlawful but were simply exercising their right to protest. The judge held that the use of the highway for picketing was not a lawful use of the highway unless it was in furtherance of a trade dispute (for which special statutory provision was made), and granted the injunction. In doing so he relied on the traditional test for lawful use of the highway laid down in Harrison v Duke of Rutland. This decision was upheld by the majority of the Court of Appeal, on the different and narrower ground that it was not certain who would win the case at trial, and that in these circumstances an injunction until trial should be granted. because on balance granting it would do less damage to the protesters than not granting it would do to the estate agents.

Lord Denning disagreed. In his dissenting judgment, he said that there was no evidence of any breach of the peace or obstruction of the highway, and that the presence of half a dozen or so protesters on a Saturday morning was not an unreasonable use of the highway. He went on to state that the main grievance of the estate agents was the placards and the leaflets, and said:

> *"We have to consider the right to demonstrate and the right to protest on matters of public concern. These are rights which it is in the public interest that individuals should possess, and indeed that they should exercise without impediment so long as no wrongful act is done. It is often the only means by which grievances can be brought to the attention of those in authority – at any rate with such impact as to gain a remedy. Our history is full of warnings against suppression of these rights. Most notable was the demonstration at St Peter's Fields, Manchester, in 1819 in support of universal suffrage. The magistrates sought to stop it. Hundreds were killed and injured. Afterwards the Court of Common Council of London affirmed "the undoubted right of Englishmen to assemble together for the purpose of deliberating upon public grievances"… Such is the right of assembly. So also is the right to meet together, to go in procession, to demonstrate and to protest on matters of public concern. As long as it is all done peaceably and in good order without threats or incitement to violence or obstruction to traffic, it is not prohibited: see Beatty v Gillbanks. I stress the need for peace and good order, but so long as good order is maintained, the right to demonstrate must be preserved."*

Lord Denning concluded that it was time for the courts to recognise the freedom to protest on issues of public concern, and not to interfere by interlocutory injunction with the right to demonstrate and to protest, any more than they interfere with the right of free speech, provided that everything was done peaceably and in good order. In his view, everything was being done peaceably and in good order by the Islington protesters, and the injunction should have been refused.

Lord Denning's dissenting judgment was followed, and its principles at last became part of the law of the land, in <u>Hirst & Agu v Chief Constable of West Yorkshire</u> (1987), which concerned two animal rights supporters taking part in a demonstration outside two shops in Bradford selling fur coats. Some demonstrators were carrying banners and others were distributing leaflets. Hirst and Agu were arrested for conduct likely to cause a breach of the peace. Other protesters who gathered round to protest at these arrests were also arrested for the same offence and for obstruction of the highway. The arrested protesters defended the subsequent criminal charges on the grounds that there was no obstruction, and that the use of the highway was not an unreasonable one. They were convicted by the magistrates, and the conviction was upheld on appeal to the Crown Court, which again applied the traditional rule as to use of the highway, and held that distributing leaflets or holding a banner on the highway was not incidental to its lawful user, and so amounted to an obstruction. However the defendants applied successfully to the Divisional Court for judicial review of the Crown Court's decision. In upholding Hirst's and Agu's application, the court adopted Lord Denning's statements in <u>Hubbard v Pitt</u> about the importance of recognising the right to demonstrate and protest on matters of public concern, and held that the correct test was not the one used by the Crown Court, but simply whether the demonstrators' use of the highway was in all the circumstances reasonable, which it was in that case.

Development of the law on demonstrations in the United Kingdom has also been influenced by the creation of the European Convention on Human Rights. The United Kingdom was one of the original parties to the Convention when it was created in 1953. However it was only much later that the Convention began to have an effect in Britain. In 2002, the Convention was made directly part of English law by the Human Rights Act 1998, so that judges in the English courts, at every level, had to take account of its provisions in deciding cases. At that point it began to fulfil a similar role to the constitution in the United States, since the Human Rights Act required all laws and executive acts to conform to the provisions of the Convention.

Between 1966 and 2002, although the Convention was not directly part of English law, the United Kingdom recognised the right of individual petition under Article 25 of the Convention, under which someone who was dissatisfied with the decision of a United Kingdom court could petition the European Court of Human Rights in Strasbourg, on the grounds that the United Kingdom was in breach of its obligations under the Convention. This was the procedure used unsuccessfully by Christians against Racism and Fascism in relation to the

London-wide ban on demonstrations in 1977. It was also used in an unsuccessful attempt to overturn a temporary ban on meetings related to Northern Ireland in Trafalgar Square while negotiations about the future of Northern Ireland were in progress (Rai, Almond and "Negotiate Now" v United Kingdom (1995)). The Convention did not lead to any direct victories for demonstrators over the UK Government in the European Court during this period, but that did not mean that the Convention had no influence on the development of English law.

Article 11 of the European Convention on Human Rights states that: *"Everyone has the right to freedom of peaceful assembly and to freedom of association, including the right to form and join trade unions for the protection of his interests. No restrictions shall be placed on the exercise of these rights other than such as are prescribed by law and are necessary in a democratic society in the interests of national security or public safety, for the prevention of disorder or crime, for the protection of health or morals or for the protection of the rights and freedoms of others. This article shall not prevent the imposition of lawful restrictions on the exercise of these rights by members of the armed forces, of the police, or of the administration of the state."*

Article 11 is in similar to terms to Article 21 of the International Covenant on Civil and Political Rights (ICCPR), which itself sets out more fully the rights guaranteed by the United Nations Universal Declaration of Human Rights. Both Article 11 and Article 21 adopt the same approach of setting out the existence of the basic right of freedom of assembly, followed by the circumstances in which it can be lawful to restrict that right. The two key features of any permissible restriction are that it must be prescribed by law, which means that it must not be arbitrary or uncertain, and that it must be "necessary in a democratic society".

The Convention has been influential in a variety of ways. Britain extended its provisions to its colonies, and included Bills of Rights based on the Convention in the independence constitutions of most of those colonies, so that the provisions were very widely disseminated around the world. In addition, because of the right of individual petition, the decisions of the European Court of Human Rights sometimes had an effect on English domestic law, either directly through a case from the UK, or, more often, because cases involving other countries gave an indication of how the Court would regard a case on the same subject if it was the subject of a petition from the UK.

However, in relation to demonstrations, the most important effect of the European Convention and the ICCPR, is that they established both the idea of freedom of assembly as a universal right, and the idea that that right could be restricted for good reasons as defined in those two Conventions. Today, debate about freedom of assembly in most democratic countries (apart from the United

States, which pays little regard to international conventions in its domestic law), is usually framed in terms of whether there is a good reason for restricting a right. The fact that the right exists in principle is usually no longer an issue.

The performance of the enforcement mechanism provided under the Convention, which for many years consisted of a preliminary screening body, the European Commission on Human Rights as well as the European Court of Human Rights itself, has been very uneven. In the early years the Commission was afraid to upset the governments of important member countries, and thereby risk the whole Convention machinery being rejected by those countries. This led to very timid decisions like Christians Against Racism and Fascism. It is likely that today a decision to ban all demonstrations in London for a period of two months would be found by the court to be a breach of the Convention, but the Court's performance in relation to freedom of assembly has been so unpredictable that it is impossible to be sure.

On the positive side, the Court gave a ringing endorsement of everyone's right to take part in a demonstration in a case from the French overseas territory of Guadeloupe, Eselin v France (1991). Roland Ezelin, a lawyer, was barred from practice for bringing the Bar into disrepute by taking part in a demonstration against punishment of two persons, described only as "militants", for criminal damage. The crowd of demonstrators was chanting the name of one police officer "BEAUGENDRE – MAKO – UN JOU OU KE PAYE" ("Beaugendre – pimp- one day you will pay") and some participants defaced buildings with paint. There was no suggestion that Ezelin had done anything other than take part in the demonstration. Reversing the decision of the Guadeloupe courts, the European Court held that Ezelin was entitled as a citizen to take part in the demonstration, irrespective of the fact that he was a lawyer. The case has some similarities with the case of De Freitas v Permanent Secretary, Ministry of Agriculture (1999), where the United Kingdom Privy Council, dealing with an appeal from the Caribbean nation of St Kitts Nevis, held that a civil servant in the Ministry of Agriculture was entitled to exercise his constitutional freedom of assembly by taking part in an anti-government demonstration, even though he was a civil servant. These similarities are not accidental. The constitutional right to demonstrate in St Kitts was itself derived from the European Convention, which the UK extended to St Kitts while it was still a British colony, and then included as a Bill of Rights in St Kitts' independence constitution.

On the negative side, in Ziliberberg v Moldova (2004) the European Court, almost in passing and without any detailed analysis, held that it was legitimate for the authorities in Moldova to fine a demonstrator for having taken part in a demonstration which was not authorised by way of prior application for a permit. In an earlier case, Rassemblement Jurassien v Switzerland, it held that there was no breach of the European Convention in requiring prior authorisation for a demonstration. These two decisions ignore important questions about the nature of a right to hold a demonstration.

Usually, a right is something that a person is entitled to do, and not something that they need permission to do. The right of free speech is not a right to speak if some-one gives you permission. Why should the right to hold an assembly be different and be subject to a permission requirement? That was the basis of William Davis's argument that he was entitled to speak on Boston Common without a permit from the city authorities (Chapter 7).

It is true that the way the law has developed in the United States, most U.S. cities today do require a permit to be obtained for a march or meeting, and the exceptions are usually cities so small and remote that no-one has ever thought of holding a demonstration there. However United States law makes it clear that a permit to demonstrate cannot be unreasonably withheld. The most important cases involving the right to demonstrate in the United States – Hague v CIO, and Shuttlesworth v City of Birmingham – both involved situations where laws which required permits for demonstrations were not being applied fairly, but were instead being abused, so as to prevent legitimate demonstrations from taking place. Since Shuttlesworth the grant of permits for demonstrations in the USA has become a formality in most cases, and is not in practice a significant restriction on the right to demonstrate there.

The disadvantage of the American system with its requirement to obtain a prior permit, is that if the permit is refused, whether for good reasons or bad, the applicant has to apply to the courts for redress, or contemplate breaking the law. Litigation is expensive and slow. Where the issue on which people want to demonstrate results from a sudden outburst of popular feeling, the need to apply for a permit in order to be legal may result in criminalisation of a completely reasonable spontaneous protest. Again, this problem is minimised in the United States, because demonstration organisers are aware of the need to apply for permits, while most city officials are aware that permits must be considered quickly so that freedom of assembly is not infringed. However it is doubtful whether such a system could work as well in a country where it was not already well-established.

English law, in contrast to United States law, does not require prior permission to be obtained for demonstrations. Instead, Section 11 of the Public Order Act 1986 requires six days' written notice of most processions (but not static assemblies) to be given to the police. If the police wish to do so, they can impose conditions on the demonstration, which are subject to a legal appeal. From one point of view there is not much difference between a need to apply for a permit which is unlikely to be refused, and the need to give notice which may result in conditions being imposed. However one crucial difference is that a notice requirement means that unless the police take positive steps to impose conditions, the procession is free to take place. A second crucial difference is that a failure to notify in compliance with a notification requirement may be an offence by the demonstration organiser, but it does not make the demonstration unlawful. No crime is committed by people who take part in a demonstration where the advance notice requirement has not been complied with.

The Public Order Act provides that the required six days' advance notice may be abridged where it is not reasonably practical to give six days' notice. It thus makes provision for spontaneous demonstrations reacting to sudden events.

This English notification system is generally regarded as having worked effectively, without either placing an unreasonable burden on demonstration organisers or giving inadequate notice to the police to enable them to deal with problems such as traffic congestion. It has been exported to Hong Kong where it has also been in force for many years without serious problems.

The decisions of the European Court of Human Rights in Rassemblement Jurassien v Switzerland and Ziliberberg v Moldova completely disregard the issue of permits versus notification. There seems no obvious explanation why, when the United Kingdom is able to manage with notifications of moving demonstrations, without any need for organisers to apply for a permit, it has been held to be a necessary restriction on freedom of assembly in a democratic society, and so not a breach of the European Convention, for the authorities in Switzerland and Moldova to require a permit.

Despite such occasional poor judgments, the overall effect of the Convention has been to encourage English court decisions to give more recognition to the right to demonstrate. An example is <u>Director of Public Prosecutions v Jones</u> (1999).

That case arose because of a new law passed in 1994, which prohibited the holding of "trespassory assemblies". The law was mainly aimed at groups of protesters assembling on private land such as military bases, and was a government response to the semi-permanent protest camps established by disarmament campaigners outside the British nuclear missile bases at Greenham Common and Molesworth. However, on 1 June, 1995, the police used the new law to arrest people who had assembled on the roadside verge of a public road, the A344 trunk road, at the point where it runs past the perimeter fence of the ancient monument of Stonehenge. Those arrested were members or supporters of groups campaigning against the restriction of public access to Stonehenge, and some were bearing banners with the slogans "Never again", "Stonehenge Campaign 10 years of criminal injustice", and " Free Stonehenge". About an hour earlier, members of another group had attempted to enter the fenced off and closed site of Stonehenge, and had been stopped and escorted away, without anyone being arrested. As the courts in due course accepted, there was no reason to believe that Dr Jones's group was doing anything other than protesting at the location outside the fence where they were arrested, without any intention of scaling the fence. However Dr Jones and his companions were charged with "trespassory assembly" on the highway, on the basis that the highway was private property and that they had no right to assemble on it for any purpose other than passing and re-passing.

The arrest and charge on this basis relied directly on the reasoning of the Victorian courts in Harrison v Duke of Rutland and Hickman v Maisey. The magistrates convicted all the defendants, but the Crown Court upheld an appeal, on the grounds that the defendants were not doing anything other than reasonably using the highway. The prosecution then appealed by case stated to the Divisional Court, which restored the conviction, on the grounds that the new statutory provision had abrogated the applicable common-law about reasonable use of the highway. The case then proceeded as far as the House of Lords, which decided by a three to two majority that a public highway may be used for any reasonable purpose, provided that it does not amount to a public or private nuisance, or unreasonably obstruct the right of the public to pass and re-pass. Harrison v Duke of Rutland and Hickman v Maisey were effectively disapproved. In giving the leading judgment for the majority, Lord Irvine expressly referred to the need to comply with Article 11 of the European Convention, which was due shortly to become part of English law with the coming into force of the Human Rights Act 1998.

The year 1999 also saw the rule in Beatty v Gillbanks reapplied in Redmond-Bate v Director of Public Prosecutions, another case involving street preachers, on this occasion on the steps of Wakefield Cathedral in Yorkshire. Mrs Redmond-Bate and her fellow evangelists were haranguing passers-by about morality, God and the Bible, although the case report disappointingly does not record their exact words. The words caused great annoyance to passers-by, and led to chants of "lock them up", and gathering of a hostile crowd of about 100 people. Mrs Redmond-Bate was asked by the police to stop. When she refused, she was arrested, and charged with obstructing a police officer in the execution of his duty. She was convicted, and her appeal to the Crown Court was dismissed.

However the Divisional Court quashed the conviction, applying the rule in <u>Beatty v Gillbanks</u> that fear of violence by others could not be a reason for curtailing the defendant's rights of free speech and freedom of assembly. This ruling, like <u>Jones v DPP</u>, was based both on common law and on the European Convention.

In the years since the Convention became part of English law in 2002 there have been two important English decisions relating to the right to demonstration, which together highlight the uneven, unpredictable and unsatisfactory manner in which the courts deal with demonstration issues. The first appears to give enhanced protection to demonstrators. The second appears substantially to erode the right to demonstrate.

<u>Laporte v Chief Constable of Gloucestershire</u> (2006) concerned the extent to which the police had power to stop demonstrators travelling to their intended demonstration site, if they anticipated that a breach of the peace would occur when the demonstrators arrived there.

Ms Laporte was one of a group of 120 demonstrators travelling on a specially chartered coach from London, to take part in a demonstration against the Anglo-American invasion of Iraq, outside the American airforce base at Fairford in Gloucestershire. The demonstration was organised by a group called Gloucestershire Weapons Inspectors, who wore white overalls as a trade+mark uniform. The coach was open to anyone who wished to take part in the demonstration. Among those on board were eight members of a violent anarchist group called the Wombles (White Overalls Movement Building Effective Libertarian Struggles), who similarly wore white overalls. Ms Laporte was not connected with this group, and, like most people on the coach, was a person who intended simply to take part in the demonstration outside the base. There had previously been attempts to invade the base, from which American bombers flew operational sorties against Iraq. When the coach carrying Ms Laporte reached Lechlade, five miles from Fairford, it was stopped by police, who searched everyone on board, and identified members of the Wombles, as well as finding a small number of items which might have been intended for use in a violent confrontation, including crash helmets and home made polycarbonate shields, as well as face masks. Three of those on board, who were due to speak at the demonstration, were permitted to leave the coach and continue to Fairford. Then the police ordered the coach with all the other passengers on board to return to London under police escort. Passengers were not permitted to leave the coach until it returned to London. The coach was prevented from stopping at motorway service stations for passengers to relieve themselves, so that some passengers suffered acute discomfort and embarrassment.

The Chief Constable of Gloucestershire defended this decision on the grounds that, because of the record of the Wombles, a breach of the peace would have been imminent when the Womble members on board the coach arrived in Fairford, although it was not imminent when the coach was stopped at Lechlade; and that while it was possible that there were some peaceful demonstrators on the coach, it was not possible for the police to know which of the passengers were members of the Wombles intent on violent direct action.

The Divisional Court, the Court of Appeal and the House of Lords all agreed that forcing the coachload of passengers to return to London was unlawful, being an unlawful detention wholly disproportionate to any possible breach of the peace. The more difficult issue was whether the police were justified in preventing the coach from carrying on to travel the five miles from Lechlade to the start of the demonstration at Fairford.

The practice of police stopping coaches carrying people to events where public order trouble was expected had developed during the 1984 miners' strike, when there had been fierce conflict, including pitched battles, between working miners and striking miners picketing the working pits. The conflict had been particularly acute in Nottinghamshire, home of a breakaway working miners' union. In Moss v McLachlan (1985), the Chief Constable of Nottinghamshire had stopped a coachload of striking miners intending to picket at a working mine, five miles away from their destination, and refused to permit them to proceed any further. The legality of this action had been upheld by the courts. As a result the police had gone so far as to prevent striking Kent miners, who wished to travel to Nottinghamshire to picket, from going beyond the entrance to the Dartford Tunnel under the Thames near London. This extreme interference with the right to travel in one's own country had not been challenged in the courts. However, in Nottinghamshire in 1984, the police had been able to justify their actions because they were faced with a situation of severe tension between two violent hostile groups, which arguably justified extreme action to prevent a breach of the peace.

In Laporte, the House of Lords relied on Albert v Lavin (1982), a case concerning powers of arrest, which held that for an arrest for breach of the peace to be lawful, the breach of the peace must be imminent. Overturning Moss v McLachlan, the House of Lords held that, as the Chief Constable had admitted that there was no risk of any breach of the peace before the coach reached Fairford, it was unlawful for him to stop it proceeding to Fairford.

Laporte thus ended one unreasonable restriction on demonstrations. Very shortly afterwards, however, an equally pernicious restriction was upheld in Austin v Metropolitan Police Commissioner (2009). This was the recently developed police practice of "kettling" demonstrators by detaining them for long periods inside a police cordon. This detention was not deemed to be an arrest. There was no requirement that the persons so detained had committed any offence or were likely to do so. It was a form of crowd control, but one that did involve effectively depriving those detained within the cordon of their liberty, sometimes for a period of hours.

On May Day, 2001, an anti-capitalism demonstration took place in central London. The police claimed to have intelligence that within the crowd of demonstrators, along with many genuine demonstrators, were groups of people, not readily distinguishable from the other demonstrators, whose aim was at the first opportunity to loot shops in Oxford Street. This police evidence was in due course accepted by the court. There had been massive criminal damage associated with May Day parades in London in 1999 and 2000 and with May Day parades in other cities in previous years, notably in Seattle. To prevent this anticipated outbreak of looting, the police threw a cordon around most of the demonstration, resulting in many demonstrators being detained in the street for hours. Ms Austin was one of those detained. She claimed that she had been refused permission to cross the police cordon and as a result had been kept there for over six hours, despite the fact that she needed to depart to collect her infant daughter from a crèche. During the period of her detention it rained. There was no shelter and no food, water or toilet facilities for those detained, who included some people who were not demonstrators at all, but were merely caught up by chance in the police cordon, including a Mr Black who brought a claim jointly with Ms Austin. The House of Lords upheld the decision of the High Court that because of the risk of an outbreak of looting the detention of Ms Austin within the cordon was lawful.

The case is perhaps most notable for remarks by Lord Neuburger, generally regarded as a thoughtful and liberal minded judge, which strongly suggested that he had never taken part in a demonstration. Being held in a police "kettle", Lord Neuburger stated in his judgment, was comparable to travelling on the motorway and being held up for several hours because of an emergency on the motorway causing a severe traffic jam. This statement fails to recognise that people stuck in a car on the motorway are warm and dry, have a degree of privacy, and can if necessary use the hard shoulder for a call of nature. It also fails to recognise the chilling effect on exercise of the right to demonstrate if any would-be demonstrator is expected to realise that he may, depending on circumstances, be detained in the street for many hours to suit police operational requirements. The "kettling" tactic has since been adopted by the Hong Kong Police, which often follows the

London Metropolitan Police in public order matters, so as to "kettle" a whole demonstration overnight in the street.

However reading between the lines in the court judgments in <u>Austin</u>, the case is not as disastrous for the right to demonstrate as it at first appears. The police evidence was that their cordon was not rigidly maintained, and that some individuals who asked to be allowed to cross the cordon, and who did not appear to be intent on looting shops, were allowed to cross and disperse. This assertion was not disputed by the lawyers for Ms Austin, who simply maintained that she had personally been refused permission to cross the cordon by an officer whom she could not identify. The judgment of Mr Justice Tugendhat in the High Court conveys a sense of scepticism as to whether Ms Austin was truly refused permission to cross the cordon, and this scepticism is likely to have affected the attitude of the House of Lords. The Lords emphasised that the use of "kettling" cordons was for exceptional emergencies. It is not far fetched to expect another case in a few years in which the police will be found to have gone too far in their use of "kettling" and to have acted unlawfully.

Far more disturbing than the House of Lords judgment was what happened when <u>Austin</u> reached the European Court of Human Rights in <u>Austin v UK</u> (2012). The petition to the European Court was brought not on the grounds of interference with freedom of assembly (Article 11 of the Convention) but of interference with liberty (Article 5). The majority of the court stated that much deference had to be given to the decisions of the police in relation to policing demonstrations, that their decisions would usually be right, and in the unusual circumstances of the particular demonstration, with the threat of very substantial criminal damage, the police action was a justifiable restriction on liberty. The court's analysis is less careful than that of the House of Lords, and the assumption that the police will usually be right, given the history of police attitudes to demonstrators described in this chapter and elsewhere in this book, shows a complacent blindness comparable to Lord Hewart at his worst.

It is tempting to feel that a court of human rights which shows so little respect for liberty is scarcely worth keeping. However such a view would be premature. The European Court of Human Rights has been highly unpredictable in the past. Its initial timidity was replaced by a very active phase at the end of the twentieth century and the first years of the twenty-first century. It may now be moving back into a more supine phase, but it still provides an additional avenue of redress for those whose rights have been infringed or abused, which may sometimes help achieve justice. However its unwillingness over many years to find against the London Metropolitan Police is striking. The European Court of Human Rights is not at present of much assistance to people in Britain seeking to exercise a right to demonstrate, though it probably does help to curb government excesses against demonstrators in some other countries such as Turkey.

Within the space of this chapter it has only been possible to sketch out briefly the issues involving demonstrations and the law which have been most prominent over the last hundred years or so. The history of these cases shows that the courts are generally unsympathetic to the right to demonstrate, always inclined to believe the police where their evidence conflicts with that of the demonstrators, and highly conservative in their interpretation of applicable law. The occasional cases where the rights of demonstrators are vindicated maintain some degree of faith in the legal system, but are also memorable because of their rarity. In the great majority of cases, the ability of a demonstration to take place unhindered depends not on the decisions of the courts, but on the decisions of the police, which are rarely subject to effective legal challenges. Accordingly, the next chapter deals in more detail with the relationship between demonstrators and the police.

CHAPTER 14

DEMONSTRATIONS AND THE POLICE

Demonstrators and the police are usually antagonists. In many countries demonstrators are most likely to come into contact with riot police, who are trained simply to chase and beat people at a word of command, or sometimes even on sight. This is still a fair description of the French and Italian riot police. In Britain, because of its long tradition of peaceful demonstrations, there is often a good deal of co-operation between demonstration organisers and the police at a senior level. At many peaceful demonstrations there will be no riot police visible. The attitude of the ordinary uniformed police on duty at the demonstration will range from good-humoured and affable to bored and disengaged, depending on the demonstration, but will not usually be aggressively hostile. However the position is quite different in cases where the demonstration involves civil disobedience or any other situation where a senior police officer decides that the demonstration or part of it has become illegal. Notorious episodes of police brutality to demonstrators in British history include Bloody Sunday in 1887, the beating up of hunger marchers in Whitehall in 1920, and more recently, the massive police violence used to suppress unlawful picketing at Orgreave and elsewhere during the 1984 miners' strike. Violent police retaliation may occur if demonstrators cross a line by, for example, committing a criminal trespass, and if the stakes are high enough.

Having said this, the police relationship with demonstrations is not just one of antagonism. A peaceful demonstration can only take place if there is a mechanism for stopping other people who may want to attack the demonstrators. The police are that mechanism. Without them, the prospects of demonstrations degenerating into massive brawls between supporters and opponents of a cause, in the style of the Salvation Army and the Skeleton Army in Weston-super-Mare in 1883, are very high. Modern-style British police forces were first set up in the early nineteenth century, just as demonstrations were becoming popular, and helped create an environment where such clashes could usually be avoided or contained.

In 1990 and 1991, a researcher embedded with the Metropolitan Police, P.A.J. Waddington, studied police interaction with demonstrators, and described his findings in his book *Liberty and order, public order policing in a capital city*. Demonstrations and the police have both changed since them, with the advent of mobile phones and internet technology, but Waddington's account still gives one of the best descriptions of demonstrations, seen from the police point of view, in a place where demonstrations are traditional.

During the period Waddington was researching there were about 150 "notified demonstrations" in London. A notified demonstration is one where the organisers have complied with the requirement in the Public Order Act 1986 to notify the police in advance. Large demonstrations disrupt traffic, and it is in the interests of safety and general public convenience that the police are given this notice. At the time of Waddington's research there would have been few organisers of large demonstrations who would not have notified the police, a situation which has changed today with "flash mob" type demonstrations. His research therefore covered nearly all demonstrations in London over a one-year period.

Waddington identified the police strategy for dealing with demonstrators as an overwhelming concern to avoid trouble. "Trouble" meant hassle and pressure for the individual senior police officer responsible for policing a particular demonstration. Trouble may erupt if the policing of the demonstration is too heavy, so that there are complaints about unjustified arrests, unjustified police obstructiveness, or brutality by arresting officers. Trouble may also erupt if policing is too light, so that there are complaints about violence or damage to property by demonstrators. Trouble may arise if the policing of the demonstration is simply inept, so that there is excessive disruption to traffic. Trouble takes the form of complaints and protests to the head of the Metropolitan Police, the Commissioner, from members of the public, the media, pressure groups and Members of Parliament. These complaints result in a need for briefing and explanation to the Commissioner from the responsible Assistant Commissioner, Commander or Chief Superintendent. A demonstration that passes off peacefully, with no arrests and minimal complaints from anyone, generates no trouble for the responsible officer. If she/he is responsible for a big demonstration which passes off without problems, it may even help the officer's promotion. In contrast, a demonstration that requires a lot of arrests, and even more one where the policing receives a lot of adverse publicity, is bad for the responsible officer's career as well as his stress levels.

Because of these inevitable pressures, the Metropolitan Police style of demonstration policing is heavily geared towards smoothing out difficulties. The police are always anxious to meet demonstrators in advance and offer to "assist" them. The assistance may be genuine, since the police may know the location and possible routes of a planned demonstration better than the demonstration organisers, and be more familiar with the kinds of practical problems which may arise. However the assistance is not disinterested. The police ideal is a march which is completed without a single complaint from any member of the public. Such a march may or may not be the most effective lawful way for the demonstrators to get their message across to the public.

Under the Public Order Act 1986, the police have power to impose conditions on a demonstration if they have reasonable grounds to foresee "serious disorder or serious disruption of the life of the community". This is a high threshold to meet, with the strong likelihood of any conditions imposed being challenged in court. The police also have a more sweeping power to ban all demonstrations in a particular area for up to three months if they foresee serious public disorder. This is obviously a draconian measure requiring strong justification. As a result, police bans on demonstrations in London are uncommon, and imposition of formal conditions is also avoided by the police if possible. What the Metropolitan Police instead aim to do is keep the risk of trouble to a minimum by extensive pre-demonstration contacts with the organisers, subtly designed to change potentially difficult demonstrations into something less troublesome.

These contacts are entirely extra-legal. There is no requirement for a demonstration organiser to meet the police beforehand. However it would be a bold decision by an organiser of a large demonstration in central London not to do so. The problem for the organiser, particularly if inexperienced, is that once dialogue with the police begins, it is difficult to resist police pressure to do things "their way".

Waddington observed how organisers were repeatedly wrongfooted by subtle police tactics. Meetings took place at police premises, never at those of the organisers. Once there, the organisers would be isolated from their supporters. (His research was before the advent of mobile phones, but despite this revolutionary aid, the psychological pressure caused by isolation in a small room at police headquarters seems likely to persist). The police would be friendly and informal, deliberately using informality to build up a friendly relationship with the visitors. One senior officer who was an enthusiastic athlete always held meetings in his room, where everyone had to step and stumble over a variety of sporting equipment and clothes to get to their seats, an experience bound to break down barriers. In this atmosphere it was often easy for confident and experienced officers to persuade demonstration organisers that the best choice for the route of their demonstration was really the one that the police suggested, and not the one that the demonstrators themselves originally planned.

The police operated on a completely different level from the law. The power to ban or restrict demonstrations was rarely discussed, and experienced public order specialists in the police regarded it as "gauche and amateur" to discuss the law's requirements with demonstration organisers. Instead they went to great lengths to persuade, pressure or fool demonstrators into agreeing to conditions which could never have been obtained through formal legal methods. An example was the police insistence that there should not be a vehicle at the head of any demonstration. This is a strange requirement, as a colourful float with the demonstration leaders and a loudspeaker or a band can be an effective way for demonstrators to attract attention, and is used in many places. The reason the Metropolitan Police refuse to allow it is that it would interfere with their practice of having a police command and control vehicle travelling slightly in front of the demonstration, monitoring the activities of the demonstrators behind it. A demonstrators' vehicle might also be turned into a barricade and rallying point if the demonstration became violent. It is unlikely that a court would uphold a vehicle ban in relation to a group with a track record of peaceful demonstrations, which many groups have. However none of the demonstration organisers Waddington observed objected strongly to this police demand. In every case the police got their way, and weakened the potential impact of the demonstration, without attempting to invoke the law, and without the demonstrators realising what was happening.

Police co-option of demonstration organisers was often combined with police willingness to overlook minor infractions of the law to ensure that the event ran smoothly. Violent confrontation was an option of last resort and an indication of police failure. Of 82 demonstrations Waddington observed, 43 had no recorded arrests, and only nine involved the arrest of more than ten people. Those nine included two which undoubtedly degenerated into riots, the 1990 anti-poll tax riot, (339 arrests) and the second anti-poll tax march (105 arrests).

Waddington's research presents a picture of relatively civilised and liberal policing, with a genuine commitment to democratic values. He cites examples of intolerant members of the public complaining to the police about demonstrations and being told "everyone has a right to express their point of view". These included instances where the police defended the rights of demonstrators, such as gay rights activists, with whom the majority of the police concerned had no personal sympathy. The police also took pains to defend demonstrators whose demonstrations were generating hostility from other members of the public. An example was a march by anti-racism activists in Eltham, near an area traditionally used as a gathering place by the far-right National Front.

However the very feature which Waddington identifies as being at the root of the conciliatory police practices he describes, the wish of police officers to avoid in the job trouble, can easily lead to suppression of the right to demonstrate when the issues are different. Waddington himself found that in situations where complaints from the rich and powerful were foreseeable, the police went far beyond what the law allowed them to do. Their respect for the right to demonstrate stopped where ceremonial was involved, and in connection with certain key locations such as Buckingham Palace and the Houses of Parliament.

In relation to ceremonial, the police commitment was to ensure that the ceremony passed off without a hitch of any kind. While admirable in principle, this aim led to such extra-legal abuses as searching persons approaching the Cenotaph on the occasion of the One Minute Silence on Remembrance Day, and confiscating any whistles on people searched. Extra-legal police action effectively prevented all protests when the Queen attended the State Opening of Parliament.

The police concern with protecting the Houses of Parliament led to a clash in 1992 with the gay rights group *Outrage*, led by Peter Tatchell, which specialised in dramatic forms of protest designed to "out" secret homosexuals and focus attention on gay rights issues, such as the (then) different ages of consent for heterosexual and homosexual sex. *Outrage* announced an intention of holding a demonstration outside Parliament to mark the State Opening. When they approached the police, they were simply told that such a demonstration would not be tolerated, although there was at the time no legal basis for prohibiting it. The group pointed out that they had a track record of orderly demonstrations, and gave an assurance that they would not obstruct the entrance to Parliament, which would have been illegal. The police remained adamant that any demonstrator who went into any part of Parliament Square, a public square to which members of the public would have access even on the day of the State Opening, would be arrested. On the day, *Outrage* members who had entered the Square anonymously attempted to unfurl banners as the Royal Carriage passed, and were all arrested. However none were charged, perhaps not surprisingly as they had not broken any law. The fact that no attempt was made to prosecute them meant that the *Outrage* demonstration was prevented by means which were almost certainly illegal, but, as no charges were laid, there was no opportunity given to test the legality of police action in court.

The Metropolitan Police's abuse of power became much more serious when Chinese President Jiang Ze Min paid an official visit to London in 1999. This was the first state visit to Britain by a president of the People's Republic of China. As such it was important for the British government that it went smoothly. Unfortunately from the government's point of view, Jiang was a highly controversial person, and China a controversial country. As described in Chapter 19 below, Jiang had been personally implicated in the Tiananmen Square massacre, which he later described in an interview in English with American television as "much ado about nothing". China's occupation of Tibet also concerned many people in Britain who wanted to protest about it. Jiang himself was violently hostile to demonstrators of any kind, and took the view that it was the responsibility of the British government to protect him from any contact with them, including visual contact. On his way to Britain, Jiang visited Geneva, where some demonstrators did manage to get within sight and sound of him to make their point. Jiang's reaction was to tell the media that, as a result of what had happened, "Switzerland has lost a good friend".

The conduct of the Metropolitan Police on this occasion was illegal and dictatorial, and caused widespread outrage. The police seized Tibetan flags from protesters who were carrying them in the street and even went into a house on the route of Jiang's motorcade procession and "ordered" the householders to remove the Tibetan flag they were flying from a window. When Jiang travelled to meet the Queen, the police blocked his view of the large number of demonstrators lining the street by deliberately parking large numbers of police vans in front of the demonstrators. The same police tactic was used in Cambridge when Jiang went there.

This police behaviour was so uncharacteristically harsh and heavy-handed as to lead to allegations of political interference with the police by the government. It was soon revealed that there had been "planning meetings" between the Metropolitan Police and the Foreign and Commonwealth Office in relating to policing Jiang's visit. An internal inquiry set up by the police purported to exonerate them from wrongdoing. However when the police were sued by demonstrators, under the auspices of the Free Tibet Campaign, for infringing their rights of free speech and freedom of assembly, the action was settled out of court on terms favourable to the demonstrators. The police admitted publicly that they had broken the law, and apologised for doing so.

The episode showed that even in the city where demonstrations were invented two hundred years previously, the traditional freedom to demonstrate was quickly suppressed by unlawful means when demonstrations were likely to have a powerful impact that the British government did not want.

In many other countries demonstrators are routinely treated much worse. This includes other democracies. The culture of the French riot police is one of extreme and brutal violence towards demonstrators. In 1961, this combined with a culture of racist hatred, for France's resident Algerian community, to perpetrate a horror as bad as some of the more notorious horrors committed by dictatorships.

Passions in France were at boiling point in 1961 over Algeria's fight for independence. Right wing opinion enthusiastically supported the white Algerian settlers, the "colons", in their bitter fight against the Arab majority fighting to end French rule. In the summer of 1961, independence negotiations were taking place in Geneva between the French government and the Algerian independence movement, the FLN, but these talks repeatedly stalled.

Hundreds of thousands of Algerian Arabs lived in France, and an increasingly violent situation developed there, with the FLN's French representatives determined to maintain a powerful hold over the French Algerian population, and FLN assassinations of police and police killings of FLN activists.

On 17 October, 1961, the FLN called a peaceful demonstration in Paris. Those taking part were asked to dress well, and prior to joining the demonstration were searched for prohibited arms by demonstration stewards. Some 25,000 Algerians (according to police estimates, which tend to underplay numbers at demonstrations) attempted to assemble at the starting point of the demonstration on the Champs Elysee.

The French Interior Minister, Roger Frey, was determined to prevent a large demonstration by Algerians in Paris, and deployed 8,000 police to break it up. The demonstration was not illegal, and there was no suggestion that the demonstrators on the day did anything to justify its suppression. However as soon as the demonstrators assembled, they were subjected to a massive, unprovoked, murderous attack by armed police, in which at least two hundred demonstrators were killed. Many were hunted down and killed by the police in cold blood as they fled. At least 1,500 demonstrators were wounded. Many bodies of murdered demonstrators were thrown into the Seine, and were washed up downstream over the following weeks.

The Paris police also arrested journalists covering the demonstration, and prevented them from filing copy. French national television was prohibited from broadcasting anything about the demonstration. As a result most French people knew nothing about what had happened, and it took years before the truth gradually emerged.

Those events were half a century ago, and it seems unlikely that an atrocity on the same scale would be committed again. However it would still scarcely cause any surprise today if the French riot police shot one or two demonstrators dead.

Italian riot police are also notorious for violence against demonstrators. Throughout the 1950s there were demonstrations in Italy associated with labour disputes, and it was commonplace for these to end with one or two demonstrators shot dead. This has become less common, but not ceased entirely. In Genoa, in July 2001, when the Group of Eight leaders of industrialised nations was meeting there, thirty thousand demonstrators marched into a zone which had been designated as a "yellow zone" in which demonstrations would not be allowed. The police responded with extreme violence, shooting one demonstrator dead, and brutally clubbing many others, including the *Sunday Times* correspondent covering the demonstration, John Elliot, who was knocked down from behind by a police truncheon. Elliot was dragged along the ground while repeatedly kicked and clubbed with truncheons on his head, body and legs. He was then arrested for resisting arrest with violence. The police conducted a raid in the middle of the night on premises called the Social Forum, where many demonstrators were sleeping, and attacked and beat them as they slept, The police later tried to justify the raid by claiming that they were searching for "infiltrators". Following public outcry, after scenes of police brutality were shown on television around the world, several policemen were tried and convicted for a variety of offences arising from these police actions.

In that respect the right to demonstrate in Italy was at least vindicated by the prosecution and conviction of those who had abused the demonstrators. The same could not be said for the right to demonstrate in the American state of Ohio. In 1974, members of the Ohio National Guard were called out by the governor of Ohio to enter and police the campus of Kent State University, where there were protests against the Vietnam War. Without any legal authority, the National Guard purported to order a ban on demonstrations on the campus, and then fired without warning on student demonstrators, killing four and wounding nine others, one of whom was paralysed for life. So popular was the National Guard, and so unpopular were the students, that it was only with the greatest reluctance that charges were eventually brought against the guardsmen and their officers, all of whom were acquitted, despite overwhelming evidence that they had fired to kill without any justification at all.

These incidents, in three countries where freedom to demonstrate is both recognised by law and part of the tradition of the society, show how fragile that freedom is. It is under continual pressure from state convenience, and is likely to survive only so long as enough citizens are willing to involve themselves to make sure that it is not suppressed. Thomas Jefferson's famous remark that "the price of liberty is eternal vigilance", applies with particular force to the continued existence of the right to demonstrate. It is a right which can only exist in societies whose culture is committed to upholding it.

A further aspect of police involvement with demonstrators which has become topical recently in the UK is that of police use of agent provocateurs. This unsavoury practice is as old as demonstrations, and indeed much older. The incitement of unlawful violence among the Lancashire weavers and the Parliamentary reformers in the early nineteenth century by the police infiltrators Castle and Oliver has already been described in Chapters 3 and 4. There is every reason to suppose that similar infiltration of demonstrating movements has continued as a police practice ever since. The Chartist leader William Lovett stated in his autobiography, *My Life and Struggles*, that infiltration of police spies into the Chartist movement was as common as it had been into the Parliamentary Reform movement at the time of Oliver and Castle. Use of agents provocateurs came to light during the hunger marches of the 1930s, and has again come to light in recent years with the confessions and outing of several undercover police officers who spent years disguised as committed activists joining in the organisation of demonstrations. The most notable of these was Mark Kennedy, who appears to have become disillusioned with his role, and whose extensive public confession has focussed much attention on the issue.

Use of informers is an important part of police work, and common sense suggests that tip-offs from informers prevent many serious crimes. If a group is genuinely planning violent illegal activity, infiltration of an informer into that group may prevent such violence. The police therefore have a justification in principle for the use of infiltrators. The difficulty is with how this tends to work in practice.

It is a natural tendency of undercover infiltrators, whether regular police or unofficial informers, to adopt a militant stance in the organisation which they have infiltrated, as a means of disguising their true purpose in being there. In many cases, an ability to report that the organisation which they have infiltrated is engaged in illegal activities provides a justification for their being posted there, so that the infiltrator has a direct job-related incentive to exaggerate and encourage illegal activity within the infiltrated group. In the worst cases, which are not rare, both the infiltrator and the more senior police personnel who have sent the infiltrator into the group, actively wish to discredit the group and suppress its activities. They therefore deliberately encourage the group along the path of illegal activity, which will in due course lead to arrests, trials, prison sentences, and the group being disbanded or effectively disabled.

Mark Kennedy's career is an astonishing example of how much damage one police agent provocateur can do, over a long period, to many organisations, without ever being suspected. The number of organisations with which Kennedy was involved in many countries, also strongly suggests that, far from being a particularly British phenomenon, the use of infiltrators like him is accepted and regarded as normal by the police in most democratic countries. Some doubt still surrounds the full extent of Kennedy's activities, but there appears to be evidence suggesting that he carried out his activities as an agent provocateur in France, Germany, Italy, Denmark, Iceland, Ireland, Japan and the United States as well as the U.K. He appears to have infiltrated or associated himself with the "Wombles" (see passage on Laporte v Chief Constable of Gloucestershire in previous chapter); with the extreme environmental group Earthfirst; with the breakaway Greenpeace group associated with the ship *Sea Shepherd* (see next chapter); with protests against genetically modified crops, and with climate change camps protesting against power stations and global warming. He was often personally involved in illegal activities as part of his role as a militant activist, committing criminal trespass and using force to cross police cordons. During much of this career, which lasted from 2004 to 2012, he was known as Mark Stone to the activists he met. He had intimate relationships with more than one female activist. Kennedy's role finally came to light during the trial of a group of activists arrested for planning to break into Ratcliffe-on-Soar Power Station, in the east Midlands. His prominent role in plotting the break-in came under scrutiny, and led to his exposure as a policeman. Following this, several other police informers in environmental protest groups have been "outed" by activists, and either their real identities or their assumed identities published. One policeman, from the same Metropolitan Police Unit as Kennedy, the "Special Demonstration Squad", fathered a child with a woman activist with whom he entered into a serious relationship in his false identity as an animal rights activist, and then disappeared from her life and the child's when his mission was over.

Kennedy's story is paralleled by that of United States police agent provocateurs who infiltrated the anti-Vietnam War protest movement. The organisation Vietnam Veterans against the War was heavily infiltrated, and a trial of eight veterans for allegedly planning to use violence in a protest attack on the Republican National Convention in 1972 – the "Gainesville Eight" – collapsed when it was revealed that FBI agents had played a key role in the planning of the alleged violence.

That police infiltration was part of a massive programme of disinformation, disruption, slander, blackmail and infiltration initiated by the Director of the FBI, J. Edgar Hoover, against all groups which campaigned against the status quo in the United States, including campaigners against the Vietnam War. Hoover infiltrated thousands of agents into groups ranging from the Communist Party to the Civil Rights Movement, and into Students for a Democratic Society, the main student campaigning group against the Vietnam War. Among many other illegal activities, Hoover arranged for the FBI to spy on extra-marital liaisons by the civil rights leader Martin Luther King, and then to send an anonymous letter to King, threatening to publicise these liaisons unless King committed suicide.

The extent of Hoover's programme, which involved law-breaking on a massive scale by the FBI, only came to light as a result of a burglary by anti-war activists of an FBI office in Media, Pennsylvania, a suburb of Philadelphia, on 8 March, 1971. The burglars, who were never caught, were apparently operating on a tip-off from someone inside the FBI. They seized over 100 classified FBI documents, which included documents about COINTELPRO, the "Counter Intelligence Programme" in question. Following the burglary and the subsequent outcry, Hoover suspended the programme.

Noteworthy among the documents seized in the Media burglary was a directive to agents infiltrated into the anti-war movement, warning agents that they "should not become the person who carries the gun, throws the bomb, does the robbery, or by some specific violative overt act becomes a deeply involved participant ... there have been cases where security informants assault police."

The need for a directive of this kind is an indication of the kind of role which the infiltrated agents were playing in the groups they infiltrated. Veterans of the anti-Vietnam War protest movement today recall how some of the most militant protesters they knew during their involvement with the anti-war movement were in due course "outed" as FBI agents.

Another striking example of the sinister role of police agent provocateurs comes from the 2011 "Arab Spring" demonstrations in Egypt, and is described by Ahdaf Soueif, who took part in many of the demonstrations, in her book *Cairo, Memoir of a City transformed*. Soueif describes how the pro-democracy demonstrators who were blocking Tahrir Square – Cairo's central square – debated the question of a compromise agreement, under which the demonstrators would withdraw from the Square in response to substantial concessions made by the Egyptian government to their demands. Many more moderate demonstrators felt that they should withdraw, and that to insist on remaining would provoke the government into using massive force to crush the demonstrations. They were opposed by hardliners who argued that the only way forward was to refuse to clear the Square, and to make more demands on the government. The hardliners won the day and the demonstration carried on. The following day government soldiers attacked the demonstration in the Square, and some of the hard-line demonstrators, who the previous day had successfully argued against the proposed withdrawal by demonstrators from the square, re-appeared "wearing the vest and headgear of the military over their civvies and chatting comfortably with the soldiers".

This pervasive use of police infiltrators in demonstrations is a major difficulty for the Gandhian style civil disobedience demonstration, and a strong argument in favour of the strictly law abiding demonstration favoured by pioneers like Thomas Attwood. In a strictly law-abiding demonstration it is often possible for stewards to ensure that individual demonstrators do not embark on law-breaking activity. In a demonstration dedicated to civil disobedience, it is much harder, and often impossible, to control a provocateur who chooses to embark on a kind of law-breaking designed to discredit the aims of the demonstration, and to alienate the public from the cause for which the demonstration is being held.

It is true that even law-abiding demonstrations face problems from police provocateurs, but they are better able to prevent the provocateurs from discrediting them. Tom Brake, a Liberal Democrat MP, has described events at protests against the Group of 20 international heads of government meeting in London on 1 April 2009. This was another occasion when "kettling" was used by the police, and Brake and others were held behind a police cordon for over five hours *"When I was in the middle of the crowd, two people came over to me and said "There are people over there who we believe are policemen and who have been encouraging the crowd to throw things at the police".* When the crowd became suspicious of the men, and accused them of being police officers, the pair approached the police cordon and passed through, after showing some form of identification to the police in the line.

Despite these sinister activities, the positive role of the police in relation to many demonstrations should not be underestimated. As already explained, police sometimes assist peaceful demonstrations by preventing them from being attacked and by helping the organisers to keep their demonstration peaceful. They also provide enormous support with regard to traffic control and other practicalities. It is easy to imagine the difference between the amount of disruption caused by a large London demonstration which takes place with prior police co-operation in its organisation, and one which takes place with no such assistance. The police role is however heavily influenced by the nature of the demonstration and its organisers. As Waddington noticed in his research, where a demonstration organiser was trusted by the police as someone who would keep an agreement with them, the police were much more willing to give positive assistance in making the demonstration a success. It is noteworthy that in <u>Austin</u>, the police evidence, which was accepted by the court, was that they had been driven to the desperate measure of kettling, in part, because of a total breakdown in communication between the police and the demonstration organisers. According to the police, they had not been able to open a dialogue with any demonstration organiser or get any clear idea of the planned route or the aim of the anti-capitalism demonstration.

Of course the police can only be expected to assist a demonstration with a basically law-abiding approach to its activities. The police cannot be expected to stand by without intervening in the face of civil disobedience such as demonstrators blocking a busy road by lying down in it.

Given these unavoidable realities, the question then arises as to the most effective method for demonstrators to achieve their goals. Sometimes images of demonstrators struggling with police can be an effective publicity tool, for example as used by Gandhi in the attempt to enter the Dharasana salt factory, and the consequent attacks on demonstrators by police guarding the factory (Chapter 11). However in the great majority of situations, scenes of dignity, peacefulness and order are more impressive, and more likely to attract more supporters to a cause, than scenes of violent struggle. This is therefore a strong argument in favour of the law-abiding demonstration rather than the civil disobedience campaign.

A further argument, already referred to, in favour of the law-abiding approach, is the almost certain presence of police infiltrators in any demonstrating movement which has any propensity or potential towards illegal action. The use of police informants is difficult to oppose in principle if serious crime may be involved, as it has been, for example, with some animal rights protests. The temptation and pressure on informants, embedded in disguise within a group of protesters, to become agent provocateurs, in order to improve their credentials with the group, and so strengthen their cover, is almost irresistible. Attempts to organise peaceful and moderate campaigns of civil disobedience are therefore highly likely to be hijacked and turned into something much more offensive to the public, who are the intended audience of the campaign, by the actions of agent provocateurs in their midst.

Finally, it should always be remembered that not all police, even in democratic countries, are democratically-minded supporters of the rule of law. As an off-duty Metropolitan Police sergeant once said to this author in casual conversation, "Never forget that there is a contingent in every police force in the world which believes that Heinrich Himmler's approach to policing was the right one". Police officers who simply hate demonstrators, and long for a chance to beat them up, will naturally gravitate towards the riot squad, and be eager for an opportunity to use their batons. Civil disobedience campaigns give such police the opportunity they are waiting for. In the case of the Dharasana Salt Works, the stakes were so high that the resultant deaths and multiple injuries were arguably worth it, for the sake of the independence of India. In the nature of things, the stakes will only be so high in a small minority of demonstrations.

In recent years these issues have often arisen in the context of environment-related demonstrations and the growth of environment-related direct action protests. It is therefore time to consider environmental demonstrations in more detail.

CHAPTER 15

ENVIRONMENTAL DEMONSTRATIONS

The first recorded environmental demonstration in Britain was the "Grand Promenade" for the preservation of the Crystal Palace, described in Chapter 8.

The next major environmental demonstration, the Kinder Scout Mass Trespass of 1932, was more controversial, and could scarcely have been more different in style.

In the nineteenth century much moorland in northern England, which had previously been open land, was enclosed and used for grouse shooting. The closure of these large areas of land to the public became a political issue. From the late nineteenth century, rambling became an increasingly popular activity, particularly at weekends among those who worked in the northern industrial cities. The ramblers understandably resented many of the best areas of walking country being entirely closed to them, in order that they could be used for a tiny minority of people to shoot grouse for a few weeks of the year. An Access to the Countryside Bill, to permit public access to the moorlands, was introduced into Parliament by James Bryce M.P. in 1884, and similar Bills were introduced every year until 1914, but were always blocked by landed interests.

The issue was most sensitive in the Peak District of Derbyshire. The moorland tops of the Peak District are desolate and largely uninhabited, as the windswept boggy land does not lend itself to agriculture. However the Peak District lies in the centre of a triangle of very densely populated areas. Close by to the north west is Manchester. Equally close to the north east is Sheffield, and to the south are Nottingham and Derby. Every weekend in the 1920s and 1930s, thousands of walkers left these conurbations for the Derbyshire hills, to find themselves excluded from the most dramatic areas as trespassers. Kinder Scout, the huge moor which sprawls across the top of Derbyshire between Edale and Glossop, was the private grouse moor of the Duke of Devonshire. Today, Edale is the start of the Pennine Way, the long distance footpath which runs on public rights of way for over 200 miles to Scotland. Few of those who walk the Pennine Way know that a battle had to be fought to allow them to set foot on Kinder Scout at all.

In 1932 a group of young Lancashire ramblers, led by Benny Rothman, had the idea of a mass trespass to try to force open access to Kinder Scout. Although there is no record that they were inspired by Gandhi, it can scarcely be a coincidence that a few months earlier, in September 1931, Gandhi himself had made a highly publicised visit to Darwen, Lancashire, to explain his cause and justify his call for a boycott of Lancashire cotton goods.

Benny Rothman was a committed Communist, and the British Workers Sports Federation, through which he organised the Mass Trespass, was a Communist- influenced organisation. Larger, more established groups, such as the Ramblers Association, did not support a mass trespass, as they believed that it would damage relations with landowners, resulting in more land being closed to ramblers, and would fail to achieve its goal of opening up Kinder Scout. This did not deter Rothman and his associates, all in their teens or early twenties, who believed that the older people in the Ramblers Association simply did not want young people walking on the same moors as themselves.

The trespass went ahead on Sunday, 24 April, 1932, starting from the village of Hayfield. One third of the Derbyshire police, under the personal command of the Chief Constable, were on duty to attempt to stop it. For several days previously, the police had been trying unsuccessfully to find Rothman to serve an injunction on him, prohibiting him from setting foot on Kinder Scout. That morning they waited for him at Salford railway station, but Rothman avoided them by cycling to Hayfield from his home.

At Hayfield about 400 mass trespassers assembled. They deliberately moved off half an hour before the stated time, to forestall any attempt by the police to stop them from starting. At 1.30 pm they marched up a road leading on to the moor which was so narrow that it was not possible for the police to overtake them and block their path. After an address by Rothman, they sang *The Red Flag* and *The Internationale*, before climbing towards Kinder Scout. As they ascended, they were met by gamekeepers, employed by the Duke of Devonshire, whose job was to stop them. There were only about 20 or 30 gamekeepers, and being so heavily outnumbered most of them did not attempt to stop the marchers. However a scuffle developed, for unknown reasons, between one group of eight gamekeepers and a group of about 40 marchers. The gamekeepers were armed with sticks and the marchers were unarmed, but the marchers, because of their greater numbers, were able to seize some of the sticks and use them against their owners. One keeper, Beevor, was knocked unconscious. On the top of the moor the march linked up with another march from Sheffield and held a victory meeting, at which Rothman congratulated the marchers, but warned them that some of them might be fined for trespass.

Nothing further happened during the march, but, on return to Hayfield, Rothman and four others were arrested and charged with conspiracy to cause an unlawful assembly, while one marcher, Anderson, was charged with the assault on Beevor. The six were tried before a judge and jury at Derby Assizes. One was acquitted, and Anderson was only convicted of common assault. However he was sentenced to six months' imprisonment, and Rothman and the other three convicted conspirators were given four months.

There was much public outrage at these harsh sentences, which greatly strengthened the movement for open access to the moors. The Ramblers Association, which had opposed the trespass, was strongly opposed to the prison sentences. A ramblers' protest demonstration against the prison sentences was held at Winnat's Pass, near Castleton, on 26 June, 1932, and attracted an attendance of 10,000 people. Two more mass trespasses were held, one in the Derwent Valley, and one at Stanage Edge on 16 October, 1932. The Stanage Edge trespass was stopped by mounted police and police using Alsatian dogs, which was then a new police technique in England. Protests were held in other parts of England, including one attended by 1,000 people at Leith Hill in Surrey, and there were also rallies in Scotland and Wales. More Members of Parliament took up the cause of open access to the countryside, including Arthur Henderson, a former leader of the Labour Party.

As a result of the Mass Trespass, the Ramblers Association and other more traditional groups were given an additional weapon in their negotiations with landowners, since they were able to threaten that, if the landowner did not give access by way of a voluntary agreement with them, he might instead be faced with the disruption and trouble of a mass trespass by Rothman and his supporters. In 1939 the Access to Mountains Act gave some additional access, but criminalised trespass, and was opposed by ramblers. However, in 1949, the National Parks and Access to the Countryside Act required local authorities to secure further access to countryside by means of agreements, orders or purchase. In the Peak District this led to large areas of land being opened up to the public, including

Kinder Scout. It could reasonably be said that by starting the momentum which led eventually to this legislation, the Mass Trespass was instrumental in achieving in its objectives. The trespass on private land was illegal, so it is an example of successful civil disobedience.

Many years later, the Duke of Devonshire, grandson of the Duke whose gamekeepers fought with the mass trespassers in 1932, issued a public apology for his grandfather's actions in trying to keep the public off the moor.

In the years after World War Two, concern about the countryside shifted, from concern about access to concern about its intensifying destruction, and demonstrations opposing motorways, airports and loss of beautiful scenery became common in the industrialised world.

For many years demonstrations which pitted people who cared about the environment against the forces favouring economic development had a poor success rate. In some countries concern about the environment became so intense that, following the failure of peaceful demonstrations, they were replaced by violent confrontations, as with the resistance to the building of Tokyo's third airport. In this respect, they followed the classic pattern, so clearly observable with women's suffrage demonstrations in Britain, where peaceful demonstrations were ignored by the authorities and were then replaced by violence. However, peaceful or violent, environmentalist demonstrations seemed to be fighting a losing battle.

Equally unsuccessful, in the 1950s and 1960s, were demonstrations against nuclear weapons. Such demonstrations were then more focussed on the threat nuclear weapons posed to human life than on the impact of nuclear technology on the environment.

In 1957, American Quaker pacifists, organised by A.J. Muste in the Committee for Nonviolent Action (CNA), illegally entered the US nuclear weapon test site in the Nevada desert to stage a protest, and were arrested and jailed. In 1958, the Committee for Nuclear Disarmament (CND) was set up in London, at a meeting convened by the philosopher Bertrand Russell. Every year since then, CND has held a march against nuclear weapons from London to the Atomic Weapons Research Establishment at Aldermaston in Berkshire. The Aldermaston March soon became an established part of the British political calendar, invariably peaceful, orderly and respectable, but failing to generate much additional support for its cause.

On 2 May, 1958, the first deliberate attempt was made to sail a boat into an exclusion zone for an atmospheric nuclear test. Organised by the Quakers, the 32-foot ketch *Golden Rule*, sailed by former US Navy captain Albert Bigelow, entered the exclusion zone around Bikini Atoll in the Marshall Islands, where a test was due to take place. The US coastguard intercepted the yacht, and Bigelow was charged with criminal conspiracy and sentenced to six months' imprisonment. There were demonstrations in his support in seven American cities and in London and Montreal, but the incident did not receive enough media publicity to generate more widespread support.

In 1960, Muste and the CNA led a march from Boston, Massachusetts to the Electric Boat Company Yard in Groton, Connecticut, where a nuclear submarine was being built. After an attempt to enter the dockyard was stopped, a small group of demonstrators paddled in front of submarines as they were being launched, swam to the vessels, and boarded them by climbing up ropes. They were arrested, and received 19-month jail sentences.

One of those who took part in the Groton march was Irving Stowe, who, by the early 1970s, was living in Vancouver, Canada, where he played a key role in setting up a new kind of campaigning environmental organisation, Greenpeace.

As its name suggests, Greenpeace brought together environmental and anti-war concerns. Vancouver was home at that time to many Americans opposed to the Vietnam War, and also to many people who had moved there because of its attractive natural surroundings. It was therefore a natural place for a group such as Greenpeace to emerge.

The first Greenpeace campaign was against American nuclear testing in the Aleutian Islands. This long chain of islands, which are part of the U.S.A, runs from the coast of Alaska far south-west into the Pacific Ocean. The islands have active volcanoes and are earthquake prone. In 1964, following an earthquake in the Aleutians, a tsunami destroyed part of Alaska's capital, Anchorage. Many of the Aleutian Islands are known for their wildlife, particularly seabirds, marine mammals and sea otters. Greenpeace came into being to oppose an underground nuclear test scheduled for the Aleutian island of Amchitka in 1969. Its first large demonstration was a 6,000-strong protest, which closed the main US-Canada border crossing between Vancouver and Seattle, at the Peace Arch monument. This was the first time since the War of 1812 that the border had been closed at that point. The Attorney-General of British Columbia warned that serious charges could be laid against the people who blocked the road, but the Canadian police made no attempt to intervene.

Despite the protest, the test went ahead the following morning, 4,000 feet below the surface of Amchitka. Reports of the destruction were alarming. The ground above the explosion rose 14 feet into the air. Two lakes were partly drained through fissures. Chunks of granite the size of houses broke off from the cliffs and fell into the sea. Seabirds which had been sunning themselves on the rocks were found with their backs broken and their legs driven through their bodies by the force of the explosion. Dead fish, otters and seals were found floating in the sea. The explosion registered as the equivalent of a 6.9 scale earthquake shockwave. These effects were well-publicised, and when the US announced plans for another explosion five times as strong as the first, opposition in British Columbia and elsewhere intensified. The Vancouver activists decided to sail a boat, to be named the *Greenpeace*, into the test area.

The Greenpeace plan was courting danger. The Aleutian archipelago is known as "the cradle of storms". The worst time of the year for storms was October and November, when the test was likely to take place. Fifty knot gales and 40 foot cresting waves were common. Gusts of wind from the Arctic, known as williwaws, reaching speeds of 100 knots, faster than a hurricane, were also a local feature. If the boat survived the storms, there were the dangers of being arrested or irradiated.

Greenpeace chartered a 66-foot halibut fishing boat, the Phyllis Cormack, named after the wife of the skipper, John Cormack, who was to be captain for the voyage. Cormack was a traditional ocean fisherman, willing to enter into the arrangement because he was short of money. He was a skilled and experienced seaman, which was essential to the success of the enterprise, as the Greenpeace activists lacked nautical skills. Their group included hippie mystics, who relied on the Chinese book of I Ching to give them guidance on difficult decisions, and many of the group were prone to sea sickness. Fortunately they also included two engineers and a doctor. Back on shore, Greenpeace did have activists with excellent media skills. The failure of the *Golden Rule* activists to publicise their cause sufficiently would not be repeated.

The intended voyage suffered bureaucratic harassment by the Canadian authorities. The Ministry of Fisheries informed Cormack that his vessel's insurance was being withdrawn as he planned to use it for a non-commercial purpose. When it appeared that the Minister of Fisheries, Jack Davies, was behind this decision, Greenpeace attacked him in the media for being a tool of the Americans acting against Canadian interests, a line which normally played well with the Canadian public. Under this pressure, Davies gave way, and the insurance was restored.

On 15 September, 1971, the Phyllis Cormack, also known as the Greenpeace, with a distinctive Greenpeace emblem on its sail, left Vancouver, and sailed up the Georgia Strait between Vancouver Island and mainland Canada. After a warm welcome at a native Canadian village, the boat headed out into the open sea. As they did so, news of their protest was reported in the Canadian media. An outbreak of sympathy protests followed across Canada. In Toronto, 100,000 students boycotted class. Protest telegrams were sent from all over Canada to

Canadian Prime Minister Pierre Trudeau and US President Richard Nixon. Even the very conservative Prime Minister of British Columbia, W.A.C. Bennett, expressed concern about the blast.

The Phyllis Cormack was about a day's journey short of the Aleutians when the planned test was postponed because of a legal challenge in the US Supreme Court. This placed the crew in a dilemma, as they had limited supplies of food and fuel. However, if they put into a port, they risked arrest or obstruction from the port authorities. They decided to risk this, and applied for permission to land at Dutch Harbour in the Aleutians. This was refused, and instead the boat was given permission to anchor off the remote island of Akutan. After some members of the crew went ashore, the US Customs arrived in the coastguard cutter *Confidence*, and told them that they had committed an offence by failing to clear customs within 48 hours of setting foot on land, in breach of the Tariff Act of 1930. The penalty was a US$1000 fine. The Phyllis Cormack was required to make radio contact with customs in Anchorage within 24 hours, and the penalty for failing to comply was a $5,000 fine and confiscation of the vessel.

Before the coastguard cutter left, one of the crewmen handed the Greenpeace crew a crumpled piece of paper, which read: *"Due to the situation we are in we the crew of the Confidence feel that what you are doing is for the good of all mankind if our hands weren't tied by these military bonds we would be in the position you are in if it were at all possible"*. Greenpeace obtained the crew's agreement to mention the note on the radio, so their action was soon known to the world. All of the 18 members who signed were disciplined, with the non-commissioned officers being reduced in rank.

The US Customs insisted that the Phyllis Cormack report to the nearest US Customs post at Sand Point, a day back, further away from Amchitka. At Sand Point, the Greenpeace team decided by a narrow vote on 13 October that they should return to Canada. The reasoning was that they had achieved as much as they were likely to achieve in terms of publicity, and that it was unwise to stay there waiting for a test for which no date had been announced. Their decision was vindicated two days later when the Canadian Parliament passed a unanimous motion against the bomb test.

Unknown to most of the Greenpeace crew, the Greenpeace organisation, during their absence at sea, had raised funds to charter a second vessel, a former Navy minesweeper called the *Edgewater Fortune*, renamed *Greenpeace II*. The two vessels met off the Canadian coast, as *Greenpeace II* left to continue the mission started by *Greenpeace 1*.

Public pressure against the tests continued to mount, and, on 2 November, 1971, British Columbian unions representing over 150,000 workers went on a half hour strike in protest at the tests. *The Washington Post* carried a letter signed by former Canadian Prime Minister Lester Pearson and other prominent Canadians, calling on the US to stop the tests. *The New York Times* declared that the thermonuclear test represented "the folly of a species that burns and poisons and blows up its own house". President Nixon nevertheless set 4 November as the new date for the test. On that day a petition against the test signed by 177,000 people was handed in at the White House, and protesters closed US-Canada border crossings and stormed US Consulates across Canada.

Greenpeace II encountered much worse weather than *Greenpeace I*, and was still 700 miles from Amchitka when, despite all the protests, the nuclear bomb was detonated under the island. However the Greenpeace boats had not failed in their mission. In February 1972, the US Atomic Energy Commission announced that the Amchitka test site would be abandoned "for political and other reasons".

After the Amchitka voyages, protest by boat was an idea whose time had come. Greenpeace had captured the public imagination, and funds and volunteers came into the organisation in sufficient numbers for it to embark at once on a similar protest campaign against the French nuclear tests at Moruroa (sometimes written as Mururoa) Atoll in the South Pacific.

The basic design of the Moruroa campaign was similar to that against the Amchitka tests, with one boat leaving from New Zealand, and one from Peru. The main differences were the vast distances of the South Pacific, and the ruthlessness and violence of the French government in responding to the protesters.

The boat from Peru was prevented from leaving through French pressure on the Peruvian government. France also put pressure on the New Zealand government, which placed numerous obstacles in the way of the Greenpeace team, but the New Zealand boat, the Vega, a 38-foot ketch, eventually managed to depart, skippered by a Canadian, David McTaggart, with a crew of five. McTaggart, who later became the president of Greenpeace, showed brilliant sailing skills in twice navigating the Vega to Moruroa by routes which avoided French vessels, which were intent on stopping him before he arrived at the exclusion zone.

On the first occasion, in 1972, after the Vega arrived at the exclusion zone, it was rammed and severely damaged by a French minesweeper, the *Paimpolaise*. McTaggart managed to sail the battered and leaking yacht as far as Rarotonga in the Cook Islands, where it had to be left for extensive repairs. The French authorities claimed that the ramming was an accident, but McTaggart had photographs which proved otherwise. He did not immediately release these, but used them later to win a case against the French government in the French courts.

The following year, McTaggart and the other members of the crew, including two women, were severely beaten by French sailors with clubs who boarded the yacht when it entered the test zone, and seized both yacht and crew. McTaggart nearly lost his sight in one eye after being struck with a club. Film taken by the Vega crew of the rammings and beatings was destroyed by the sailors. However one woman, Anne-Marie Horne, hid a film, first on the boat and then in her vagina, before she was taken away into custody. She later managed to pass the film to other Greenpeace supporters. The French government attempted to explain away McTaggart's eye injury by announcing that McTaggart had hurt his eye falling over a cleat while attempting "to throw our sailors back into the sea" and that "our men boarded his vessel unarmed and without striking a single blow". Greenpeace then revealed the truth to the world's media by showing Horne's film, although it was not seen on the French media, as it was excluded by government censorship. The political damage to France was great, but not enough to stop the tests permanently.

The Greenpeace leadership were consciously inspired by Gandhi's civil disobedience philosophy, and by the American civil rights movement. According to Rex Weyler, an early Greenpeace activist who later wrote a history of Greenpeace, other influences included the Quakers, with their tradition of "bearing witness"; Marshall Macluhan, with his teachings about the importance of the medium to convey the message; American Catholic workers' rights advocate Dorothy Day; and Saul Alinsky who had organised slum dwellers in Chicago to obtain improvements in their own conditions.

Early on in the movement a philosophical split developed between those who were firmly committed to non-violence, and those who felt that the moral strength of the cause they stood for, and the ineffectiveness of much non-violent protest, justified some use of violence. This split became evident in the course of Greenpeace's next two campaigns, both of which were immensely popular with the public and ultimately very successful. These were *Save the Whale*, and the campaign to end the clubbing to death of baby seals for their fur in the annual seal hunt in Newfoundland and Labrador.

The *Save the Whale* campaign involved finding whaling ships at sea, and then placing Greenpeace crew members, in motorised inflatable dinghies called Zodiacs, between the whales and the harpoon guns of the whaling vessels. This was slow work, as finding the whaling ships in the middle of the Pacific Ocean was not easy. At first Greenpeace searched for the whaling ships by listening for their radio communications. However the whaling ships could often detect the Greenpeace ship as soon as it could detect them, and, being faster, could take avoiding action. When Greenpeace did find the whalers, it was difficult for its photographers to hold a camera in a bouncing dinghy to record the carnage of the whale killing and the Greenpeace intervention, although they eventually became skilled at doing this.

Greenpeace repeatedly tracked down the Soviet factory ship *Dalniy Vostok*. It was helped in doing so by a secret source in Washington DC, who provided American intelligence information. However the source never provided information about Japanese whaling ships, which were more numerous, and so a more important target from Greenpeace's point of view. The reason appears to have been related to Cold War attitudes. Anything which might embarrass the Soviets was tacitly welcomed by the US government, while embarrassment to the US's staunch ally, Japan, was not welcome.

As a result of the falling numbers of whales, and world pressure generated by Greenpeace, the Soviet Union decided to give up whaling. Iceland followed suit after similar Greenpeace tactics against Icelandic whalers. However these difficult and time-consuming missions were not enough for some Greenpeace activists, who broke away from Greenpeace to form their own direct action organisation. The most prominent of these activists was a Canadian, Paul Watson, who had sailed to Amchitka on the *Edgewater Fortune*.

Watson achieved worldwide prominence during the Greenpeace campaign against the killing of baby harp seals. Most of that campaign involved going out on to the ice floes where the seal hunt took place, photographing the hunters killing the baby seals with their special killing picks and skinning them in front of their mothers, arguing with the hunters if the opportunity arose, and occasionally trying to stand between the hunters and their victims with limited success. These confrontations were usually attended by Canadian fisheries protection officers, anxious for the hunt to continue, and eager to pounce on any infraction of Canada's seal protection laws, which prohibited anyone except a licensed hunter from touching a seal. Greenpeace's opposition to the seal hunt was unpopular in Newfoundland and Labrador, so Greenpeace generally made efforts to keep within the law, in order to reduce the authorities' opportunities for making difficulties for them. Most Greenpeace activists therefore did not touch the baby seals even in an attempt to save their lives. Paul Watson however, picked up a baby seal and carried it to safety. This action, for which he was charged and fined, provided Greenpeace with wonderful film footage for its campaign.

Watson's action in touching the seal was less controversial than his action against the whalers. Having left Greenpeace, he raised money to buy his own vessel, the *Sea Shepherd*, intended specifically to hunt down whaling ships. The ships he hunted were illegal "pirate whalers" which did not obey the rules laid down by the International Whaling Commission (IWC). Watson filled the bow of the *Sea Shepherd* with three tons of concrete, and in July 1979, under his command, the *Sea Shepherd* deliberately rammed the illegal Spanish whaler *Sierra*, off the Azores, staving in 45 feet of the whaler's hull, and putting it out of business. The *Sea Shepherd* was caught by a Portuguese destroyer and taken into harbour in the Azores. There Watson scuttled it, to keep it out of the hands of Japanese fishing companies which were suing him.

Watson's action was almost universally popular. Even a publication as mainstream and conservative as *Time* magazine cheered the demise of the illegal whalers and called the ramming a "victory at sea". However the action did raise serious issues about how far the ecological movement was justified in going. As Rex Weyler put it, "Greenpeace played on a dangerous edge between Gandhian satyagraha and militant aggression". Paul Watson had gone far beyond that edge.

Ironically from the point of view of the rule of law, it is easier to construct a legally plausible defence for Watson's very dangerous and controversial action in ramming the whaler than for his harmless action in lifting up the baby seal. The whaler was killing whales illegally. By acting illegally on the high seas the whaler was in some ways acting like a pirate, and use of force against pirates has always been respectable. Moreover, use of reasonable force has always been a defence to any charge of violence, from common assault to murder. Legally, it could be argued that it is just a small step, from using force to prevent the killing or injuring of a person, to using it to prevent the illegal killing or injuring of a legally protected animal. In contrast, the touching of the seal had no such possible legal defences, and was in breach of Canadian law which specifically prohibited it.

However from the point of view of Gandhian civil disobedience things look different. Deliberate peaceful disobedience to an unjust law is at the heart of the Gandhian philosophy. The Canadian Seal Protection Law was not necessarily unjust in itself. It was a compromise protection measure intended to limit the number of people slaughtering baby seals. However the law was being applied in such a way as to restrict an anti-seal hunt protest. For those who believed that all hunting of baby seals was immoral and should be stopped, picking the seals up, and taking them away to prevent the hunters killing them, was very much in the tradition of a non-violent Gandhian satyagraha.

The reason that Watson's action did nevertheless cause controversy among other Greenpeace activists was related to the practicalities of the situation, and the fact that, although it turned out to be a propaganda coup, it risked destroying the whole anti-seal hunt operation. It gave the fisheries protection officers an opportunity to intervene and stop anyone from Greenpeace being present during the seal hunt. In addition, defying the rule of law was dangerous against a background of fierce local hostility to the Greenpeace operation. These were essentially tactical objections to Watson's action, rather than objections of principle.

Ramming the whale ship was fundamentally different. Every seafarer knows that ramming a ship is inherently very dangerous. Watson did deliberately give warning of his intentions before he rammed the *Sierra*, by swinging his bows in close and scraping the whaler before coming in a second time to ram it. This is said to have made his intentions clear to the whaler's crew. The fact remains that Watson had either great skill or great luck to be able to steer the *Sea Shepherd* so that he disabled the *Sierra* without sinking her. If he had sunk the Sierra, and members of her crew had drowned, world reaction to the ramming would have been less euphoric.

Watson might perhaps have justified his action by quoting the Chinese proverb "Righteousness lies in the heart". This saying means that whatever the formal rights and wrongs of a situation, judged in terms of law or other formal ways of analysing things, people know in their hearts where justice lies. The illegal whalers were very bad. Their actions were illegal even by the lax rules of the IWC. Their whale killing was physically loathsome, and no other method of protest would have stopped it. There was rejoicing at the ramming because everyone knew in their hearts that it was just.

Unfortunately, "righteousness lies in the heart" is not an adequate moral justification for a mass movement. It is significant that the phrase comes from China, where the rule of law scarcely exists. Everyone's assessment varies of where the balance of righteousness lies. Inevitably actions which strike a chord in most people's hearts will be followed by others on which opinions of reasonable people differ, and some which many people will consider unacceptable. This is indeed what has happened with many other direct action environmental protests. An example are the direct action protests against logging by the group Earthfirst. Greenpeace had begun such protests with the original "tree-hugging", to prevent the felling of redwood trees in British Columbia. Earthfirst "spiked" the trees to achieve the same effect. By placing a metal spike in a tree which is to be felled, it is possible to break the links of a chainsaw. It is claimed that, as a result of Earthfirst spiking, loggers have been killed. Not surprisingly, Earthfirst is regarded as an extremist organisation and has little popular support. Quite apart from being morally wrong in most people's eyes to cause a death in this way, such action is likely to diminish, not increase, support for the environmentalist cause.

In addition, a demonstration at sea, just like a traditional street demonstration, depends on general acceptance of the rule of law to take place safely. If an environmental demonstration uses force, it lowers itself from the plane of reasoned argument on which it must operate to be effective. It encourages use of much more powerful force by those who specialise in force, and who are only too happy to operate outside the rule of law to achieve their ends. This eventually happened to Greenpeace in 1985, when the French Secret Service blew up the Greenpeace ship, *Rainbow Warrior*, in Auckland Harbour, with a booby trap double explosion, killing a crew member who went back to retrieve his belongings after the first explosion. Mines had been attached to the ship by professional divers, after the location of the ship and its plans had been obtained by a French secret agent infiltrated into Greenpeace. Greenpeace was perhaps fortunate in the circumstances that its loss of life was limited to one person, although unlucky in that Greenpeace itself, as opposed to its radical offshoots, had never used violent direct action, and had done nothing to invite retaliation against it. The *Rainbow Warrior* affair proved to be a costly own goal for France, and brought closer the day when testing at Moruroa would end. However this does not alter the fact that generally direct action by environmental protesters risks retaliation in kind which may involve loss of life.

Even environmental protests strictly limited to the Gandhian model of civil disobedience raise ethical issues different from those faced by Gandhi. Both in South Africa and in India, Gandhi was campaigning against systems which were fundamentally unjust, and which could not be changed through the usual channels of democratic political activity. It was civil disobedience or nothing. This is not the position in relation to many environmental issues. Whether a power station should or should not be built is, in a democratic country, a decision which can, and normally should be, taken through political campaigning, elections and informed public debate. Some people feel deeply and passionately that they do not want a power station built, but the democratic view of the majority may well be that a power station is needed, and has to be built somewhere. Such a view is not necessarily wrong, and it may be anti-democratic and even selfish to oppose it by illegal means.

This point was made by Lord Denning, a judge with a notable record of supporting small people against big organisations, in R (CEGB) v Chief Constable of Devon and Cornwall, a case brought by the Central Electricity Generating Board against a Chief Constable for refusing to remove demonstrators from the site of a proposed power station in Cornwall. "This sort of problem", said Denning, "is recurrent in modern society. The country as a whole needs to be provided with reservoirs for water, with military areas for defence, with airports for travel, with prisons for criminals, and so forth. The local inhabitants object most strongly. But it still does happen from time to time that their objections have to be overruled. It is much to be regretted, but, if the national interest demands, they must give way remembering that they are to be fully compensated, so far as money can do it, for any property that is compulsorily acquired or any injurious effect to persons or property."

Lord Denning was probably being unfair to the demonstrators in that case in suggesting that they were all motivated by a "not in my backyard syndrome". At most demonstrations in Britain against nuclear power a substantial number of the demonstrators will be motivated, not by personal or local considerations but by a belief that nuclear power anywhere is unacceptably dangerous. However he made a valid point that a direct action demonstration in a fully functioning democracy, which achieves its objectives by breaking the law, may be undemocratic and against the public interest, even where it is based on attractive rallying calls such as protection of the countryside or stopping introduction of dangerous industries.

Lord Denning's view is not far-fetched. In France blockades of motorways by farmers, seeking better prices for their produce or imposition of tariffs on import competition, have become commonplace in recent years. These farmers are employing the same civil disobedience techniques pioneered by Greenpeace. However they are employing them not for the public good, but purely for their own sectional interest. In this sense they are no different from a picket blockading premises as part of industrial action. Farmers in France are not an under-privileged section of the community. By no stretch of the imagination can it be said that "righteousness lies in the heart" in relation to their blockade action.

The answer may be that Greenpeace-style protests work best in an international environment, particularly where the government of one country is riding roughshod over the interests of the global community, and where there are no other effective means of taking action. Nuclear test explosions in the USA and France fall into this category.

Greenpeace protests, just like Gandhian civil disobedience, are not effective against completely ruthless and powerful opponents. Greenpeace China, although it has been in existence for many years, has not attempted to mount civil disobedience-style protests in China. It knows that they would lead to the immediate suppression of the organisation.

Greenpeace-type protests may however be effective, and perhaps the only effective means of achieving results, in corrupt democracies, where the approved constitutional channels for citizens to voice their concerns and safeguard their interests do not work, or only work so badly that they are unlikely to prevent environmental destruction.

A good example of such a democracy is India, where hundreds of national and state elected legislators are indicted felons awaiting trial, likely to escape justice because of the slowness and corruption of the Indian legal system. The number of Indian legislators likely to respond to local concerns about the environment in the manner of a British Member of Parliament, by articulating those concerns and demanding a meeting with the responsible minister, is quite small. In many cases the Indian Member of the Legislative Council will be part of the very same corrupt clique which is intent on destroying a forest for commercial gain, and against which the demonstrators wish to protest.

This is the environment in which the Chipkos emerged in India and achieved great success with their Greenpeace-style demonstrations. "Chipko" means "hug" in Hindi, and the Chipkos are tree-huggers. They are Gandhian civil disobedience activists, many of them women, originally inspired by Greenpeace's protest against the felling of redwood trees. In 1980 they began a long-running campaign against deforestation of the Indian Himalayan foothills through excessive logging. Over the years they have achieved a lot of success in halting logging projects and saving areas of forest. The Chipkos have deliberately attempted to invoke religious imagery to assist their cause, with marches known as "padyatras", a traditional name for religious pilgrimages. They have also disrupted auctions where plots of forest were to be sold to timber contractors for logging, and have staged mass sit-ins and blockades.

The Chipkos' most memorable series of demonstrations were in the Doon Valley, the famous valley around Dehradun in Uttarakhand, between 1986 and 1988. A quarry had been responsible for depleting water resources in the area, through operations which interfered with the only water supply to nearby villages. The Chipkos forced the quarry to stop operations by burying themselves up to their waists in the middle of the only access road, so that any lorry attempting to reach the quarry would have had to run them over. Being dug in, they could not be simply dragged away, as with participants in a conventional street blockade, but had to be dug out, a process taking several hours. They were of course at risk of a crazed driver mowing them down. Fortunately this did not happen, and the quarrying operation was successfully stopped as a result of the protest.

Tree-hugging type protests are quite common around the world. In England one of the most famous was the campaign against the Newbury by-pass in 1996, when protesters camped in tree houses high in mature oak trees, and lived in tunnels under the site of the proposed road in the hope that this would make it impossible for the road to be built. After months of confrontation, the protesters were slowly removed, with the assistance of paid specialist climbers to remove them from the tops of the trees. The protest was non-violent and the removal of the protesters was eventually effected without casualties.

The Newbury by-pass campaign raised in an acute form the issue of the role of environmental protest demonstrations in a highly developed democracy such as the United Kingdom. The campaign was not really a civil disobedience campaign in the Gandhian sense. It involved every form of political activity, as the demonstrations at the site were linked to a huge public campaign in the media. Many different forms of protest were attempted at the site during the months of confrontation there, and this included some direct action involving criminal offences such as criminal damage. Generally, however, the conduct of the demonstrators was lawful. It was not intimidatory, and so could not justify the use of the recently enacted Criminal Trespass Act 1994, aimed at hunt saboteurs, which criminalised trespass liable to intimidate those carrying out lawful activities on land. Most of the demonstration activities constituted, at most, civil trespass, rather than commission of criminal offences. However the protest was aimed at halting the building of the by-pass road through making it too difficult and costly for the building to proceed, even though polls showed that the majority of local people wanted the road built, to relieve traffic congestion and reduce accidents on existing roads. There were local campaigners in favour of the building of the by-pass, who received much less publicity than the anti-by-pass protesters. The local Liberal Democrat M.P. supported construction of the road.

It could be said that the Newbury protesters, many of whom campaigned under the organisation "Third Battle of Newbury" (a reference to the first two battles of Newbury in the English Civil War) lost the battle, but won the war. Although the by-pass was built, the cumulative effect of the massive protest, and of other similar protests (notably the earlier protest against the building of the Winchester by-pass over Twyford Down) turned the national climate of opinion against major road building projects. This change was also connected with growth of concern about carbon dioxide emissions contributing to climate change, and with the gradual realisation that building more and more roads was not a viable long-term transport policy. The Newbury protest, which itself helped to publicise those wider issues, undoubtedly made a major contribution to changing attitudes.

Is civil disobedience direct action justifiable, or likely to be effective, in this kind of situation? It is worth emphasising that civil disobedience was only a minor part of the generally law-abiding Newbury protests. However many other environmental groups are explicitly dedicated to civil disobedience-type direct action. An example is the anti-airport expansion group "Plane Stupid". Another example is the climate camp which was infiltrated by the undercover agent provocateur Mark Kennedy. The furore at the disclosure of Kennedy's role has overshadowed what the climate change camp he infiltrated was actually planning, by way of direct action at Ratcliffe-on-Soar Power Station.

That plan, which Kennedy joined in and actively encouraged, but as far as is known did not originate, was to stop the operation of the power station entirely, by suspending a protester inside one of the cooling towers, while the station was temporarily shut down, so that it could not be re-started. This was to be achieved by means of a cradle-like contraption known as a "bat tent". The idea was that the power station operator would not be able to switch on the power station with a live protester inside one of the chimneys. It was hoped that the protester, who would have food and water with him, would be able to remain inside the chimney for up to a week, keeping the power station shut down the whole time, while the power station operator and the police searched for a way of removing him without killing him. The plan was foiled by Kennedy's reports, and the resultant arrest of most of the activists the night before the planned action, while they were asleep in a nearby school hall.

This seems a clear example of a kind of civil disobedience which cannot rationally be justified by any democratically-minded demonstrator. Most people agree that high emissions of greenhouse gases from coal-fired power stations contribute to global warming and are bad for the environment. Agreeing on a viable alternative is enormously more difficult. Nuclear power and wind power have their own environmental issues and their own strong critics. Until there is some agreement, it is not clear how coal-fired power stations can be phased out. Even if they were to be phased out, that is something different from an unplanned shutdown. If the shutdown, attempted by demonstrators at Ratcliffe, were to be done successfully at several power stations, it would probably lead to power blackouts with consequent disruption. Almost certainly, that is something which the majority of citizens do not want to happen. Nor does the stoppage of a power station by any method, let alone one as dangerous as suspending a demonstrator inside a cooling tower, seem likely to increase support for the demonstrators' cause. A traditional demonstration, handing out leaflets about the arguments for closing coal-fired power stations, would seem far more likely to achieve that goal. However the task of such traditional demonstrations is of course made harder, if the police and other authorities are suspicious that they may be hijacked by direct action activists. In this situation respect for the right to demonstrate is rapidly eroded.

For these reasons environmental direct action demonstrations are usually wrong in principle in a properly functioning democracy, and are generally unlikely to help their cause.

The question then arises as to what techniques and tactics are most likely to make a traditional demonstration a success. This is considered in the next chapter.

CHAPTER 16

WHAT MAKES A SUCCESSFUL DEMONSTRATION?

The first requirement for any peaceful demonstration is good organisation. It must have some of the characteristics of a disciplined army. The participants have to be properly informed as to why they are demonstrating and how the demonstration is to be carried out. They all have to know that it is to be non-violent, and the organisers have to be sure that this non-violent policy will be adhered to by everyone. The participants also have to be persuaded to come, and to know when and where to turn up.

The London Corresponding Society, which first organised a deliberately peaceful mass meeting to make their points, told people to come unarmed, and people seem generally to have done what they were told.

Exactly how the London Corresponding Society got so many people to come to their open-air meetings is not entirely clear. It seems likely that the Society had large numbers of handbills printed and also advertised the meeting in some of the newspapers of the day. Their advertisements told people that they should come unarmed as the meetings were to be strictly peaceful, which was how they turned out.

As demonstrations became more common in the early nineteenth century they were usually organised through a variety of local meetings. In London, parish vestry meetings were a venue at which a planned demonstration could be publicised, as was done by John Powell and Thomas Bowker for their pro-Reform Bill demonstration in 1831. In Lancashire, the meetings of trade unions, which also emerged in their modern form in the early nineteenth century, were also an important avenue for organising demonstrations, such as those which led up the Peterloo Massacre in 1819. By the time of the Chartists, information about planned demonstrations was coming increasingly from the media, with the Chartists' own newspaper, the *Northern Star* providing a means of informing supporters. The Suffragettes organised through their network of branches, as many other organisations have done since. Today, with instant mass communication by way of social media such as Facebook and Twitter, communicating with others to organise a demonstration has never been easier.

Another aspect of organisation is control and direction. Common sense suggests that clear direction from a central point is likely to make any demonstration more disciplined and more effective. As described in Chapter 4, the Lancashire Parliamentary Reform meetings were tightly organised, with one person leading every row of demonstrators, and leaders leading contingents of various sizes. This was the start of the practice by which most large modern demonstrations have stewards, often wearing armbands or other signs to make them visible, helping, organising, and keeping order among the demonstrators. Some type of organisation for keeping order, assisting with problems, and relaying information is probably essential for any large demonstration.

Another essential requirement for a successful demonstration is to be able to send a clear message to its intended audience, which will consist both of persons in authority and of the uncommitted general public. This means that the demonstration must either use banners and placards, with easily comprehensible slogans, or some other, more inventive way of conveying its message. It usually also means, except perhaps with a very small local demonstration, that there must be a way of getting information about the demonstration to a wider audience than those people who happen to see it in the street. It is again no coincidence that the emergence of demonstrations coincided with the emergence of the first mass circulation newspapers, Cobbett's *Political Register* and *Twopenny Trash,* both of which gave full reports of contemporary Reform mass meetings and marches.

Today, there are so many demonstrations that the organisers of any one demonstration will have to take active steps to ensure that they get the publicity they want. At least one media officer is essential, to make sure that all relevant media are aware that the demonstration is going to happen, and also to receive photographs and videos afterwards. For a large demonstration, a whole media team is needed. Greenpeace have been a particularly successful example of how to use the media to maximum effect.

These are the basic essentials of a modestly successful demonstration. In many situations more, often much more, is needed to generate enough impact to make a difference. Many factors come into play, but four key recurring themes of successful demonstrations are novelty, symbolic power, leadership, and timing. In the remainder of this chapter I consider a number of demonstrating movements which succeeded either because of the novelty of their approach, or because of the power of their symbolism, or both. I then go on to consider the issues of leadership, and of timing.

The Womens' Suffragists in Britain and the United States benefitted from the novelty of what they were doing, as they organised the first large peaceful demonstrations ever which were attended overwhelmingly by women. It was to persuade hesitant women and their families to support this novel approach that they emphasised images of feminine beauty and dignity. This emphasis had a powerful effect, which certainly generated increased support for their cause.

The National Unemployed Workers Movement organised the first long-distance marches in Britain by hungry unemployed people to publicise their plight, and the novelty, combined with the moving plight of many of the marchers, succeeded in gaining support for changes to the unemployment benefit system which the NUWM was campaigning for.

Gandhi not only organised the first deliberately peaceful large scale civil disobedience demonstrations. He also himself, as noted in Chapter 11, was a powerful symbol, deliberately dressing in a very simple traditional Indian homespun cloth, to emphasise his own frailty. This deliberate frailty and humility, as he stood against the might of the world's largest empire, brought his movement millions of new supporters, both in India and around the world.

The quality of symbolism can transform the impact of a demonstration. Dignity and humility usually strike a chord with many observers, and others, as well as Gandhi, have used an approach which emphasised those virtues to great effect. The Civil Rights March through the police lines at Birmingham, Alabama (Chapter 12), is one of many examples.

Another powerful demonstration weapon is absolute silence. Henry Cockburn noted the "terrible silence" at the 30,000 strong 1832 Reform Bill demonstration in Edinburgh. A striking record of a silent demonstration in nineteenth century India is contained in a letter from the then Lieutenant-Governor of Bengal, John Peter Grant, dated 17 September, 1860, reporting on a silent demonstration by indigo-growing peasants protesting against exploitation by landlords:

"I have myself just returned from an excursion to Sirajganj on the Jamuna river where I went by water for objects connected with the line of the Dacca Railway and wholly unconnected with indigo matters. I had intended to go up the Mathabhanga and down the Ganges; but finding on arrival at the Kumar that the shorter passage was open, I proceeded along the Kumar, and the Kaliganga, which rivers run in Nadia and Jessore, and through that part of the Patna District which lies south of the Ganges.

Numerous crowds of raiyats [peasant farmers] appeared at various places, whose prayer was for an order of the government that they should not cultivate indigo. On my return a few days afterwards along the same two rivers, from dawn to dusk, as I steamed along these two rivers for some 60 or 70 miles, both banks were literally lined with crowds of villagers, claiming justice in this matter. Even the women of the villages on the banks were collected in groups by themselves; the males who stood at and between the river-side villages in little crowds must have collected from all the villages at a great distance from either side. I do not know that it ever fell to the lot of any Indian officer to steam for 14 hours through a continued double line of suppliants for justice; all were most respectful and orderly, but were also plainly in earnest. It would be folly to suppose that such a display on the part of tens of thousands of people, men, women and children, has no deep meaning. The organisation, and capacity for combined and simultaneous action in the cause, which this remarkable demonstration over so large an extent of country proved, are subjects worthy of much consideration."

Unfortunately no-one seems to have given the demonstration the consideration it deserved. History seems to have no record of who organised it or how this was done.

Another demonstration movement which used dignity, humility, and silence together with indomitable persistence, until it ultimately achieved its main aims, was that of the Mothers of the Plaza de Mayo in Argentina.

They were protesting about the disappearance of their children at the hands of the Argentinian military junta. The "disappeared" were in fact almost all dead. In the 1970s, the Argentinian Junta fought what it itself called a dirty war against Leftist political activists or people whom it saw as such. Applying techniques perfected by the Nazis, they kidnapped people and killed them without anyone ever knowing what had happened to them. Many were thrown to their deaths over the sea from helicopters or aircraft. Others were shot and buried in hidden graves. Thousands were killed in this way.

The Plaza 25 de Mayo is the large open square outside the Argentinian Presidential Palace, known as the Casa Rosada ("the Pink House"). The mothers began assembling there with placards demanding to know the fate of their children. A small group of 14 women came together on 30 April, 1977 to demand information. They had met in government offices, prisons and courts while looking for their sons and daughters. They slowly became an identifiable group. At first they used Catholic symbols to identify themselves, carrying a carpenter's nail on their backs in memory of "Christ's sacrifice". Later, in an important move, they began wearing white head kerchiefs in order to be able to recognise each other and be recognisable to others, as well as carrying pictures of their kidnapped children around their necks or in their hands. They walked slowly in a circular procession around the Square, with their eyes turned upwards in supplication, deliberately giving their demonstration an air of religious devotion.

The fact that the protesters were mothers, and were making their protest as mothers, gave them a degree of protection even in a society as repressive as Argentina under the junta, since the junta had built up its political credibility as a supposed protector of Christian and family values against Communism. Gunning down defenceless mothers would not have gone well with that image. Instead, as it could not use such open violence, the junta tried to dismiss the mothers as "crazy old women", while individually the mothers were threatened by junta operatives both in their homes and on their way to and from the Square.

As the Mothers maintained their protest, the numbers joining them grew. More people were disappearing, more people were hearing about the protest, and more people were gathering the courage to come forward. By July 1977, the number of protesting Mothers had reached 150. They came from different social classes, from different religious backgrounds, and from all parts of Argentina. At this stage, with the junta still firmly in power, the majority of Argentinians ignored them, either out of hostility or out of fear, and people would cross the road to avoid encountering them. Some passers-by insulted them, but others whispered words of support.

On 5 October, 1977, the Mothers placed an advertisement in the leading Argentine daily newspaper, *La Prensa,* demanding the truth about 237 disappeared persons, together with photographs of the disappeared people and signatures and identity card numbers of the women in the movement. They received no response. Ten days later, hundreds of women delivered a petition to the Casa Rosada, bearing

24,000 signatures, demanding an investigation into the disappearances. The police tried to disperse the demonstrators, spraying them with tear gas, shooting into the air, and detaining over 300 of them for questioning. Foreign correspondents covering the event were also arrested. No Argentine media attended.

At this point, as a result of coverage in the foreign media, the Mothers began to gain important international recognition and financial support, with help from human rights groups in the Netherlands, Sweden, France and Italy. President Jimmy Carter of the USA sent Patricia Derian, US Assistant Under-Secretary, to investigate the accusations of disappearances. As a result of her report the US cut military aid to Argentina, and cancelled $270 million in loans. This led the junta to take more desperate steps to try to stop the Mothers. In December 1977 it kidnapped some of the Mothers, three of whom, including the Mothers' leader and key organiser, Azucena Villaflor de Vicenti, were permanently "disappeared". Despite this terrifying act, the remaining women returned to the Plaza and continued demonstrating.

The Mothers continued their demonstrations through 1978. They were held weekly, every Thursday, despite regular harassment and detention of demonstrators by the police. In 1979, the Plaza was cordoned off by heavily armed police in a final attempt to stop the demonstrators. The Mothers could only dash across, trying to get as far as they could before they were stopped by the police. This cordoning off of the Plaza might possibly have stopped the demonstrations if it had been done earlier, but by the time it was attempted support for the Mothers internationally had gained such momentum that they continued. Added momentum was also provided in 1979 by the decision of the Inter-American Human Rights Commission to visit Argentina to obtain evidence about the disappearances. The Mothers brought thousands of witnesses from all over Argentina to testify before the Commission. When the junta realised it was unable to stop this, it began organising its own counter-demonstrations. They put up posters and used people to carry billboards with the punning slogan "Somos derechos y humanos" (We are [politically] on the Right and are human).

In 1980, the Mothers, for the first time, made their organisation into a formal association, the Association of the Mothers of the Plaza de Mayo. Their demonstrations became increasingly large and dramatic, involving up to 200,000 people. In 1983, following Argentina's defeat in the Falklands War with Britain, the junta fell from power. The Mothers continued to demonstrate and demand information about their children and punishment for those who had ill-treated them. They continued for many years to walk in circular process round the Plaza, holding their last rally in 2006.

Very slowly, over the years, the Mothers' campaign met with substantial success. An amnesty law passed just after the fall of the junta in relation to crimes during their period in power was repealed, and many of the perpetrators of the "disappearances" were tried and sentenced to long prison terms. Forensic investigation of remains of bodies identified many of the "disappeared", including Azucena Villaflor de Vicenza, whose remains have now been reburied in the Plaza de Mayo, next to a monument to the work of the Mothers.

The eventual great success, of the Mothers' demonstrations, albeit at huge personal cost, led to them being imitated in many other countries facing a problem of disappearances or secret killings by the authorities. So far, however, such groups as the Mothers of Tiananmen Square in China and similar groups in Sri Lanka have not achieved comparable success.

This is mainly because in Argentina the repressive regime fell, while in China it remains in power. The Chinese regime will not let anyone who even looks like a demonstrator stand in Tiananmen Square. Any demonstrator who appears is immediately arrested, and faces severe consequences. So far, therefore, what worked against the Argentinian Junta, which had some vestigial respect for traditional ideas of motherhood, has not worked against China's even more ruthless regime.

The lack of comparable success by other groups of demonstrating mothers is however not only due to the nature of the regimes they face. The Argentinian Mothers' demonstrations undoubtedly had more impact internationally because of their novelty. Anyone who starts a similar group now in any country will be following a well-worn path and will not be newsworthy in the same way. Novelty was therefore critical to the Argentinian success.

Another example of a demonstration which achieved great success because of its novelty, was also organised by a celebrated mother. This was the first known large demonstration by children.

Systematic use of children in demonstrations is liable to be exploitative, as children will often not understand why they are there, or want to be there. However the position is different where the demonstration is on behalf of the children themselves. The great pioneer who organised the world's first children's demonstration on behalf of children was the American labour organiser, Mary Harris Jones, known as "Mother Jones."

Mother Jones was an indomitable campaigner for her causes, and was memorably described by the novelist Upton Sinclair as "the walking Wrath of God". She lost her husband and her own children in a scarlet fever epidemic, and later became a labour organiser as a result of her sense of outrage at the Haymarket trial (Chapter 7). Much of her work involved organising miners across America by visiting their remote mining camps. However, when she learned of the appalling conditions in which children were working in cotton mills in Pennsylvania, she decided to campaign to outlaw child labour in factories, and to do so by way of a demonstration march from Pennsylvania to New York by the factory children themselves. Her own description, in her autobiography, of the March of the Mill Children cannot be bettered:-

"In the spring of 1903 I went to Kensington, Pennsylvania, where seventy five thousand textile workers were on strike...At least ten thousand were little children... Every day little children came into Union Headquarters, some with their hands off, some with the thumb missing, some with their fingers off at the knuckle. They were stooped little things, round shouldered and skinny. Many of them were not over ten years of age, although the state law prohibited their working before they were twelve years of age... The Liberty Bell that a century ago rang for freedom against tyranny was touring the country and crowds were coming to see it everywhere. That gave me an idea. These little children were striking for some of the freedom that childhood ought to have, and I decided that the children and I would go on a tour. I asked the parents if they would let me have their little boys and girls for a week or ten days, promising to bring them back safe and sound. They consented. ... A few men and women went with me to help with the children. They were on strike and I thought they might as well have a little recreation.

The children carried knapsacks on their backs, in which were a knife and fork, a tin cup and a plate. We took along a wash boiler to cook the food on the road. One little fellow had a drum and another had a fife. That was our band. We carried banners that said, "We want more schools and less hospitals", "We want time to play", "Prosperity is here. Where is ours?"

We started from Philadelphia where we held a great mass meeting. I decided to go with the children to see President [Theodore] Roosevelt to ask him have Congress pass a law prohibiting the exploitation in childhood. I thought that President Roosevelt might see these little children and compare them with his own little ones who were spending the summer on the seashore at Oyster Bay. I thought too, out of politeness we might call on Morgan in Wall Street, who owned the mines where many of their fathers worked.

The children were very happy, having plenty to eat, taking baths in the brooks and rivers every day. I thought when the strike is over and they go back to the mills they will never have another holiday like this. All along the line of the march the farmers drove out to meet us with wagon loads of fruit and vegetables. Their wives brought the children clothes and money. The inter-urban trainmen would stop their trains and give us free rides. I would go ahead to the towns and arrange sleeping quarters for the children, and secure meeting halls. As we marched on it grew terribly hot. There was no rain and the roads were heavy with dust. From time to time we had to send some of the children back to their homes. They were too weak to stand the march.

We were on the outskirts of Trenton, New Jersey, cooking our lunch in the wash boiler, when the conductor on the inter-urban car stopped and told us the police were coming down to notify us that we could not enter the town. There were mills in the town and the mill-owners didn't like our coming. I said "Alright, the police will be just in time for our lunch".

Sure enough the police came and we invited them to dine with us. They looked at the little gathering of children with their tin plates and cups around the wash boiler. They just smiled and spoke kindly to the children and said nothing at all about not going into the city. We went in, held our meeting, and it was the wives of the police who took the children and cared for them that night, sending them back next morning with a nice lunch rolled up in paper napkins.

At one town the mayor said that we could not hold our meeting because he did not have sufficient police protection. "These little children have never known any sort of protection, your honour", I said, "and they are used to going without it". He let us have our meeting...

From Jersey City we marched to Hoboken. I sent a committee over to the New York Chief of Police, Ebstein, asking for permission to march up Fourth Avenue to Madison Square because I wanted to hold a meeting. The Chief refused and forbade our entrance to the city. I went over to New York and saw Mayor Seth Low... I asked him what the reason was for refusing us entry to the city, and he said that we were not citizens of New York".

This feeble statement was not enough to deter Mother Jones, and the children were in due course allowed to enter New York and march up Fourth Avenue. They held a meeting in Twentieth Street, with Mother Jones introducing individual children to the crowd and telling the crowd about them. The next day she took the children to the beach at Coney Island. However even this treat was turned into a demonstration. The children visited a menagerie with the support of the owner, and were photographed for the press locked inside animal cages, *"to represent American employers' attitudes to their workers"*, according to Mother Jones, in front of a giant picture of a Roman Emperor giving the "Thumbs Down" sign, and with the sound of lions roaring in the background.

The March of the Mill Children succeeded. Shortly afterwards, Pennsylvania passed an effective child labour law that ended the practice of employing children under 14 in the mills.

The impact of the march was enormous and enduring. Mother Jones' techniques caught on and became widespread, and are still in use today. In modern India, where child labour remains a major issue, protesters have organised several marches by children to campaign against the practice, deliberately modelled on the Mill Children's March of 1903. These included the Global March against Child Labour in 1998, organised by Kailesh Satyarthi from India, which was a children's march through countries of Asia and Europe, starting in Manila, and ending in Geneva during a meeting of the International Labour Organisation.

In the 1970s, when disabled people in the USA began to publicise their plight by way of demonstrations, they, like the Mothers of the Plaza de Mayo and the Mill Children, had powerful advantages of novelty and symbolism on their side.

A driving force behind these demonstrations by disabled people was Reverend Wade Blank, a veteran civil rights and anti-Vietnam War activist, who founded the Atlantis Community, to provide attendant care to people with severe disability who wanted to live independent lives. An issue which arose at once was the need for accessible public transport, particularly for wheelchairs. At that time disabled people in wheelchairs were routinely asked to leave restaurants, theatres and other places on the ground that they were a "fire hazard", and were arrested if they refused to comply. Wheelchair users did not have access to most housing, most shops, classrooms, places of worship or places of employment. Polite requests for special arrangements to be made met with disappointing responses.

On 5 July, 1978, 45 people in wheelchairs surrounded two city buses in Denver, Colorado, bringing traffic at a busy intersection to a halt. Nineteen people held the buses hostage throughout the night. Shocked into awareness by this action, the Denver Regional Transit Department agreed to provide wheelchair lifts on all its buses.

Having won in Denver, the disabled campaigners moved on to tackle the rest of the United States. They raised money to enable transport to be provided to bring severely disabled people from around the country to a location where a demonstration was planned, known as an "action site". Atlantis staff members served as volunteers, trainers and attendants. After brief classroom instructions, which included an outline of the strategy for the demonstration, the Atlantis staff would lead the disabled demonstrators in conducting direct action. A favourite type of demonstration was the "crawl-in". Disabled people would arrive outside a recalcitrant restaurant which had declined to accommodate the disabled, throw themselves out of their wheelchairs on to the ground, crawl across the pavement, in through the door of the restaurant and across the restaurant floor to the tables. The pressure this placed on the targeted restaurant owner to change his attitude was powerful. Another favourite type of demonstration was the blocking of entrances and exits to national transport conventions by demonstrators in wheelchairs.

In 1983, Reverend Blank's group became American Disabled for Accessible Public Transport (ADAPT). ADAPT's campaigning for a better deal for the disabled reached a climax in March 1990, with a demonstration in Washington. One thousand people marched or wheeled themselves along Pennsylvania Avenue. At the Capitol Building, 60 of those who had taken part abandoned their wheelchairs and dragged themselves up the 83 marble steps of the entrance to the building. They then occupied the Capitol Rotunda, chaining their wheelchairs to fixed objects in such a way that it took four hours of police work to free them. The police arrested 104 participants in the demonstration.

On 27 July, 1990, in response to the ADAPT demonstrations, and the waves of sympathetic publicity which they generated, the US Congress passed the Americans with Disabilities Act, introducing extensive legal requirements for access to be provided for the disabled.

The forms of symbolism which can be used for a demonstration are almost infinite, with new forms liable to emerge in response to new issues. In Saudi Arabia, where women are prohibited from driving, a simple and obvious symbolic demonstration was conducted by 47 women in Riyadh who just drove a procession of cars. All were arrested, and many were punished by being sacked from their jobs. In the short-term the demonstration was counter-productive, in that the informal ban which had existed before the demonstration was replaced by an official ban. However, if women do in due course obtain the right to drive in Saudi Arabia, those women demonstrators will be remembered as the pioneers who started the changes which made it possible.

In 2007 President Lucio Guttierez of Ecuador became unpopular because of allegations of corruption. Demonstrators used a clear and simple form of symbolism to make their point. They marched past the presidential palace all holding aloft rolls of toilet paper. The president resigned. Since then, demonstrations using rolls of toilet paper have been used elsewhere so often that they are in danger of become a cliché.

However the power of even a simple symbol, endlessly repeated, should not be under-estimated. A final striking example comes from Hong Kong, where in 2003 the unpopular leader, C.H. Tung, attempted to introduce laws which would have seriously restricted free speech. Half a million people, out of Hong Kong's then population of six million, turned out to demonstrate against this. The demonstration was extremely orderly, and marched past Tung's office, where he was seated inside watching. Many of the demonstrators, as they passed, held up a double-page spread from a popular opposition newspaper, *Apple Daily*. This spread was a photograph of Tung, with an exploding cheese pie superimposed on his mouth. The effect of hundreds of thousands of these cheese pie photos was infinitely more effective, as well as more dignified, than if someone had actually thrown a cheese pie at Tung. Key ministers in Tung's government resigned the next day, and Tung himself did not last much longer. The plans for repressive legislation were abandoned. The demonstrators with the cheese pie pictures had won.

It can be seen, from these accounts of several successful demonstration campaigns, that most of them used demonstrations as part of a wider campaign, also involving mobilisation through the media, contacts with politicians or other influential people, and lobbying for legislation to be enacted or abandoned. This is normal and inevitable. Demonstrations take place to achieve an objective, and rational campaigners for that objective will use all available means which may help to achieve it. However, as the Hong Kong example shows, a huge and dramatic demonstration can be absolutely decisive in bringing a campaign to a successful conclusion.

The examples of the Mothers, the Mill Children, the Hunger Marchers and ADAPT all illustrate that demonstrations can be particularly effective when drawing the situation of marginalised groups to a wider public. This remains one of the major roles of the peaceful demonstration, as it is one of the few ways that groups whose concerns would otherwise be of little interest to the wider public can draw attention to themselves and their needs.

Turning from novelty and symbolism to leadership, the four demonstration movements just referred to would not have succeeded, and possibly not even started, but for the initiative and leadership shown by Azucena Villaflor de Vicenti, by Mother Jones, by Wal Hannington, and by the Reverend Wade Blank. Leadership is obviously critical to the success of many demonstrations. However good leaders are rare, and finding effective leadership for a demonstration movement presents many problems.

Most, though not all, of the successful demonstrating movements described in this book have had a single strong overall leader. However this is not a necessity, as there was no one overall leader for the Reform Bill demonstrations in 1830 to 1832. Thomas Attwood was the most prominent figure in Birmingham, but numerous other leaders played a part across Britain, with no one person being pre-eminent.

On the other hand, there have been several notable demonstrating movements which failed because of a divided leadership which lacked cohesion. The division between the ANC and the PAC doomed the 1961 direct action protests in South Africa, while divided leadership gravely weakened the Tiananmen Square student movement[44]. In an extreme case, a divided leadership has meant that agent provocateurs can take over a movement and lead it in the direction of disaster, as in the incident with the 2011 demonstrations in Tahrir Square, Cairo, described in Chapter 14.

These problems of a weak or divided leadership are matched by different problems which can arise where a demonstrating movement has a single strong leader. Leaders are by definition strong personalities with strong opinions, who often do not suffer fools gladly. Many find it difficult to operate within the constraints of a democratic organisation. This can lead to ironic contrasts when such leaders are spearheading a campaign for greater democracy but are themselves autocrats. Mrs Pankhurst is perhaps the classic example.

On top of this difficulty, there is the effect of power. As the nineteenth century English historian, Lord Acton, put it, "All power tends to corrupt", and the power of swaying thousands with one's oratory, or controlling an organisation that can bring thousands of demonstrators on to the streets, is no exception to this universal rule. A good example of this rush of power to the head of a demonstration leader was the behaviour of Walter Waters in the later part of the Bonus Campaign.

---

44   Chapter 19 below

Waters was so deeply committed to democracy and the rule of law at the outset that he required everyone in his B.E.F to swear allegiance to the US constitution. Despite that, before the end of the campaign he was unmistakably showing signs of megalomania, with his assumption of dictatorial powers over the marchers, his setting up of the "Khaki Shirts", and his approving references to Mussolini and "Hitler". In fairness to Waters, he was never corrupted in the financial sense. As he put it in his memoir. *"I sold out to no-one. I was bankrupt when I started the march. I was bankrupt and in debt when I went home afterwards."* Other demonstration leaders have not resisted financial temptation. Controversy still surrounds the status of Father Gapon because of his willingness to accept a regular payment from the Czarist police.

The most outstanding example of a leader who was never corrupted by power was Gandhi, who declined numerous offers to form part of the Congress Party administration. When Congress gained power at Indian independence, Gandhi again declined to be part of the government, and continued to live his modest life, dressed in his dhoti. That deliberate rejection of political power when it was offered is part of Gandhi's greatness. However personalities like Gandhi's are obviously extremely rare.

On balance, the risks of an over-powerful leader betraying a demonstrating movement or leading it astray are , in the view of this author, so great that it is better to have some degree of democratic control over the leader, however great the leader's talents. The aim must be to harness those talents, but ensure that the movement is always greater than the person who leads it. That way the movement will survive both the leader's weaknesses and the leader's demise. However finding the right balance will always be difficult.

Timing is sometimes an aspect of good leadership. Gandhi recognised his own "Himalayan blunder" in calling for a hartal against the Rowlatt Act, when he did not yet have the organisation to mount a nationwide peaceful protest. Robert Sobukwe committed a similar mistake, with even more serious consequences, when he embarked on his civil disobedience campaign against the South African pass laws, before the PAC had grown to an adequate size to organise an effective nationwide campaign. The 1989 Tiananmen Square students movement, in contrast, made an inspired choice in the initial timing of their demonstration, which was planned to coincide with the anniversary of another much respected demonstration movement, the May 4 Movement, seventy years previously. That timing gave their movement a resonance and a moral authority that enabled it to grow at once into a huge nationwide movement.

Often however, the benefits or disadvantages of timing are something which depends on external factors beyond the control of the demonstration organisers. A classic instance of this is the success of the Reform Bill demonstrations from 1830 to 1832. Those demonstrations succeeded, where the earlier Reform movement of the years after Waterloo had failed, because of a conjunction of unrelated factors which in themselves had nothing to do with Reform. Firstly, the granting of Catholic Emancipation by the Duke of Wellington, in response to Daniel O'Connell's campaign, had removed what had been another divisive political issue, and had also showed that big constitutional changes were possible. Secondly, the peaceful July 1830 Revolution in France removed the fear that reform would lead to revolutionary terror, which had terrified many people in England between 1791 and 1830. This was what led the *Edinburgh Review* to write that "*The battle of English liberty has been fought and won at Paris*". The passage of the Reform Bill was still a very close run thing, but the Reformers had a chance because of those two favourable extraneous factors.

Another striking example of fortunate timing involved the first effective demonstration in the Soviet Union after the suppression of civil liberties there by the Bolsheviks in the 1920s. This was the "Glasnost meeting", a demonstration held in Pushkin Square in Moscow in December 1965, to protest against the trial for treason of the Russian writers Andrei Sinyavsky and Yuli Daniel.

Unlike the victims of Stalin's show trials in the 1930s, who were all tried for involvement in non-existent "plots" against the state, Sinyavsky and Daniel were put on trial because of the contents of their literary works, and for statements critical of the regime which they had put into the mouths of fictitious characters. This was a novel and alarming departure for Russia's small community of writers, academics and intellectuals, a few of whom felt that they should speak out to protest. However they were well aware that in the Soviet Union any kind of protest was highly dangerous and often suicidal. Only a few months earlier the Soviet authorities had used army troops to shoot down striking workers at Novocherkassk. They had also forcibly broken up a student demonstration in April 1965, which appears to have been the first opposition peaceful demonstration to take place in the Soviet Union since the 1920s. The student demonstration had been organised by a group called SMOG, an acronym from the first letters of the Russian words for courage, thought, depth and form, to demand freedom of artistic expression and the right to circulate ideas. Several hundred young people marched from Mayakovsky Square in Moscow to the Union of Writers Building to present a petition to a Union official. However on the way many students were attacked, beaten up, and arrested, and their banners destroyed, by KGB agents, assisted by hostile members of the public. There was therefore every likelihood that a demonstration in support of Sinyavsky and Daniel would meet the same fate as the students, and quite possibly the same fate as the Novocherkassk workers.

The driving force behind the Glasnost meeting was Alexander Esenin-Volpin, a mathematician. Esenin-Volpin believed that he could embarrass the authorities by demanding that Sinyavsky and Daniel receive a public trial in conformity with the human rights provisions of the Soviet Constitution. Those provisions had only been included in the 1935 "Stalin" constitution as a form of propaganda against the Western powers, and had been uniformly ignored by Soviet officialdom ever since being enacted. Esenin-Volpin's idea was that demanding that the regime comply with its own laws would be a more viable and effective form of protest than openly opposing the regime, or criticising its actions on other grounds not related to the law.

Esenin-Volpin enlisted the help of the writer Vladimir Bukovsky, who had already been subjected to a period of detention in a mental hospital because of expression of views that were unacceptable to the authorities. Bukovsky in his memoirs described Esenin's idea as:

> "Both inspired and insane. The suggestion was that citizens who were fed up with terror and coercion should simply refuse to acknowledge them... The inspiration of this idea consisted in eliminating the split in our personalities by shattering the internal excuses with which we justified our complicity in all the crimes [of the Soviet state]. It presupposed a small core of freedom in each individual, his "subjective sense of right", as Volpin put it. In other words a consciousness of his personal responsibility. Which meant, in effect, inner freedom."

Bukovsky joined in the organisation of the demonstration but was arrested three days before it was due to take place. Esenin-Volpin and others however went ahead. At about 6.00 pm on 5 December 1965, a date which was designated as "Soviet Constitution Day", about 200 demonstrators and supporters gathered in Pushkin Square. Many of those who attended were wary about actually joining the demonstration. One demonstrator was carrying a pair of skis, in order to be able to claim if arrested that he had not been attending the demonstration, but merely passing through and happening to stop and watch. However a handful of the demonstrators committed themselves by holding up posters. One read "For your freedom and ours". Another read "Respect the constitution". Within minutes the people holding the posters were arrested by the KGB. They were released after some hours of interrogation, but Esenin-Volpin was subsequently committed to a mental hospital.

The use of psychiatric hospitals, rather than labour camps or the firing squad against Esenin-Volpin and Bukovsky, was a sign that the form of their protest had wrong-footed the Soviet authorities to some extent. The authorities were used to dealing with supposed conspiracies or violent opponents, but completely unused to dealing with people who claimed to be upholding the authorities' own laws. Bukovsky was told by one of his interrogators, *"You keep talking about the Constitution and the laws, but what normal man would take Soviet laws seriously? You are living in an unreal world of your own invention, you react inadequately to the world around you"*. Esenin-Volpin's psychiatric diagnosis, used to justify his detention, was "pathological honesty".

In earlier years, the appearance of a handful of demonstrators with posters, and the detention of the demonstration organisers in psychiatric hospitals, would have attracted no attention. However, in terms of its timing, the Glasnost meeting was extremely lucky. By 1965, enough time had elapsed since Stalin's death in 1953 for a generation to grow up in the Soviet Union with no direct experience of Stalin's terror. The older generation of intellectuals, who remembered the terror, were determined to do what they could to prevent it from returning, and were particularly disturbed by the Sinyavksy and Daniel trial. In addition, beyond the Soviet Union's borders, far fewer people in the West held the idealised and mistaken views of the Soviet Union which had been common at the height of Stalin's show trials in the 1930s. Events in the Soviet Union were watched from afar by many, and the trial of Sinyavsky and Daniel had attracted international attention and criticism. As a result Esenin-Volpin's demonstration was noticed, both within and beyond the Soviet Union. Because it was noticed it led directly to the emergence of a group of determined and persistent domestic critics of the Soviet Union, known as "dissidents", which was soon joined by the distinguished physicist Andrei Sakharov. The issues raised by the dissidents, and the attention they received internationally, led to increasing pressure on the Soviet Union in relation to human rights, and in due course to the inclusion of respect for human rights in the Helsinki Accords signed by the United States, the Soviet Bloc nations and the nations of Western Europe in August 1975. The Helsinki Accords in turn provided Soviet dissidents with a further important statement of Soviet commitment, to which they could attempt to hold the Soviet government. Thirteen years elapsed between the Helsinki Accords and the introduction by Soviet Union General Secretary Mikhael Gorbachev of his free speech policy of "glasnost" in 1988, but there is no doubt that the ideas which came from the Glasnost Meeting, via the dissidents and the Helsinki Accords, had an important influence in bringing about Gorbachev's fundamental policy change, and all the historic events which followed from it. The Glasnost Meeting was therefore a tiny demonstration which changed the world because of its lucky timing.

Having considered these ingredients of successful demonstrations, it is obvious that the absence of these success factors is likely to result in failure. Poor advance notice, and poor organisation and control make failure very likely. Lack of novelty or inventive symbolism mean that a demonstration is much less likely to make an effective impact. Poor leadership is liable to ruin a demonstrating movement, and this can include failure to take account of timing. Sometimes, however, events require an immediate response by way of a demonstration, to reflect public feelings, and whether the timing turns out to be good or bad is quite outside the control of the organisers.

Demonstrations of various kinds have also tended to fail, or at least to achieve much less than their supporters might have hoped, irrespective of the qualities of the demonstration itself, where they are organised by both sides in a highly divided community. The problems of such communities are too intractable to be resolved by something as simple as demonstrating, even though numerous demonstrations will inevitably take place there.

Another situation where peaceful demonstrations have occasionally succeeded, but where they have more often resulted in catastrophic failure, with large-scale loss of life, is where the aim of the demonstration is to topple a repressive regime.

These two situations are described more fully in the next two chapters.

CHAPTER 17

NORTHERN IRELAND

Northern Ireland is a divided community where the issue of provocative demonstrations is always live. For this reason, it is a good place to consider both the effectiveness of demonstrations in a divided community, and also to look further at the advantages and disadvantages of the American strict protection of free speech, on the one hand, and the reasonable restrictions approach of English and European law on the other, as already discussed in chapter 13.

The tradition of sectarian marching in Northern Ireland has continued, without much change, since the time of the nineteenth century "orange lily" court case of Humphries v Connor. It goes back at least as far as the foundation of the Protestant Orange Order in 1795. Many marches are held on 12 July, and commemorate the victory of the Protestant William of Orange, by the then King William III of England– "King Billy" – over the exiled Catholic King James II –"King Jimmy" – at the Battle of the Boyne in 1690. From shortly after the order's foundation, its marches were associated with attacks on Catholics and inter-communal violence.

In the nineteenth century Britain tried to prevent the worst excesses of procession-related violence by banning Orange marches, by the Party Processions Act 1845. However that Act proved unenforceable, and it was repealed in 1869. Between then and 1922 the British government's official policy was one of "equal marching rights", whereby parades by both Protestant and Catholic communities were allowed to proceed but were restricted, at least in theory, to non-contentious areas. However parading was much more part of the Protestant than of the Catholic tradition, with hundreds of Orange Lodges across Northern Ireland, most of which were involved in holding Orange Parades. British government acceptance of parading by either community as being lawful therefore represented, in practice, a major victory for the Orange Order and its parade-related culture.

In 1922, most of Ireland became independent from Britain as the Irish Free State, but the six Protestant majority counties of Ulster remained in the UK, but with internal self-government, forming the new political entity of Northern Ireland.

From the creation of this new Northern Ireland, with its own government and parliament, until the imposition of direct rule on Northern Ireland from London in 1972, the political dominance of the Protestants, known as Unionists, was institutionalised. The police, the judges, and the whole of the government machinery were overwhelmingly Protestant. In this situation, the Orange and other Protestant parades were an assertion of police-backed Protestant power over the Catholic minority. In some places, notably at Portadown, marches were deliberately routed through predominantly Catholic areas, with the apparent intention of giving as much offence as possible to the Catholic community, thus generating continuing resentment and risk of violence.

This situation of entrenched Protestant superiority was challenged in the late 1960s by a new kind of march. Directly inspired by the American Civil Rights Movement, the Northern Ireland Civil Rights Association (NICRA) was formed by a coalition of different non-sectarian groups. Its objectives were defined in its constitution being "to defend the basic freedoms of all citizens, to protect the rights of individuals, to highlight all possible abuses of power, to demand guarantees for freedom of speech, assembly, and association, and to inform the public of their lawful rights". The main issue on which it inevitably focused was the second-class citizen status of Catholics in Northern Ireland.

NICRA generated fierce opposition from militant Protestants, led by the Reverend Ian Paisley. NICRA's first planned march was banned by the Minister of Home Affairs, William Craig, but the organisers went ahead regardless. Serious rioting occurred, during which the police baton charged demonstrators, who included Members of Parliament, and were televised hitting them with their batons. This episode raised tension all over Northern Ireland. On 30 November, 1968, the Prime Minister of Northern Ireland, Terence O'Neill, who had shown himself more understanding towards Catholic concerns than his militant predecessors, made a conciliatory speech calling for restraint. In response to that speech, NICRA announced a one month suspension of marches from 11 December, 1969. However another civil rights group, People's Democracy, set up by students at Queen's University, Belfast, decided to go ahead with a civil rights march from Belfast to Londonderry, on 1 January, 1969.

The People's Democracy march was directly inspired by Martin Luther King's march from Selma to Montgomery five years earlier, and was designed to focus as much attention as possible on the injustices of the Northern Ireland political system. It was intended to be through strongly Protestant areas of County Antrim and County Londonderry, by way of a deliberate exercise of controversial civil rights. To that extent it was provocative in the same way that the Orange Order marches were provocative. However it was a wholly peaceful march designed to draw attention to injustices.

The march set out from Belfast with about 40 people taking part. A close associate of Ian Paisley, Major Ronald Bunting, held a protest rally in Belfast against the march and made it clear that he and his supporters intended to harass the marchers along the whole length of their route. On the first day the march proceeded unhindered as far as the strongly Protestant town of Antrim, where the road was blocked by a police barricade. The Northern Irish police - the Royal Ulster Constabulary (RUC) – refused to remove the barricade, and after a lengthy delay and minor scuffles the marchers were driven in police vehicles to a community centre where they spent the night, interrupted by a bomb scare.

The next day the marchers set off for Randalstown, but found their way blocked by Major Bunting and a hostile crowd of protesters. The RUC refused to remove the protesters, and the marchers were eventually transported to Toome by car. At Toome they were welcomed, and after lunch set out for Maghera. After 30 minutes, the march was halted by the police and routed away from the strongly Protestant village of Knocklaughlin. Two miles further on protesters again blocked the marchers' route, again led by Major Bunting. Another stand-off developed as locals arrived to support the marchers. Eventually the RUC asked Major Bunting's group to stand aside, which they did, and the march continued towards Maghera. On learning that a large "reception committee" armed with clubs and sticks, was waiting to meet them at Maghera, the marchers diverted to Brackaghreilly, where they spent the night.

On the third day the marchers marched without incident as far as Dungiven. Outside Dungiven they were halted by the RUC, who told them there was a protesters' roadblock a mile up the road. A civil rights supporter then arrived from that direction and told them that there was no such blockade. The marchers continued and found that their informant was correct, and the RUC information untrue. The marchers spent the night in a village hall which was attacked by Unionists, who were in turn driven off by local people.

When the marchers reached Burntollet, seven miles from Londonderry, on 4 January, 1969, they numbered about 500. They were stopped briefly by the RUC, who told them that there were a few protesters ahead but that they could continue. As they continued the marchers came under a hail of stones from about 300 Unionists, waiting to ambush them on a slope above the road. The marchers turned to flee, only to find their retreat blocked by a second group of Unionists. As marchers fled into fields on either side of the road they were chased and beaten by Unionists, who threw several marchers into the nearby river Faughan. The beatings all occurred under the eyes of the RUC, who made no attempt to intervene. Seventeen marchers required hospital treatment. Later investigations proved that a large number of the Unionist attackers were off-duty policemen, belonging to a force of part-time constables called "B Specials", an exclusively Protestant unit intended solely for protection of the Protestant community in times of sectarian conflict.

Those marchers who were able to continue their march after the attack at Burntollet were again ambushed and attacked after they entered Londonderry. Again off-duty police took part in the attack and the RUC did nothing to stop it. A rally in the centre of Londonderry, which was intended to be the culmination of the march, was broken up by the RUC.

The events at Burntollet changed the political scene in Northern Ireland. For many Catholics, Burntollet proved conclusively that peaceful non-sectarian protest, which offended a significant element of the Protestant community, would not be permitted. It also confirmed the police, in many Catholic eyes, as enemies of the Catholic population. Moderate people were disheartened, and extremist elements in both Protestant and Catholic communities were strengthened. The Orange marches in the summer of 1969 degenerated into massive, serious and continuing rioting in which whole streets of houses were burned out. On 14 August, 1969 the RUC told the government that it could no longer cope, the civil authority requested assistance from the military, and British troops were sent to Belfast and Londonderry to restore order.

The British troops were initially seen by the Catholics as liberators from oppression by Protestant mobs. This changed in 1970, when no steps were taken by the Northern Irish or British governments or the Army to restrict the annual 12 July Protestant marches commemorating the Battle of the Boyne. A ban on all marches was then introduced on 23 July, 1970, to run until the end of the year, but this was too late to restore the confidence of the Catholic community. Sectarian attacks, violence and murder continued to increase. Across Northern Ireland, in the first seven months of 1971, there were 55 violent deaths, over 300 explosions, 320 shooting incidents, and over 600 people treated in hospital for violence-related injuries. The situation was then disastrously worsened in August 1971 by the decision of the British and Northern Irish governments to introduce detention without trial, known as internment, of suspected members of the Irish Republican Army (IRA) the Irish nationalist para-military organisation whose objective was a united Ireland and the end of Northern Ireland as a separate entity. Internment resulted in the detention of hundreds of innocent people, and caused violent rioting in Catholic areas, in which Protestants were burned out of their homes. There were also further burnings of Catholic homes in Protestant areas. Some 7,000 people were left homeless. Internment acted as a powerful recruiting sergeant for the IRA and, as the IRA grew, Protestant para-military organisations such as the Ulster Defence Association (UDA) also grew up to fight it. A state of near civil war developed, with 174 violent deaths in 1971.

On 2 January, 1972, with many people still interned, an anti-internment march was held in Belfast. The Prime Minister of Northern Ireland, Brian Faulkner, responded on 18 January, 1972 by banning all parades and marches until the end of the year.

On 22 January, 1972, before the ban came into effect, an anti-internment march was held at Magilligan Strand, County Londonderry, near the site of an internment camp. Several thousand marchers took part. As the march reached the vicinity of the camp, it was stopped by soldiers, who used barbed wire to close off the beach along which the marchers were walking. When it appeared that the marchers were going to go round the end of the wire, the soldiers fired rubber bullets and CS gas at close range into the crowd. A number of witnesses claimed that soldiers severely beat protesters and had to be physically restrained by their own officers.

A further anti-internment march was planned to be held in Londonderry on Sunday, 30 January, 1972. This was the first large march to be affected by the new Faulkner ban. The organisers were NICRA and the local MP, Ivan Cooper. Frank Laggan, Chief Constable of the RUC, recommended to the Army that the march be allowed to go ahead. However a decision was taken by the Army to stop the march and to arrest those taking part.

Ten thousand people are estimated to have attended the march in Londonderry on 30 January. It began at about 2.30 pm, from Central Drive in the city's Creggan Estate, and proceeded towards the City Guildhall, where a rally was planned. However, because of the march ban, the Parachute Regiment had sealed off the approaches to Guildhall Square. To avoid trouble, the march organisers therefore led most of the demonstrators down Rossville Street towards "Free Derry Corner" at the bottom of the street, a traditional location for protests.

A group of protesters from the march stayed behind to confront the soldiers at the barricades sealing off Guildhall Square, throwing stones and other missiles at them. Stoning of the soldiers was not new, but had been happening intermittently for some weeks. In response the soldiers used rubber bullets, CS gas and a water cannon. The CS gas caused many of the remaining protesters to move away and take refuge in the Bogside area of the city. Acting under orders to move in and arrest as many of the civil rights protesters as possible, the paratroopers then advanced down Rossville Street and into the Bogside. Then, at about 4.10 pm, without any prior warning, soldiers of the Parachute Regiment opened fire on the crowd of demonstrators, using live ammunition and firing at them for about 25 minutes. Thirteen demonstrators were killed and a fourteenth died later of his injuries. No soldier suffered serious injury.

The Army persistently claimed that the soldiers opened fire after a sniper opened fire on them from the Rossville Flats overlooking the demonstration. This claim has been exhaustively investigated by the Saville Inquiry set up many years afterwards, which concluded that an IRA sniper had indeed fired at the Army, but that the circumstances did not provide any justification for the soldiers opening fire on the crowd. The inquiry found that the firing on the crowd happened because of a breakdown of discipline on the part of the soldiers.

These killings, which became instantly notorious as "Bloody Sunday", caused understandable worldwide outrage. In Dublin the British Embassy was burned down by a mob. The British Government responded by demanding that Faulkner hand over to it his responsibility for security matters in Northern Ireland. When Faulkner refused, the British government suspended the operation of the Northern Ireland government and parliament and imposed direct rule on Northern Ireland from London, for the first time since 1922. Direct rule then continued for over 25 years until 1997.

"Bloody Sunday" ensured that there would be no peace in Northern Ireland for many years to come. It also led to a long campaign of IRA bombings in Britain, which cost many lives, beginning with the bombing on 22 February, 1972, less than a month later, of Aldershot Military Barracks, the headquarters of the Parachute Regiment.

The 25 years of British direct rule in Northern Ireland continued to see violent sectarian clashes every year associated with the "marching season" of Unionist marches. The clashes continued despite the gradual decline in the general level of violence in Northern Ireland in the 1980s and 1990s. In 1996, high hopes of a general cessation of violence were dashed by trouble over the annual Orange Order march to Drumcree Church at Portadown. This had taken place along the same route since 1807, through an area which by 1996 was strongly Catholic. That year the Chief Constable of the RUC required the march to alter its route, the day before the parade, to take it away from the Catholic area. On the morning of the parade police blocked the path of some 4,000 Unionist demonstrators. Four days of riots and disruption by Unionists across Northern Ireland followed, leaving the police seriously overstretched. Numbers of protesters facing the police at the "stand-off" at Drumcree kept growing over several days, until the Chief Constable felt compelled to give way and let the marchers through. This at once precipitated a week of serious rioting by Catholics.

The chaos and disruption caused by events at Drumcree led the British government to set up a general review of the handling of parades and marches in Northern Ireland. The review's recommendations were made law as the Public Processions (Northern Ireland) Act 1998. Under the new law, responsibility for regulating parades was taken away from the police and given to a new body, the Parades Commission, which is responsible for taking decisions concerning imposition of conditions on parades and re-routing of contentious parades. The Commission does not have power to completely ban a parade, but its power to impose conditions and re-route gives it effective power to change the nature of a parade if it considers it necessary. It has published procedural rules and guidelines as to how it operates, as well as a code of conduct for parades. Anyone who wishes to object to the form of an intended parade may refer the parade to the Parades Commission, and any controversial parade is therefore likely to come before the Commission's scrutiny.

The Orange Order strongly opposed the setting up of the Parades Commission, claiming that it would infringe people's freedom of assembly under the European Convention on Human Rights. However so far no successful challenge to the Commission has been made before the European Court, in the years since the 1998 Act was passed. This is probably because the Act's structure is designed to fit with the formula used in Article 11 of the European Convention, whereby the right of peaceful assembly is subject to reasonable limitations when necessary for reasons such as public order and protecting the rights of others.

The operation of the Parades Commission has not removed all tension from the issue of marches in Northern Ireland but it has substantially reduced it. It is generally agreed to have acted even-handedly and fairly in most of its decisions. With Unionist and Catholic politicians now in government together the political background has also changed dramatically. It remains to be seen whether the

Commission is a permanent or only a temporary solution to a centuries-old problem. The signs however are optimistic. There has been an easing of tension over the years of the Commission's existence which has coincided with a growing recognition that the right to march should not be absolute but should be subject to reasonable restrictions. It seems, therefore, that abandonment by many Protestants of their previous strict view that it was their right to express themselves by marching anywhere they wanted to, has led to a more peaceful society, without any significant diminution of the right to demonstrate. During these years the number of parades from a broadly Nationalist background has risen somewhat while the number of parades from a broadly Unionist background has stayed about the same. The reduction in the risk of riots and violence may actually have made peaceful parading more popular, so that freedom of assembly is actually being exercised more widely, as a result of the restrictions which have been placed on the most controversial marches, in the interests of peace. There is surely a lesson here for advocates of the American-style absolute free speech approach to demonstrations which gave rise to the events at Skokie in 1977, as described in Chapter 13.

Because of the improvements in the situation in Northern Ireland, a demonstration such as the People's Democracy March of 1969 would certainly be able to be held today without being broken up in the way that march was broken up at Burntollet Bridge. The changes in Northern Ireland in the intervening years have gone far to right the injustice against which People's Democracy were marching. However this has only happened after 25 years of low-level civil war and some 3,500 deaths. The People's Democracy was determinedly non-sectarian, but because it was campaigning against injustices to the Catholic community, it was inevitably seen by most Protestants as a march by "the other side" in a divided community. In these situations marches perceived by one side as supporting the other side are likely to achieve little, except, perhaps, by helping to maintain a long-term campaign in existence until progress can be made by some other means.

CHAPTER 18

DEMONSTRATIONS AND REVOLUTION

The relationship between demonstrations and revolutions is complicated. History shows that peaceful demonstrations cannot achieve their objective against an absolutely ruthless state. Sometimes, however, demonstrators, at great personal risk, have stood up against a ruthless dictatorship, and to general surprise the dictatorship has suddenly given way. In some of these cases the regime has actually been overthrown as a result of the peaceful street protests, so that the demonstration has turned into a peaceful revolution. Two examples of this have already been mentioned, the July 1830 peaceful overthrow of the Bourbon monarchy in France (Chapter 5) and the International Women's Day demonstration which turned into the first stage of the Russian Revolution in February 1917 (or March by the Western calendar) (Chapter 8). Such cases are however very rare, and whether they will arise out of a particular situation can be impossible to predict.

Sometimes cruel repression of a demonstration causes such outrage that it brings about a revolution that would not otherwise have happened. A classic example of this was the Cossack massacre of Father Gapon's demonstrators in 1905, which precipitated the first Russian Revolution of 1905, described in Chapter 8. A similar instance, causing not a revolution but a massive and irreversible movement towards independence, was the Amritsar Massacre (Chapter 10). Indeed, in the colonial situation, repression of demonstrations has frequently been a trigger for the movement which led to independence, as described further in Chapter 20. It was also the killing of demonstrators in Tahrir Square in 2011 which raised the momentum of protests against Hosni Mubarak to the point where his regime fell.

In 2014, similar killings in Independence Square in Kiev were the catalyst for the fall from power of Viktor Yanukovich.

However on a depressing number of other occasions, there is no such reaction to a massacre of demonstrators, and the perpetrators continue as before. This is sometimes because the majority of the public do not care enough, sometimes because the perpetrators succeed in suppressing knowledge of what they have done, sometimes because the perpetrators succeed in falsely blaming the violence on the demonstrators, and sometimes all three of these factors. Massacres understandably terrorise as well as enrage the population in the country where they happen. Usually the people remain in a state of terror and silent rage. Occasionally, and unpredictably, as in Russia in 1905, rage gains the upper hand and the regime is shaken.

As explained in Chapter 14, these types of massacres of demonstrators happen in democracies as well as dictatorships, as happened in France in 1961, even though in democracies the general public usually have access to better information about what has happened.

The list of occasions when dictatorial regimes have successfully suppressed potential revolutions by massacring demonstrators is a long one. Perhaps the most well-known within living memory is the Tiananmen Square massacre in Beijing, which is described in the next chapter, but the same result was achieved by massacres of demonstrators at Sharpeville in 1961, in Thailand in 1976, in South Korea in 1980, in Burma in 1988, in Uzbekistan in 2005 and in Guinea in 2009. In Syria, in 2011, massacres of demonstrators, notably at Tremseh in Hama, transformed a situation of peaceful demonstrations into a civil war which continues at the time of writing. The massacre of Uighur demonstrators by the Chinese Government at Gulja in Xinjiang province on 5 February, 1997 successfully suppressed peaceful protest and maintained Chinese control of Xinjiang, but did much to boost the clandestine violent anti-Chinese Uighur resistance movement which has since been increasingly active. In Egypt, on 14 August, 2013, General Abdul Fatah Al Sisi, having seized power in a coup, broke the supporters of the elected Muslim Brotherhood–led government by a massacre of over 1,000 demonstrators. This massacre, known as the Raba'a massacre, where the number of victims was probably more than double the numbers killed in the Tiananmen Square massacre, has at the time of writing effectively crushed opposition to Sisi's rule.

Total suppression of peaceful demonstrators was also successfully achieved in 1968 by the government of Mexico, which at that time was often described as a "façade democracy", by a massacre carried out in order that the protesters would not spoil Mexico's image as it hosted the Olympic Games.

The period of the run-up to the 1968 Olympic Games saw an escalating struggle between the Mexican authorities and a left-wing demonstration movement led by a National Strike Committee (CNH). An initial brutal suppression of a student demonstration was followed by suppression of other demonstrations, each of which provoked bigger demonstrations in protest. This was in a country with no previous tradition of large peaceful demonstrations. Indeed, one of the key demands of the protesters was the repeal of a law that prohibited more than three people from meeting together without permission. Mexico had at that date been governed since its 1910 revolution by the Institutional Revolutionary Party (PRI), through rigged elections and institutionalised corruption. No effective opposition was permitted, and when such opposition arose, it was treated as intolerable by the PRI. Even more intolerable was the possibility that demonstrations might distract attention from the Olympic Games, which were intended to show off Mexico to the world, and to show off the Mexican government to its own citizens.

On 2 October, 1968, troops and plain clothes police attacked a large demonstration of several thousand people in the Plaza de las Tres Culturas in Mexico City, next to the ancient ruins of Tlatelolco. The army surrounded the square, then fired without warning and continued shooting for several hours, during which time they also tried to prevent anyone leaving the square. The weapons used by the army included machine guns and tanks. Hundreds of arrests were made, with those arrested being brutally beaten, and in many cases stripped naked before being taken away to prison. Estimates of the dead vary between 44 and some 300, including young children and old people, many of whom had simply been in the square at the time and were not demonstrators. Many more people were wounded.

The Mexican government claimed that sharpshooters on nearby roofs had fired on the police. Demonstrators who survived denied that any demonstrators were armed, and claimed that sharpshooters who had been on the roofs were connected in some way with the authorities, as shown by their behaviour and the way they were treated by other officials. The demonstrators' testimony was collected in a moving book, *The night of Tlatelolco*, by Elena Poniatowska. Many years later, the PRI lost power in Mexico, and secret government papers relating to the Tlatelolco massacre became available. These confirmed the accounts of the demonstrators. The sharpshooters were a specially recruited government plain clothes force, instructed to fire into the square when a signal was given by the firing of flares in the air, and so to provide a supposedly plausible reason for the assembled troops to fire on the crowd.

The massacre and subsequent mass arrests of the surviving demonstrators completely broke the demonstration movement, and enabled the Olympic Games to take place without further interruption. Tlatelolco was possibly the first occasion on which a government strafed peaceful demonstrators with machine guns from a low flying helicopter, something which has since also happened in Libya in the early stages of the movement which led to the fall of Colonel Gaddafi.

Against this background of utterly ruthless killing of demonstrators in many countries, it is a relief to turn to the most famous example in recent times of a dictatorial regime being directly brought down as a result of huge street peaceful demonstrations. This was the first "People Power" revolution in the Philippines in 1986, which ended the dictatorship of Ferdinand Marcos. This was such a rare event that it is worth considering in some detail.

"People Power" began in response to President Marcos' blatant rigging of the results of the vote in the February 1986 presidential election. A nationwide body of election observers, organised by the Philippines National Citizens Association of Monitors for Free Elections (NAMFREL) produced overwhelming evidence that the true winner of the election was the opposition candidate, Mrs Corazon ("Cory") Aquino, widow of Benigno Aquino, the previous leader of the opposition, who had been murdered by the Marcos government.

On 16 February, 1986, Mrs Aquino launched a nationwide civil disobedience campaign to persuade Marcos to stand down, at a rally in Rizal Park in the centre of Manila, attended by an estimated one million people. She called on Filipinos to boycott "crony establishments" i.e. businesses run by associates of the president, which included many of the largest businesses in the country, such as San Miguel beer.

The movement was greatly helped, and Marcos correspondingly weakened, by the stance of the international community, particularly the United States. US President Reagan, after initially causing consternation by appearing to welcome Marcos's re-election, changed his position, on the very same day as the Rizal Park rally, publicly announcing, while the rally was in progress, that there had been massive fraud in the election.

The United States had been the colonial power in the Philippines prior to the Second World War, and still wielded enormous influence. The timing and content of Reagan's statement therefore gave a huge boost to the civil disobedience movement. It also persuaded some members of the Marcos government that the United States, which had previously backed Marcos uncritically, would now support regime change. The European Community, Australia, New Zealand, Japan, and the Association of South-East Asian Nations (ASEAN) also expressed concern about the elections. Despite this Marcos made it clear, in his public announcements, in response to these international expressions of concern, that he intended to use military force to enforce his "mandate".

In the next few days, it looked as if the Aquino civil disobedience movement might run out of momentum and fail, despite a slight drop in the sales of San Miguel beer as a result of the cronyism boycott. However on the afternoon of 22 February, the Catholic radio station, Radio Veritas, interrupted its programme to cover an emergency news conference given by Marcos's defence minister, Juan Ponce Enrile, and the Armed Forces Vice-Chief of Staff, General Fidel Ramos, at Enrile's headquarters at Camp Aquinaldo on the eastern side of Manila. Enrile and Ramos both announced that they had withdrawn their allegiance from Marcos as president of the Philippines, and that they had barricaded themselves in, after learning that Marcos intended to arrest them. They stated that they would defend their barricades to the death.

That evening, Marcos broadcast to the nation on television. He announced that there had been an attempted coup led by Enrile and Ramos, and called on them to "stop this stupidity" and surrender. Cory Aquino's younger brother, Agapito "Butz" Aquino, responded to the broadcast by calling on pro-democracy groups to gather around Camp Aguinaldo and provide street support to Enrile and Ramos. The head of the Catholic Church in the Philippines, Cardinal Jaime Sin, followed suit by calling on people to go out into the street, send food into the camp, and block any movement of hostile troops.

Within an hour of Cardinal Sin's call, thousands of men, women and children had ringed the gates of both Camp Aguinaldo and nearby Camp Crame. Ramos considered Camp Crame, which had a smaller perimeter than Camp Aguinaldo, to be more defensible, and shortly afterwards he moved there, while Enrile remained at Camp Aguinaldo. The ten lane highway between the two camps, Epifanio de los Santos Avenue ("EDSA"), became the focus of events as it filled up with people arriving to block the route of hostile troops.

The situation remained static until the following morning, when Enrile followed Ramos across the avenue to Camp Crame. At that stage they had only three battalions of soldiers supporting them, totalling less than 500 men.

Shortly afterwards Radio Veritas, which had been giving support and coverage to the demonstrations, was knocked off the air by a pro-Marcos saboteur, but was replaced by a makeshift radio station broadcasting information, advice and requests for help to the crowds of protesters, one of whom later described EDSA as having " a radio every square metre".

Families camped out on EDSA with their friends and with food and drink. Most people wore yellow ribbons or other yellow objects as the symbol of the people power movement. The atmosphere was initially festive, but was gradually replaced by fear, as rumours swept the crowd that tanks were coming. Trees were felled to make tank barricades across the road, and other barricades were made from vehicles, lamp posts and drainage grills. One eye-witness reported a new Mercedes Benz car placed in line to form part of a barricade. Instructions were given over the radio about how to make a bus into a more effective barricade, by letting its tyres down and turning it over on its side.

Eventually, not tanks, but half-tracked armoured personnel carriers (APCs) appeared on Ortigas Avenue, a mile from Camp Crame, carrying armed marines with orders to storm the camp. A crowd, consisting mainly of women, rushed towards the vehicles and threatened to lie down on the road in their path if they advanced any further. The APCs, commanded by Marine General Tadiar, halted. A tense stand-off followed, with at least 4,000 people immediately in front of the APCs, including men, women and children, and many priests and nuns. Behind them, in the section of EDSA adjoining Ortigas Avenue, were an estimated 100,000 demonstrators. The number of People Power supporters on the streets in and around the two camps was probably in excess of two million.

Tadiar announced that people had half an hour to disperse. The time elapsed without anyone moving. Then Tadiar's vehicles several times revved up their engines and acted as if they were preparing to move forward and crush the human barrier in front of them. Military helicopters flew low over the crowd. One of those present in front of the APCs later described the scene:

> "At the very front, within arm's length of the APC, three nuns are kneeling, praying, They are puny and incongruous in front of the APCs and the soldiers… One of the marines atop the APC seems especially belligerent. When someone tosses a packet of cigarettes up to him, a peace offering, he stares balefully at the person. He is booed and hissed. He gathers himself up to his full height, deliberately turns his back on the crowd, and viciously jabs his hand into the air in an obscene gesture. He heads for one of the far hatches, opens it, takes out an Armalite, pointedly lays it on top of the hatch. The gesture is not lost on the crowd… the soldier now walks back to the near edge of the APC. Arrogantly he turns his back on us, signals to

*the driver. The engine comes to life again, coughing black smoke...
I link arms with men on either side of me. Some of us are weeping.
Some are also cursing.*

*The APC jerks forward again. Men brace themselves against
the advancing metal wall, trying to hold it back. Behind them the
nuns stay on their knees, praying. I am ...behind the nuns, but the
APC is so huge it seems to loom over me. I wonder how many will
be crushed before they realise we mean to stay, or before the pile of
bodies makes it impossible for the APC to continue.*

*All around us, the horde of people... begins to chant angrily
"Cor-ee! Cor- ee!", as if the name alone had the power to stop
arrogant men and metal.*

*Just as I am about to hear the first shriek of agony, a miracle...
the APC stops, its engine winds down. Cheers and wild applause. We
have won again. The soldiers glare down at us. Again the thousands
chant Cory's name.*

*The APC's engine starts again and my heart sinks. But this time
it does not intend to try us again. It only wants to turn and join the
rest of its unit. The General knows he cannot pass this way."*

The stand-off between the blocked columns of troops and the millions of
demonstrators continued all day on 23 February, through the night, and for most
of Sunday, 24 February. At about 5.00 pm on 24 February, the US Ambassador
sent a message to Ferdinand Marcos from President Reagan that the United
States would not tolerate the use of heavy weaponry against the crowds. News
of this message began to trigger additional defections from the army to Enrile
and Ramos, including a group of helicopter pilots, who landed their machines in
Camp Crame.

Only one violent incident occurred throughout Manila during the whole
crisis. Near a television station controlled by Marcos loyalist soldiers, snipers fired
into the crowd wounding a number of people. Soldiers supporting Enrile and
Ramos then attacked the soldiers in the television station, who surrendered after
killing one of the attackers. Apart from this, People Power was entirely peaceful.

By the end of 24 February, continuing military defections swung the balance
of power heavily to Cory Aquino, and she decided to proceed with her presidential
inauguration the next day. Ferdinand Marcos also decided to proceed with his, so
there were alternative inaugurations on the same day, Marcos in the Malacanang

Palace and Aquino at the Manila Country Club. However later that day Marcos fled the country, never to return, and Aquino took over the government.

The People Power revolution was immensely influential around the world, as an inspiring example of peaceful regime change through citizen action. It was replicated elsewhere in Asia, notably in South Korea from 1987 to 1989, and in 1989 in the Velvet Revolution in Prague. However it would not have happened without the critical interventions of the United States on the side of the demonstrators, causing key defections from Marcos's forces. Even so it was a close call, despite the huge numbers of demonstrators, reflecting the support of the large majority of the population of the Philippines. The Catholic Church played a major role in organising the demonstrations, and some of the Catholic writing about the demonstrations by their supporters is infused with semi-mystical allusions, as if what happened was a divinely inspired miracle. However the factor which led to the triumph of the demonstrators was the defection of key elements of the military, influenced by the US intervention. Without those defections, the military would certainly have been used to massacre the demonstrators, as happened in so many other places.

Sadly the Aquino government was a great disappointment. As well as disappointing hopes of sweeping and overdue reforms, it showed itself almost as insensitive to civil liberties and human life as Marcos had been. On 22 January, 1987, the Peasant Movement of the Philippines (Kilusang Magbubukid ng Pilipinas) held a 10,000 strong march on the presidential palace to protest at the lack of progress on land reform. Their way was blocked by riot police at the Mendiola Bridge, and when the farmers tried to force their way through the roadblock the riot police fired on them, killing thirteen farmers and wounding 80 others. No police were prosecuted, despite recommendations for prosecution by an independent commission of inquiry.

The People Power Revolution was replayed as farce in 2001 when crowds again assembled in Manila to demand the resignation of President Joseph Estrada, on account of his massive corruption. As the crowds kept growing, Estrada, who lacked Marcos's ruthlessness and political skill, simply fled the palace, allowing his defeated (and also very corrupt) election opponent, Gloria Magapagal Arroyo, to declare herself president. This was a demonstration-driven regime change which weakened Philippines democracy, engineered by demonstrators who may well not have represented majority opinion, and by-passing existing constitutional procedures for removing a president. It showed the scope for "People Power" to degenerate into an abuse.

Despite this subsequent history, the People Power example continues to influence demonstrators around the world who want regime change, as shown by the colour revolutions of the first decade of the twenty first century, the "Orange Revolution" in Ukraine and the "Rose Revolution" in Georgia. It has directly inspired some tragic demonstrators who, unlike "People Power", were not helped by outside pressure or defecting military, and who, as a result perished in large numbers, when the army shot them down en masse. This happened two years after "People Power" in Burma, and three years afterwards in China.

What general conclusions can be drawn about demonstrations and revolution? First of all, using a demonstration to bring about a revolution in a democratic country where the rule of law is observed is quintessentially anti-democratic, and incompatible with the concept of a demonstration as the exercise of a legally guaranteed right. Secondly, when dealing with a dictatorship, whether overt, or concealed under façade of rigged elections as in Mexico of 1968 or Hosni Mubarak's Egypt in 2011, there may be few or no alternative methods of attempting regime change. However an attempt to change a repressive regime will always be extremely dangerous, with multiple deaths and defeat a more likely outcome, on historical precedents, than victory. Thirdly, in that kind of repressive situation, the distinction between abiding by the rule of law and engaging in civil disobedience, so important in democratic countries, diminishes almost to vanishing point. People so desperate that they are willing to risk death, by demonstrating against a regime that is likely to shoot them down, cannot realistically be expected to worry about such legalistic concepts as obstruction of the highway, trespass, or interference with a police officer in the execution of his duty. The fact that " People Power" was part of Cory Aquino's civil disobedience campaign against Ferdinand Marcos's rigged elections has to be set in this context. It is not a reason for adopting civil disobedience tactics except in the situation of a desperate struggle to remove a dictatorship.

Perhaps the final conclusion about movements such as "People Power" is the scope which they offer for abuse, by way of anti-democratic overthrow of an elected government, as seen in the second People Power movement.

Further examples of such abuse of the power to demonstrate were the sustained, and partly successful, street protests against the democratically elected – although authoritarian and corrupt – former prime minister of Thailand, Thaksin Shinawatra, which eventually led to Thaksin's departure from Thailand. The Thai middle classes in Bangkok who demonstrated against Thaksin, and against his sister and successor, Yingluck, almost certainly represented a minority of the country. It is ironic that they were an educated and rule of law-minded minority, since by their protests they promoted a system of change of government through pressure from the streets which is incompatible with modern ideas of democracy. It is not surprising that this sustained street pressure on a fragile democracy resulted, in 2014, in a military coup.

In the Arab world, in the years before the Arab Spring, the expression "democracy of the streets" was sometimes used about the traditional ability of rioting mobs in Arab cities to bring down authoritarian regimes. This was not democracy in the sense of legislators who represent the will of the people, but simply an ability of violent street protesters to overthrow a government.

If "People Power" becomes a regular means of unseating democratic prime ministers by whichever movement can organise a large enough demonstration in the capital city, it, like Arab street mobs, will weaken democracy and democratic institutions, increase instability, decrease respect for the rule of law, and ultimately decrease respect for rights, including the right to demonstrate. It will do all these damaging things even if, unlike the Arab street mobs, it remains a peaceful movement.

Every revolutionary situation is slightly different from others, and general precepts can be no substitute for careful analysis of the facts of a particular case. In Ukraine for example, further inquiry is still needed into the exact circumstances in which Viktor Yanukovich relinquished power and fled in February 2014, after a vote calling for his resignation was passed by the Ukrainian Parliament, with enormous crowds of demonstrators outside, and apparently some inside the building. It is not yet entirely clear to outside observers whether what happened was intimidation by mob rule, as claimed by Yanukovich and his Russian allies, or a free and legitimate democratic vote to remove Yanukovich, carried because many of his own former supporters were disgusted by the fatal shootings of many demonstrators over the previous days.

However it is certain is that the removal of a democratically-elected government, like that of Yanukovich, by demonstrations, can only be justified in the most extreme circumstances, where the government has ceased to be democratic, and where there are no constitutional methods available to bring about change. Demonstrations as a way to bring about a revolution are a game of last resort only, played for the highest possible stakes.

CHAPTER 19

DEMONSTRATIONS AND CHINA

The 1989 Tiananmen Square demonstrations were partly inspired by the People Power movement in the Philippines and similar events in South Korea. Students at Beijing University had access to better information than most Chinese people, and were aware of world events. However the demonstrations also had roots going back deep into Chinese history. These roots need to be understood, to appreciate how the demonstrations appeared to those taking part in them, and also how they appeared to the Chinese government.

Throughout the millennia of Chinese civilisation, rulers were absolute, subject only to retaining "the mantle of heaven". The ancient Chinese philosophers, Confucius and Mencius, taught that the people had the right to overthrow an unjust ruler, who through his actions had lost the mantle of heaven. Their books, containing these dangerous doctrines, were ceremonially burned, along with many others, by the Chin emperor, in 213 BC, in the notorious event known as "the burning of the books". From 213BC onward, for over two thousand years, the old teachings, about the right to overthrow an unjust ruler, were replaced by imperial neo-Confucianism, which emphasised absolute obedience to the emperor, enforced by imperial rescripts which ended with the words "Tremble and Obey". This philosophy, and the imperial system based on it, endured until the end of Imperial China at the beginning of the twentieth century.

There was no role in such a system for legitimate political opposition. All opposition was by definition illegal and clandestine. As a result, conspiratorial movements and secret societies, bent on the overthrow of the dynasty, became part of the national culture. The notorious Triad societies of southern China, are today merely non-political criminal gangs. However they still show their historic origin, in secret seventeenth century political societies dedicated to the restoration of a previous Imperial dynasty, when they swear in their initiation ceremonies that they will "Uphold the Ming, overthrow the Ching".

Despite the Chin emperor burning the books, the concept of losing the mantle of heaven remained well-known and influential through Chinese history. However Confucius and Mencius were not precise in describing the situations in which the mantle of heaven would be lost. Any person who thought it had been lost and raised the standard of rebellion was gambling heavily that his assessment was right. If he was wrong he would be killed. If he was right he would found a new dynasty, which would then be as intolerant of dissent as its predecessors.

Over the centuries certain characteristics emerged, which identified people who believed that the mantle of heaven had been lost. The appearance of large numbers of such people then indicated to others, who were themselves uncommitted, the possibility that the emperor's mantle might be about to disappear. These identifiable people were often adherents of religious or semi-religious mass movements. Thus the Ching dynasty was weakened in the late eighteenth century by the religious rebels of the White Lotus Society (1796-1804). It was then again further severely weakened in the mid-nineteenth century by the rebellion of the Taipings, whose leader, Hong Xiuquan, claimed to be the younger brother of Jesus Christ, who would lead his followers to the promised kingdom. The Taipings were only suppressed after fifteen years of war and the loss of 30 million lives.

Understanding the idea of the mantle of heaven, the intolerance of peaceful opposition, and the tradition of repression, rebellion and revolution, is necessary to understand what happened in Tiananmen Square in June, 1989, even though on a formal or explicit level the issues were very different.

Another important factor, which has to be understood in connection with the Tiananmen Square events, is the special historical role of students in Chinese society. When the students protested in 1989, they were not embarking on an unprecedented activity, but were consciously following a tradition of student protest thousands of years old.

Students had always had a role as a kind of tribune of the people, in a society with no legislature or popular representation. As far back as the first century BC, students had protested against punishment of an honest official by the emperor. Student movements occurred in the Han dynasty (the Roman era in Europe), and were common in the Sung dynasty (the Middle Ages in Europe). A notable student-led protest, which seems to have had all the characteristics of a modern peaceful demonstration, occurred in the last year of the Northern Sung dynasty,

1126 A.D, when the armies of the nomadic Jurchen people were threatening the capital city of Kaifeng. The peace faction in the government secured the dismissal of the minister Li Keng, who was a leading proponent of a last-ditch fight against the Jurchens, as a way of appeasing the Jurchens and clearing the way for a settlement with them. Led by Chen Tung (1086-1127), a member of the staff of the Imperial College (where students studied for the examinations to become mandarins), thousands of scholars, students, soldiers and citizens of the capital assembled at the gate of the Imperial Palace, and beat the drum traditionally placed at the entrance of an official's yamen, or court, for the use of anyone demanding that his grievance be heard by the authorities. The demonstrators then formally presented a memorial to the authorities, protesting against the dismissal of Li Keng. Their demonstration was successful in that Li Keng was then reinstated in his post, although he proved unable to hold back the Jurchens, with whom the Sung emperor was forced to sign a humiliating peace.

Students in the earlier part of the Ming dynasty (1368-1643) were continuously involved in the feuds of political factions, and it seems likely that some of these feuds involved demonstrations. However the tradition of student activism died out before the end of the Ming dynasty, and was not recorded for most of the Ching dynasty. For a period of some three hundred years students ceased to play any part in politics.

Then, near the end of the Ching dynasty the tradition revived. Under the leadership of Kang You-Wei, candidates for the imperial civil service examinations signed a ten thousand word petition in April 1895, protesting against the Treaty of Shimonseki, which China was forced to sign after being defeated by Japan in the Sino-Japanese War, and under which Taiwan was to be ceded to Japan. The petition was known as the Gonche Shangshu, meaning "Public Vehicle Petition", a name taken from the ancient practice in the Han dynasty of providing public transport for civil service candidates from various provinces to take the examinations. After the Ching government rejected the petition, thousands of students and other citizens demonstrated in Beijing against the Treaty of Shimonoseki on 2 May, 1895.

Kang You-Wei and his associates continued to campaign for reform of the antiquated system under which the late Ching dynasty China was governed. They were nationalists humiliated by China's weakness in relation to the European powers and Japan, and also modernisers who wanted China to adopt a more modern system of government. As well as wishing to see the modernisation of China's government and army, they were strong supporters of introducing Western systems of education to replace the training in the Chinese classics on which the civil service examinations were based.

In 1898, Kang You-Wei presented a memorial to the emperor calling for a comprehensive modernisation of China, including replacement of the mandarin examinations by modern Western education. For a few months the emperor in response began reforms, with Kang You-Wei as a member of his council. Then conservative interests at court, led by the Dowager Empress Cu Xi, organised a palace coup, and the leading reforms were either executed, like the political philosopher Tan Si Tong, or, like Kang himself, fled overseas. The reforms which had been introduced were mostly repealed, with the exception of the foundation of Beijing University as a Western style university, replacing the old Imperial University which taught students for the old civil examinations. From its foundation Beijing University became a stronghold of modernising ideas in China. In the 1910s and 1920s a modernising movement, the New Culture Movement, emerged, many of whose leading members were Beijing University staff members. Against this background, it is not surprising that the first modern mass demonstration movement in China was organised by students. The May 4 movement in 1920 arose from Chinese outrage at the terms of the Treaty of Versailles ending World War One. The important port of Qingdao had been a German possession under one of the "unequal" nineteenth century treaties made by the European powers with the Ching dynasty. By the Treaty of Versailles, all Germany's former colonies, including Qingdao, were taken away from Germany, and given to countries which had fought on the winning side in World War One. China had been on the Allied side in World War One from 1917, and therefore hoped to be given back Qingdao. Instead the victorious allies gave Qingdao to Japan, which had also entered the war on the Allied side, and had occupied Qingdao since 1914, after defeating its German garrison.

Anger was widely felt in China, both at the great powers which had imposed this arrangement on China, and on ministers in the Chinese government who were thought to have weakly failed to stand up for their country's rights.

On 4 May, 1919, some 3,000 students, from Beijing University and 12 other educational institutions in Beijing, held a mass demonstration outside Tiananmen, the south gateway to the old Imperial Palace, known as the Forbidden City. This was very close to the location of the Tiananmen Square demonstrations in 1989, although, following the Communist takeover in 1949, the layout of the area had been changed to create the present huge square.

This large student demonstration was entirely peaceful, and its good organisation, sincerity and self-discipline impressed both Chinese citizens and foreign observers[45]. The students handed out a "Manifesto of All the Students of Beijing", which called for the return of Qingdao and the removal of the ministers who had permitted it to be given to Japan. After the rally at the Tiananmen Gate, the students marched off in procession. At the head of the procession were two huge five-coloured national flags, together with a pair of Chinese funerary scrolls on which were written traditional Chinese mourning phrases adapted for the occasion: *"The names of Tsao Ju Lin, Lu Tsung–Yu and Chang Tsung-Hiang (three pro-Japanese cabinet ministers) will stink for 1000 years/ The students of Beijing mourn them with tears)."* The students carried white flags made of cloth or paper, with slogans written in Chinese, English and French, and caricatures expressing the purpose of the demonstration. Slogans included "Return our Tsingtao!", "We may be beheaded but Tsing Tao must not be lost!", "Boycott Japanese goods!", "International Justice!", "Don't just be patriotic for five minutes!"

Although the demonstration itself was peaceful, some students went on to burn the house of a pro-Japanese Cabinet minister and to beat up the Chinese Minister to Japan. The police were initially sympathetic to the students and only intervened when they received orders to do so from higher commanders. Fighting followed between students and the police, and one student later died from his wounds. Thirty-two students were arrested and martial law was declared in the area where the fighting had taken place.

That demonstration on 4 May, 1919, was followed by more demonstrations around the country over the next few days, including at Shanghai, Nanjing, Wuhan, Fuzhou and Canton. However, after the success of these demonstrations, the students stopped using demonstrations as their main method of organising. Instead they organised strikes, teams to distribute patriotic leaflets and make speeches to the general public, and a movement to boycott Japanese goods on a sufficient scale to damage Japanese trade with China for at least a year.

The government, led by the pro-Japanese president, Hsu Chi-Chang, decided to suppress the boycott, and at the beginning of June it started arresting students who were helping the boycott by selling Chinese goods. By 4 June, 1919, the government had about 1,150 student prisoners. This led to massive sympathy strikes for the students, and increasing pressure on the government. Matters came to a climax on 9 June, with a 20,000-strong sympathy demonstration in Tientsin, followed by the start of a general merchants' strike. Bankers warned the government that the financial markets would collapse if the situation continued.

---

[45]   These observers included the American philosopher John Dewey, who compared the students favourably with American college students.

The government under pressure then accepted the resignations of the three ministers widely blamed for the loss of Qingdao and the pro-Japanese policy. On 28 June, under continuing public pressure, the Chinese government formally refused to sign the Treaty of Versailles, and so refused to accept the Japanese annexation of Qingdao. To this extent the May 4 Movement succeeded. Although Qingdao remained in Japanese hands, the Chinese government did not accept the position as it otherwise would have done.

The May 4 Movement was the broadest demonstration of popular national feeling that China had ever seen. It was led by intellectuals committed to Western ideas of science and democracy. After the end of the active phase of the movement, its idealistic activists moved in different political directions and into other kinds of reform activities, but the fact that the students had come together for a national cause remained a profound source of inspiration for future generations.

Another patriotic student demonstration movement, on a smaller scale, was the May 30th movement, inspired by protest against the killing of 13 demonstrators by police under British command in the International Settlement of Shanghai on 30 May, 1925.

In 1931 and 1932 the Beida (short form of the Chinese name for Beijing University) Demonstration Corps and Petition Corps also organised demonstrations against Japanese aggression. This was after open war between the two countries had broken out following the 1931 fighting outside Beijing known as the Marco Polo Bridge incident.

Student protesters in China therefore had a strong tradition of being seen as patriotic. China is a society with a strong sense of history, and this tradition was well-known to Beijing students in 1989. This was so despite the fact that unofficial demonstrations stopped happening in China after the Communist takeover in 1949. From then until 1987 the only demonstrations which were tolerated were those organised by the ruling Communist Party.

The most dramatic and extreme government organised demonstrations in China were those of the Cultural Revolution from 1966 to 1976. These were widely misunderstood in the West at the time. Apparently spontaneous, they were in fact Mao Tse Tung's way of preserving himself in power after the catastrophe of his "Great Leap Forward", the agricultural and industrial policy which led to the deaths of 15 million people in a man-made famine in 1962 and 1963. Other leading figures in the Communist Party, such as Liu Shao Chi and Deng Xiao Ping, were aware of Mao's disastrous blunders, and might have moved to restrain his power, if he had not moved against them first.

Mao used the apparatus of the Communist Party, and its organs in every institution, to encourage groups of young militants, called Red Guards, to identify and persecute teachers and other intellectuals, who would otherwise have been the most likely to speak out about Mao's shortcomings. Those whom the Red Guards singled out for denunciation were savagely beaten, paraded through the streets in dunce's caps, forced to take part in grossly humiliating public self-criticism sessions, and often killed. The campaign escalated until it led to the systematic humiliation and disgrace of Liu, Deng and other party leaders. It then went wildly out of control, with rival gangs of Red Guards fighting each other as miniature armies.

In 1968, the chaos became so great that Mao called on the People's Liberation Army to take over, and abolished the Red Guards. Significantly, in carrying out Mao's orders to suppress the Red Guards, the People's Liberation Army did not use firearms at all, although the chaos caused by the Red Guards was incomparably greater than the disruption caused by the Tiananmen Square student demonstrations in 1989.

After Mao's death in 1976 and the overthrow of his widow, Chiang Ching, the men who had been humiliated in the Cultural Revolution gradually returned to power. Deng Xiao Ping, after gross public humiliation by student Red Guards, had spent the Cultural Revolution cleaning pigsties. His son, Deng Pu Fan, had been thrown from a window by Red Guards, and as a result became a paraplegic. By 1989 Deng, although officially retired as president of China, was in fact the real ruler of the nation.

The 1989 demonstrations began during a period of rapidly rising social unrest, caused by the forces unleashed by Deng Xiao Ping's economic reforms. Inevitably, the economic progress visible during the 1980s led to talk of possible progress in the direction of greater freedom. This had been a theme of China's dissidents ever since the end of the Cultural Revolution. It had surfaced during the period of protest associated with the "Democracy Wall" movement in 1978-79, when the dissident Wei Jing Sheng had been imprisoned after calling for democracy as "The Fifth Modernisation".

The students of 1989 knew little about the Democracy Wall movement, as information about it had been censored and written out of history. This was to show at a late stage of the 1989 demonstrations when veterans of that movement who came forward to join the students were treated with suspicion and little respect. However the issues which concerned the "Democracy Wall" protesters were the same issues which concerned students in 1989.

The idea of a new student demonstration movement arose early in 1989, in informal discussions held by Beijing University students and teachers, at the university's "Democracy Lawn", in front of the statue of Cervantes. One idea was to start the movement on 4 May, the exact seventieth anniversary of the May 4 Movement of 1919. Wang Dan, who later emerged as the leading public face of the Beijing University students, was already active at this stage.

Organising students for large demonstrations is easier in Beijing than most places. They traditionally live in communal dormitories, sharing many activities, and, once a proposal was debated by a group of students, it was likely that most of them would join in an agreed course of action. This tendency to join in what had been agreed was reinforced by Chinese attitudes favouring communal harmony, and by the ideology of Communism. Beijing also has a huge student population, much of it concentrated in one district, Haidian in the north-west of the city. Mobilising large numbers of students for marches to the centre of the city could therefore be done more easily than if the universities had been more dispersed.

The Communist authorities were very concerned that the liberalising economic forces that they had themselves encouraged were going to lead to an increase in crime and social disorder. The "Tiananmen papers", internal documents later leaked to Western researchers, show that, as well as concerns about assaults and robberies, they were concerned, even before the student movement started, about increased cases of "demonstrations, public petitioning and other disruptions of public order".

On 15 April, 1989, former Communist Party Secretary-General Hu Yao Bang died suddenly of a heart attack. He had been the leading reformist within the Communist Party hierarchy, but had resigned in 1987. He had been forced to resign to take the blame for tolerating student demonstrations which had occurred that year in some cities. His funeral, and the opportunity to pay tribute to his memory, was therefore also an opportunity for supporters of democratic reform to make their feelings known.

Within a day of the announcement of Hu's death, people began gathering at the Monument to the People's Heroes in Tiananmen Square with wreaths, flowers and signs praising Hu as a reformer and a democrat. In Shanghai protest posters to the same effect appeared on university campuses. On the afternoon of 17 April, 600 students from Beijing's Chinese University of Politics and Law entered the square with mourning banners and wreaths and shouted slogans in favour of freedom, democracy and the rule of law.

The movement to commemorate Hu as a beacon of democratic reform spread rapidly among students across China. It spread at a tense and symbolic time of year, as both the students and the government were well aware that the significant date of 4 May was only a few days away. The obvious parallel between the students of 1919 and those of 1989 made the student movement an immediate object of public sympathy and respect.

In late April 1989, the Communist leadership was deeply split in its attitude towards reform. The Party General Secretary, Zhao Zhiyang, was a reformer, sympathetic to student demands for more democracy, less Communist party control of daily life and eradication of corruption, particularly corruption involving sons and daughters of the top leadership. Other party leaders, including the Prime Minister, Li Peng, were orthodox Communists, who wanted the student agitation forcibly suppressed. The real final arbiter behind the scenes, although officially retired, was Deng Xiao Ping.

On 26 April, while Zhao Zhiyang was on an official visit to North Korea and not directly in touch with events in Beijing, the *People's Daily*, the official mouthpiece of the Chinese government, published an editorial condemning the students for causing turmoil. The word "turmoil" has very negative connotations in Chinese politics. It is widely used to describe the situation during the Cultural Revolution. The principal author of the line taken in the editorial was Li Peng. This condemnation caused outrage among the students, who regarded themselves as heirs to the patriotic, though Westernising, inheritance of the May 4th movement. It also caused the students to fear that if they gave up their movement at that point they would be harshly punished. The editorial also outraged many people in the wider community, and so generated more support for students. Demonstrations supporting the students took place in almost every large city in China, and the demonstrations in Tiananmen Square became much bigger.

On 3 May, Zhao Zhiyang, back from North Korea, made a conciliatory speech, celebrating the 70th anniversary of the May 4th Movement, and praising the role of youth. In a critical passage he affirmed the patriotism of the 1989 student demonstrators and the legitimacy of their desire for democracy and opposition to corruption. This speech had some effect in mollifying student and public anger about the *People's Daily* editorial. However the fact that it differed markedly from hardline statements still being made by official spokespersons made it obvious that the government and party were divided. This in turn encouraged student reformers to press their demands.

On 4 May, tens of thousands of students from 51 campuses marched along Chang An Avenue, which runs east-west through the centre of Beijing and across Tiananmen Square. They broke through police cordons which had been set up around the square, and converged there carrying drums and banners, chanting slogans and singing. At about 3.00 pm, a student leader standing under the banner of the Autonomous Federation of Students – a new and officially illegal body formed by the students themselves, as opposed to official student organisations set up by the Communist Party – read out a "May 4th Declaration". This stated that the current student movement was a continuation and development of the great patriotic student movement of 70 years earlier, and that it shared with the government an ultimate goal, China's modernisation. The students stood for the May 4th values of democracy, science, freedom, human rights and the rule of law. They called on the government to accelerate political and economic reforms, guarantee constitutional freedoms, fight corruption, adopt a press law, and allow the establishment of privately run newspapers. The Declaration stated that important first steps would include institutionalising the democratic practices that the students themselves had started on their campuses, conducting student-government dialogue, promoting democratic reforms of the government system, opposing corruption, and accelerating the adoption of a press law. It stated that the students had already achieved a series of unprecedented victories for the cause of democracy and the May 4th spirit, but that the victories were fragile, and that it was necessary to continue the struggle.

After the reading of the Declaration, the AFS representatives announced that the students would return to classes, but would continue to negotiate with the government over their demand for dialogue. Depending on the outcome of those negotiations, they might organise further action. They also announced that students would go forth among the citizens of Beijing, explaining the May 4th Movement.

If the student movement had indeed paused then, and the students returned to classes, it is possible that confrontation might have been avoided, and the future of China been very different. Behind the scenes, Zhao Zhiyang was struggling with his Communist comrades to obtain more sympathy for the students. If their action had ended then, or even stopped for a limited period, Zhao's strategy would have gained credibility with his colleagues.

Unfortunately, however, just as the Communist hierarchy were divided, the students were also divided and suspicious of their leaders. It was easy for more militant students to label those who wished to avoid further confrontation as sell-outs. Moreover the history of Communist China left room for legitimate differences of view as to whether student restraint would lead to their acceptance as patriotic reformers, or simply give the Communist Party time to get ready to crush them.

In the event, the students did not stop their demonstrations, but intensified them, by way of a hunger strike in Tiananmen Square in support of democratic reform. This was a disastrous miscalculation. It destroyed Zhao Zhiyang's credibility with the Communist leadership, and led directly to his downfall. Soviet Communist Party leader Mikhail Gorbachev was due to arrive in Beijing two days later on an official state visit, intended, by both sides, as a triumphal healing of years of bad relations between the Soviet Union and China, Gorbachev would have been formally greeted in the Square. Instead he had to be met elsewhere, and the Chinese leadership had to explain the reason to him. This was a humiliation of a kind which an authoritarian regime could not accept. At the same time, the hunger strike itself generated a great deal of additional support for the student movement among the citizens, to whom it was a proof of the students' sincerity in a cause which most people supported.

The hunger strike was led by a fanatical extremist, Chai Ling, who described herself as "General Commander of the Tiananmen Square Hunger Strike Headquarters". The Headquarters announced that the government must recognise the movement as patriotic and democratic, and that if the government continued to ignore their demands some students would burn themselves to death. Chai's behaviour was so extreme and so damaging to the democracy cause that it is tempting to wonder if she was an agent provocateur. The Chinese security services use agents provocateurs to infiltrate demonstrations (including those in Hong Kong) in much the same way as the security services of other nations have done. However in Chai Ling's case there seems to be no evidence that she was anything other than a disastrously misguided fanatic.

On 17 May, two days after Gorbachev's visit, Deng Xiao Ping, whose only official post was chairman of the Central Military Commission, decided, with the support of the majority of the party elders, to declare martial law and if necessary to use force to clear Tiananmen Square. On that day, a demonstration 1.2 million strong took place in Beijing in support of the hunger strikers, accompanied by large demonstrations in most other cities. A further demonstration, over a million strong, took place the next day.

On 19 May, Zhao Zhiyang visited the hunger striking students in the Square and begged them without success to call off the hunger strike. The same day Zhao took sick leave on grounds of exhaustion. Later that evening, martial law was announced, to begin the following day, in the urban areas of Beijing. Under the terms of the martial law proclamation "demonstrations, student strikes, work stoppages, and all other activities that impede public order" were banned, and people were forbidden from networking, making public speeches, distributing leaflets or "inciting social turmoil". At 10.30 that evening the students voted to call off the hunger strike, but it was too late. The decision to crush the student protest had been taken.

The declaration of martial law led to protest demonstrations in 116 Chinese cities and in British-administered Hong Kong, where 600,000 people demonstrated on 21 May. It also caused the immediate resignation of Zhao Zhiyang, who was not prepared to implement it. Deng Xiao Ping shrewdly concluded that replacing Zhao directly with his hardline rival, Li Peng, would provoke further unrest. Zhao was therefore replaced by the Shanghai Communist Party leader, Jiang Ze Min, who had gained favour with Deng and other hardliners by his sacking of the editor of the Shanghai newspaper, *World Economic Herald*, for expressing support for the student movement.

Following the declaration of martial law, large numbers of troops began to arrive in the city. Both students and other citizens began building barricades to halt their progress. It was at this point that increasing numbers of workers began to become involved with the resistance movement, some of whom set up the Beijing Autonomous Workers Union. The troop movements were halted by students and citizens, who attempted to persuade the soldiers to support them. Many soldiers, particularly those in the 38th Army, appeared receptive to persuasion. An uneasy lull ensued, as if both sides were unsure what would happen next.

The students again debated evacuating the Square. They were again persuaded not to do so by Chai Ling, but as the days passed the numbers there gradually fell. The declaration of martial law made many feel that a crackdown was coming and that further protest was hopeless. Others were alienated by Chai Ling's extreme and authoritarian attitude. However the protest was given new momentum on 29 May by the erection of a 37-foot high statue called the "Goddess of Democracy", directly modelled on the American Statue of Liberty, which had been made by students at the Beijing Central Academy of Fine Arts. The statue was placed in the square, facing the square's huge portrait of Mao Tse Tung.

Protests around China also declined in size and number, although in Taiyuan, capital of Shansi Province, 200,000 students demonstrated on 30 May, ostensibly in memory of the 30th May movement of 1925, while from Nanjing a group of several hundred students set off to march to Beijing in a "Long March for Democracy". This title was obviously meant as a comparison with the famous 1934 Long March of the Communists, when Mao led them out of encirclement by their enemies, the Kuomintang, and eventually to their future stronghold at Yanan. At the same time the government began to organise pro-government rallies against turmoil, among farmers in the area outside Beijing. At some of these rallies "Uncle Sam" appeared as a sinister puppet-master manipulating Chinese dissidents from behind the scene.

On 2 June, the Communist Party leadership decided to clear Tiananmen Square by force, and on 3 June large numbers of additional troops began entering Beijing, both uniformed and in plain clothes. Tension rose sharply after a road accident on the night of 2/3 June, when a People's Armed Police jeep ran onto a pavement at Muxidi in western Beijing, killing three pedestrians. A crowd of several hundred people quickly gathered. Their suspicions were aroused because the jeep had no licence plates, and when police arrived the perpetrators were immediately taken away without any attempt at investigation. The crowd stormed the vehicle, and inside it found military uniforms, maps and mobile phones.

As the news spread that troops were entering the city, groups of students and citizens converged on many major intersections, blocking the path of army vehicles, overturning them, or puncturing their tyres, Many columns of troops came to a halt. About 500 soldiers were reported as being trapped by the crowds. Soldiers were angrily asked why they were attacking the people. Some were stoned. Others were stripped of their weapons and equipment. It seems clear that at this stage the soldiers had no orders to use their weapons, and that some units contained soldiers who were unhappy about what they were being asked to do.

At about 5.00 pm the Autonomous Federation of Students Tiananmen Command Centre, which had developed as a co-ordinator of support given by workers to the students, began issuing "self-defence weapons" to students and citizens, including cleavers, clubs, steel chains, and sharpened bamboo poles. At about the same time, the Communist leadership took a decision to clear the Square come what may, using lethal force if necessary.

Later that evening, troops advancing into Beijing from the west were faced by a solid crowd of thousands of demonstrators at Muxidi, who had set up a barricade across the road. The troops fired tear gas and rubber bullets, but these were not sufficient to break the blockade. They then tried to baton charge the demonstrators, but were beaten back by a hail of bricks. Then rows of troops rushed forward, firing alternatively into the air and into the crowd, killing people. Each time the firing began, the demonstrators took avoiding action, but as soon as it stopped they stood up and attempted to stand their ground. After about 10 minutes the surviving demonstrators were slowly driven back over Muxidi Bridge by the troops. As the troops pushed forward, people in the buildings on either side of the road shouted abuse at them and pelted them with rocks. Some soldiers hit by rocks lost all self-control and fired at any civilians they saw. At least 100 civilians were killed in the area around the Underground station east of the bridge. These included three residents in nearby buildings, one of whom was the son-in-law of a minister, who had made the mistake of watching what was happening from an upstairs window without first turning off the light.

Shortly after midnight on 4 June, 1989, the first troops entered Tiananmen Square. They entered from many directions in overwhelming numbers. Unknown to the demonstrators, Deng Xiao Ping had given orders that there was to be no killing in the Square itself. The students public address systems were smashed and army public address systems ordered the students to leave. Attempts by a famous Taiwanese singer, Hou De, to mediate, were ignored by the army. All street lights around the square were switched off, and then switched on again at 4.20 am to show the square full of tanks and armoured cars. The troops and armoured vehicles gradually pushed forward, pushing the students before them, and crushing the Goddess of Democracy under the wheels of a tank. The students were slowly forced out of the square under blows from soldiers' batons.

Around the Square, and in other parts of Beijing, killings by soldiers continued into the morning of 4 June. Some soldiers were also killed when their vehicles were set on fire by enraged civilians. The death toll from the violence in Beijing that night is not known. Hotly disputed official figures put deaths at 241 including 23 military personnel. The true figure may never be known but seems likely to be higher.

The news of the massacre caused enormous protests the next day in every city in China, in Hong Kong, and among Chinese communities overseas, as well as from foreign governments. However the protests had no effect on the course of action the Chinese government had embarked on, which was a complete crushing of the democracy movement. Leaders of the movement who were caught were given long prison sentences. Some workers' organisers were executed. Many of the democracy movement leaders managed to hide and then flee China. Wang Dan and Chai Ling both ended up in the United States, the former after many years imprisonment in China. The third well-known student leader, Wuerkaixi, escaped and settled in Taiwan. Zhao Zhiyang remained under house arrest until his death in 2005. The Chinese Communist Party appears stronger than it has ever been, and the portrait of Mao still hangs in the same place in Tiananmen Square.

Despite the crushing of the democracy movement, there are still street demonstrations in post-1989 China. However they are usually local and without any wider significance. Most are desperate protests by workers made unemployed by closure of their local factory, in a country with no state benefits or social security. Some are defused by local administrative compromises. Others are met by a violent crackdown by the police, to which the demonstrators frequently respond with retaliatory violence. All are classified by the police as illegal, despite the existence of a right to demonstrate in a little known section of the Chinese constitution. They do not appear to represent any threat to the continuing iron grip of the Communist Party. Periodic calls are made by courageous individuals in China to "reverse the verdict on the Tiananmen Square movement", but the movement remains a taboo subject about which information is systematically suppressed by the authorities. When this author gave a talk about human rights at Beijing University in 2008, he was mobbed by students desperate to find out what had really happened in 1989.

Tiananmen Square was a disastrous setback for freedom in China and in the world. Because the democracy movement was so thoroughly crushed, the new, much richer and more powerful China which has developed as a result of Deng Xiao Ping's economic reforms, is a highly authoritarian state, whose government is profoundly hostile to democratic values. There seems no reason why this was inevitable. Despite China's long authoritarian traditions, support for democracy in China in 1989 was very strong. If the students had helped and supported Zhao Zhiyang, instead of adopting more extreme postures when he tried to negotiate with them, history might have been very different. However judging when to stand firm and when to compromise in such a tense situation requires leadership skills of a high order, which the Tiananmen students did not have. This was not surprising, given their youth and inexperience, and their lack of all contact with the older dissident movement in China.

Since the arrival of the internet and cyberspace, China has constructed the most comprehensive and sophisticated system of internet censorship in the world, known as the "Great Firewall of China". There is much that the Chinese government wishes its citizens not to know, but possibly the most important single secret is the truth about Tiananmen Square. Given the length of historical memories in China, they will have to keep the secret excluded for a long time, if they are to prevent the memories of 1989 from generating new reform movements in China, just as memories of 4 May, 1919 generated May 1989.

This is particularly so, as on one corner of Chinese soil the memories are still kept alive publicly. In Hong Kong, freedom of speech is guaranteed until 2047 under the Sino-British Declaration on the Future of Hong Kong, signed by Margaret Thatcher and Deng Xiao Ping in 1984, and under Hong Kong's mini-constitution, the Basic Law. On 4 June every year, a huge candle-lit vigil is held in Victoria Park, Causeway Bay, on Hong Kong Island, to remember the victims of Tiananmen Square. Attendances of many thousands are normal, and on occasion up to 80,000 people have attended. Predictions at the handover of Hong Kong to China in 1997, that the vigils would soon be suppressed, or would just wither away as memories faded, have so far proved wrong. Year after year, parents bring their young children to learn about what happened in 1989. Everyone holds candles aloft to commemorate those who died, and songs are sung which were sung in Tiananmen Square in 1989, songs which are themselves sometimes adaptations of former Communist or nationalist songs, given new words in support of democracy. Pro-democracy leaders give speeches, and huge screens are used to beam videos with speeches by former Tiananmen leaders such as Wang Dan. Wang Dan has been repeatedly refused permission to enter Hong Kong to attend the vigil in person. As well as the vigil there is also a smaller annual commemoration march through the centre of Hong Kong. It is to be hoped that these commemoration events in Hong Kong will eventually help bring about a "reversal of the verdict", but whether this will happen is impossible to predict.

As this book was going to press, Hong Kong erupted in a massive civil disobedience campaign, intended to force the Beijing government to grant Hong Kong real democracy, as opposed to Beijing's plans for a pretend democracy where people would be allowed to vote for the Chief Executive, but to choose only from among candidates pre-selected by Beijing. The campaign involves three organisations, "Occupy Central with Peace and Love, an organisation created for the campaign, and led by Benny Tai and the Reverend Chu Yu Ming; Hong Kong university students, led by Alex Chow and Lester Shum, and a well-organised school students organisation, Scholarism, led by seventeen-year-old Joshua Wong.

The main focus of the campaign is occupation of the streets of the central business districts of the city, in order to stop the city and force Beijing to make concessions. Many thousands of peaceful demonstrators are sitting or lying in the main roads of the city, bringing them to a complete standstill. At the time of writing the campaign appears to have overwhelming popular support, and the occupation is in its sixth day. The demonstrations follow the tradition of Hong Kong demonstrations, which are notable for their exceptional peacefulness and good order. An attempt on the second day to break up the demonstration with police baton charges and tear gas failed. The demonstrators, who were prepared with masks against tear gas, were too numerous and too determined. The riot police were then withdrawn, and it appears that the Hong Kong government, which has agreed to talk to the leaders of the demonstrations, is hoping to defuse the protests by waiting for the demonstrators to tire, and possibly then offering minor concessions to get them to disperse. It seems therefore that dire predictions of another Tiananmen Square massacre, this time in Hong Kong, will probably not be fulfilled. However the situation remains extremely volatile and unpredictable. After the demonstrations had been in progress for five days, the students in some demonstration locations were attacked by Triads, members of Hong Kong's criminal gangs, who often have links to well-connected influential people. The students showed impressive discipline, stoicism and self-control, in refusing to allow themselves to be provoked into responding to violence with violence. Gandhi would have been proud of them. After massive outcry at police inaction in the face of these Triad attacks, nineteen people were eventually arrested in connection with them, eight of whom were said by the police to have known Triad backgrounds.

By the time this book is being read, the outcome of these Hong Kong democracy demonstrations will be known. If the demonstrations are broken up with lethal violence, the participants in "Occupy Central with Peace and Love" will be more tragic victims, like those who are recorded in the dedication of this book. However if they succeed in their objective, they will have joined the ranks of the successful demonstrations which have changed the world.

CHAPTER 20

DEMONSTRATIONS AND EMPIRES

The Chinese Government committed two major massacres of demonstrators in 1989. As well as the one in Tiananmen Square in June, which received massive worldwide publicity, there was also the very much less well known but equally bloody one in Lhasa, capital of Chinese-occupied Tibet, in March.

China invaded and occupied Tibet in 1950. It entered into a treaty with the Tibetan Government in 1951, known as the 17 Point Agreement, which provided for substantial autonomy, but which it never had any intention of honouring. After repeated breaches of the agreement by China, the Tibetans rose in revolt in 1959 but were ruthlessly crushed by the Chinese People's Liberation Army. The young Tibetan spiritual leader, the Dalai Lama, had to flee to safety over the Himalayas, to begin a lifelong exile in India. Tibet has remained under Chinese military subjugation since then.

China claims that Tibet is an inalienable part of ancient China, that its invasion in 1950 was liberating the Tibetan people from the oppressive feudal rule of "the Dalai Lama clique", and that its rule has brought economic benefits. The reality is that while Imperial China usually claimed suzerainty over Tibet, this was a distant relationship comparable to the role of the Holy Roman Emperor in medieval Europe. For most of Tibet's history it was independent. The Chinese invasion conquered and subdued a culture completely different from that of China, with its own ancient language, religious traditions and proud sense of identity. Under Chinese rule, the natural resources of Tibet have been remorselessly exploited for the benefit of the Chinese state.

China always angrily denies that Tibet is a colony, and attributes the idea to evil Western propaganda. However Tibet's relationship with China shares all the characteristics of the former relationship of European colonies with the European countries which conquered them. There is the same cultural gulf, the same repression of the aspirations of the indigenous Tibetans and their culture, and the same exploitation of the resources of the territory for the benefit of the coloniser.

Chinese propaganda about Tibet also shares the myths and justifications of the European colonisers in relation to non-European territories. British, French, Dutch, Belgian and American colonisation were similarly justified on the basis that they were bringing economic and educational benefits to "backward" Africans or Asians. Just as Tibet is said by China to be an inalienable part of China, Algeria when it was a French colony was always said by the French government to be "an inalienable part of France". It is therefore appropriate to consider the 1989 Tibetan demonstrations in Lhasa in the same context as other demonstrations by colonised people against the empire which was colonising them.

Tibetan public feeling towards Chinese occupation has always been one of bitter antagonism, evidenced, despite the absence of any free media in Tibet, by the steady stream of refugees every year, risking death in winter to cross the high passes of the Himalayas into exile in India or Nepal. Usually the repression within Tibet is so strong that there is no public outlet for Tibetan feelings. However the position changed in the late 1980s when there were encouraging signs of possible reform in China. The reformist Hu Yao Bang favoured a more conciliatory approach towards Tibet, following his visit there as Secretary-General of the Communist Party in 1980. In 1987, when students began to demonstrate for reforms in several parts of China – a development which led the Communist leadership to force Hu Yao Bang to resign – pro-independence demonstrations also began in Tibet, culminating in the police firing on a demonstration on 1 October 1987, and the expulsion of all foreigners from Tibet including all journalists. On 5 March, 1988, a large demonstration again took place in Lhasa, and was again fired on by the police, with eight Tibetans being killed.

Tension in Tibet began to mount again in February 1989, following the death of the 10th Panchen Lama. The Panchen Lama was the second most important Tibetan spiritual leader after the Dalai Lama. Both the Dalai and the Panchen Lama were chosen by an elaborate traditional selection process, but many Tibetans feared, with good cause, that China would manipulate the selection process for the new Panchen Lama to ensure that the chosen individual would be pliant and subservient to Beijing. A further reason for rising tension was that a few days before the unexpected death of the 10th Panchen Lama, he had denounced China's role in Tibet in the presence of the Tibetan secretary of the Chinese Communist Party, Hu Jin Tao. Many Tibetans believed that he had been murdered because of his outspoken criticism. Anti-Chinese demonstrations by Tibetans became frequent, with Tibetan monks, the guardians of traditional Tibetan culture, playing a prominent part in them, as they had in earlier protests. On 5 March, the police opened fire and killed a group of demonstrators in Lhasa. The response by the Tibetans was a massive increase in the number and frequency of demonstrations.

Exactly what happened next is hard to establish with certainty, as on 7 March the Chinese Government forced all foreign journalists, tourists and diplomats to leave Lhasa as the People's Liberation Army took control of the city from the civil administration. The main source of available information about the days following 7 March, 1989 comes from a Chinese journalist Tang Da Xian who is now a dissident living in Paris.

Mr Tang was at that time the correspondent in Lhasa for the China Journalists Association, the China State Council, the United Front Department of the Chinese Communist Party, and other Chinese Government bodies. He was thus a trusted member of the Chinese Communist political establishment with access to internal information not generally available. However two months later Tang fled the country, believing that he was suspected of having leaked inside information to the student demonstrators in Tiananmen Square.

Having fled China, Tang then revealed to the Western press details of what he had seen in Lhasa in March. It appears that Hu Jin Tao, who later became president of China, was determined to crack down mercilessly on the Tibetans, in order to impress the top leadership in Beijing with his toughness and reliability, while at the same time keeping his options open by distancing himself slightly from the violence of the actual suppression of the demonstrations, in case that violence was later criticised. Hu therefore left Lhasa on a visit at the critical moment when the demonstrations were suppressed, having delegated responsibility for public order to the People's Armed Police.

According to Tang, large numbers of police agent provocateurs joined the demonstrators in Lhasa, which until then had been mainly peaceful, disguised as monks. The agent provocateurs engaged in violent rioting and setting fire to buildings, which gave the People's Armed Police, on orders from their national commander in Beijing, General Li Lianxu, the pretext for a massacre of demonstrators. Again according to Tang, a secret document belonging to the People's Armed Police to which he had access recorded that the police killed 82 monks, injured 37, and arrested or detained 650, and killed 387 other Lhasa citizens, mainly by shooting, injured 721, and arrested or detained 2,100. The total official death total was therefore 469. Official death tolls of massacres by the authorities are usually understated. However as this was a secret report intended for internal information it may be more accurate than would normally be the case from a published official source.

The massacre was effective in the short term in halting the wave of demonstrations and unrest in Tibet. It also led the Chinese paramount leader, Deng Xiao Ping, impressed by Hu Jin Tao's toughness, to name him as his choice to be the next president of China after Jiang Ze Min, and in 2002 Hu Jin Tao did indeed become president.

The scale and brutality of the massacre in Lhasa in 1989 is startling, as is the lack of detailed knowledge about it. However when considered in the context of other massacres of demonstrators by colonial powers, it was not exceptional on a world scale. The Amritsar massacre in India by General Reginald Dyer in 1919 has already been described in Chapter 11, as has the massacre by Russian cavalry of peaceful demonstrators in Warsaw in 1905 (Chapter 8). Despotic and dictatorial empires have usually crushed peaceful demonstrations in predictably brutal ways. However the French Empire, which was the empire of a democratic country and paid lip service to humanitarian ideals, was in practice little better. The British Empire, was arguably a partial exception in that it alternated between incidents of destructive and self-defeating brutality such as the Amritsar massacre, and attempts at a more benign and co-operative approach, which occasionally even involved meetings demands of demonstrators.

Space does not permit a full account of all demonstrations involving colonial empires. However it is instructive to consider and compare four very well known instances, two from the British Empire, one from the French, and one from the Ottoman.

As the idea of demonstrating spread around the world from the British Isles in the nineteenth century, one place where it became established fairly early was Egypt. Egypt was officially part of the Ottoman Empire until 1911, ruled by a viceroy known as the Khedive. However it was in reality a British colony from 1882, when British forces intervened to frustrate the nationalist ambitions of the nationalist Prime Minister, Ahmed Arabi, and to protect passage of ships through the Suez Canal. In the years following the British occupation, elements of the Egyptian upper class became influenced by many aspects of English culture, including the use of peaceful demonstrations for political protest. Student demonstrations began to occur in Egypt by the end of the nineteenth century, and by the early twentieth century the peaceful demonstration was adopted as a major campaigning weapon by the then nationalist leader, Dr Zaghloul Pasha.

Britain first attempted to deal with Zaghloul in 1919 by arresting him and exiling him to prison in Malta. This provocative act precipitated a popular revolt against British rule in which British soldiers were killed. The British Prime Minister, Lloyd George, was anxious to defuse the situation and avoid adding another colonial headache to the many he was dealing with. He therefore appointed General Edmund Allenby, who had defeated the Turks in Palestine in World War One, to be British High Commissioner in Egypt, with a remit to stop the revolt by conciliation. Dr Zaghloul was released and permitted to return to Egypt, where he resumed his campaign for independence. Part of this campaign was based on civil disobedience and boycotts, and may well have been directly inspired by Gandhi. It also involved numerous large peaceful demonstrations. An attractive feature of these demonstrations was a deliberate show of Muslim-Christian unity. Zaghloul did not want Britain to be able to divide and rule Egypt by setting the Muslim majority against the large Coptic Christian minority. Demonstrators therefore marched with banners with the Islamic Crescent and the Coptic Cross stitched together. Zaghloul maintained the pressure, until Britain became so frustrated that it again exiled him, this time to the Seychelles. Again, his exile was counterproductive, and shortly afterwards Allenby announced that Egypt would henceforth, from 22 February, 1922, be independent, but with four "reservations", which effectively left Britain in control of defence and foreign policy. Zaghloul was elected the first prime minister of the new semi-independent Egypt.

Zaghloul's campaign was successful because in Allenby it faced an intelligent opponent, whose conscious aim was to reduce tension by making concessions. The particular situation of Egypt, where Britain's main interest was protection of the Suez Canal and ability to use Egypt as a military base, also meant that there was much room for negotiation, as well as an obvious British need to avoid the sort of domestic turmoil which could interfere with its international trade or defence interests. The relatively peaceful and successful outcome in Egypt was unusual. Few colonial administrators had Allenby's vision, and most empires had no tolerance at all of indigenous opposition.

At the other end of the spectrum from Allenby's response to the Egyptian nationalists was the response of the Ottoman Sultan Abdul Hamid to demonstrations in the Ottoman capital, Constantinople (now Istanbul) in 1895.

In 1895 the idea of holding peaceful street demonstrations was completely new and alien to the Ottoman Turks. However the minority Christian Armenians took up the idea, probably because they were culturally influenced by Russia, where the practice of street demonstrations had already become well-known.

Most Armenians lived in eastern Turkey, close to the border with present-day Armenia (which was formerly part of Imperial Russia and of the Soviet Union), but many also lived in Constantinople. Like other Christian subjects of the Ottomans, they were tolerated, but were always second class citizens, with a subordinate status in relation to Muslims, and few rights. They were forbidden to bear arms, and were frequently robbed and killed by armed Muslims, particularly by Kurdish tribesmen in eastern Turkey.

In the late nineteenth century other Christian subjects of the Ottomans, the Serbs, Roumanians and Bulgarians, successfully broke away and became independent nations. This encouraged the Armenians to demand greater rights. They were supported by the Christian European powers, partly out of genuine feeling, but mainly as a way of weakening and pressurising the Ottoman Empire. The Ottoman Sultan, Abdul Hamid, became determined to teach the Armenians a lesson, and to show Europe that he was master of his own empire, by deliberately organising mass killings of Armenians. The first of these, a terrible massacre of thousands of villagers at Sassoun in south-eastern Turkey in 1894, led to European demands for a commission of inquiry. An inquiry was set up by Abdul Hamid, but was a farce, as it predictably exonerated the perpetrators and claimed that the Armenians had been rebels and criminals. The European powers then turned their attention to pressing the Sultan to adopt a reform programme giving greater civil rights to the Armenians. A package of reform proposals was put forward in May 1895.

In October 1895, Armenians in Constantinople decided to demonstrate in support of these proposals, and in protest at the lack of punishment of the perpetrators of the Sassoun massacre. The demonstration was organised by the Hunchak party, one of the two main Armenian political parties. The Hunchaks favoured constitutional means of campaigning rather than violence, which was the alternative more favoured by their main Armenian opponents, the Dashnaks. The demonstration was attended by about 4,000 Armenians, and involved a march to the Sublime Porte, the seat of the Ottoman Government, where the demonstrators intended to hand in a petition. The Sublime Porte is called in Turkish "Bab Ali", the Gate of Ali, and this demonstration has since been known to history as the Bab Ali demonstration.

The Hunchak petition demanded equal civil rights, equitable taxation, guarantees for life, property and honour, deliverance from attacks by the Kurds, and permission to bear arms if the Kurds could not be disarmed. It was the first time in the history of the Ottoman Empire that a demonstration against the government had taken place in Constantinople.

When the demonstration arrived at the Sublime Porte, the chief of police refused to allow the petition to be delivered, and addressed the Armenians in provocative, insulting language. This inflamed the demonstrators. A fierce altercation then took place between a Turkish officer and an Armenian demonstrator, which eventually provoked the Armenian into the disastrous action of pulling out a gun and shooting the officer. This act, a response to what appears to have been deliberate incitement by the police, acted as the signal for a massive murderous attack on the whole demonstration by the police and by large numbers of Muslim Turkish civilians armed with iron tipped clubs. The massacre was not limited to the demonstrators, but extended to many of the Armenian population of Istanbul over a period of several days.

There is no reliable figure for the number of Armenians killed following the Bab Ali massacre, but contemporary estimates by foreign observers are of up to ten thousand murdered. The frenzied atmosphere is captured in a report by the French Ambassador, Paul Cambon, *"On Monday these fine gentlemen of the Foreign Ministry have themselves trampled to death with their kicks an expiring Armenian who was cast into the courtyard of the ministry after the demonstration. Can you imagine our young people at the Quai D'Orsay* (French Foreign Ministry) *kicking a wounded person for pleasure after a disturbance"?*

The reaction of the European powers to this massacre was one of ineffectual hand-wringing, which encouraged Sultan Abdul Hamid in his belief that he could safely get away with more massacres of the Armenian population. He continued to carry out massacres for a further year, during which it is estimated that 100,000 Armenians were killed. The fact that Abdul Hamid managed to get away with these atrocities, without serious consequences, in turn generated a sense, in Turkish governing circles, that Armenians could be massacred with impunity. This in turn led to the 1915-16 genocide against the Armenians, carried out by the revolutionary Young Turk regime which had overthrown the Sultanate in 1908, in which over a million Armenians died.

Another effect of the Bab Ali demonstration massacre was to discredit the Hunchak party and all Armenians who believed in peaceful protest, and to strengthen support for their rivals, the Dashnaks, who were influenced by Russian anarchism and believed in violent revolution. A Dashnak seizure of a bank in Constantinople in 1896 predictably resulted in renewal of massacres against the Armenian community. From the point of view of Sultan Abdul Hamid, protest was unacceptable and would be suppressed with maximum force. Whether it was peaceful or not was irrelevant to him. However, it is still significant that events in Constantinople conformed to the general rule, evidence from the Women's

Suffrage campaign in the UK, the Amritsar massacre, the Sharpeville massacre, and the 1997 Gulja massacre in Xinjiang (Chapter 18) that suppression of peaceful demonstrations, or intransigent opposition to their demands, inevitably results in an upsurge of violence. Tibet has so far been an exception to this rule, because of the deep religious commitment of many Tibetans, and the Dalai Lama in particular, to non-violence.

The Bab Ali demonstrators were seeking greater civil rights, rather than a separate state, which would have been scarcely practicable, given how scattered Armenians were in the Turkish Empire, with so many in the Imperial capital. This was probably a doomed venture, given the old-fashioned despotic nature of the Ottoman Empire, and the Turkish Muslim religious hatred of Christians. It was therefore a case where the savage repression following the demonstration ultimately led to genocide and complete defeat for Armenian aspirations. However, in other cases where empires have been dealing with an overseas population, culturally different from that of the metropolis, the result of savage repression has often been to ensure the ultimate end of Imperial rule. Amritsar was a classic example. Another example is what happened when a peaceful demonstration was suppressed in French Algeria in 1945.

Algeria, the jewel in the crown of the French colonial empire, was officially classified by the French government as part of metropolitan France, and divided into the three metropolitan "departements" of Algiers, Oran and Constantine. This reflected the fact that Algeria, across the Mediterranean from the south of France, had been subject of massive settlement by European colonists. Most colonists were in fact of Italian or Spanish origin, but all intensely identified with French culture. The majority of these "colons" regarded the indigenous Algerian Arabs and Berbers with contempt and were determined to keep them as a subject underclass. Because of this huge settler population, Algeria was in a quite different position from the other French North African territories of Morocco and Tunisia, to the west and the east respectively, and from the French empire in Sub-Saharan Africa.

Algeria had a turbulent time during World War Two, with the colons troubled by conflicted loyalties, and the Arabs suffering badly from the economic downturn, which was causing starvation by the end of the war. Admiral Darlan, the Governor-General appointed by the Vichy French Government, was assassinated in 1942, and in November that year Anglo-American forces successfully invaded Algeria, and recognised General De Gaulle as Algeria's ruler. The loss of French prestige, as a result of defeat by Germany in 1940, followed by the American invasion and contact with American anti-colonialist views, gave a huge boost to Arab nationalism. Then, in January, 1944, General De Gaulle gave a speech at Brazzaville in French Congo, in which he said that it was French policy to lead colonial peoples to development that would permit them to administer themselves and later to govern themselves. De Gaulle did not give any time-scale, but his speech aroused hopes among nationalists throughout the French empire, and corresponding fears and defensiveness among the Algerian colons.

The Algerian nationalist movement was split between two leaders, Messali Hadj, a socialist revolutionary orator, and Ferhat Abbas, who started his career as a liberal moderate, but gradually became more extreme and committed to nationalism as a result of repeated refusals by the French administration to agree to any reforms. Abbas was imprisoned in 1943 for producing "The Manifesto of the Algerian people", calling for immediate and effective participation of Muslims in government, and the establishment of a constitution providing for liberty and equality for all Algerians. However he was released at the end of the year.

This background led to a crisis when Algeria, like France, planned to celebrate the final defeat of Nazi Germany in 1945. The celebration by the colons of "liberation" had a hollow and hypocritical ring to Algerian Arabs. Many of the colons had in fact happily supported Darlan's pro-Nazi Vichy government and had not been liberated from anything they disliked. The colons also bitterly opposed any form of liberation for the Arabs from their status as a downtrodden underclass. As Victory in Europe (VE) Day approached in spring 1945, threats against the colons were scrawled on walls and there were incidents of colons being stoned. The French authorities believed that Messali Hadj might be planning an insurrection, and exiled him to an oasis in the desert. The colons generally reacted to these Arab expressions of nationalism with scornful and racist responses which raised the emotional temperature further.

Algerian Muslims in Setif, a medium sized, overwhelmingly Muslim town on the inland plateau south of the coast, decided to hold a peaceful march to mark VE Day.

The stated purpose of the march was to lay a wreath at the town war memorial, to commemorate the sacrifice of local Algerian troops killed fighting for France during the war. The small minority of colons in the Setif area were terrified by the prospect of such a march, likely to be many thousands strong. Normally the administration would have had no hesitation in banning such a large Muslim gathering, but it was unthinkable to ban a celebration commemorating the war dead on VE Day.

The mayor of Setif, M. Butterlin, accordingly gave orders that the march could go ahead but, unrealistically, that no political slogans were to be uttered or displayed. The marchers began assembling outside a mosque shortly after dawn. The organisers gave an order that weapons were to be left behind in the mosque, though it seems that this order was ignored by some participants, carrying weapons being very traditional for Algerian peasants. Some 3,000 marchers assembled, but less than a hundred weapons were deposited in the mosque.

The march proceeded along the main street of Setif, then called the Avenue George Clemenceau. At its head were Scouts, Muslim Algerian troops, carrying a wreath to lay at the war memorial. Behind them were a group of supporters of Messali Hadj. Despite the prohibition on political banners, they were displaying banners reading "Vive Messali" "Free Messali", "We want to be equal" and "Long live the United Nations".

The police presence at the march was light. However as the marchers reached the crossroads at the centre of the town, where there was a police post, some marchers displayed the green and white flag which had been the symbol of Abd El Kader, the nineteenth century leader of resistance against the French invaders, and which later became the flag of the twentieth century Algerian liberation movement. They also displayed a banner reading "For the Liberation of the People, Long Live Free and Independent Algeria!" The police, apparently acting on orders from the mayor, attacked the demonstrators holding this flag and banner, and attempted to seize them by force.

This attempt was the spark that started murderous, armed combat. Historians have flatly disagreed about how it started and who fired first. The most detailed recent study, by Jean-Louis Planche, concludes that it was the police who fired first, with a police inspector shooting dead the man carrying the green and white flag. As the flag-bearer fell, some of his companions drew pistols and fired back, without hitting anyone. This provoked a fusillade of firing from the police, and from French civilians watching the march from balconies overlooking the street. The marchers at the head of the procession, in front of the Messali Hadj supporters, carried on to the war memorial, where they laid their wreath. The great majority of demonstrators, who were behind the part of the column which the police had attacked, ran back the way they had come, in order to escape the firing. By extreme bad luck, they ran straight into a coachload of twenty gendarmes who had just arrived in the town, and who, believing themselves under attack, opened fire on the crowd.

The effect of this volley of fire was to drive the surviving demonstrators back into town where some, infuriated by the deaths of their co-demonstrators, began killing Europeans, who were vastly outnumbered. The killings were purely racial, and the victims included some Europeans known for their pro-Arab sympathies.

By 10.30 am, the arrival of a troop of Algerian infantry restored order in the town. The death toll from the killings before order was restored was never fully established. Twenty-nine Europeans were known to have been killed. The figures for the demonstrators killed by the police were between 20 and 40. However this figure does not include an unknown number of other demonstrators killed by European civilians.

The response to the killing of Europeans by the French authorities was the indiscriminate killing of an unknown number of Algerian villagers over a wide area around Setif, some by aerial dive bombing of their villages, some by entry of troops into the village and summary execution of most of the inhabitants. The best estimate of the death toll from this repression is between 1,000 and 1,300. Only a small minority of Algerian Arabs around Setif, perhaps 5%, were involved in support for the demonstrators, so the overwhelming majority of the population was innocent of even an indirect connection with the killings of Europeans which had taken place.

In the short-term the French authorities cowed and subdued the Arabs of the Setif area by their reign of terror. However, across Algeria, their actions there convinced large numbers of Algerian Arabs that they must have independence and must fight to get it. The liberal Algerian Arab poet, Kateb Yacine, spoke for huge numbers when he wrote: *"The shock which I felt at the pitiless butchery that caused the deaths of thousands of Muslims, I have never forgotten. From that moment my nationalism took definite form."* Almost every one of the Nationalist leaders who emerged in the 1950s, leading the Algerian liberation struggle, traced their commitment to the struggle from learning about the massacres around Setif. Even the responsible French general, Duval, who had carried out much of the repression, was under no illusion as to what he had achieved. He reported to Paris, *"I have given you peace for ten years. But don't deceive yourselves".* Nine and a half years later, in 1954, the Algerian civil war broke out, and in 1962 Algeria became independent, a course which was irrevocably set in 1945 in Setif.

Three years later, in 1948, Britain also destroyed the prospect of any long-term continuation of its African empire by its conduct in suppressing a peaceful demonstration. Even after Gandhi's inspirational campaigns had made Indian freedom a certainty, it was not accepted either by Britain or by other colonial European powers that the age of European empires was drawing to a close. Britain assumed that it would go on ruling much of the rest of its empire after the independence of India in 1947. In Africa, in particular, there was no expectation of any moves to independence in the foreseeable future, nor any general popular demand for it. All this was changed by brutal and stupid suppression of one peaceful demonstration, with murderous loss of life, although not on the scale of Setif.

The Gold Coast was Britain's model African colony. It had been subject to British influence since 1665, from the British castle at Cape Coast. Its biggest export had always been gold, rather than slaves, unlike several other territories along the West African coast, although the Ashanti kingdom which controlled the goldfields had also been a big slave-trading empire. The crushing of the Ashanti by the British, in the Ashanti wars of the nineteenth century, had been brutal, but colonial rule afterwards had turned the Gold Coast into an economically successful territory, with one of the most educated populations in Africa. English was widely spoken, and large numbers of Gold Coast men had fought for Britain in World War Two, distinguishing themselves in the campaigns against Italy in East Africa, and against Japan in Burma.

In February 1948, the Ex-Servicemen's Union of the Gold Coast announced that they intended to march to Christianborg Castle in Accra, the seat of the colonial government of the Gold Coast, to deliver a petition about their grievances. The nub of the ex-servicemen's complaint was that at the end of World War Two, after years of fighting for Britain, they had simply been demobilised and told to go home, without any financial compensation or pension. Some had not been able to find jobs in civilian life and were unemployed. One ex-serviceman, Geoffrey Aduamah, later described their feelings:-

> "What the British did was very bad indeed. We arrive off ships and there is a small officers' camp. The officers just give you your discharge money, give you some money for your fare to your home town, and that is the end of it… We feel very bad, very bad indeed, that the British have actually deceived us. Because during the war they were telling us how Hitler was so bad and when Hitler comes to rule other countries they were treated like animals… He does not like the black man at all. So we should fight, to see that Hitler doesn't rule the world. When we came back, and we saw that they were not doing anything to help us to re-establish ourselves in life, we thought they have made fools of us.. What hurt us more was that our chiefs who pushed us to support the British were backing the British for not doing anything for us. That was very painful for us".

Despite this disillusionment, and despite contact with Indian supporters of Gandhi while stationed in India, the ex-servicemen were not demanding independence for Ghana, or even greater political rights. Their demand was simply for a pension for their military service. In that respect their situation was not dissimilar from that of the Bonus marchers in the Depression-era United States, who like them, had also been war veterans.

Christianborg Castle, to which the ex-servicemen intended to march, was also known as Government House. It had been the colonial government headquarters for many years, and is today the seat of government of independent Ghana. Marching to Christianborg Castle to deliver a petition was therefore the exact equivalent, in the Gold Coast, of British people marching to Westminster to deliver a petition to the British Parliament. The Gold Coast Ex-Servicemen were planning to do exactly what John Wilkes, the Reform Bill demonstrators, the Chartists, the Suffragettes and the Jarrow hunger marchers had all done in Britain. It was a respectable, traditional, non-violent way of making their strong feelings known to the authorities.

The colonial authorities in Accra reacted to the planned demonstration with myopia, amnesia and crass ignorance as to its cultural origins. They announced that a street demonstration would be permitted, but under no circumstances would the demonstrators be allowed to present their petition at the castle, or to approach the castle.

Undeterred, the demonstrators set out, carrying banners and singing. As they marched towards the castle, they were confronted by a line of police across the road, who refused to let them proceed any further. When the demonstrators would not disperse, the colonial police officer in charge, one Imrie, first ordered his men to fire on the demonstrators, and, when they disobeyed orders and refused to do so, himself fired several shots into the crowd, killing three of the ex-servicemen and wounding several others.

Just as in India, after the Jallianwalla Bagh massacre in 1919, outrage at the gunning down of peaceful demonstrators transformed the population of the Gold Coast, from people who had been generally content to remain under British rule indefinitely, to people determined to accept no substitute for early independence. The immediate reaction to the shooting was several days of violent rioting in Accra, in which over two hundred people were killed. The response of the British government was to set up a commission of inquiry, the Watson Commission. This commission appears to have been fooled by the Gold Coast colonial authorities into accepting their version of events surrounding the shootings. Records held in Rhodes House Library in Oxford show that the part of the report of the Watson Commission dealing with the shootings is lifted directly from an Accra Government House internal memo.

The Watson Commission did, nevertheless, recommend big changes to the government of the Gold Coast to make it more representative. The British government, in fire-brigade mode, appointed a much more able replacement governor, Charles Arden-Clarke, to implement the Commission's recommendations as soon as possible. However it was too late to restore the previous acceptance of British rule. The die was cast for independence. Moreover, once Ghana became independent, as it did in 1957, other British African colonies were bound to follow. Britain's failure to respect the ancient right of petition, or its own established tradition of peaceful demonstrations, therefore led directly to the loss of its African colonies.

The lesson of the colonial experience thus shows that in almost all cases repression of peaceful demonstrations by the colonial authorities has been counter-productive, giving a huge boost to independence movements, which have often as a result become irresistible. This is a further situation in which peaceful demonstrations act as a safety valve, so that blocking the safety valve, by using force to suppress such demonstrations, is liable to lead to an explosion of hostile popular feeling.

CHAPTER 21

CONCLUSION

T wo hundred years after the idea of peaceful demonstrations was born, demonstrations remain controversial in most places. Even in Britain, where they were invented, it is easy to find people who think that demonstrators are nothing more than a tiresome nuisance who clog up the traffic and could sensibly be banned. Many people on the political Right see demonstrations as predominantly Left-wing, agitating for causes they disapprove of, and potentially violent and disruptive. Police attitudes are often obsessed with the possibility of violent disorder. As recently as the 1980s the ultra-conservative Prime Minister of the Australian state of Queensland, Johannes Bjelke-Petersen, attempted to ban any demonstrations from taking place in Queensland. His attempt eventually failed, but only after several years of peaceful demonstrations being violently broken up by the police[46].

In addition to this long-standing hostility to demonstrations from complacent and ignorant people, from vested interests and the political Right, there has been a disillusionment with the traditional peaceful demonstration among demonstrators and campaigners for causes, and an upsurge in support for "direct action" type protests involving deliberate lawbreaking.

---

[46] In some ways Bjelke-Petersen resembled Eugene "Bull" Connor, of Birmingham, Alabama, in his attitude to demonstrations, with the difference that "Bull" Connor would not tolerate demonstrations by black people, while Bjelke-Petersen would not tolerate demonstrations by anyone. "The day of street marches is over", he said in 1977, "Don't bother applying for a march permit. You won't get one. That's government policy now."

Much of this upsurge can be traced to the failure of probably the world's largest ever campaign of peaceful demonstrations, held in 2003 against the Anglo-American decision to go to war against Saddam Hussein's Iraq.

Demonstrations against the planned invasion of Iraq began as soon as U.S. president George W. Bush signed into law a Joint Congressional Resolution authorising war on Iraq, on 2 October, 2002. A worldwide day of protest against the war was arranged for 15 February, 2003. This idea of simultaneous demonstrations worldwide in different cities, was comparable to the nineteenth century plan for worldwide labour demonstrations every year on May Day. However it was infinitely more effective in generating support. This was because of the invention of e-mail and social media, which enabled details of demonstrations to be circulated instantly worldwide and to reach anyone who had access to a computer. The intensity of feeling against the U.S. and UK decision to go to war also contributed to huge turnouts at demonstrations in many countries. Traditional anti-war activists formed coalitions with Muslims opposed to invasion of Muslim lands by non-Muslim forces, and with large numbers of people who were opposed not to war as such but to a war started unilaterally by the U.S. and its allies, without the backing of a United Nations resolution, which would have made an invasion of Iraq legal under international law.

The demonstration in London was organised by the Stop the War Coalition, the Campaign for Nuclear Disarmament (CND), and the Muslim Association of Great Britain. A common slogan on many of the demonstrators' placards was "Not in my name!" The plan was for two processions, one from the Embankment (for people coming from the south), and one from Gower Street (for people coming from the north), to converge on Hyde Park for a rally. In a curious echo of events at the time of the Hyde Park riots in 1861, the minister responsible for the Royal Parks, Tessa Jowell, at first announced that she was banning the rally in Hyde Park, on grounds of safety and possible damage to the grass. Under pressure, however, Jowell gave way and reversed her decision, so that the marches and rally were able to go ahead as planned. The lowest estimate of attendance is 750,000, which would make it substantially larger than the great Suffragette rally on 21 June, 1908, and easily the biggest demonstration in British history. However the true figure is almost certainly over a million, as many who attended the Hyde Park rally did not enter Hyde Park with the main body of the marchers. The two marches were so long that those at the rear only reached Hyde Park long after the main speakers had spoken and departed. The speakers included a large number of traditional speakers at Left-wing protest rallies in Britain, such as the veteran Labour politician Tony Benn, and the political activist Bianca Jagger.

However in terms of moving public opinion to support the demonstrators' cause the most important speaker was probably the Liberal Democrat leader, Charles Kennedy, who made it clear that he was opposing the war because of its illegality in the absence of a United Nations Resolution. Despite the enormous numbers, the event was entirely peaceful, with almost no arrests.

An even larger demonstration took place simultaneously in Rome, which is estimated to have been the largest demonstration ever in history, with 3 million attending. At least 300,000 demonstrated in Berlin, at least 100,000 in Paris, at least 700,000 in Madrid, 350,000 in Barcelona, over 100,000 in Montreal, and many millions worldwide.

In New York, in an unprecedented move, a Federal District judge issued an order banning a planned march past the United Nations Building, on the grounds that the police could not guarantee public order. A stationary rally was instead arranged, but as some 300,000 people went to the rally, many along the route which would have been the march route, they in effect constituted the march which had been banned.

Despite this outpouring of worldwide feeling, the war went ahead. Protests and demonstrations continued, generally with smaller numbers, as the war started and so long as it continued. However the failure of the biggest demonstrations in world history to persuade the American and British governments to change their minds discouraged many people from believing in peaceful demonstrations as a way of achieving things.

This failure was not total. In Montreal, numbers demonstrating rose after February 2002, probably because President Bush made remarks about France's failure to join the war coalition which were interpreted as anti-French. In response to the mounting demonstration pressure, the Canadian government changed its mind about sending Canadian troops to participate in the war. To that extent the Canadian demonstrations succeeded. However since even a movement many millions strong had not been able to persuade governments to alter course or slow down, many felt the whole exercise had been pointless.

This view was almost certainly wrong. As the history of earlier demonstration campaigns shows, immediate success is very much the exception rather than the rule, and many campaigns which do not succeed at first do often succeed eventually, with demonstrations contributing to that ultimate success.

The years following 2003 have seen a great increase in protests deliberately designed to break the law in order to have a dramatic impact. Many have been related to environmental concerns, including climate change, genetically modified crops, air pollution and excessive aircraft noise. The philosophy behind some of these demonstrations is that the democratic political system is broken, as supposedly evidenced by the failure of the Iraq war demonstrations, or in any event is incapable of dealing with new and urgent environmental dangers. This, it is argued, gives rise to a moral imperative to break the law to draw attention to those dangers. It is also sometimes wrongly argued that in breaking the law demonstrators will be following in the footsteps of the early Parliamentary Reform demonstrators. A representative of "Plane Stupid", which campaigns against expansion of Britain's airports, told an audience in 2009, including this author, that the meeting attacked at Peterloo in 1819 had been an illegal meeting. By implication "Plane Stupid" in carrying out lawbreaking direct action protests was following in the footsteps of Henry Hunt and the Lancashire reformers. As Chapter 4 makes clear, this is a gross distortion of what happened in the run-up to Peterloo, and is simply incorrect about what Hunt and the Lancashire Reformers believed. The philosophy of the early nineteenth century campaigners who invented the modern demonstration was encapsulated in the words of the marching song of the Birmingham Political Union in 1832, *"No swords we draw. We kindle not war's battle fires. By union, justice, reason, law. We'll gain the birthright of our sires."*

Possibly "Plane Stupid" will modify their views about the rule of law after an opposing group, perhaps called "Plane Lovely" and campaigning for more airports, organises a counter-demonstration in opposition to them, at the same time and at the same place as one of their demonstrations, and a destructive brawl ensues.

However unless and until there is a change in the fashion for direct action law-breaking protests, it is certain that the authorities will continue to react with draconian and unreasonable restrictions on the right to demonstrate, justified on the grounds of preventing illegality, but in practice placing unreasonable restrictions on every demonstration.

A notable example of a new British law which over-reacted to perceived threats from demonstrators was Section 138 of the Serious and Organised Crimes and Police Act 2005. This was partly a reaction to the noisy one-man non-stop anti-war protest by Brian Haw, who remained camped outside Parliament with a loud hailer and banners from 2003 until shortly before his death in 2011. However it was also influenced by the police wanting to have tight control over the area around Parliament. It provided that there could be no demonstration of any kind within one kilometre of Parliament while Parliament was sitting, except for the traditional demonstration venue of Trafalgar Square, which was excluded from the restricted area. Following the enactment of this law, an anti-war campaigner, Maya Evans, was arrested and prosecuted for standing by the Cenotaph (the national war memorial in Whitehall, close to the Houses of Parliament) reciting the names of British soldiers killed in Iraq. Her appeal against conviction was dismissed.

Both Brian Haw's protest and Maya Evans' protests directly impacted on Tony Blair, the Prime Minister who took the decision to go to war in Iraq. As soon as Blair was replaced as Prime Minister by Gordon Brown, the Government announced that it was not committed to maintaining the one kilometre restriction on demonstrations and that it was setting up a review. This was completed under the Coalition Government which took power in 2010, and resulted in the repeal of Section 138 by the Police Reform and Social Responsibility Act 2011, which abolished the restriction on demonstrations near Parliament, simply prohibiting use of amplification equipment or camping in Parliament Square.

In Parliament Square the new law seems to strike a good balance between the right to demonstrate, the important right of elected legislators to debate without interruption, and the need to maintain one of London's most famous squares, rather than it being turned into a camp-site, which had occurred with the "Democracy Village" movement in 2010. However this happy outcome does not alter the fact that demonstrations which take direct action that impinges on the rights and freedoms of others are likely to generate further restrictions on the right to demonstrate, even if those restrictions are eventually abandoned.

This book has aimed to show how the right to hold a peaceful demonstration is a good and valuable thing, capable of achieving impressive results in many different kinds of situation. Time and again, a demonstration in support of a just but seemingly hopeless cause, started by a tiny group of people, has eventually resulted in huge changes for the better which might not otherwise have occurred. One striking example is the brave stand of the Mothers of the Plaza de Mayo against the Argentine Junta. Another, equally brave, was the Moscow dissidents' "Glasnost Meeting" demonstration in 1965. Few would then have predicted, that from that one small demonstration, internal opposition to the Soviet Union would grow in less than 30 years to a point where the Soviet Union ceased to exist.

I have also tried to show how the coming of the peaceful demonstration has been a natural evolution from earlier forms of protest, a change which happened in parallel with other forms of change in society, notably wider literacy and the arrival of cheap mass media, but also the development of modern trade unions and modern police forces.

Peaceful demonstrations started in the London of the age of the French Revolution, as a way for English reformers to show that they were not violent revolutionaries.

The French Revolution and the fear which it brought to the English upper classes brought to an end what was previously the commonest form of protest in eighteenth century London, the political riot.

That eighteenth-century justification for rioting disappeared when Britain became a democracy. While demonstrations played a huge part in bringing democracy to Britain, the spread of democracy and the spread of demonstrations have tended to travel in parallel. It is in democracies that the practice of holding demonstrations is generally prevalent today, and it is in countries which are not democracies that the right to demonstrate is usually suppressed. In the democratic world, the peaceful demonstration has replaced the political riot in the same way that the automobile has replaced the horse and cart, and for similar reasons. In each case the new invention is more convenient and cost-effective than its predecessor. Peaceful demonstrations should be, and generally are, occasions when people can express their views effectively without anyone getting hurt, with far less disruption to the life of a community than that caused by a riot. Those who disparage demonstrations as a way of doing things should remember what they have replaced.

It is worth noting in passing the practice of some undemocratic countries which try to pretend that they are democratic, and to fake support for the regime's views, through managed or manipulated demonstrations or riots. We have seen how the Chinese government paid farmers to hold counter-demonstrations against the Tiananmen Square student demonstrations in 1989. The practice of supposedly spontaneous demonstrations which are in fact state organised, with demonstrators being paid to attend and bussed to their destination, is well-entrenched in China. Other examples there include the attacks on the US Embassy in China in the aftermath of the NATO bombing of the Chinese Embassy in Belgrade in 1999, when the U.S. consulate in Chengdu was set on fire by demonstrators, and the 2012 outbreak of anti-Japanese demonstrations in connection with Chinese claims to the Senkaku or Diaoyutai Islands. Iran is likewise a master of the non-spontaneous spontaneous demonstration, and this political art form also seems to be undergoing a revival in Putin's Russia.

At the same time, there is danger in the anti-democratic potential of some demonstrations, which try to force their view on the public, ignoring the fact that they do not have majority support. This has been discussed in the context of the growth in direct action environmental demonstrations but the issue is a wider one. Demonstrations complement the ballot box in a free society. They can never be a substitute for the electoral process, however slow and cumbersome that often is.

In Germany, which lacked any significant tradition of peaceful demonstrations until after the Second World War, and where the rise of Nazism developed out of violent street battles between Nazis and Communists, demonstrations were regarded with deep suspicion by many liberal minded people for years afterwards. Democracy and the ballot box were felt to be the only way to solve political issues. They were not to be solved in the street, which was the domain of the thugs of the Far Left and the Far Right. Similar suspicion also prevails in German-speaking Switzerland. A study by Dominique Wiesler and Hans-Peter Kriesi found contrasting public attitudes to demonstrations in Geneva and in Zurich, with Geneva more tolerant and supportive. They concluded that this was mainly because Zurich had a very well-developed system of "Burgerinitiative", citizens' initiative laws which enabled a relatively small number of citizens to get a proposal for legal change on to the ballot paper, to be voted on by the whole voting population of the Canton of Zurich. In Geneva, in contrast, such initiatives had only recently been introduced and were not part of the culture of the city in the way that they were in Zurich. The popular perception of demonstrations in Zurich was that they were undemocratic because anyone who had any significant support for their view could get the matter on the ballot paper as a "Burgerinitiative", and did not need to go out into the street to look for support.

This view from Zurich is mistaken, and misunderstands one of the most useful functions of a demonstration. It is true that some demonstrators may demonstrate for a cause when they could equally well obtain a change in the law by other means. However often demonstrators will represent a minority view which has little chance of obtaining a change in the law through the ballot box. Just because a view is a minority view, and likely to remain one, does not mean that the view should not be heard. The stability of society depends on people being able to bring their grievances to public attention by lawful means.

A person who can make his voice heard through a peaceful protest is less likely to express his frustration in a violent protest or other illegal action. More importantly, issues sometimes only affect a minority in society. Without the publicity which a demonstration gives to that minority's cause, the minority will have no chance of bringing it to the attention of their fellow citizens, and so no chance of winning a ballot on an issue which affects only them. Examples of issues of fundamental importance to minorities were the U.S. civil rights marches of the 1960 and the demonstrations by the disabled, organised by ADAPT. Other examples are issues relating to the unemployed, or to gay rights.

The Women's Suffragists did not represent a minority, but they represented a half of society that was completely shut out of the political process. Suffrage demonstrations kept the issue of women's suffrage high on the political agenda, where it would not otherwise have been. The battle for women's suffrage has been won in most of the world, but there will always be downtrodden or marginalised sections of society for whom a demonstration offers a good opportunity to highlight their problems.

The ability for a group of citizens to walk together through the street, to a government building or prominent meeting place, to express their views on an issue, is a force for good in any society. It brings problems to the notice of officialdom, which may otherwise be unresponsive. It focusses public attention on important matters which have been overlooked by the mainstream political parties and media. It gives expression to powerful emotions in a manner which is dignified and meaningful. If the ability to do this is suppressed, those emotions are likely to work themselves out in more harmful ways.

The right to demonstrate is particularly important for those who have few other means of publicising their grievances. People who are poor, inarticulate, unconfident, or lacking in language skills can make their concerns known by means of a demonstration. In that sense, demonstrations give a voice to the voiceless. Again, the ADAPT demonstrations by the disabled were a classic example. For these reasons, peaceful demonstrations serve an important purpose, and should remain every person's right.

This book records great demonstrating movements which have ended in success and others which have ended in failure. The Parliamentary Reformers, the Australian Eight Hour Day demonstrators, the Suffragists, the American Civil Rights Movement, Gandhi, People Power in the Philippines, and ADAPT were all movements that succeeded. The cynicism which followed the failure of the anti-Iraq war demonstrations in 2003 is misplaced. The Chartist Great National Demonstration of 1848 was also felt at the time to have been a failure, but almost all of the Chartists demands for changes in the voting system were eventually met. A demonstration or a series of demonstrations will often be an effective part of a wider political campaign, keeping an issue in the public eye, and reinforcing the solidarity and commitment of those who support the campaign.

The final conclusion of this book is that the right to demonstrate is fragile. While it was being written, peaceful demonstrations were broken up with tear gas near the Parthenon in Athens, often regarded as the birthplace of democracy, as demonstrators protested against the austerity measures being imposed on Greece by the European Union.

This violently hostile reaction by the Greek authorities was a reminder that, while lip service is paid by many governments to the right to hold a peaceful demonstration, demonstrating is still a dangerous business. Rights of all kinds are precarious, and the right to demonstrate is more precarious than most. Lord Acton pointed out that all power tends to corrupt. This is so regardless of time and place. Those in power appear to have an almost irresistible temptation to overstep the mark, and infringe the rights of those they rule. This applies even to those who come to power with the best of intentions, but the intentions of many who come to power are very bad from the outset. That is why, over two hundred years ago, just as the first peaceful demonstrations were being held, Thomas Jefferson correctly noted that the price of liberty is eternal vigilance. As the early twentieth century historian H.A.L. Fisher put it, "Progress is not a law of nature. What is gained by one generation may be lost by the next". Freedom will only survive so long as people are willing, when necessary, to come out into the street to raise banners to protest.

Oxford, March 2014

2021 Hong Kong Update

Seven eventful years have gone by since the first edition of this book was completed in October 2014.

When I wrote then, the *Occupy Central* civil disobedience protest was in progress in Hong Kong and it was not yet clear how it would end although its prospects of success were not looking good.

Looking back now, some of the conclusions in the book look prophetic. I said that it was impossible for any peaceful-demonstrating movement to succeed against a regime that was so powerful and utterly intransigent. That is the kind of regime that the *Occupy Central* movement was opposing. The Hong Kong Government had no power to respond meaningfully to the movement's demands for full democracy. All power rested with Beijing, and Beijing was inflexible. Eventually, after eight weeks of closing the streets of central Hong Kong by its sit-in, the three leaders of the *Occupy Central* movement called off the protest, realising that it was not going to succeed, and being anxious not to alienate support by continuing to disrupt daily life. They were later charged with conspiracy to carry out an unlawful assembly and were convicted. Benny Tai and Chan Kin Man were imprisoned; Chu Yu Ming, who was over 70, was spared imprisonment on account of his age but given a suspended sentence.

I also stated that when peaceful demonstrators with a legitimate grievance are ignored or treated with hostility, peaceful demonstrations will tend to become discredited and people will be attracted instead to violent protest and deliberate lawbreaking. This happened with the Chartists, the Suffragettes, the PAC and the ANC in South Africa, and the Northern Ireland Civil Rights Movement and the IRA in Northern Ireland. It has now happened in very much the same way in Hong Kong. The defeat of *Occupy Central* led to widespread disillusion with peaceful protest and the rise of violent protest of a kind and intensity not seen in Hong Kong since the 1960s. When this book appeared in Hong Kong in 2015,

I was told not to expect big sales, because peaceful demonstrations were now a discredited technique which people did not want to hear about.

The rise of this feeling coincided with the first violent riot in Hong Kong for many years on the night of 8 to 9 February 2016, the eve of Chinese New Year.

The Hong Kong Government Food and Environmental Hygiene Department, which is responsible for keeping the streets clean and has extensive power to remove obstructions, removed traditional Chinese New Year hawker stalls in the Mong Kok area of Kowloon. Twenty-five-year-old Edward Leung, leader of a new political group, Hong *Kong Indigenous*, called on people via social media to defend the hawkers. Many came to the area to do so, and a pitched battle developed between an outnumbered police contingent of between 30 and 60 and somewhere between one hundred and two hundred protesters. The protesters threw missiles at the police causing many injuries. Edward Leung was convicted of rioting and assault on the police, and sentenced to 6 years' imprisonment.

Hong Kong Indigenous broke with the democratic party traditions in Hong Kong of aiming to bring democracy to the whole of China, and instead concerned itself specifically with Hong Kong, which it wishes to see governed democratically by the people of Hong Kong for the people of Hong Kong, with minimal if any control from Beijing. Edward Leung coined the phrase "Liberate Hong Kong – revolution of our times". As some of the hawkers whose stalls he was protecting sold fishballs the riot is sometimes referred to as the "Fishball Revolution".

The other major difference between Edward Leung and the Hong Kong anti-Communist politicians and activists who came before him was that Edward Leung did not follow their strong tradition of legality and non-violence. Calling on supporters to use physical force to protect the street hawkers against officials and the police crossed a line which had not previously been crossed. It marked the beginning of the replacement of peaceful demonstrations by violence, as was bound to happen after the failure of *Occupy Central*.

However the Mongkok riot was just a taster or overture for the massive protests which shook Hong Kong in 2019, and continued until the coronavirus epidemic in early 2020.

Those protests started because the Hong Kong Government decided to introduce an Extradition Bill in the Legislative Council which would, for the first time, have permitted extradition of criminal suspects from Hong Kong to Mainland China. The trigger for the Bill was a murder in Taiwan, which also has no extradition treaty with Hong Kong. The prime suspect who has confessed to the killing was a Hong Kong resident, as was the victim, his girlfriend. Although it is not certain, it seems likely that the Chief Executive of Hong Kong, Carrie

Lam, deliberately seized upon this as an opportunity to secure extradition both to Taiwan and, more importantly, to the Mainland, an act which she assumed would be welcomed by the national leadership in Beijing. There appears to be no evidence that the Bill was an initiative from Beijing.

The pro-government parties have had a majority in the Hong Kong Legislative Council at all times since 1997. There should therefore have been no difficulty for them in passing the Extradition Bill. However the Bill caused huge concern in the community.

Extradition procedures in Hong Kong at the time were similar to those in other common-law countries such as the UK. All that was required was some evidence that the person whose extradition was requested had done something which was a crime in both Hong Kong and the country requesting the extradition, and that the extradition was not for a political offence. A challenge to an extradition could be brought in the Hong Kong courts, but if the formal requirements for an extradition were met the Hong Kong courts would not investigate the strength of the case against the accused.

This is a system that can work reasonably well with countries which have the rule of law, if the courts in Hong Kong can be sure that the evidence will be tested in a proper trial in the country to which the extradited person is being sent. But it cannot work in Mainland China, which does not have the rule of law, and where the verdicts and sentences for cases are decided by the Communist Party before the accused enters court. An allegation can be wholly fraudulent, designed either to bring a political enemy within the jurisdiction of the Mainland, or to lock up a commercial rival or to take personal revenge for a bad business deal.

This was why most of the Hong Kong community, including the usually pro-government business community, felt extreme concern at the Extradition Bill. Large peaceful demonstrations were organised by the Civil Human Rights Front and other groups, and businesses including the American Chamber of Commerce spoke out against the proposal. However the Hong Kong Government was impervious to either the demonstrations or the representations by business and reiterated its determination to pass the Bill.

Matters came to a head on 9 June, 2019, when one of the largest demonstrations ever held in Hong Kong took place against the Bill. The organisers, the Civil Human Rights Front, claimed one million people attended this peaceful demonstration. It was much bigger than the 500,000-strong demonstration against Article 23 legislation in 2003 which brought down the government of C.H. Tung. Many wore white – the colour of funerals in Chinese culture – to symbolise the death of Hong Kong.

Startlingly, the response of Carrie Lam was not to resign or make concessions but to issue a statement that nothing would change as a result of the demonstration and that the debate on the Bill would go ahead on 12 June as planned. This was crass rigidity of a kind guaranteed to raise tension to a new level.

On 12 June another huge demonstration took place. Although still predominantly peaceful, it was accompanied by unsuccessful attempts to break into the Legislative Council and the mood of the demonstrators was angrier than it had been three days earlier. Controversially the police broke up the demonstration with the use of tear gas not far from the Council building.

In response to the 12 June demonstration Carrie Lam announced a temporary pause in consideration of the Extradition Bill three days later. This was an inadequate response, and resulted in a further demonstration the following day, 16 June, in which according to the organisers some two million people took part. Other observers estimate this number at one and a half million, which still makes it the largest demonstration in the history of Hong Kong, three times as big as the 2003 demonstration which stopped the Article 23 legislation, one and half times as big as the largest demonstration in support of the Tiananmen Square students in 1989, and involving a very significant proportion of Hong Kong's total population of between 7 and 8 million.

Carrie Lam did not make any further concession in relation to that demonstration. As a result of her intransigence the mood of the city changed and belief in non-violent protest ebbed away and was replaced by anger and a determination to fight. The parallel with Asquith's rigid refusal to make any concession to the Suffragettes after their giant demonstration of 21 June, 1908 is striking.

On 1 July, 2019 demonstrators stormed and systematically vandalised the Hong Kong Legislative Council Building. Symbols of China's sovereignty were defaced and pro-democracy and anti-China slogans scrawled as graffiti. These included the memorable statement: "You taught me that peaceful protests are useless". The demonstrators occupied the building for several hours, but then left without waiting for any attempt to evict them.

The shock of the storming of the Legislative Council building in previously peaceful Hong Kong is hard to underestimate. It made it very unlikely that the Extradition Bill would be restored, and reinforced an impression that where peaceful protest had failed, violent direct action would bring results.

At this point the demands of the protesters morphed into calls for Lam to meet five demands – complete withdrawal of the Extradition Bill, an inquiry into police behaviour, an amnesty for those arrested in connection with the demonstrations, withdrawal of references to events on 12 June as being riots, and universal suffrage.

The protests continued and became increasingly violent, with protesters blocking roads, attacking businesses thought to be pro-Beijing or Mainland-controlled, and attacking the police.

These violent protests had several notable features new to Hong Kong and distinctive in terms of demonstrations in general. A high proportion of demonstrators were very young, with many secondary school students involved. There were scenes of crowds of schoolchildren changing out of school uniform into the black clothes, black face masks, goggles and helmets which became the unofficial uniform of the protesters. Children as young as 12 were involved, and many 14-year-olds played key roles in the ongoing violence.

A second notable feature was the strong support given to the demonstrators by the older generation, even after the demonstrations became very violent. There was a widespread view that non-violence had failed, and that violence, in the form of storming the Legco, had actually brought success.

A third feature was the lack of any obvious leader of the protests. Protests were mainly organised via very decentralised social media networks, particularly LIHKG (sometimes referred to as the Hong Kong equivalent of Reddit) and the encrypted network, Telegram. These networks enabled large numbers of protesters to assemble at particular locations at short notice and to divert very quickly to other locations if messages spread that they were needed there. The police did not have ready access to some of these networks so that the protesters were able to remain one step ahead of them. The protests thus built on the "flash mob" style of demonstration which had already developed in London and elsewhere as a result of the arrival of social media.

The violence and destruction increased dramatically after 21 July, which was the day of another large demonstration. Demonstrators returning from that demonstration were attacked and brutally beaten at Yuen Long railway station by large numbers of men in white shirts wielding rattan canes and clubs. The police were nowhere to be seen, save for two officers who appeared briefly and then walked away. A video of their departure from the scene was widely circulated. The men in white had the appearance of Triad gang members. Significant numbers of police arrived just after the attackers in white had departed leaving dozens of returning demonstrators injured, some of them severely.

This incident looked like police collaboration with Triads to attack demonstrators, and raised feelings against the police among demonstrators and their supporters to boiling point. Many also pointed the finger of blame at a fiercely pro-Beijing politician, Junius Ho, who was photographed shaking hands with some men in white who looked like the Yuen Long attackers a few days before the attack took place. The feelings of fury resulted in protesters turning much of Hong Kong into a war zone during the period from August to November 2019. In August, the international airport was occupied by demonstrators and brought to a standstill, with hundreds of flights cancelled. In the autumn the aim of the demonstrators became to paralyse the economic life of the city by disrupting transport links.

Far, far too late, Carrie Lam in September announced the permanent withdrawal of the Extradition Bill, but this did not stop the protests. Trains were burned, the tollbooths of the Cross-Harbour Tunnel were burned, university campuses were occupied, and brick walls were built across major roads. Violence reached a climax with a pitched battle lasting several days between the police and demonstrators occupying the campus of the Hong Kong Polytechnic University near the Cross-Harbour Tunnel in Kowloon. The eventual police occupation of the campus and the arrest of thousands of protesters did not stop the violence, which continued sporadically until the arrival of the coronavirus in early 2020 brought it to a halt.

An excellent detailed account of the protests from their origin in the murder in Taiwan to their halt in early 2020 is contained in the *South China Morning Post* publication, *Rebel City*, edited by Zuraidah Ibrahim and Jeffie Lam.

Throughout the months of demonstrations, Carrie Lam only met the demonstrators once, at a consultation held at Queen Elizabeth Stadium, Wanchai, on 26 September. Her rigid stance went down badly with those present. A school student addressed her as follows, "Have you ever been sympathetic toward people who were tear-gassed or beaten by police? You only care about turnstiles in MTR stations which were vandalised. You have taught me, a naïve person, that peaceful protests cannot make a difference."

When the movement became violent, it bitterly divided the community. Supporters of the demonstrations are known as "yellow", opponents as "blue". The demonstration movement supported "yellow" businesses, such as restaurants and cafes, and boycotted and often vandalised larger businesses identified as "blue". "Blue" supporters, most numerous among the better-off, pointed angrily to the disruption of the city, the economic damage, and the damage to the city's reputation as a peaceful place. Many called the demonstrators "cockroaches" and wanted them to be crushed. Calls for them to be shot were not uncommon.

A central focus of the "yellow" movement in its later stages was on the brutality of the police. Police discipline undoubtedly deteriorated during the protests and there were many cases of excessive police violence. There was significant use of tear gas, including an incident when it was discharged by police inside Kwai Fong Underground station, and Britain even halted tear gas exports to Hong Kong during the protests. Substitutes, whose chemical composition was unknown, were imported from China. There were also shocking scenes at Prince Edward Station when police chased protesters into the station and onto a train, using their batons freely in all directions and striking passengers who were not demonstrators. Unfortunately yellow supporters were often silent about serious acts of violence committed by some yellow activists.

In dealing with acts of extreme violence committed in the context of a demonstration movement it is always important to remember the traditional use of agents provocateurs by nearly all the police forces of the world. There were instances during the 2019 Hong Kong demonstrations when suspected agents provocateurs were identified and attacked. Some of these individuals were in fact not agents provocateurs, and acts of gratuitous brutality by demonstrators took place against them. It is safe to assume however that at least a few police agents were operating as infiltrators within the demonstration movement. There is no doubt that on at least one occasion police dressed as demonstrators joined in the arrest of genuine demonstrators.

However I do not believe that agents provocateurs were responsible for the acts of violence which caused most horror among the general public. This is partly because infiltrators are rarely trained to commit serious criminal acts themselves. I quote in Chapter 14 the FBI's directive to its agent infiltrators that they should not "become the person who carries the gun, throws the bomb, does the robbery, or by some specific act becomes a deeply involved participant". This is common sense for agents of a law enforcement body, and one would expect similar instructions to have been given to agents in Hong Kong. For this reason it is very unlikely that the demonstrator who threw a corrosive liquid over a police officer at Tuen Mun on 11 June, 2019, causing him severe injury, was any kind of police agent. The same applies to a policeman's finger being bitten off by a demonstrator at Sha Tin on 14 July, and the stabbing of a police officer in the neck with a box cutter on 13 October.

It is also not likely that infiltrators were responsible for other acts of violence which have all the hallmarks of powerful feelings bursting into physical attacks. This applies to the beating up of people who expressed opposition to the demonstrators, which happened several times. It also applies to events at Sheung Shui in the northern New Territories on 13 November where demonstrators were using bricks to build a barricade across a road near the North District Town

Hall. A group of local people attempted to remove the barricades and a fight developed between them and about 20 demonstrators. A man of 70 called Luo started filming the fight on his mobile phone. A demonstrator turned and threw a brick at him, which hit him on the head causing serious injury from which Luo later died in hospital.

There was thus serious crime on the side of the protesters. On the police side there were two incidents where the police shot and seriously wounded individual protesters. In one case it appears that the policeman who fired was under violent attack by a demonstrator armed with an iron bar. In the other the policeman claimed that he thought the demonstrator was going to seize his gun. Whether it was necessary to fire a gun to stop him is debatable. However some of the worst incidents alleged against the police have not so far been substantiated by evidence. Thus it became and remains widely believed in Hong Kong that the police killed three protesters at Prince Edward MTR station on 31 August, 2019, and then spirited away their bodies never to be heard of again. However there are no missing persons' reports which could relate to anyone disappearing at that incident. It is highly unlikely that three people could just disappear in Hong Kong without generating any reports from relatives, friends, work colleagues or any other source. Over two years has now gone by since the incident and in the absence of anyone reported missing it seems reasonable to conclude that no-one was killed and disappeared. Despite that flowers are still regularly placed at Prince Edward Station in memory of the supposed dead.

Another widely publicised allegation of police brutality related to detention of arrested demonstrators at the San Uk Ling Detention Centre in the New Territories. After a short period detentions at that location were stopped. When Hong Kong's Independent Police Complaints Council produced a report on the protests in May 2020 (itself highly controversial), it devoted a whole chapter to San Uk Ling. The Council has been accused of being too pro-police and reluctant to get beneath the surface of the police explanations. However it does seem significant that according to their report, while there were justified complaints of the remoteness of the location and of inadequate facilities, there was no actual complaint laid against the police in relation to detention at San Uk Ling. Admittedly many people are so disillusioned with Hong Kong's ineffective police complaints system that they would not bother to make a formal complaint. Nevertheless, the absence of a single complaint or specific first-hand allegation of brutal policy behaviour tends to suggest that the reports which appeared on-line about events at the Centre were all incorrect or seriously exaggerated. In 2021 one Poon Yung Wai admitted in court falsely spreading a claim on-line that a friend in the police had told him that people were being murdered and raped inside the Centre, when in fact he had no such friend or information. Poon was competently defended in court and there is no doubt that his admission of spreading false information is genuine.

In this context it is hard to overestimate the effect of the internet. Anyone can place any assertion on line, and it can be relayed instantly to thousands of people. In these circumstances fake news is a huge problem. There seems to have been an additional problem in that the police were slow and limited in using on-line media to put their version of events or rebut allegations which they were in a position to rebut.

What conclusions can be drawn from the events of 2019? Extremely bad leadership by the Hong Kong Government converted initially peaceful demonstrators into warriors fighting the police. The police were placed in an invidious position not of their making by government intransigence.

In the case of the demonstrators the problem was not so much bad leadership as absence of leadership. This was a deliberate strategy adopted by many demonstrators in order to facilitate rapid action and reduce the chance of leaders being arrested. Once the Civil Human Rights Front, with its long record of peaceful demonstrations, was no longer organising, and the traditional leaders of the democratic movement were sidelined, there was no-one to calculate a coherent strategy to be used to secure durable progress. There was no Gandhi, or Martin Luther King, or even Emmeline Pankhurst. If instead of the uncontrolled violence of summer and autumn 2019 there had been a leader who could have negotiated with the authorities, and called a pause in demonstrations while she/he did so, it might have been possible to see the withdrawal of the Extradition Bill followed by a return to normal daily life. That would have been a meaningful victory for the democratic forces. Instead, leaderless and violent, they have succeeded in losing more ground than ever before since 1997.

On 1 July, 2020 the Beijing Government imposed on Hong Kong a Chinese national law, entitled the Hong Kong National Security Law, creating widely drawn new offences of sedition, secession, subversion, theft of state secrets and collusion with foreign powers. All Hong Kong laws are declared to be subordinate to this law. Prosecution decisions are taken by a special unit overseen by the Mainland. Trial by jury is removed, and serious cases can be taken to Mainland China and tried under Mainland Chinese law. This is far worse than the Article 23 legislation against which half a million people successfully marched in Hong

Kong in 2003, and worse than the 2019 Fugitive Offenders Bill, which at least provided for some sort of extradition process before a person was removed to the Mainland It effectively ends free speech in Hong Kong, as it criminalises the significant minority of younger Hong Kong people, many of them demonstrators in 2019, who support an independent Hong Kong. The British Government and many observers consider the law a blatant breach of the 1984 Sino-British Joint Declaration on the Future of Hong Kong, and it has led many countries to suspend their extradition arrangements with Hong Kong.

This National Security Law would never have happened but for the sustained destructive violence of summer and autumn 2019. That violence was successfully used by pro-Beijing forces to persuade much of the Hong Kong establishment that such a law was needed. This persuasion was linked to the fantastic idea, widely propagated in the Chinese national media and Hong Kong pro-Beijing media, that the protests were organised by foreign forces, meaning the United States and Britain. Anyone who has spent any time with the demonstrators knows that they were demonstrating because of deeply held personal views and not for any other reason. Unfortunately, this motivation is itself incomprehensible, and so unbelievable, to Beijing. All of the crimes committed by demonstrators during those protests, from criminal damage to rioting to murder, were punishable under existing Hong Kong law with heavy maximum penalties and the Hong Kong courts were well able to deal with them without a new law. Some 14,000 people have been arrested as a result of the protests and many have been charged and convicted, none of them under the new National Security Law. The aim of the National Security Law is not to restore order but to crush peaceful political opposition to Beijing's world-view and make Hong Kong obedient to its wishes. It may now succeed in this aim.

A further negative side effect of last year's events is that it is now much harder to hold any peaceful demonstration in Hong Kong. Organisers of meetings of more than 50 people or marches of more than 30 people are required to obtain a notice of no objection from the police. Such letters were usually given before 2019 to many groups with a record of peaceful protest, including the Civil Human Rights Front. A legal challenge to the system in 2005 failed because the court found that in practice the system allowed the right to demonstrate to exist. Since the second half of 2019 it has been much harder to obtain a notice of no objection even for very traditional marches. The police objection is usually that violent protesters will use the cover of the peaceful protest to commit acts of violence or vandalism. This may well be true, but if this is to be the test for depriving peaceful people of the right to demonstrate the right has been effectively abolished. Good stewarding and a clear end time for a demonstration could prevent this type of hijacking, but at present it seems there is neither the will on the part of demonstration organisers to put good stewarding in place, nor the will on the part of the authorities to accept that arrangements could be made to prevent violence on the fringes.

The movement has probably changed demonstrating around the world for a long time. The style of the 2019 protest movement, with its flash mob characteristics, referred to in Chinese by the slogan "Be water", its protective helmets, goggles, masks and black uniform, and its disregard for the law and commitment to property destruction and vandalism, has been widely copied round the world, most prominently in Iraq, Lebanon, Chile and the UK. For those like this author, who have campaigned for years to ensure that the right to demonstrate is recognised as a legally protected human right, this is very depressing, as one cannot have a legally protected right to break the law.

Summing up my review of the last seven years, I am surprised at how much events have confirmed my conclusions in Chapter 20. Peaceful demonstrations have a vital role to play in drawing attention to issues, providing an outlet for strong emotions, and as part of a wider movement for political or social change. But they must be peaceful and they must be intelligently led. Hong Kong 2019 will always be a salutary warning of what happens when demonstration movements abandon the rule of law and turn into leaderless urban guerrillas.

Freedom's Banner: Bibliography

General

American Civil Liberties Union, The Right to protest
Fenwick, Helen, Civil Liberties and Human Rights, Cavendish Publishing, 2001
Galligan, Dennis: The right to protest, University of Southampton Institute of Criminal Justice, 1989
Le Bon, Gustav: The crowd: a study of the popular mind, Ernest Benn, 1896
Mead, David: The new law of peaceful protest, Hart, 2010
Powers et al: Protest, power and change: An encyclopedia of non-violent direct action, Garland Press, 1997
Stephen, James: A history of English criminal law, 1883, Burt Franklin, New York

Chapter 1: The London Corresponding Society

Cestre, Charles: John Thelwall, a pioneer of democracy and social reform in England during the French revolution, Swan Sonnenschein, New York, 1906
Davies, Michael (ed), London Corresponding Society, Collected Papers: Pickering and Chatto, 2002
Goodwin, Albert: The Friends of Liberty, The English democratic movement in the age of the French Revolution, Harvard University Press, 1979

Chapter 2: Origins

Acton, John Frederick, Lord: Essays on the History of Freedom, 1907

Bate, W. Jackson: Samuel Johnson, Counterpoint Press, 1998

Bowen, Catherine Drinker: The lion and the throne, the life and times of Sir Edward Coke: Little, Brown, 1991

Gilmour, Sir Ian: Riots, risings and revolution: Governance and Violence in eighteenth century England, Pimlico, 1992

Hibbert, Christopher: King Mob, Longmans, 1958

Holdsworth, William: History of English Law, vols 1 & 2, London, Methuen 1903-38

Holmes, Geoffrey: The Sacheverell riots, London, Past and Present No 72

Holt, J.C: King John: Historical Association, 1963

Holt, J.C: Magna Carta, Cambridge University Press, 1992

Jephson, Henry: The Platform, its rise and progress, London, Frank Cass, 1892

Rude, George: The crowd in history: A study of popular disturbances in France and England, 1730-1848

Sedley, Stephen (ed): A spark in the ashes, the pamphlets of John Warr: Verso, 1992

Thompson, E.P: Customs in common: Merlin Press, 1991

Zaret, David: Origins of democratic culture: printing, petitions and the public sphere in early modern England; Princeton, 2000

Chapter 3: Spa Fields

Belchem, John: "Orator" Hunt, Breviary Stuff Publications, 2012

Darvall, Frank: Popular disturbances and public order in Regency England, Oxford, 1934

Goodwin, Albert: The Friends of Liberty, The English democratic movement in the age of the French Revolution, Harvard University Press, 1979

Hunt, Henry: Autobiography (Nuffield College Library, Oxford)

Sutton, David: The Spa Fields Riots of 1816, Internet Essay

Chapter 4: Peterloo

60 Geo III and 1 Geo IV Seditious Meetings and Assemblies Act 1819

Bamford, Samuel: Passages in the life of a radical, 1844, Macgibbon & Kee Ltd, 1967

Belchem, John: "Orator" Hunt, Breviary Stuff Publications, 2012

Darvall, Frank: Popular disturbances and public order in Regency England, Oxford, 1934

Hunt, Henry: Autobiography (Nuffield College Library, Oxford)

Holdsworth, William: History of English Law: Methuen, 1939

Read, Donald: Peterloo, the massacre and its background, University of Manchester Press, 1958

Jackson, Thomas: Trials of British Freedom: Lawrence and Wishart, 1945

Marlow, Joyce: The Peterloo Massacre: Panther: 1969

Thompson, E.P: The making of the English working class, Penguin, 1963

Trial of Henry Hunt, 1820: State Trials

Working Man's Friend and Political Magazine: 18 May 1833

Chapter 5: Demonstrations come of age: the Reform Bill

Brock, Michael: The Great Reform Act, Hutchinson, 1973

Butler, J.R.M.: The passing of the Great Reform Bill, Longmans, 1914

Cobbett, William: Twopenny Trash (Nuffield College Library, Oxford)

Ingrams, Richard: The Life and Adventures of William Cobbett; Harper Collins, 2005

Moss, David J: Thomas Attwood, biography of a Radical: McGill-Queens University Press, 1990

Pearce, Edward: Reform – the fight for the 1832 Reform Act, Pimlico, 2004

Smith, Dr E.A: Lord Grey and the 1832 Reform Act, Internet Essay

Chapter 6: The demonstrating habit spreads

The Annual Register, British Newspaper Library

Harrison, Brian: Drink and the Victorians, Pittsburgh University Press, 1972

The Journal of the New British and Foreign Temperance Society, 1839 (James Turner Collection, Senate House Library, University of London)

Charlton, John: The Chartists, Pluto Press, 1997

Lovett, William: Life and Struggles of William Lovett: Macgibbon & Kee, 1967

Irish identity website: "When Tara greeted the liberator"

University College Cork Multitext project in Irish History

Australian Dictionary of Biography: Serle & Ward, Melbourne, 1976

Clark, Manning: A history of Australia, Melbourne University Press, 1978

Crawley, Frank: A documentary history of colonial Australia, 1841-1874, Nelson, 1980

Ebbels, R.N: The Australian Labour Movement, 1850-1907; Australasian Book Society, Sydney, 1960

Hughes, Helen: The eight-hour day and the development of the labour movement in Victoria in the 1850s: Historical Studies, vol 9, No 36 (May 1961)

Internet website of Victoria Museum

Ross et al: Chronicle of Australia: Penguin Books, 2000

Chapter 7: Demonstrations come to America

Avrich, Paul: The Haymarket Tragedy; Princeton, 1984

David, Henry: The history of the Haymarket Affair; New York, Russell & Russell, 1936

Foden, Philip S: A History of May Day, International Publishers, New York, 1985

Plawiuk, Eugene: The origin and tradition of May Day, Le Gauche Review

Davis v Massachusetts 167 US 43 (1897)

Chapter 8: Demonstrations come to Europe

(a) France

Tartakowski, Danielle: Les manifestations de rue en France 1918-1968

Tilly, Charles: The contentious French, Belknap Press, Harvard, 1986

Willard, Claude: La fusillade de Fourmies; Editions Sociales, Paris, 1957

(b) Russia

Ascher, Abraham: The Russian Revolution of 1905: Stanford, 1988-1992

Galai, S: The impact of war on the Russian Liberals, 1904-5; Government and Opposition, vol 1, 1963-66

Schapiro, Leonard: History of the Soviet Communist Party: Methuen, 1970

Unger, Arieh: Constitutional Development in the Soviet Union, Methuen, 1981

(c) Germany

Diehl, James: Paramilitary Groups in Weimar Germany: Indiana University Press, 1977
Lidke, Vernon: The outlawed party: Social Democracy in Germany, 1878-1890: Princeton University Press, 1966

Chapter 9: Demonstrations and votes for women

Marlow, Joyce: Votes for women: Virago, 2000
Marx, Karl: Demonstration in Hyde Park, Marxengels.public-archive.net
Mulvihill, Margaret: Charlotte Despard, a biography: Pandora, 1989
Pankhurst, Emmeline: My own story: Eveleigh Nash, London, 1914
Pankhurst v Jarvis, The Times, 2 December 1909
Pugh, Martin: The Pankhursts, Penguin, 2002
Purvis, June: Emmeline Pankhurst; Routledge, New York, 2002
Van Wingerden, Sophia A: The women's suffrage movement in Britain, 1866-1928; Palgrave Macmillan, 1999

Chapter 10: Marching on Washington

Adams, Katherine H, and Keene, Michael L: Alice Paul and the American Suffrage Campaign, University of Illinois Press, 2008
Barber, Lucy G: Marching on Washington, the forging of an American political tradition, UCLA Press, 2002
Dickson, Paul & Allen, Thomas B: The Bonus Army, an American Epic: Walker & Co, New York, 2004
Hague v CIO US 496 (1939)
Jones, Daniel P: From military to civilian technology: the introduction of tear gas for civil riot control: Technology and Culture, Vol. 19, No 2 (April 1978), John Hopkins University Press
Lisio, Donald J.: The president and protest; Hoover, MacArthur and the Bonus Riot, Columbia, University of Missouri Press, 1974

Schwantes, Carlos A: Coxey's Army, an American Odyssey; University of Idaho, 1994

Waters, Walter & White, William: The B.E.F, the whole story of the Bonus Marchers: John Day, New York, 1933.

Chapter 11: Gandhi

Thoreau, Henry David: Civil Disobedience

Brown, Judith: Gandhi, prisoner of hope, Yale University Press, 1989

Edwards, Michael: The Last years of British India, Cassell, 1963;

Payne, Robert: The life and death of Mahatma Gandhi, Bodley Head, 1969.

Chapter 12: Gandhi's Legacy

(a) Rosenstrasse protest

Stolzfuss, Nathan "Resistance of the heart", Rutgers University Press, 2001

(b) Sharpeville

Davenport, Rodney & Saunder, Christopher: South Africa, a modern history, Macmillan, 2000

Frankel, Philip: An ordinary atrocity, Sharpeville and its massacre, Yale University Press, 2001

Karis, Thomas and Carter, Gwendoline: Documents of African Politics in South Africa, 1882-1964

Pogrund, Benjamin: Sobukwe and apartheid: Rutgers University Press, 1960

(c) Civil Rights Movement

Abernethy, Ralph: Freedom of Assembly and Association, University of South Carolina Press, 1961

Cogan, Neil H: The complete Bill of Rights, Oxford University Press, 1997

Davis v Massachusetts 167 US 43 (1897)

Edwards v South Carolina 372 US 229

Fairclough, Adam: Better day coming, Blacks and Equality, 1890 -2000

Lutz, Donald S (ed.): Colonial Origins of the American Constitution, Liberty Fund, 1998

Marbury v Madison 5 US 137 (1803)

Newman, Mark: The Civil Rights Movement; Edinburgh University Press, 2004

Shuttlesworth v City of Birmingham 382 US 87

Young, Andrew: An easy burden: Harper Collins, 1996

Chapter 13: Demonstrations and the Law

Albert v Lavin [1982] AC 546

Aldred v Miller [1925] JC 21

Austin v Metropolitan Police Commissioner [2005] EWHC 480; [2009] UKHL 5

Beattie v Gillbanks (1882) 9 QBD 308

De Freitas v Permanent Secretary, Ministry of Agriculture 4 BHRC 563

Director of Public Prosecutions v Jones [1999] AC 240

Duncan v Jones [1936] 1 KB 218

Elias v Passmore [1934] 2 KB 164

Harrison v Duke of Rutland [1893] 1 QB 142

Hickman v Maisey [1900] 1 QB 752

Hirst & Agu v Chief Constable of West Yorkshire (1987) 85 Cr App R 143

Hubbard v Pitt [1976] QB 142

Humphries v Connor (1864) 17 ICLR 1

Laporte v Chief Constable of Gloucestershire [2006] 2 WLR 46

Moss v McLachlan [1985] IRLR 76

Redmond-Bate v Director of Public Prosecutions [1999] All ER (D) 864

Thomas v Sawkins [1935] 2 KB 249

Westminster City Council v Haw Queen's Bench Division, Gray J., 4 October 2002

Wise v Dunning [1902] 1 KB 167

Christians against Racism and Fascism v UK (1984) No 8440/78 21 DR 138

Ezelin v France (1991) 14 EHHR 362

Rai, Almond and "Negotiate Now" v UK (1995) 19 EHHR CD 93

Ziliberberg v Moldova ECHR Applic. 61821/00, 4 May 2004

Chaplinsky v New Hampshire 315 U.S. 131 (1966)

Doe v University of Michigan 721 F. Supp. 852 (E.D. Mich. 1989)

Kunz v New York 340 N.Y. 273, 90 N.E. 2nd 455 (1950)

Near v Minnesota 283 U.S. 697 (1931)

New York Times v United States 403 US 713 (1971)

Rockwell v Morris 12 App. Div. 2nd 272, 211 NYS 2d 25 (1961)

Texas v Johnson 491 US 397

United States v Eichman 1990 436 US 310

Ewing, K.D. and Gearty, C. A.: The struggle for civil liberties. Political Freedom and the Rule of Law in Britain, 1914-1945

Strum, Philippa: When the Nazis came to Skokie, University Press of Kansas, 1999

Chapter 14: Demonstrations and the Police

Ackerman, Kenneth: Young J Edgar, Hoover, the red scare and the assault on civil liberties, Cape Press 2007

Baldwin, Paul: "Chinese express anger at protests", Guardian Unlimited, 22 October 1999

Black, Ian "Anger and relief as Jiang waves goodbye", Guardian Unlimited, 23 October 1999

Blackstock, Nelson: CONTELPRO, The FBI's secret war on political freedom, New York, Pathfinder, 1988

Della Porta, Donatella & Reiter, Herbert, eds: Policing protest: the control of mass demonstrations in Western democracies, University of Minnesota Press, 1988

Doward, Jamie and Townsend, Mark: "Police 'used undercover men to incite crowds'", Observer, 10 May 2009

Evans, Rob and Lewis, Paul: Undercover, the true story of Britain's secret police, Faber & Faber, 2013

Ewing, K.D. and Gearty, C. A.: The struggle for civil liberties. Political Freedom and the Rule of Law in Britain, 1914-1945

Gordon, Wiliam A: Four Dead in Ohio, North Ridge Books, 1995

Hannington, Wal: Never on our knees, Lawrence and Wishart, 1967

Hartley-Brower, Julia: "No pressure on police to quell Jiang visit demos", Guardian Unlimited, 25 October 1999

Hartley-Brower, Julia: "Met accused of Tibet protest whitewash", Guardian Unlimited, March 18, 2000

Keller, William W: The Liberals and J. Edgar Hoover, Princeton University Press, 1989

Simon, Jeffrey: "Police admit breaking law on anti-China protests", Guardian Unlimited, May 3, 2000

Soueif, Ahdaf: "Cairo, Memoir of a city transformed", Pantheon, 2014

Morgan, Jane: Conflict and Order, the police and labour disputes in England and Wales, 1900-1939, Clarendon Press, Oxford, 1987

Theoharris, Athan: Spying on Americans: Political surveillance from Hoover to the Huston Plan, Philadelphia, Temple University Press, 1978

Waddington, P.A. J. Liberty and Order, public order policing in a capital city, UCL Press, 1994

Woodward, Will: "Police action at Tibet rally unlawful", Guardian Unlimited, 4 May 2000

Chapter 15: Environmental demonstrations

The Annual Register

Bhatt, Chandi Prasad: A chipko experience

Bohlen, Jim: Making waves; Black Rose Books, 2001

King, Michael: The death of the Rainbow Warrior, Penguin 1986

R v Chief Constable of Devon and Cornwall ex parte Central Electricity Generating Board [1982] 1 QB 458

Rothman, Benny: The Kinder Scout Mass Trespass\ a personal memoir, Willow Publ, Altrincham, Chesh, 1982

Routledge, Paul: Terrains of resistance, Praeger, 1993

Weyler, Rex: Greenpeace, Rodale, 2004

Chapter 16: What makes a successful demonstration?

Bonafina, Hebe de: Historia De Las Madres De Plaza De Mayo, conference speech, 6 June 1988, madres.org website

Buckland, C.A: Bengal under the Lieutenant-Governors, Calcutta, 1900

Encyclopedia of Non-violent Direct Action – entry on ADAPT

Gorn, Elliot J: Mother Jones, the most dangerous woman in America: Hill & Wang, New York, 2001

Autobiography of Mother Jones: Chicago, Charles H. Kerr Publishing Co. 1996

Internet pages of Associacion de Madres de Plaza de Mayo (Spanish)

Navarro, Maryse: The personal is political: the Madres de Plaza de Mayo, in Susan Eckstein (ed): Power and popular protest, Latin American Social Movements

Rubinstein, Joshua: Soviet dissidents: Their struggle for human rights: Beacon Press, Boston,

Taylor, Diana: The mothers of the Plaza de Mayo in Cohen-Cruz: Radical Street Performances, an international anthology

Chapter 17: Northern Ireland

Bloody Sunday Trust Internet Pages

CAIN Web Service: The civil rights campaign 1964-72 – a chronology of main events

CAIN Web Service: Burntollet

Guardian Unlimited: Drumcree, a brief explainer

Hennessy, Thomas: A history of Northern Ireland, 1920-1996, Macmillan, 1997

IRIS Magazine, November 1988: Interview with Anthony Coughlan

Northern Ireland Veterans' Association, Internet pages

Parades Commission Northern Ireland: (1) Parade Organiser's Guide; (2) Public Processions and Parades; (3) Guidelines: (4) 6th Annual Report, 2003-4

Report on Parades in Northern Ireland (the North Report)

Sinn Fein Submission to the Review of Parades

Chapter 18: Demonstrations and revolution

Mercado, Monina & Tatad, Francisco: People's Power, an eye witness history, James B Reuter Foundation, Manila, 1986

Poniatowska, Elena: Massacre in Mexico, Viking, New York, 1975

Chapter 19: Demonstrations and China

Brook, Timothy: Quelling the People: Oxford University Press, 1992
Calhoun, Craig: Neither Gods nor Emperors, University of California, 1994
Chow Tse-Tsung: The May 4th Movement, Intellectual Revolution in modern China, Harvard, 1960
De Bary, William T: A plan for the prince: The Ming-I Tai-Fang-Liu of Huang Tsung-His, Columbia (doctoral thesis), 1953
Fairbank, John King: China, A new history, Belknap Press, 1992.
Nathan, Andrew: Chinese Democracy, Tauris, London, 1986
Nathan & Link, ed: The Tian An Men papers, Little, Brown & Co, 2001
Wasserstrom, Jeffrey: Student protests in 20th century China, Stanford, 1991

Chapter 20: Demonstrations and empires

Ajayi, J.F.A: History of West Africa, Longman
Dadrian, Vahakn N: History of the Armenian Genocide, Berghahn Books, 1995
Eleven Shadows Tibet website
Freedom Now website, Interview with Geoffrey Aduamah
Horne, Alastair: A savage war of peace, New York Review Books, 2006
New York Times Archives, 14 August 1990 "Chinese said to kill 450 Tibetans in 1989"
Planche, Jean-Louis: Setif 1945, Histoire d'un massacre annonce, Perrin, 2006
Report of the Commission of Enquiry into the Disturbances in Gold Coast, 1948 (Rhodes House Library)